D1453073

The Ukraine, 1917–1921: A Study in Revolution

Taras Hunczak, editor

with the assistance of John T. von der Heide

The Ukraine, 1917–1921:
A Study in Revolution

Distributed by Harvard University Press
for the
Harvard Ukrainian Research Institute   1977

Publication of this volume was made possible in part by the financial support of the Ukrainian National Association, Jersey City, New Jersey.

947.77084
UK7
106421
Sept. 1978

The Harvard Ukrainian Research Institute was established in 1973 as an integral part of Harvard University. It supports research associates and visiting scholars who are engaged in projects concerned with all aspects of Ukrainian studies. The Institute also works in close cooperation with the Committee on Ukrainian Studies, which supervises and coordinates the teaching of Ukrainian history, language, and literature at Harvard University.

Preface

THIS BOOK ORIGINATED in a conference dedicated to the fiftieth anniversary of the Ukrainian Revolution, which was held in New York at the Ukrainian Academy of Arts and Sciences on May 25–26, 1968. After the conference, additional contributions were solicited from scholars who, for the most part, had dealt with some aspect of the Ukrainian Revolution in their previous work. We hope that the quality of the individual contributions will compensate for the lack of a unifying thesis, a problem common to all symposia.

The Ukrainian Revolution of 1917–1921 represented the culmination of the Ukrainian national revival, which had slowly gained momentum in the nineteenth century to become a political force in the twentieth. During the prolonged turmoil that followed the fall of the Romanov and Habsburg Empires, Ukrainian leaders were faced with the task of building a national political community whose *raison d'être* they frequently confounded with dogmatic adherence to ideologically inspired sentiments. Such an attitude, so characteristic of the intelligentsia in general, distracted Ukrainian political leaders from the urgent task of building a viable state system based upon the broad masses of the population. Indeed, this preoccupation with ideology separated the Ukrainian leadership from the vast majority of the politically inarticulate Ukrainian population, for whom more tangible social, economic, and ethnic considerations were more understandable and therefore more acceptable.

The short experience with independence and the eventual loss of sovereignty has become the focal point of Ukrainian political history in the twentieth century. Initially, the literature was characterized by polemics from both partisans and detractors of the Ukrainian state, who portrayed those features which best suited their own ideological purposes. As Western archives became accessible, there arose a pressing need for new analyses based on the latest available documentation. The first objective study on the subject was Professor John S. Reshetar's *The Ukrainian Revolution, 1917–1920,* published in 1952, and since its appearance several monographs of high quality, though of limited scope, have been published in the West. It is hoped that the present volume, based on a wide variety of sources, will further our understanding of this crucial period in modern Ukrainian history.

This volume deals primarily with the eastern Ukraine and only tangentially with developments in the western Ukrainian lands of Galicia, Bukovina, and Carpatho-Ukraine. This orientation corresponds to the real division between eastern Ukrainians, whose activities, centered in Kiev, were concerned with the problem of a Russian state, whether Bolshevik or White, and western Ukrainians, who were engaged in a bitter struggle with the successor states of the Austro-Hungarian Empire. However, this approach should not obscure the contrasts that did exist between the two parts of the Ukraine, symbolized by the act of union on January 22, 1919. It is hoped that a second volume, focusing on the western Ukraine, will complete the picture of the Ukrainian Revolution.

Special appreciation is extended to the staff of the Harvard Ukrainian Research Institute for editorial and technical assistance. I feel particularly indebted to Mrs. Luba Prokop of the American Geographical Society for her dedication and care in preparing the map for this volume. Similarly I wish to thank John T. von der Heide of Drew University, who was very helpful in the initial stage of this project. Unless indicated otherwise, all dates are given according to the New Style. Transliteration of Ukrainian and Russian names follows, with only a few changes, the system used by the Library of Congress.

Taras Hunczak
Chatham, New Jersey
June 1975

Contents

The Ukraine, 1917–1921: A Study in Revolution

Introduction

Richard Pipes

ALTHOUGH THE RUSSIAN Revolution was no surprise—it had been talked about and anticipated for decades—almost everything that occurred once it got under way turned out to be unexpected. Russian political thought to the left of center had been for so long under the spell of the history of the French Revolution that there was general expectation that the coming revolution in Russia would closely resemble the French model: specifically, that it would be "bourgeois" in character and bring to power a middle class that would transform Russia into a country like those of the contemporary West. Among the distinguishing characteristics of the "bourgeois" phase of history was understood to be the creation of a centralized national state. All the oppositional parties in pre-1917 Russia expected that the revolution would "solve" the nationality question in the sense that, by abolishing the disabilities imposed by the imperial government on the minorities and offering them generous opportunities for political and cultural self-fulfillment, it would induce all of the Empire's ethnic groups to cooperate with Russians in creating a democratic and socialist society.

Almost the instant the monarchy collapsed it became apparent that the nationality question would not vanish that simply. The mistake committed by almost all Russian liberals and socialists lay in treating nationalism as an exclusively negative force, a by-product of oppression and discrimination, and ignoring the strong affirmative factors present in all national movements. Western history in the nineteenth century had given ample proof that the stirring of democratic sentiments among the masses of the population invariably assumed national forms of expression: that the aspiration to popular sovereignty was accompanied by an awareness of national identity and a demand for some kind of national self-determination. And yet, for all their knowledge of history and respect for its lessons, the leaders of Russian liberal and socialist parties ignored this particular evidence. Hence their surprise and perplexity when in 1917 nationalism suddenly raised its head in all parts of the Empire, presenting an added difficulty in the already formidable task of administering a country whose expectations had gotten far ahead of its capabilities.

The Ukrainian problem was the first to confront the Provisional Government; indeed, it represented the first serious crisis of any kind confronted by the new authority. It was met in a characteristically temporizing fashion. The Provisional Government tended to treat Ukrainian demands with particular suspicion because it was well aware of the efforts of the Austrians and Germans to exploit Ukrainian nationalism for their own purposes. As the year 1917 rolled on to its explosive climax, it became increasingly apparent, however, that what lay behind the movement was not enemy propaganda and money, but the ground swell of a genuine mass movement: it was the expression of a democratic revolution among a people who by virtue of their historic traditions and specific economic interests developed aspirations different from those of the Russians and other nationalities.

It is my impression that if Russia had remained a democratic republic, the Ukrainian national movement would have been content with broad territorial autonomy, at least for some time to come. The idea of independent statehood was not as yet strongly inculcated, at any rate in the eastern half; and the Ukrainian intelligentsia, raised on the same intellectual fare as the Russian, was also inclined to view nationalism with a certain embarrassment. The Bolshevik *coup d'état* changed the situation overnight. Henceforth, nothing short of independence could satisfy Ukrainian national aspirations. For one, the Bolsheviks themselves, by their irresponsibly demagogic use of the slogan "national self-determination," had encouraged the idea of a complete disintegration of the Empire—at any rate, until they themselves were in power. Second, with the unleashing of the Civil War, it became a matter of plain self-preservation to seek independence as a means of escaping the bloodbath. And, finally, the spectacle of a dissolving Austro-Hungarian Empire and the emergence on its ruins of sovereign national states provided an irresistible inspiration to follow suit.

The record of the Ukrainian national movement from 1917 to 1920 indicates that events moved too swiftly for it; that the disintegration of the Russian Empire occurred too soon, before the Ukrainian forces were prepared to move in and fill the political vacuum. The Ukrainian intelligentsia was small and politically fragmented. It had lacked the opportunity before 1917 to engage in discussion of aims and methods and to work out a minimum program acceptable to the majority of politically active nationalist groups. The rapidity with which the country fell apart caught everyone by surprise, forcing those suddenly thrust into positions of authority to act before they had a clear notion of what it was they wanted. Hence the ineffectiveness of the Ukrainian movement during the Revolution, and its readiness to pursue opportunistic tactics by forming alliances with such dubious friends as the Bolsheviks (October–November, 1917) and the German occupation forces (1918). Hence the absence of disciplined followers. Hence the ugly explosions of racial hatred directed against Jews and Poles, or (in the case of Makhno) against all who bore the stamp of urban civilization.

By one of those strange twists that history is prone to make, the proclamation of Ukrainian independence in early 1918 marked not the *dénouement* of the process of nation-forming in the Ukraine, but rather its serious beginning. The clarification of national aims and the penetration of Ukrainian nationalism into the masses occurred in earnest only *after* the Revolution, after the first and dismally unsuccessful try at gaining political freedom. Everything that had preceded was only preparation. The record of the Revolution in the Ukraine provides a valuable insight not so much into the national movement itself as into the conditions under which it was born. The papers that follow analyze this complicated event in greater depth than has ever been done in the scholarly literature, and they furnished a basis for understanding the Ukraine at the instant of its entry onto the stage of history as a self-conscious political entity.

CHAPTER ONE

Ukrainian National Aspirations and the Russian Provisional Government

Wolodymyr Stojko

THE COLLAPSE OF the Russian tsarist autocracy in March 1917[1] created a situation of flux. For the various peoples within the Russian Empire, it provided a new oportunity for the realization of their national aspirations. The Ukrainians were among the most active in asserting their national rights and in laying the foundations for a new relationship with Russia. The development of Ukrainian-Russian relations, particularly between the Russian Provisional Government and the Ukrainian Central Rada,* is the subject of this study.

Ukrainians actively participated in the March revolution in Petrograd. The Volynskyi regiment, composed chiefly of Ukrainians, was the first to join the civilian demonstrators,[2] thus marking the turning point of these revolutionary developments. Ukrainian students in Petrograd formed a Temporary Ukrainian Revolutionary Committee, which issued an appeal to the Ukrainians in that

---

* Since the word *Rada,* meaning "council," is used extensively throughout this book, it will not be italicized as all the other foreign words.

[1] All dates in this study are given according to the Gregorian or new style calendar.

[2] O. Lototskyi, *Storinky mynuloho,* Vol. III (Warsaw: Ukrainskyi Naukovyi Instytut, 1934), p. 315. As one of the soldiers later told Tsereteli, "In the February days . . . Ukrainian soldiers of the Petrograd garrison were the first to go to the side of the revolution, since we suffered enough persecution of Ukrainianism under the old regime." I. G. Tsereteli, *Vospominaniia o fevralskoi revoliutsii,* Vol. II (Paris: Mouton & Co., 1963) p. 103. See also V. Vynnychenko, *Vidrodzhennia natsii,* Vol. I (Kiev-Vienna: Vyd. Dzvin, 1920), p. 252.

city calling for self-sacrifice "not for foreign political rights but for the national and political rights of the Ukrainian people."[3] And when the Petrograd Soviet of Workers' Deputies was formed, the Ukrainian colony in Petrograd sent representatives.

On March 22, 1917, the Petrograd branch of the Ukrainian Progressivist Association (TUP) issued a declaration demanding national-territorial autonomy for the Ukraine, and three days later Ukrainians in the city staged a demonstration to commemorate the Shevchenko Anniversary, at which some thirty thousand civilians and soldiers participated.[4] On March 30, and again on April 3, 1917, delegations of Petrograd Ukrainians, who by that time had organized a Ukrainian national committee, visited Prince Lvov, the Prime Minister and Minister of the Interior of the newly created Provisional Government. They requested the appointment of Ukrainians to all governing positions in the Ukraine, the creation of a commissar for Ukrainian affairs in the Provisional Government, the satisfaction of cultural and educational needs, and the introduction of the Ukrainian language in the administration of churches, courts, and schools of the Ukraine. The need to free arrested Galician and Bukovinian Ukrainians was also discussed. Although he agreed with many of the demands, the Prime Minister declined to make any commitments, "as if events were not rapidly passing by and as if there were no need for life to catch up with them."[5]

The first uncertain news about the collapse of the tsarist regime reached Kiev on March 13, 1917. Once confirmed, it spread rapidly, triggering enthusiasm and an outburst of national activities in the Ukraine, as well as in Ukrainian settlements in other parts of the Empire and in the Armed Forces.[6] Considering that the tsarist Russian government had denied Ukrainian nationality and pro-

---

[3] Lototskyi, Vol. III, p. 327.

[4] For a detailed account of Ukrainian activities in Petrograd, see *ibid.* and D. Doroshenko, *Istoriia Ukrainy, 1917–1923 rr.*, Vol. I (2nd ed.; New York: Bulava Publishing Corporation, 1954).

[5] Lototskyi, Vol. III, p. 243; Doroshenko, Vol. I, p. 49. In some cases Ukrainians were appointed as gubernia commissars as well as to positions in the county administration of the Ukraine.

[6] On Ukrainian activities in the eastern part of the Empire, for example, see, I. Svit, "1917 Rik na Dalekomu Skhodi," *Zoloti rokovyny* (Jersey City—New York: Vyd. 'Svoboda,' 1967), pp. 151–164.

hibited even its most elementary manifestations, the extent of this spontaneity caught many by surprise.

In Kiev, the Ukrainian Rada, which had been organized on March 17, 1917, assumed the leadership of the Ukrainian national movement.[7] At this point, the Rada apparently looked forward to successful cooperation with Russian democracy and was "confident," as it stated in its telegraph to the Prime Minister, Prince Lvov, "that the just demands of the Ukrainian people and their democratic intelligentsia will be fully satisfied."[8] A similar telegram was also sent to A. Kerensky. This note of optimism also resounded in the Rada's declaration of March 22, 1917: "Liberty has come to all peoples and to all oppressed nations of Russia" and for ". . . the first time, you, the thirty million Ukrainians, will have the opportunity to say for yourselves who you are and how you wish to live as a separate nation."[9]

Kiev again became a center of Ukrainian national life. On April 1, 1917, an impressive demonstration was held to celebrate a "Holiday of Freedom." Some hundred thousand people participated.[10] Ukrainian political, cultural, military, and other organizations made their headquarters in Kiev, and numerous congresses were held there. Various Ukrainian periodicals appeared again. Publishing houses previously closed by the tsarist regime resumed their activities, and new ones were established.

The culminating point of Ukrainian organizational activity came in Kiev when on April 19–21, 1917, the Rada convened the All-Ukrainian National Congress. Nine hundred delegates with mandates, along with some six hundred other participants, attended the Congress. The delegates represented peasant, professional, military, and cultural-educational organizations, in addition to

---

[7] V. Manilov (ed.), *1917 god na Kievshchine; khronika sobytii* (Kiev: Gos. Izd. Ukrainy, 1928), p. 6; Doroshenko, Vol. I, p. 42.

[8] R. P. Browder and A. F. Kerensky (eds.), *The Russian Provisional Government, 1917: Documents,* Vol. I (Stanford: Stanford University Press, 1961), p. 370; Doroshenko, Vol. I, p. 42.

[9] *Ibid.,* p. 43.

[10] Manilov, p. 19; V. Chernov, *The Great Russian Revolution* (New York: Russell and Russell, 1966), p. 266. The text of the resolutions adopted on this occasion expressed support of the Provisional Government and demanded immediate broad autonomy in order "to implement immediately all measures in order to give a national character to public institutions in the Ukraine. . . ." Browder and Kerensky, Vol. I, p. 371.

political parties, municipalities, and *zemstvos* within as well as outside of the Ukraine.

The All-Ukrainian National Congress reorganized the Rada, recognizing it as "the supreme national authority with a duty to protect the rights and liberties of the Ukrainian people, to prepare plans for Ukrainian autonomy, and to take steps for its realization."[11] The Rada was empowered to initiate the formation of a union comprised of all peoples in the Empire who, "like the Ukrainians, demand national and territorial autonomy on the principles of the democratic Russian republic." At the same time, the Congress recognized the right of the All-Russian Constituent Assembly to sanction "the new state order of Russia." However, the Ukrainians, in cooperation with the national minorities, also would lay immediate foundations for an "autonomous existence." The resolutions stated that all nations have the right to self-determination and that "frontiers between states must be established in accordance with the will of the borderland population." Finally, the Congress protested against Polish "claims to non-Polish lands" (i.e., eastern Galicia) and asked that the Ukraine be granted a seat at a future peace conference.[12]

While demands for territorial national autonomy[13] received the support of all Ukrainian congresses, this did not necessarily represent the unanimous opinion of Ukrainians. Virtually all the congresses contained voices demanding complete independence. For example, at the Ukrainian Military Congress (May 18–21), writes R. Pipes, "the general tone of these sessions was so extremely nationalistic that Vynnychenko, the delegate of the Rada, and a leading member of the USD [Ukrainian Social Democrats], felt forced to plead with the delegates to remain loyal to the Russian democracy...."[14]

---

11 N. Avdeev, *Revoliutsiia 1917 goda: khronika sobytii*, Vol. II (Moscow: Gos. Izd., 1923), p. 24.

12 Text of the resolutions in Browder and Kerensky, Vol. I, pp. 372–373. A slightly different version appears in Doroshenko, Vol. I, pp. 58–59.

13 The President of the Rada, M. Hrushevskyi, defined autonomy as "the right to live according to your own laws and not under foreign laws and government." In the case of the Ukraine, this autonomy would "more or less approach a state of independence." M. Hrushevskyi, *Iakoi avtonomii i federatsii khoche Ukraina* (Vienna: Nakl. Soiuza Vyzvolennia, Ukrainy, 1917), pp. 3–4.

14 R. Pipes, *The Formation of the Soviet Union* (Cambridge: Harvard

Ukrainian goals as put forth at that time reflected the thinking of the Ukrainian Social Democratic Labor Party (USDLP), the Ukrainian Party of Socialist-Revolutionaries (SR's), and the Ukrainian Progressive Association (TUP), which later was reorganized into the Ukrainian Party of Socialist-Federalists (UPSF).[15] These parties commanded the leadership of the Ukrainian national movement and steered it within autonomist limits. Some of the Social Democrats feared, according to Vynnychenko, that if they crossed beyond that demand, it would break up "the revolutionary forces of all Russia."[16] The Ukrainian Socialist-Revolutionaries were more outspoken in their national demands, though at the time they did not go beyond the formula of "national territorial autonomy."[17] On the other hand, many intellectuals in the Ukrainian Progressivist Association considered reorganization of the Russian Empire into a federation as only a beginning. A European federation would follow in which the Ukraine would play a leading role.[18]

Since this policy has often been criticized, subsequent explanations by leading participants have tended to play down ideological motivations. Rather, they argue that a cautious and more practical policy was necessary during this period, because the Russian military was strong in the Ukraine, particularly in the western war zone, where troops could be deployed against the Ukrainians.[19] Further-

---

University Press, 1964), p. 56. See also K. M. Oberuchev, *Vospominaniia* (New York: Oberutcheff Publishing Fund, 1930), pp. 226–227, and Chernov, p. 272.

[15] For a brief description of Ukrainian parties, see *Ukraine: A Concise Encyclopedia,* Vol. I (Toronto: University of Toronto Press, 1963), pp. 728–730.

[16] Vynnychenko, Vol. I, pp. 543–544.

[17] S. M. Dimanstein (ed.), *Revoliutsiia i natsionalnyi vopros, fev.–okt. 1917,* Vol. III (Moscow: Izd. Kommunisti-Cheskoi Akademii, 1930), pp. 137–138.

[18] S. Yefremov, *Istoriia ukrainskoho pysmenstva,* Vol. II (Kiev-Leipzig: Ukrainska Nakl., 1919), pp. 242–244. For the July 1917 platform of the Ukrainian Party of Socialist-Federalists, see Dimanstein, Vol. III, pp. 167–168.

[19] It should be noted that during the summer of 1917 there were three million Ukrainians in the Russian Army of ten million. Further, "the Ukrainian contingent was concentrated, in principle, on the southwestern and Rumanian fronts." The breakdown of the army on the Rumanian front, according to nationality, was: "Russians—33%, Ukrainians—23%, Muslims—16%, Belorussians—8%, Poles—7%, Moldavians—5%, etc."

more, there was also a shortage of trained Ukrainian administrators and officials, so that time was needed in order for the national revival to achieve greater organizational strength and to allow Ukrainians to improve their position in the large cities, where Russians and Russified elements predominated.[20]

The last point, due to its direct relevance to the problem discussed, merits additional consideration. The Soviet historian Popov, writing about the pre-war period, observed that "large landowners in the Ukraine . . . were by nationality mostly Russian. And together with the large army of Russian officials—Russificators, Russian soldiers, the clergy, and in part the commercial bourgeoisie . . . [they] formed the cornerstone of Russian chauvinism in the Ukraine. . . ."[21] For obvious reasons, Popov failed to include the Russian proletariat in his list. The revolution, in this respect, changed little. In their orientation toward Petrograd, the Russians and Russified elements paid little attention to the national needs and aspirations of the Ukrainian people. A. A. Goldenveyzer gives a good picture of this in his memoirs: "In the first weeks (following the revolution)," he writes, "we did not know and didn't wish to know anything about Ukrainianism and about its national aspirations. Every reminder about it from interested circles was received by us as rude tactlessness."[22]

The Russians and other pro-Russian minorities in the Ukraine, observed Chernov, the leader of the Russian Socialist-Revolutionaries, "found it difficult . . . to cease considering themselves masters

---

A. H. Tkachuk, "Krakh sprob Tsentralnoi Rady vykorystaty ukrainizovani viiskovi formuvanniia v 1917 r," *Ukrainskyi istorychnyi zhurnal*, XI, 8 (Kiev, 1967), p. 76, n. 7; L. Shankovsky, "Disintegration of the Imperial Russian Army in 1917," *The Ukrainian Quarterly*, XIII, 4 (New York, 1957), pp. 305 ff.

[20] B. Martos, "First Universal of the Ukrainian Central Rada," *The Ukrainian Quarterly*, XXIV, 1 (New York, 1968), pp. 23 ff. M. Kovalevskyi, *Pry dzherelakh borotby* (Munich: 'Biblos,' 1960), pp. 285–286. For a different interpretation, see L. Shankovskyi, "Ukrainska natsionalno-vyzvolna revoliutsiia," *Almanakh provydinnia na rik 1967* (Philadelphia: Vyd. 'America,' 1967), pp. 124–156.

[21] N. N. Popov, *Ocherk Kommunisticheskoi Partii (b) Ukrainy* (Kharkov: Izd. Proletarii, 1929), p. 26.

[22] A. A. Goldenveyzer, "Iz kievskikh vospominanii (1917–1921 gg.)," in *Arkhiv russkoi revoliutsii*, Vol. VI (Berlin, 1922), p. 168. See also S. I. Goldelman, *Zhydivska natsionalna avtonomiia v Ukraini, 1917–1920* (Munich: 'Dniprova Khvylia,' 1967), p. 16 ff.

of the situation, accepting the position that national minorities were content with the usual guarantees of minority rights."[23] Having control of institutions based in the large cities, such as the Councils of United Civil Organizations and the Soviets, they turned them into centers of support for Russian rule. For example, the Kiev Executive Committee of the Council of United Civic Organizations (IKSOO) was, according to Chernov, "in its overwhelming majority . . . alien to the Ukrainian movement," and "a rallying point for the Russian minority in the Ukraine."[24] The Provisional Government recognized this body, without qualification, as its local representative.[25] At the same time, it disregarded the Rada, which commanded the general support of the Ukrainian people.

At the end of May 1917, the Rada, strengthened by the support it received from the First Ukrainian Military Congress (May 18–21), decided to present its views and demands directly to the new Russian authorities. A ten-man delegation, headed by V. Vynnychenko, was sent to Petrograd. They were greeted at the railroad station by Ukrainian military representatives from the Petrograd garrison, a military orchestra, and two units of Ukrainian soldiers as honorary guards.[26] But any warmth derived from this welcome soon dissipated, since the delegation was accorded a cold reception by the Provisional Government and the Petrograd Soviet.

The Memorandum or, as it was then called, the "Declaration of the Ukrainian Central Rada," submitted by the delegation to the Provisional Government and the Petrograd Soviet, explained at length the nature and the problems of the Ukrainian national revival. It pointed out the hostility that Ukrainians encountered from the Russian minority, noting that they apparently were forgetting that the few cities in which they predominated were only small islands in a sea of Ukrainians. Eventually, these cities would succumb to Ukrainianization. The Declaration asserted that the Rada, an elected representative body, "was the voice of the or-

---

[23] Chernov, p. 276. On the opposition of the minorities, see: Vynnychenko, Vol. I, *passim;* Kovalevskyi, pp. 290–309; Dimanstein, Vol. III, pp. 144–149.

[24] Chernov, p. 266. See also Manilov, pp. 3–4, and Tsereteli, Vol. II, p. 90.

[25] Oberuchev, p. 113.

[26] Kovalevskyi, pp. 334–335.

ganized people." Specific demands which the Rada felt should be realized without delay were formulated in nine points: 1) recognition in principle of autonomy for the Ukraine; 2) participation of Ukrainian representatives in the peace negotiations, particularly with reference to the question of Ukrainian territories in Galicia; 3) creation of a commissar on Ukrainian affairs in the Provisional Government for the purpose of informing it about opinions and measures concerning life in the region (*Krai*); 4) the addition of a commissar with a regional council (*Kraieva Rada*) to consolidate government measures in all gubernias with a Ukrainian population; 5) the formation of separate Ukrainian army units in the rear and, as far as possible, at the front; 6) the extension of Ukrainianization (already approved by the Provisional Government for elementary schools) to secondary and higher educational establishments; 7) the appointment of responsible civil and ecclesiastical leaders who were acquainted with Ukrainian life, speak the Ukrainian language, and enjoy public confidence; 8) placement at the disposal of the Rāda necessary funds from the Provisional Government treasury; and 9) permission both to allow unjustly deported Ukrainians to return to their native land and to aid Ukrainian prisoners of war from Galicia by resettling them in Ukrainian gubernias.[27]

Tsereteli, then Minister of Post and Telegraph, recognized in his *Memoirs* that, considering the circumstances created by the war, the Ukrainian demands were moderate and it might have been possible to reach an agreement satisfactory to both sides.

Why did not Tsereteli, as a member of the government, support an agreement with the Ukrainians? His explanation is that they (i.e., Tsereteli and his colleagues from the Petrograd Soviet) did not give sufficient attention to the Declaration of the Rada because of other urgent matters, did not understand the real position of the Rada in the Ukrainian national movement, and did not recognize the growing importance of the national question.[28] Works of other contemporaries tend to uphold these assumptions. Chernov, writing after the Revolution, was critical of the Provisional Gov-

---

[27] Dimanstein, Vol. III, pp. 143–149; Browder and Kerensky, Vol. I, pp. 374–376. Interestingly, there was no reference, in either the Memorandum or the negotiations, to the Pereiaslav Treaty (1654) as a possible basis for the Ukrainian demands or as an assumption that the abdication of the tsar freed the Ukranians from the obligations imposed by it.

[28] Tsereteli, Vol. II, pp. 89 ff.

ernment's policy toward the Ukraine. Miliukov seemed to indicate that he would have favored an even tougher policy, while Kerensky, commenting briefly on the national question, suggested that he stood behind the course followed by the Provisional Government.[29]

All three major Russian parties in the Provisional Government made pronouncements on the nationality problem. The Socialist-Revolutionaries expressed their support for the "federal democratic republic, with territorial-national autonomy" based on an ethnographic principle.[30] The Mensheviks recognized the need for "national-cultural autonomy" and for an ill-defined local self-government. Nevertheless, they stressed the necessity to preserve the unity of the Russian state.[31] The Kadets opposed a federation based on national autonomy, but favored national-cultural autonomy and administrative decentralization based upon some form of *zemstvo*-type local self-government.[32] Miliukov, the party's leader, explained that the "preservation of the unity of the Russian State is the limiting factor conditioning the decision of the Party."[33]

The Ukrainian delegation soon discovered that the principle that emphasized the "preservation of the unity of the Russian State" guided the decisions not only of the Kadets but of the new Russian leadership in general. It took the delegation three days to arrange a meeting with the Executive Committee of the Soviet. When they finally met, the Soviet avoided taking a stand on the Ukrainian question and directed the delegation to the Provisional Government. The Ukrainian delegation was particularly frustrated by the fact that "not a single" newspaper of the Russian "revolutionary democracy" (i.e., socialists) would publish the Rada's memorandum. The members of the Provisional Government listened politely to the delegation's demands and explanations,

---

[29] See particularly Chernov, *Great Russian Revolution;* P. Miliukov, *Vtoraia russkaia revoliutsiia* (Sofia: Rossiisko-Bulgarskoe Knigo-Izd., 1921–24) and his *Political Memoirs, 1905–1917* (Ann Arbor, Mich.: The University of Michigan Press, 1967); A. F. Kerensky, *Russia and History's Turning Point* (New York: Duell, Sloan and Pearce, 1965) and his *The Catastrophe* (New York: D. Appleton and Co., 1927).

[30] Dimanstein, Vol. III, pp. 88–89.

[31] *Ibid.*, pp. 96–97; P. Khrystiuk, *Zamitky i materialy do istorii ukrainskoi revoliutsii, 1917–1920,* Vol. I (Vienna: Vernay, 1921), p. 128, n. 19.

[32] Dimanstein, Vol. III, pp. 83–84; F. F. Kokoshkin, *Avtonomiia i federatsiia* (Petrograd: 'Svoboda,' 1917).

[33] Browder and Kerensky, Vol. I, p. 317.

then passed the whole problem to a commission of judicial experts who were to consider the legal aspects of the problem.[34]

The commission questioned the legal validity of virtually every Ukrainian demand,[35] and after a few meetings the delegation left Petrograd empty-handed. Their return to Kiev was arranged to coincide with the opening of the All-Ukrainian Peasant Congress held on June 10–15, 1917. On the first day of the Congress, before 2,200 participants, the delegation submitted a report that aroused great indigation and an upsurge of anti-Russian feeling.[36]

On June 14, the Rada received a telegram that summarized the Russian position: "The Provisional Government does not consider it possible to satisfy the demands of the Central Rada, since all questions concerning the autonomy of the Ukraine and other nationalities must be decided by the Constituent Assembly."[37] In an official communiqué on this question, the Provisional Government also noted that inasmuch "as this Rada has not been elected by popular vote, the Government could hardly recognize it as the spokesman for the true will of all the Ukrainian people."[38] Since neither the Provisional Government nor the Petrograd Soviet had a popular mandate, it is clear that the Provisional Government attempted to apply different standards to itself than to the Rada.

In general, the reply of the Provisional Government received the support of the Russian press and of the Russian and pro-Russian minorities in the Ukraine.[39] On the other hand, it further strengthened Ukrainian determination. This was particularly underlined in the remarks by the president of the Rada, M. Hrushevskyi, who read the Russian reply before the Peasant Congress on June 15,[40] as well as in the adopted resolutions by that congress. The resolutions that were dispatched to Petrograd supported all the demands of the Rada and advised that body to carry out its plans

---

[34] *Ibid.*, p. 374; Vynnychenko, Vol. I, pp. 157 ff.; Kovalevskyi, pp. 335 ff.

[35] The deliberations of the commission can be found in "Iz istorii natsionalnoi politiki Vremennogo Pravitelstva," *Krasnyi arkhiv*, Vol. XXX (Moscow: Gos. Izd., 1928), pp. 49–55.

[36] Doroshenko, Vol. I, p. 83. See also, Vynnychenko, Vol. I, p. 174.

[37] Manilov, p. 99.

[38] Text of the communiqué is in Browder and Kerensky, Vol. I, pp. 376–377.

[39] *Ibid.*, pp. 377–379; Khrystiuk, Vol. I, p. 64; Vynnychenko, Vol. I, pp. 189–190; Chernov, p. 276; Doroshenko, Vol. I, p. 93.

[40] Manilov, p. 102.

without further delay.[41] Some participants even insisted on a proclamation of Ukrainian independence.[42]

After consideration of the Provisional Government's position, the
Rada resolved on June 16 that the Provisional Government "deliberately acted against the interests of the toiling people of the
Ukraine and contrary ... to the principle of self-determination of
nations." It also decided "to appeal to the Ukrainian people to step
up organizational activities and to begin immediately to lay down
foundations for an autonomous order in the Ukraine."[43] Vynnychenko explained the Rada's tactics as "neither rebellion nor
submission, but steady, untiring organization of our forces," and
"systematically laying foundations of autonomy."[44]

The Russian-Ukrainian conflict was intensified further when
Kerensky, then Minister of War, prohibited the convening of the
Second Ukrainian Military Congress on the grounds that it was
"untimely." Nevertheless, the Congress met on June 18, 1917, and
was subsequently legalized by a telegram from the Provisional
Government, which was greeted with triumphant laughter by the
delegates.[45] A total of 2,308 delegates, representing 1,600,000 men
of the Armed Forces, participated.[46]

---

[41] For the text of the resolutions, see Dimanstein, Vol. III, pp. 150–153;
Khrystiuk, Vol. I, pp. 65–68.

[42] Chernov, pp. 275–276; Doroshenko, Vol. I, pp. 86–87; Manilov, pp.
95–96.

[43] Tsereteli, Vol. II, p. 96.

[44] Vynnychenko, Vol. I, p. 193.

[45] The text of Kerensky's telegram is in Browder and Kerensky, pp. 379–
380. It should be noted that Kerensky received complete support from
Izvestiia, the organ of the Soviets. See the editorial on June 15, 1917,
ibid., pp. 381–382. A different opinion on the position of the Soviets appears in Tsereteli, Vol. II, pp. 97–98. On the other hand, Lenin attacked
Kerensky in *Pravda* (June 15, 1917), asking "whether such treatment of
oppressed nationalities is even compatible with the dignity of simple
democracy, let alone of Socialism." *Ibid.*, pp. 382–383. It should be
stressed that the Bolshevik branch in Kiev was less willing to support
the Ukrainians. Manilov, pp. 26, 104–105, 113–114, 119–122.

[46] Vynnychenko, Vol. I, p. 200. National spirit was particularly strong
among Ukrainian soldiers. For a description of the Ukrainian military
movement, see a special chapter on this subject in Doroshenko, *Istoriia
Ukrainy.* There is also a well-documented article by Shankovskyi, pp.
305 ff. See also Tsereteli, Vol. II, pp. 93 ff. The Russian Commander of
the Kiev Military District, K. M. Oberuchev, was opposed to the forma-

In its resolutions, the Congress called upon the Ukrainian Rada, "our supreme representative body," not to confer any longer with the Russian Provisional Government but, in conjunction with the national minorities in the Ukraine, to initiate at once vigorous organization of the country and the realization of autonomy. "The Congress, by itself, guarantees decisive and most active support to all undertakings of the Central Rada and calls on all organized Ukrainian people to fulfill all orders of the Central Rada in unity and without delay."[47]

The Military Congress thus provided a convenient stage for the Rada's next act, the proclamation on June 23, 1917, of an official manifesto, the First Universal.[48] "Let the Ukraine be free! Without either separating from Russia or breaking with the Russian State, let the Ukrainian people on their own territory have the right to manage their own life. Let a National Ukrainian Assembly (*Soim*) elected by universal, equal, direct and secret balloting, establish order and harmony in the Ukraine." The Universal enumerated all the demands of the Rada that had been rejected by the Provisional Government, and noted that since the desires of the Ukrainian people could not be realized in agreement with Russia, "we, the Ukrainian Central Rada, issue this Universal to our entire nation and proclaim that from this day forth, we ourselves shall direct our own lives." Further, the people were called upon to undertake a "great national effort" and hope was expressed that non-Ukrainians would also help in establishing an autonomous Ukraine. The Universal promised to convoke a Ukrainian Territorial Assembly that would represent all the people and draft laws that would later be confirmed by the All-Russian Constituent Assembly. It also introduced, as of July 1, 1917, a special "tax" for the activities of the Rada.[49]

The Congress greeted the Universal with enthusiasm that "reached the point of ecstasy,"[50] and soon assurances of support

---

tion of separate Ukrainian units. Oberuchev, pp. 220 ff. General impressions of the Congress, as described in the Russian newspaper *Kievskaia mysl*, are reproduced in Vynnychenko, Vol. I, pp. 206 ff.

[47] Text of the resolution in Vynnychenko, Vol. I, pp. 200 ff.

[48] This term was used previously by the Ukrainian Cossack hetmans for their official decrees or proclamations.

[49] Doroshenko, Vol. I, pp. 89 ff.; Browder and Kerensky, Vol. I, pp. 383 ff.; Chernov, p. 277.

[50] Vynnychenko, Vol. I, p. 225.

and contributions for the Rada came from Ukrainians throughout the country.[51] Shortly thereafter, an executive body, the General Secretariat, headed by V. Vynnychenko, was established to carry out the decisions of the Rada.[52]

Russian reaction to this turn of events indicated both dismay and anger. The Judicial Commission of the Provisional Government which met on June 26, proposed a declaration blaming the Rada for having unilaterally proclaimed Ukrainian autonomy and denying any validity to the First Universal, calling it "an act of open revolt."[53] In the Russian press, developments in the Ukraine were labelled a "betrayal," and the Ukrainians were accused of giving a "stab in the back to the revolution."[54] Russian and pro-Russian minorities in the Ukraine held similar views at first, but witnessing the broad support that the Rada had received, some, like the IKSOO, began to explore possibilities for achieving an understanding with it.[55]

The Provisional Government issued on June 28 a milder proclamation to the Ukrainian people than the declaration proposed by its Judicial Commission. In it, the Provisional Government promised cultural self-determination, removal of all traces of oppression, and other measures. It pleaded with the Ukrainians not to split up "the forces of emancipated Russia" and asked them to await the meeting of the Constituent Assembly for its decision on the nationality question.[56] If the declaration was intended to split the Ukrainian people from the Rada by vague promises, it failed. Characteristic was the response from the All-Ukrainian Council of Peasants' Deputies, which in its resolutions stated that the Provisional Government could achieve understanding with the Ukrainian democracy only by recog-

---

[51] Doroshenko, Vol. I, p. 94; Tsereteli, Vol. II, p. 99; and especially Khrystiuk, Vol. I, pp. 132–134.

[52] Doroshenko, Vol. I, pp. 95–96; Tsereteli, Vol. II, p. 99.

[53] *Krasnyi arkhiv,* Vol. XXX, p. 55; Tsereteli, Vol. II, p. 104.

[54] Doroshenko, Vol. I, pp. 94–95; reproduction of comments on the First Universal in the Russian press—*Rech, Volia naroda,* and *Izvestiia* —in Browder and Kerensky, Vol. I, pp. 386–389. Some maintained that the Universal was a product of German intrigue. Chernov, pp. 278–279.

[55] Tsereteli, Vol. II, pp. 100 ff.; Vynnychenko, Vol. I, pp. 240 ff.; Khrystiuk, Vol. I, pp. 62–64, 88–89; Manilov, pp. 118–122, 127–128.

[56] Browder and Kerensky, Vol. I, pp. 385–386; Manilov, p. 484.

nizing the Rada as the legitimate spokesman of the Ukraine and by entering into close cooperation with it.[57]

The Rada ignored the appeal of the Provisional Government. On July 6 it confirmed the newly formed General Secretariat, and four days later expressed confidence in the Secretariat's program, as presented in its first declaration.[58]

In the meantime, the worsening of Russian relations with the Ukraine and Finland, as well as the growing impatience of non-Russian peoples in other parts of the Empire, forced the first All-Russian Congress of Soviets of Workers' and Soldiers' Deputies to give attention to this problem. Although it relegated the final solution of the national question to the Constituent Assembly, the Congress did recognize the seriousness of the situation and recommended a number of steps to be introduced immediately by the Provisional Government.[59] On July 5, the Congress resolved "to give full support to the Ukrainian revolutionary democracy in its efforts to achieve democratic autonomy for the Ukraine, with protection of the rights of national minorities." Until an All-Russian Constituent Assembly would meet, the Congress urged the Provisional Government to come to an understanding with Ukrainian democracy for the purpose of forming a territorial (*kraievyi*) organ for the Ukraine and also for taking concrete measures to meet the national needs of the Ukrainian people.[60]

The Provisional Government followed the initiative of the All-Russian Congress of Soviets of Workers' and Soldiers' Deputies and decided to send a delegation to Kiev. Tsereteli observed that even the Kadets could not oppose this move, since "general opinion was extremely alarmed by the growing conflict with the Ukrainian people of thirty million so close to the war zone."[61] At first, the government considered forming a delegation composed of prominent members of various Russian parties. But

---

[57] Doroshenko, Vol. I, p. 110.

[58] Manilov, pp. 133, 139–140. Text of the declaration is in Dimanstein, Vol. III, pp. 164–166.

[59] *Ibid.*, pp. 98 ff.; Tsereteli, Vol. II, pp. 107 ff. These sources also include the opinions of those who opposed the resolutions either for going too far or for not going far enough with regard to national demands.

[60] Text of the resolution in Tsereteli, Vol. II, pp. 130–131.

[61] *Ibid.*, p. 133.

since such a group would have limited authority, it was given up as a waste of time, and government members were chosen instead.[62] On July 11, two members of this high-level delegation, M. Tereshchenko and I. Tsereteli, arrived in Kiev; they were joined the next day by A. Kerensky.[63]

The delegation first contacted representatives of various local institutions and political groups. Then they met with the chief Ukrainian negotiators, M. Hrushevskyi, V. Vynnychenko, and S. Petliura. After three days of discussion, a compromise agreement was reached.[64] The terms were embodied in a declaration of July 15, 1917, which stated that the Provisional Government had decided:

> To appoint a special organ, the General Secretariat, in the capacity of a higher organ for the administration of regional affairs in the Ukraine, the membership of which shall be determined by the Government in agreement with the Ukrainian Central Rada and augmented on an equitable basis with democratic organizations representing other nationalities inhabiting the Ukraine. The Government shall work through the designated organ in carrying out measures dealing with the life and administration of the region.

Moreover,

> the Provisional Government shall respond favorably to the elaboration of bills by the Ukrainian Rada, in such forms as the Rada itself finds correspond most closely to the interests of the region, regarding the national and political status of the Ukraine, and, also, regarding the methods of settling the land question in the Ukraine, for the purpose of submitting these bills to the Constituent Assembly.[65]

The last part of the declaration contained an agreement on military matters. Ukrainian representation would be established in the Russian War Ministry, in the General Staff, and with the Supreme Commander so as to coordinate Ukrainianization, and where the Minister of War found possible, to form Ukrainian

---

[62] Miliukov, Vol. I, pt. 1, p. 231.

[63] Another member of the Government, N. Nekrasov, was also present in Kiev for the first two days. Tsereteli, Vol. II, p. 134.

[64] For an account by participants on opposing sides, see: *ibid.*, pp. 133 ff.; Vynnychenko, Vol. I, pp. 273 ff.; Doroshenko, Vol. I, pp. 111–113.

[65] Browder and Kerensky, Vol. I, pp. 389–390; Ukrainian text in Doroshenko, Vol. I, pp. 114–115.

units. Ukrainian military committees could continue their functions in harmony with other public military organizations, but for the duration of the war the unity of the army was to be preserved under Russian command.[66]

On July 16, the Rada issued its Second Universal and informed the Ukrainian people of the provisions of the agreement with the Provisional Government. The latter recognized the right of self-determination for all people, but the final decision regarding the future form of the Russian state would have to be taken by the Constituent Assembly. Until that time, the Ukraine should have no intention of arbitrarily establishing its autonomy.[67]

The agreement met opposition both in Russia and in the Ukraine. Within the Provisional Government itself, strong opposition was voiced by the Kadet ministers. After the agreement was approved by a majority, three Kadet ministers resigned from the cabinet and the remaining Kadet, N. Nekrasov, who favored the agreement, submitted his resignation to the party. According to the Kadet organ *Rech,* in the opinion of those who resigned, "the agreement created a chaotic relation between the Government and the organs of government in the Ukraine, opening the door for the Rada to make of the Ukraine, in a legal way, an autonomous state."[68]

Two days later, on July 18, the Central Committee of the Kadet party issued an explanation stating that the delegation went to Kiev "for preliminary negotiations with the Ukrainian Central Rada, but it concluded a ready-made agreement, so that it was impossible to make amendments to it..." The Kadets recognized "the necessity of preparing a plan for the territorial autonomy of the Ukraine for submission to the Constituent Assembly" and suggested that "the Committee has even started

---

[66] *Ibid.*

[67] Browder and Kerensky, Vol. I, pp. 392–393. The passage in the Universal which assumed that the Ukrainians would wait for the Constituent Assembly before final realization of autonomy was included solely to placate the Russian delegation, since, as Vynnychenko contends in his memoirs, *de facto* autonomy already existed in July 1917. Vynnychenko, Vol. I, pp. 284–285.

[68] F. A. Golder (ed.), *Documents of Russian History, 1914–17* (New York-London: The Century Co., 1927), p. 441. For an account of the Provisional Government meeting, see Tsereteli, Vol. II, pp. 149 ff.; Browder and Kerensky, Vol. I. pp. 390–392.

work on this measure." But the Party's Central Committee also maintained that "the immediate creation of a local government, responsible to a local public organization with indefinite authority over an undefined area, and premature approval of such a project of territorial autonomy by the Government. . . . is inadmissible."[69] At this point it appears that the Kadets either failed to realize or refused to admit that vagueness in certain parts of the document could work both ways. However, they soon made use of this vagueness to their own advantage.

In Kiev, the Declaration of the Provisional Government and the Second Universal were read before a plenum of the Rada. The chief negotiators received friendly applause and M. Hrushevskyi remarked: "We are rising to a higher level and achieving actual autonomy of the Ukraine with legislative and administrative bodies—the Rada and Secretariat".[70] The importance of this agreement has been continuously disputed among Ukrainians. The Second Universal did bring Russian acquiescence to the demands which were rejected only a short period before[71] and did give legitimacy to the Ukrainian organs, but it also imposed a brake on further development of the Ukrainian national revolution.

Vynnychenko recognized that this newly won legitimacy was a "cooling off" in the revolutionary process, but concluded along with the supporters of the agreement that in general the gains outweighed the losses.[72]

There were others, though, who did not share this view. Particularly critical were the nationalists, whose ranks were growing. Since they had little trust in the Russians, they advocated the realization of complete independence to better serve Ukrainian interests. The Ukrainian Democratic-Agrarian Party program, adopted in June, stated their goal as "complete sovereignty for the Ukrainian people." During the same month, the Union of Ukrainian Statehood held a meeting at Kiev in which over 2,500 participants

---

[69] Golder, pp. 441–443. Space limitations prevent a fuller presentation of the arguments on both sides, but for criticism by the Kadets and the reply of the Government delegation see Tsereteli, Vol. II, pp. 156–158.

[70] Doroshenko, Vol. I, pp. 115–116.

[71] Y. Zozulia, "Druhyi Universal Ukrainskoi Tsentralnoi Rady i ioho pravno-istorychna vartist," *Vilna Ukraina,* XIV, 55–57 (New York, 1967), p. 12.

[72] Vynnychenko, Vol. I, pp. 274–275.

adopted resolutions calling for the proclamation of an independent Ukrainian republic.[73] A direct response to the agreement, it would seem, came from the Second Ukrainian Polubotok Regiment.[74] On the night of July 17, it swiftly took control of Kiev as the first step in seizing power. Dissatisfied with having "freedom only on paper or only half of the freedom,"[75] the leaders were planning to proclaim the independence of the Ukraine, to call Ukrainian soldiers back from all fronts, and to conclude a separate peace treaty with the Central Powers. They hoped that the Rada would not only support their plan but also provide the leadership for its realization. The Rada, on the other hand, apparently satisfied with its last negotiations with the Russians, took a stand against the uprising. The First Ukrainian B. Khmelnytskyi Regiment, which was to have taken part in the uprising, decided after serious hesitation[76] to support the Rada. This forced the Polubotok Regiment to abandon plans for a takeover and to submit also to the orders of the Rada.

Soon after, the Polubotok Regiment was sent to the front,[77] and the Rada proceeded to expand its own authority in accordance with an agreement of July 16. An understanding was completed with the national minorities, and their representatives entered the Secretariat and the Rada.[78] "The Statute of the Higher Administration of the Ukraine" was then drafted, and a delegation of three men, V. Vynnychenko, Kh. Baranovskyi, and M. Rafes (who represented the Jewish Social Democratic *Bund* in the Secretariat), went to Petrograd in the last days of July to have the statute approved by the Provisional Government.[79]

The proposed statute defined the Rada as the organ of "revolu-

---

[73] For texts see Dimanstein, Vol. III, pp. 159–160.

[74] Mlynovetskyi maintains that the decision was taken by a special Committee formed earlier at the initiative of the Union of Ukrainian Statehood. P. Mlynovetskyi, "Do tak zvanoho Polubotkivskoho perevorotu," *Almanakh-Kalendar Homonu Ukrainy na rik 1962* (Toronto, 1962), p. 161.

[75] Miliukov, Vol. I, pt. 1, pp. 80 ff.; Manilov, p. 153.

[76] Shemet, "M. Mikhnovskyi," *Khliborobska Ukraina*, bk. 5 (Vienna, 1924–25), p. 21.

[77] Doroshenko, Vol. I, p. 368.

[78] Doroshenko, Vol. I, pp. 119 ff. The number of non-Ukrainian members in the Rada was to be 202 and 51 candidates out of a total of 822. *Ibid.*, p. 123; Manilov, p. 184

[79] Manilov, p. 171.

tionary democracy" for all nationalities of the Ukraine, which was to prepare the country for the establishment of autonomy. It was to govern until the convocation of both a Ukrainian Constituent National Assembly and the All-Russian Constituent Assembly. The General Secretariat, described as the highest administrative organ, was to be formed by the Rada and to consult with it on more important questions. The Secretariat was to be responsible to the Central Rada and, when that body was not in session, to the *Mala Rada*. The Secretariat was to be confirmed by the Provisional Government and included fourteen general secretaries (interior, finance, military, food, land, justice, education, nationalities, trade and commerce, telegraph, labor, transport, a controller general, and a general clerk). The Secretary of Nationalities was assigned three assistant secretaries, representing the major minorities in the Ukraine—Russians, Jews, and Poles. According to the statute, all administration in the country was to be subordinated to the General Secretariat, and non-elective governmental posts were to be filled by that body or by its subordinate organs.

A Secretary of State was to be appointed to the Provisional Government (with the approval of the Rada), and his duty was to protect Ukrainian interests in Petrograd. If the Secretary deemed it necessary, he would send drafts of laws and budgetary estimates through the General Secretariat for the Rada's examination. The Ukrainian budget and all the laws approved by the Rada were to be submitted by the General Secretariat to the Provisional Government for its sanction. The funds used by the General Secretariat would be drawn from a budget at the disposal of the Rada.

The remaining points of the statute deal with such things as the authority of the Rada over cases of disagreement or the resignation of members from the General Secretariat. The statute ended with the statement that all orders and laws of the Provisional Government (with the exception of emergency cases) had to be published in an official organ before becoming effective in the Ukraine, and that they had to be published not only in Ukrainian but also in Russian, Yiddish, and Polish.[80]

The arrival of the Ukrainian delegation in Petrograd came at a time when a new government coalition was being formed.[81] When

---

[80] *Ibid.*, pp. 489 ff.; Doroshenko, Vol. I, p. 124 ff.; English text in Browder and Kerensky, Vol. I, pp. 394 ff.

[81] With the Kadets' resignation from the Provisional Government because of the Ukrainian question, there were also other withdrawals, par-

the coalition finally was organized, it followed a hard centralist line on the national question. Kerensky became Prime Minister, but he avoided the Ukrainian delegation. After some delays, the Ukrainians were met by N. Nekrasov, Minister of Finance, and by legal advisers, including Baron Nolde, who was well known for his strong criticism of the agreement of July 16.

The negotiations were tense and, according to Vynnychenko, "the Ukrainian delegation at times was considering leaving Petrograd."[82] According to P. Miliukov, the Russians tried to weaken the original agreement as much as possible.[83] Proposals and counter-proposals were exchanged without reaching an agreement.[84] At times, the Provisional Government debated the Ukrainian problem behind closed doors, and on August 17 it issued "Temporary Instructions for the General Secretariat of the Provisional Government in the Ukraine."

The "Instruction" defined the General Secretariat as the highest organ of the Provisional Government's local administration in the Ukraine until such time as the All-Russian Constituent Assembly made the final decision on what would constitute the future regional administration. It provided that the General Secretariat be appointed by the Provisional Government on the recommendation of the Rada and confined the authority of the General Secretariat to the provinces of Kiev, Volhynia, Podillia, Poltava, and Chernihiv (excluding the districts of Mhlyny, Surazh, Starodub, and Novozybkiv). Thus, even the provinces of Kherson, Tauria, Katerynoslav, and Kharkiv were now excluded, though as a result of the understanding reached by the negotiations in the July 16 agreement, they were, according to Tsereteli,[85] to be regarded as part of Ukrainian

---

ticularly those of A. I. Konovalov over labor policy and Prince Lvov over agrarian policy. Chernov, p. 282; Doroshenko, Vol. I, p. 128.

[82] Manilov, p. 193.

[83] Miliukov, Vol. I, pt. 2, p. 86.

[84] Even while negotiations were under way, the Ukrainian delegation was instructed that the Statute should be approved by the Provisional Government without changes that might alter the nature of any principles. Such changes could be made only with the consent of the *Mala Rada*. This instruction was adopted by the Ukrainian members of the *Mala Rada* over the opposition of the representative of the minorities, who regarded it as an ultimatum to the Provisional Government. Khrystiuk, Vol. I, note on pp. 113–114.

[85] Tsereteli, Vol. II, pp. 140–141.

territory.[86] Any extension of the Secretariat's authority to the other provinces was possible only upon the request of the local *zemstvos* formed in accordance with the laws of the Provisional Government. The number of secretaries was set at nine rather than fourteen as in the original statute. Supply, Posts and Telegraph, Justice, Transport, and Military were removed from its jurisdiction, and at least four (later reduced to three) of the nine secretaries had to be of non-Ukrainian nationality.[87] The General Secretariat was to prepare and submit bills pertaining to the life and administration of the Ukraine for approval by the Provisional Government. Those bills could be submitted first for consideration by the Rada. The "Instruction" stated that "the authority of the Provisional Government over matters of local government which lie within the competence" of the recognized General Secretaries should be exercised through them. At the same time, the local regional authorities should refer in all these matters to the General Secretariat, "which on communication with the Provisional Government shall relay the orders and instructions of the latter to the local authorities."[88] Thus, the reduction of the General Secretaries to intermediaries was made quite clear. As for appointments to governmental positions, the General Secretariat was to recommend nominees for appointment by the Provisional Government. A Commissar for Ukrainian Affairs was to act as laison between the Provisional Government and the General Secretariat, which was to have executive power over all matters in the specified provinces of the Ukraine. Only in urgent cases could the Provisional Government communicate directly with local authorities, though it was expected to inform the General Secretariat of such action.

---

[86] This only intensified Ukrainian activities in those provinces that were not placed under the General Secretariat. Vynnychenko, Vol. II, pp. 48–49; Doroshenko, Vol. I, p. 139.

[87] After the "Instruction" was issued, the Ukrainian negotiators, Mickiewicz and Zarubin, notified the Rada that the Provisional Government had reduced non-Ukrainian positions in the Secretariat from four to three and had also promised not to issue orders directly to local officials (except in an emergency of war) and to appoint the Ukrainian Commissar in Petrograd only after consultation with the General Secretariat. Manilov, p. 503; Browder and Kerensky, Vol. I, p. 396.

[88] Texts in Manilov, p. 503; Browder and Kerensky, Vol. I, pp. 396–397.

The "Instruction" shifted the center of authority from the Rada to the General Secretariat, making its cooperation with the former mandatory while at the same time reducing the Secretariat's extent of territorial jurisdiction and limiting the degree and the scope of its authority by reducing the number of secretaries and by retaining the power of decision-making in Petrograd. The "Instruction" thus was, with some minor exceptions, received favorably in Russia.[89] On the other hand, the Ukrainian public, irritated by the news that Russian soldiers shot at a Ukrainian regiment as it departed for the front,[90] received it with great discontent. For a few days the members of the Rada argued sharply about the "Instruction." There were motions to reject it, to ignore it, or to accept it with a proper statement. A leading advocate of the last proposal was Vynnychenko, who argued that, despite its limitations, the "Instruction" constituted a gain and presented a legal base for further struggle in the realization of Ukrainian goals. To do otherwise would lead to an estrangement with the national minorities and would possibly influence the conduct of the war, neither of which would be beneficial for the Ukraine. Furthermore, he added, it was only a temporary arrangement that could be changed under different circumstances.[91] In this moment of decision, no doubt, many felt the absence of the two Ukrainian regiments which had been dispatched from Kiev to the front only a short time ago, while Oberuchev, the Commander of the Kiev Military District, strengthened the city's garrison with Russian troops.[92]

On August 22, 1917, a resolution was adopted by a majority vote. Without a statement of acceptance or rejection of the "Instruction," it pointed out, among other things, that the "Instruction" was in sharp contradiction to the agreement of July 16; that it was based on distrust, it manifested Russian imperialism, and it did not meet

---

[89] Miliukov, Vol. I, pt. 2, p. 92. The Russian Senate refused to publish the instruction. See its statement in Browder and Kerensky, Vol. I, pp. 397–398.

[90] Manilov, p. 180.

[91] Vynnychenko, Vol. I, pp. 330 ff., and Vol. II, p. 471; a summary of discussion is in Khrystiuk, Vol. I, pp. 142–151. Richard Pipes ascribes the importance of the "Instruction" to the fact that "for the first time in history a Russian government had recognized the national principle as a base for the administrative division of the state . . ." Pipes, p. 65.

[92] Vynnychenko, Vol. I, pp. 325–326.

the needs of either the Ukrainians or the national minorities. And it urged the Provisional Government to implement the July agreement at the earliest possible time.[93]

Summing up the situation, Vynnychenko noted: "Everyone knew that it was not a peace, but a temporary truce, that a struggle would and must follow."[94] While his assessment proved to be correct, at the time there were no indications of Ukrainian preparations for a showdown. There was nothing comparable to the unity and determination present in June, when the Provisional Government rejected initial Ukrainian demands.

Considering the position A. Kerensky held in the Provisional Government, his remarks on the nationality question in the opening address to the State Conference in Moscow on August 25, 1917, provide additional insight into the thinking of the Russian leadership on this question. After pointing out the sacrifices of the Russian people for "the good of all peoples inhabiting our country," he turned to the non-Russian nations of the Russian Empire and asked: "Why do we fail to hear your voices casting your lot with us unconditionally, with no bargaining, in the fight for common freedom against a great terrifying despotism? We do not hear them because . . . the suspicion and hatred toward the old regime" have been transferred to the new one. Nevertheless, Kerensky maintained, "we will continue to keep our promise" and not to retract what we gave and what will be given by the supreme master of the Russian land, the Constituent Assembly." But, those that would "try to take advantage of our difficulties" he warned to keep their "Hands off!" The more defiant Finns and Ukrainians were especially singled out. In relation to the Ukrainians, he expressed faith that they ". . . in spite of many grievances and differences, perhaps due to misunderstanding, will never follow the course that would justify our saying: 'And why, my brother, dost thou kiss me? And who gave thee thirty pieces of silver?' "[95]

The Estonian representative at that conference, Mr. Pipp, appeared to express the feeling of many non-Russian participants: "The statement by the head of the Provisional Government harbors no kind words toward us" and "this attitude . . . is profoundly un-

---

[93] Manilov, p. 503; Browder and Kerensky, Vol. I, pp. 398–399; Khrystiuk, Vol. I, pp. 118–119.

[94] Vynnychenko, Vol. II, p. 37.

[95] Browder and Kerensky, Vol. III, pp. 1459–1460.

just."[96] Given the circumstances, these remarks seem strange indeed from a leader of a multi-national state in the midst of revolutionary developments and in the fourth year of a war. Kerensky apparently felt that the fruits of the revolution were simply gifts of the Russian people and not the result of a common effort. Not only did he not make any commitments to meet the aspirations of the non-Russian peoples, but he even reproached them for having asked their national rights. There apparently was a fundamentally opposite understanding of the meaning of the revolution, since, for the non-Russian nations, as Mr. Pipp observed, the desire "to satisfy the most vital and urgent national demands" did not mean "ruining the revolution" but rather consolidating "its gains."[97]

There is no substantiation to Kerensky's allegation that the non-Russian peoples shrank from carrying their share of a common burden. Tsereteli himself noted in his *Memoirs* that "the national movements manifested the greatest readiness to take into account the difficulties" of the Russian democracy.[98]

It is hardly clear what promises to the non-Russian peoples the Prime Minister had in mind. Prior to the State Conference, the Provisional Government made no proposal on the overall solution to the nationality question, stating that it would be determined by the Constituent Assembly. Only on October 8, 1917, a month and a half after the Conference, did the Provisional Government include a statement on this question in its declaration of policy.[99] The promise was hardly convincing to Ukrainians, who were frustrated over the discrepancy between what they had expected from the mid-July agreement and what they actually received in the "Instruction."

The Ukrainian Rada did not participate in the Moscow State Conference. It turned down the invitation, partly because it was allotted only five delegates, but primarily because it felt that the bourgeois composition of the Conference and the way in which it was selected could not be representative of the entire state and could not strengthen the gains of the Revolution. A resolution of the Rada stated that only the All-Russian Constituent Assembly and the Ukrainian Constituent Assembly "could express the true wish

---

[96] *Ibid.*, Vol. III, p. 1500.

[97] *Ibid.*, Vol. III, pp. 1500–1501.

[98] Tsereteli, Vol. II, pp. 79, 86. At times their willingness to cooperate worked to the detriment of their own interests.

[99] Text in *ibid.*, Vol. III, p. 1716.

of the people" and could form "a democratic order in the democratic federated republic."[100] In spite of these reservations, some Ukrainians from the provinces did participate, but Kerensky's remarks warning Ukrainians not to become Judases and his allusions to Russian chauvinist allegations that the Ukrainian movement was financed from abroad continued to irk many Ukrainians,[101] particularly since they were denied the floor when they wanted to reply.[102]

Thus, the last months of existence of the Provisional Government were marked by a steady deterioration in Ukrainian-Russian relations. Though the General Secretariat was reorganized according to the "Instruction" and was approved by the Provisional Government, Petrograd did not communicate with the Secretariat, nor through it with local officials. The Provisional Government did assign 300,000 rubles for the activities of the General Secretariat, but the money was not made available. Finally, no ministry of the Provisional Government ever informed those provinces under the General Secretariat about the meaning of the "Instruction."[103] True, such negligence allowed the General Secretariat a free hand, but it was slow in realizing this and displayed little initiative or determination. Meanwhile, economic conditions worsened, the Russian Army disintegrated further, and there was an increase in the number of wandering, uncontrolled soldiers.[104] Vynnychenko blamed the Provisional Government, which in his opinion hardly responded to the situation.[105]

In order to develop a common program and, presumably, to exert greater pressure upon the Provisional Government, the Rada organized a People's Congress in Kiev, on September 21–28, 1917. Ninety-three delegates representing thirteen nationalities attended.

---

[100] Vynnychenko, Vol. II, pp. 29–31.

[101] Chernov discusses this question and shows that the Rada even rejected those funds collected among the Ukrainian prisoners of war in Austria and Germany. Chernov, pp. 278–279.

[102] V. Andriievskyi, *Z mynuloho*, Vol. I, pt. 1 (New York: Ukr. Vyd. 'Howerla,' 1963), pp. 124–125.

[103] Doroshenko, Vol. I, p. 139; Vynnychenko, Vol. II, pp. 40, 52, 54.

[104] A conference called by the General Secretariat on October 16, 1917, with the participation of some eighty commissars from districts and provinces of the Ukraine, drew a clear picture of this situation. Doroshenko, Vol. I, pp. 150–151.

[105] Vynnychenko, Vol. II, pp. 49 ff.

The principle that all nations have a complete right to self-determination served as the basis for deliberations.[106] It decided that the Russian state should be reorganized into a federative republic based upon a national-territorial principle, that nationalities such as the Jews, who were dispersed among other peoples, would benefit by the right to obtain extraterritorial personal autonomy, that a "Council of Nationalities" should be attached to the Provisional Government, and that a "Council of Peoples" should be formed, preferably with a seat in Kiev.[107]

Meanwhile, pressure on the General Secretariat to assume more power in the Ukraine was growing, and it finally decided to broaden its authority and to deal with mounting problems. Its proposals presented to the *Mala Rada* on October 10, 1917,[108] were received by it with full satisfaction. Only the representative of the Russian Kadets, Krupnov, was opposed, and alone voted against it.[109]

One of the more important demands made at various congresses and meetings at that time concerned the early convocation of a Ukrainian Constituent Assembly. This was particularly a subject of sharp debate at the sixth session of the Rada held on October 23, 1917. Representatives of the national minorities argued that the way in which the Ukrainians formulated resolutions regarding the sovereignty of a Ukrainian Constituent Assembly indicated that their goal was independence. The Ukrainians denied this, though

---

[106] M. Porsh, "V edinenii nasha pobeda," *Kavkaz*, No. 26/2 (Paris, 1936), p. 28. Materials of that Congress are published in the first issue of the organ of the Council of Peoples, *Svobodnyi soiuz*, Kiev, October, 1917.

[107] Dimanstein, Vol. III, pp. 443–450; Doroshenko, Vol. I, p. 154.

[108] Doroshenko, Vol. I, pp. 140–147; Khrystiuk, Vol. II, p. 34; Manilov, pp. 267–268. Doroshenko, Vol. I, pp. 147–148; text of the declaration is in Manilov, pp. 514 ff. The demand to extend the jurisdiction of the General Secretariat over all provinces and to increase its competence by adding five secretaries was expressed at virtually every Ukrainian congress and meeting. The delegation of the Rada to the Democratic Conference in Petrograd, September 26–30, 1917, was instructed to voice this demand. Vynnychenko, Vol. II, pp. 32–34. It might be noted that, following the Petrograd Conference, a Russian Provisional Council of the Republic was created. The Ukrainians received only seven seats and refused to participate in it. Vynnychenko, Vol. II, p. 34; Khrystiuk, Vol. II, p. 192.

[109] Doroshenko, Vol. I, p. 148; Manilov, p. 268. Shortly thereafter, the Russian Kadets withdrew from the Rada. The text of their statement is in Dimanstein, Vol. III, pp. 199–201.

some speakers added that either Russian policy toward the Ukraine or altered circumstances might force them to take such a step. Finally, a compromise stated that the will of the peoples of the Ukraine for self-determination could only be expressed through a Ukrainian Constituent Assembly, which would be in accord with the will of the peoples of the Russian Empire as expressed at the All-Russian Constituent Assembly.[110]

Neither this compromise nor Vynnychenko's assurance in a letter to *Kievskaia mysl* that the aim of the Ukrainian democracy was a federated Russian state in which the Ukraine would participate as an equal member, alleviated the differences between Kiev and Petrograd.[111] The question of a Ukrainian Constituent Assembly strained relations even further. The Ukrainian leadership apparently felt that a Ukrainian Constituent Assembly would give them a new and strong mandate to deal with the situation. The Provisional Government recognized the possible consequences and decided to act. It ordered the Russian prosecutor in Kiev to investigate whether any laws were being violated by the Secretariat and requested that Vynnychenko and two other secretaries, Zarubin and Steshenko, come to Petrograd to explain "reports of agitation in the Ukraine in favor of convoking a sovereign Constituent Assembly."[112] Some press reports gave rise to rumors that the Provisional Government intended to arrest the members of the delegation. The nomination of K. Vasilenko as Commissar of the city of Kiev increased the tension even more.[113]

The Third Ukrainian Military Congress of November 2–12, 1917, attended by some 3,000 delegates, was opposed to the Provisional Government's nominee. The Congress resolved to ignore Vasilenko and to consider detrimental and inadmissible the appointment of someone without consultation with the Rada. "In view of this, the Ukrainian Military Congress suggests that all military units and persons refuse to carry out the orders of the head of the district until he is appointed with the approval of the Central Rada."[114] The Congress also advised members of the Secretariat not to go to Petrograd, while the Council of the Kiev Ukrainian garrison sent a telegram to the Provisional Government which protested the

---

[110] Manilov, pp. 287–288; Doroshenko, Vol. I, pp. 155–156.

[111] Doroshenko, Vol. I, p. 156.

[112] Browder and Kerensky, Vol. I, p. 401; Manilov, p. 298.

[113] Doroshenko, Vol. I, p. 157; Khrystiuk, Vol. II, p. 40.

[114] Browder and Kerensky, Vol. I, pp. 401–402.

summoning of the three Secretariat members and promised to support the Rada and General Secretariat with all means at its disposal.[115] However, on November 3, the General Secretariat did decide to send the three-man delegation to Petrograd. Vynnychenko explained to the Military Congress that such a delegation had been planned for some time because pressing problems had to be dealt with.[116] The delegation left on November 4, 1917, but it arrived at the Russian capital when the Provisional Government was in its last hours of existence. The Bolshevik take-over of Petrograd was progressing successfully, and, faced with this new situation, the Ukrainian delegates rushed back to Kiev.

It is clear that during the process of change set in motion by the March Revolution the rebirth of subjugated nations emerged as one of the strongest underlying forces. However, the response of the Russian Provisional Government revealed a deep political and emotional commitment to the preservation of a "one and indivisible Russia." Considering that the leaders of the Rada sincerely wanted to build a democratic order in close cooperation with the Russian democracy, the Provisional Government had an unusual opportunity to initiate a new era in Russian-Ukrainian relations. By developing a just and equitable relationship, it would have had a greater opportunity to strengthen and preserve justice and democracy in Russia itself. The Provisional Government's recourse to an All-Russian Constituent Assembly as the only authority competent to resolve the national question appeared to the Ukrainians as an attempt to postpone the problem to a more opportune time,[117] particularly since, when it redounded to their benefit, the Russians were able to overcome such legalistic scruples as those involved in "predetermining" the Polish question or in proclaiming Russia a republic.

Turning to the Ukrainian side, as in every revolution, the role of leadership was of crucial importance. The national revival after a long period of subjugation had to be molded into an effective state-building force. To accomplish this in such complicated circumstances, the leadership had to possess revolutionary skills, a clear

---

[115] Dimanstein, Vol. III, p. 202, Manilov, p. 303.

[116] Manilov, pp. 303–304; Doroshenko, Vol. I, pp. 153–157.

[117] Regarding this question, see the minutes of a most revealing discussion by the Juridical Council in *Krasnyi arkhiv,* Vol. XXX, pp. 56–71.

understanding of national goals, and a strong determination to achieve them.

The demands put forth by the parties that were leading the Ukrainian national movement represented the pre-war minimal program. In the period of tsarist autocracy these demands might have provided revolutionary inspiration, but the request for na-tional-territorial autonomy, to be approved by an All-Russian Constituent Assembly, could hardly inspire or sustain national efforts in a period of intense nationalism and rapid revolutionary change. As a result, the Ukrainian revolution outran its leaders and forced them to proclaim in June 1917 that "from this day forth, we ourselves shall direct our own lives." But they failed to maintain the momentum and retreated to "normalcy" and legitimacy, rely-ing on the justice of their claims. To set only minimum goals was also a tactical error. It greatly restricted the possibilities in their negotiations. Finally, this constant stressing of the alleged need for unity with Russian revolutionary democracy caused a dulling of vigilance and awareness among the Ukrainian people of both the Russian danger and the approaching military confrontation.

CHAPTER TWO

Hrushevskyi and the Central Rada: Internal Politics and Foreign Interventions

Ihor Kamenetsky

THE ESTABLISHMENT of the Rada government, its assertion of power in the Ukraine, and its demise after one year of existence must be considered within the context of the stormy internal and external circumstances that followed the February Revolution. The Rada also must be evaluated in terms of the performance of its leaders and the behavior of the Ukrainian masses.

The February Revolution, which transformed the autocratic tsarist system into a self-professed democracy with a weak central government and increased freedom of self-expression, revived problems that previously had been suppressed in the Ukraine. There is little doubt that among the specific issues was a desire for what might be called cultural autonomy, and that it was particularly stimulated by the inconsistent tsarist policy of concessions and repressions between the years 1905 and 1917.

The symptoms of tension that developed as the tsarist regime tried to suppress manifestations of Ukrainian self-consciousness, whether they appeared in the form of political petitions or in various forms of cultural activities, were numerous. Outstanding examples of such policy were the prohibition throughout the Ukraine of the 1914 celebrations marking the 100th anniversary of the poet Taras Shevchenko, and the suppression of riots that developed when police tried to disperse defiant demonstrators. No less significant were the suppression of the Ukrainian press and the severe restrictions placed upon Ukrainian cultural life shortly after the outbreak of the First World War. Not even those Ukrainian organizations that pledged loyalty to the government and campaigned in support of the Russian war effort were spared. The peak of this repressive policy was reached when all Ukrainian cultural activity was banned in those parts of the Austro-Hungarian Empire occupied by the Russian army during the early stages of the war. This policy, as well as the deportation of thousands of Ukrainian leaders from Galicia to Russia, was a blow to any hope that Ukrainians might secure essential cultural rights on the basis of piecemeal legislation from the Russian government. This feeling was strengthened by the relative indifference and even outright hostility of many Russian organizations which stood for basic civil rights and fought against social injustices, but which refused to recognize the right of Ukrainians for cultural development. Ukrainian legal petitions on behalf of these rights were numerous, especially during the war, but their results were equally unimpressive.[1] These background circumstances may provide some explanation for why the action of Ukrainian parties and organizations went from usual government lobbying procedures to demands for territorial autonomy following the February Revolution.

When Hrushevskyi arrived in Kiev on March 27, 1917, to assume leadership of the Rada, that body was already organized and included representatives of various Ukrainian political parties as well as professional and civic organizations. The political line that Hrushevskyi promoted might be described ideologically as a combination on the one hand of the Socialist Revolutionary preoccupation with the peasant masses and land reform, and on the other, of a Fabian-type socialism that respected democratic processes and gradualism in its efforts to achieve a more just and equalitarian society. In practice, this meant broad popular representation in the government and no discrimination on the basis of ethnic, religious, or social criteria. Hrushevskyi, however, insisted that a Ukrainian National Congress should be called to provide a still broader representation. For this purpose, a National Congress, or Rada, met in Kiev on April 19, 1917, to which about 900 delegates representing various organizations and parties were invited. When the territorial autonomy of the Ukraine was proclaimed, the ethnic minorities were also invited to provide delegates. Decisions in plenary sessions of the Rada and its executive Committee, the *Mala Rada* (Little Rada), were made by majority vote, and the same applied to the Rada's Cabinet (General Secretariat), which was

---

[1] Dmytro Doroshenko, *Istoriia Ukrainy, 1917–1923 rr.*, Vol I (2nd ed.; New York: Bulava Publishing Corporation, 1954), pp. 12–13.

created at the suggestion of Hrushevskyi in June 1917. A general election, based on a secret ballot and universal male suffrage, was intended to provide a Constituent Assembly for a new Rada scheduled for January 1918, but it could not take place in those parts of the Ukrainian People's Republic already occupied by the Bolsheviks.

Another policy that Hrushevskyi pursued without any tangible success was an attempt to transform provincial and local governments into organizations that would represent a cross section of organized society.[2] Such a design of the government would provide, at least theoretically, an opportunity for a democratic solution of conflicts within society, thus correcting many of these abuses which had contributed to the outbreak of the Revolution. Also, the widely discussed land reform in the Ukraine was considered from the popular as well as from the practical point of view. The Ukrainian Socialist Revolutionary Party took some preparatory steps, not only to outline the ideas for land reform but also to draw the organized peasants into its planning and implementation. For this reason, though also for the purpose of strengthening their party's influence, the Ukrainian Socialist-Revolutionaries organized an impressive network of peasant cooperative organizations (*Selianska Spilka*) in the countryside and sponsored the First All-Ukrainian Peasant Congress in Kiev during June 1917. The Congress prepared a Resolution on Land Reform as a guideline for the General Secretariat for Land, which was created by the Rada in June. The essential portion of the Resolution read:

> All land in the Ukraine shall be transferred free of charge to the Ukrainian Land Fund, which shall be at the free disposal of the people through the Ukrainian *Soim* (Diet), the districts, and the village land committees, all of which are to be elected on a democratic basis. The All-Russian Constituent Assembly shall confirm the legislation of the Ukrainian *Soim*. The beneficiaries of this Fund

---

2 Széchényi and Czernin: "Die Übersendung eines Berichtes über die Bildung der ukrain. autonomen Republik im Rahmen eines russ. Föderativstaates, über die Machtbefugnisse der ukrain. Zentralrada und über die Agrarfrage," Beilage zum Bericht der k. und k. Gesandtschaft in Kopenhagen, Nr. 47/P E, August 21, 1917, Haus- Hof- und Staatsarchiv, Politische Abteilung, Vienna, Austria (hereafter: H-H-SA/PA), cited in T. Hornykiewicz (ed.), *Ereignisse in der Ukraine, 1914–1917, deren Bedeutung und historische Hintergründe*, Vol. I (Horn: Ferdinand Berger und Söhne, ORG, 1966), pp. 262–266.

shall be only those cultivating the land with their own hands. It will be indispensable to set a land norm which would be not less than the norm of consumption and not larger than what an agricultural producer would be able to manage without outside help. Within the limits of this norm, all agricultural producers may keep their land ... The expenses connected with the land reform will be paid by the state.[3]

As may be perceived, the statement reflects a radical reform within the framework of moderation, and in a sense corresponds to the principles of Hrushevskyi's political thinking. It appealed to peasants of various status, for it was chiefly concerned with expropriating the land of the non-toilers. Further, by delegating primary authority for the distribution and administration of the land to the various Ukrainian authorities instead of to the All-Russian Constituent Assembly, the Resolution stressed the interest in land distribution as well as in autonomy.[4]

With the fall of the Provisional Government in Petrograd, the Rada moved toward a status of *de facto* independence. At this stage, the Rada was faced with unanticipated new challenges, and the weaknesses and omissions of previous policy became more obvious. Yet it would hardly be correct to assume that the independent existence of the Ukrainian government was from the very beginning a lost cause. The chances for the Rada to assert itself certainly had not passed. Both competitors for power, the supporters of the Provisional Government and the Bolshevik Party in the Ukraine, were even weaker than the Rada. The strength of the first was melting away, and the ascendance of the second was slow. Considering the indecisive Soviet leadership in Petrograd, the Rada still had an opportunity to reconsider its policy and to take proper measures to strengthen its position. For this reason, it will be useful to explore the conditions existing in the Ukraine during the last stage of the Provisional Government's existence and to note how the Rada viewed itself in the face of the new challenges and opportunities.

The eve of the October Revolution was marked by an increase in Bolshevik organizations and propaganda, as well as by a turn toward the left in the Rada's policies. Partially, this situation corresponded to a general leftward shift of the political spectrum in Russia that followed the futile rightist *coup d'état* of General

---

[3] Doroshenko, Vol. I, p. 86.

[4] Illia Vytanovych, "Agrarna polityka ukrainskykh uriadiv (1917–20)," *Ukrainskyi istoryk,* IV, 3–4 (New York-Munich, 1967), p. 18–19.

Kornilov. However, there was another reason for the Rada's leftist orientation—namely, the growing friction with the Provisional Government, which consistently undermined and obstructed Ukrainian efforts.

At the same time, the rapid disintegration of the Provisional Government's control, especially over the armed forces, transportation, and legal system, created a power vacuum into which the General Secretariat might step as the only alternative authority. With the Provisional Government's decline, two somewhat mutually exclusive alternatives were open to the Rada. It could either continue the radicalization of its program by trying to deepen the Revolution and hope to win more spontaneous support from the masses, or it could emphasize the principle of "law and order" by slowing down the revolutionary process and defying revolutionary excesses in an effort to gain more support from the middle class and the wealthier portion of the peasant population. From all appearances, the Rada made a feeble attempt to follow both courses at the same time. Thus, on the one hand, during the second All-Ukrainian Peasant Congress, which met September 2–5, 1917, the Rada made it clear that a more radical land reform[5] than that which had been previously anticipated was in preparation. On the other hand, it relied to an increasing degree upon the Free Cossack organizations, which were largely composed of and controlled by the well-to-do peasants. These militia-like organizations were supposed to restore law and order in the countryside, yet they watched the radical turn of the Rada with suspicion and saw in it one of the very causes of unrest and disorder.[6]

When the Provisional Government was overthrown, the Rada found itself confronted by a struggle for power between Russian garrison troops faithful to the Provisional Government and local Bolshevik forces, which staged an uprising against them in Kiev. The neutrality of the Rada government in this struggle is understandable in view of both its own military weakness[7] and the

---

[5] M. Hrushevskyi, *Iliustrovana istoriia Ukrainy* (Kiev-Vienna: Dniprosoiuz, 1921), pp. 539–540.

[6] Doroshenko, Vol. I, p. 146.

[7] *Ibid.*, pp. 152–153. The organization of the Free Cossacks was by no means homogeneous or centralized, and it happened that here and there the Free Cossack detachments were led by radical, revolutionary, and sometimes adventurous elements. But, on the whole, the movement could be characterized as being of a conservative-moderate nature.

implications of an eventual victory by either of the two contestants. Taking into consideration the previous relations between Kerensky and the Rada, and the antagonistic attitude of Russian circles in Kiev which sided with the Provisional Government, the victory of these forces could have meant an almost certain end to the Rada's authority. Lenin's official position toward the Rada was more friendly at this stage, but the program of the Bolshevik organizations left little doubt that they aspired to a complete monopoly of power.

After its temporary victory in the contest between the Provisional Government and the Bolsheviks, the Rada was confronted with two very obvious objectives. First, it had to avoid or at least postpone any direct military confrontations, and secondly, it had to use the time gained to consolidate its internal strength. The first objective was, of course, most urgent under the given circumstances, and the Rada initially pursued it with a certain measure of success. By not recognizing Lenin's government as a legitimate All-Russian government, the Rada could legally assert its independence from the Soviet in Petrograd. It could also expect at least a neutral attitude from those Russian circles and military units already engaged in combat with the Bolsheviks or preparing for such action in the near future. At the same time, by recognizing the *de facto* existence of the Soviet government in those portions of Russia proper under its control, the Rada was able to avoid any immediate conflict with the Bolsheviks.

The Third Universal, which the Rada proclaimed on November 19, 1917, was motivated by many reasons, not merely by the desire to appease the Rada's potential enemies. Nevertheless, its final effect must be considered a conciliatory gesture. While proclaiming itself the "Ukrainian People's Republic" and assuming most of the prerogatives of a sovereign state, the Rada at the same time pledged federation with Russia, although this pledge was bound by the condition that a constitutional All-Russian government must first be created. For Russians of Bolshevik and non-Bolshevik persuasion who were opposed to the separation of the Ukraine, such a proposition held the possibility of a peaceful settlement. Since elections to the Constituent Assembly were scheduled for the end of November 1917, with the newly elected body prepared to meet in Petrograd in January 1918, the waiting period may have appeared reasonable for most of those involved. The Soviet Russian Government initially had two motivations for avoiding any military confrontation with the Rada. On the one hand, there was the prospect that control of the future All-Russian government would mean control of the Rada by implication. On the other hand, there was a possibility that the Bolsheviks, then operating freely in the Ukraine with various communist front organizations, might be able to seize control from the inside. Only with the unfavorable outcome of the elections and the growing realization that the Bolshevik organizations in the Ukraine were too weak to seize power by themselves did the Red Guards, following Lenin's ultimatum to the Rada of December 17, 1917, invade the Ukraine.

Preceding this confrontation, the Rada government could still claim some diplomatic successes. It subordinated the commanding generals of the southwestern and Rumanian fronts to its authority[8] and reached an agreement with the Commander in Chief of the Russian army, General Dukhonin, concerning the transfer of ethnic Ukrainian troops on Ukrainian territory.[9] It also received diplomatic recognition by Great Britain and France[10] and initiated preliminary talks with the Central Powers aimed at achieving a separate peace treaty.[11] However, none of these successes could be translated into the immediate military or material help that was necessary to stop the Bolshevik invasion, and the Rada's successes in domestic affairs were, unfortunately, even less impressive.

Between the fall of the Provisional Government and the Bolshevik invasion, the Rada accomplished two significant achievements: it prevented the Bolshevik leaders in Kiev from utilizing the

---

[8] "Storck an Czernin: Abschrift eines Berichtes über die Entwicklung der agrarpolitischen und militärischen Lage in der Ukraine (Zentralrada)," Nr. 23.289, "Ukrainische Angelegenheiten; Baden, October 4, 1917," H-H-SA/PA, 1042, Kr. 58. Reprinted in Hornykiewicz, Vol. I, p. 273. See also Doroshenko, Vol. I, pp. 163–168, and V. Kedrovsky, "Ukrainizatsiia v Rossiiskii Armii," *Ukrainskyi istoryk*, IV, 3–4 (New York-Munich, 1967), pp. 76–77.

[9] Vytanovych, pp. 30–31. See also Doroshenko, Vol. I, p. 177.

[10] Vytanovych, pp. 30–31.

[11] Concerning British recognition of the Ukraine, see "Mérey an das k. u. k. Min. d. Äussern: Über die Ankunft der Delegierten der Kiewer Zentralrada sowie Bedenken gegen ihre Zulassung zur nachträglichen Unterzeichnung des Waffenstillstandsvertrages, Brest-Litovsk, Dec. 16, 1917," H-H-SA/PA, Vienna, Kr. 70/6, in Hornykiewicz, Vol. II, p. 3. For the background and the French part in the recognition, see Doroshenko, Vol. I, pp. 230–240, 436–437.

Congress of Soviets of Workers', Soldiers' and Peasants' Deputies (December 17, 1917) to seize power, and it achieved victory over the Bolsheviks in the Ukrainian elections to the All-Russian Constituent Assembly. In the Congress, the Ukrainian parties that specifically supported the Rada gained approximately two-thirds of the votes, mostly among the peasant delegates.[12] In general, the Ukrainian parties were able to secure fifty-three percent of all votes cast in the Ukraine, as opposed to the ten percent obtained by the Bolsheviks.[13] This indicated the relative popularity of the Rada, but it did not reveal the extent of peasant commitment. As future events proved, the vote did not mean that the overwhelming number of those who voted for the Rada were also willing to fight for it, and this was particularly true of the peasants, whose sympathies were then lukewarm toward any government. In addition to the transformation of peasant sympathy for the Rada into a more reliable political force, there were other essential aspects of internal consolidation that were equally crucial, including the building of a reliable administrative apparatus and the organization of efficient police and armed forces necessary for the maintenance of internal and external security. For various reasons, the Rada's efforts in those fields were either inadequate or miscalculated.

Since popularity and support for the leading Ukrainian socialist parties came primarily from the countryside, Lenin's seizure of power in Petrograd and his announcement of an immediate division of land posed a serious dilemma. Because the machinery for an orderly and immediate distribution of land was non-existent, the members of the Rada knew that distribution could not take place on short notice within the prevailing revolutionary situation. In this competitive context, the idea of satisfying the desires of the overwhelming majority of the peasants immediately appeared to be an irresistible political gimmick. The Rada faced two alternatives. One was to pursue a policy of gradual, peaceful, and rational implementation of land reform, which would require the resolution and violent suppression of all illegal land acquisitions in the Ukraine. Ironically, the success of this alternative could turn a considerable

---

[12] "Gautsch an das k.u.k. Min. d. Äussern: Bericht über die erste Besprechung mit den ukrain. Delegierten," (n.d.) H-H-SA/PA, Vienna, Kr. 70/6 in Hornykiewicz, Vol. II, pp. 6–7.

[13] Jurij Borys, *The Russian Communist Party and the Sovietization of Ukraine: A Study in the Communist Doctrine of the Self-Determination of Nations* (Stockholm, 1960), p. 173.

section of the Ukrainian peasants against the Rada, at least temporarily. The second choice was to give the appearance of legality to large-scale property seizures, hoping to regain control over the land situation, while at the same time safeguarding against a loss of popularity.

The Rada followed the second alternative, partially sacrificing the practical aspects of reform for the sake of political considerations. Its new pronouncements on the land question were yielding enough to appeal to the peasant masses, yet they were also vague enough to reserve a place for the eventual implementation of controls. This approach is reflected in the comments made at the plenary session of the Rada held on November 12, 1917, which referred to the basic principle for the new agrarian law proposed by the General Secretariat for Land and which provided for the transfer of land from the owners of big estates and from state ownership to the land committees.[14] The Third Universal, which was read personally by Hrushevskyi on November 19, 1917, indicated the degree of radicalization of the Rada's stand with regard to the land question.

The new radical agrarian reform did not turn the peasants *en masse* into active supporters of the Rada; however, the reason for their hesitation did not lie in the fact that Ukrainian peasants were more impressed by the Bolshevik land programs than by those of the Rada. Evidence shows that the peasants were largely neutral in the political struggle. Undoubtedly, the fact that both the Rada government in Kiev and the Soviet Ukrainian government in Kharkiv offered Ukrainian statehood and the free distribution of land made it difficult for some of the peasants to realize just what was at stake. But, in most cases, the major reason was the parochial outlook of the average Ukrainian peasant and his undeveloped sense of responsibility for nationwide issues. Thus, as it frequently happened during the civil war, Ukrainian villages rose up against the Soviet authorities, particularly when they were burdened and outraged by forced food requisitions. When successful, they would drive Soviet officials from their own land, even from some of the neighboring villages, but they hardly considered it their duty to exert themselves on behalf of more distant villages or larger cities, which they frequently considered either foreign or hostile.[15]

---

[14] Oliver H. Radkey, *The Election to the Russian Constituent Assembly of 1917* (Cambridge, Mass.: Harvard University Press, 1950), Appendix.

[15] Vytanovych, pp. 31–35.

In the struggle between the Bolsheviks and the Rada for the control of the Ukraine, the neutrality of the peasant masses and the social and economic disintegration of the countryside was more detrimental to the latter. The Rada looked mainly toward the peasants for support, while the Bolsheviks drew their most important activists from among the workers, who for various reasons were not easily accessible to the Rada's appeals. With military operations in the Ukraine conducted mainly for control of large cities and railway lines, the workers, although numerically less significant, proved to be an important factor in the enhancement of Bolshevik strength.

Another unanswered set of questions involved the degree to which the Rada would be able to take advantage of the Ukrainianized troops in the Russian army, the goodwill and professional skills of the middle class, the wealthier part of the peasantry, and the former tsarist bureaucrats and officers. Despite his idealistic conceptions of brotherhood and federated nation-states, Hrushevskyi realized the necessity of a standing army, especially when the Ukraine found itself in an exposed international situation after attaining independence.[16] However, there is some indication that Hrushevskyi and his socialist associates in the government relied to an exaggerated degree on Ukrainianized troops as a substitute for a regular standing army. As later events repeatedly showed, the former imperial troops were often too demoralized to be of a prolonged military value to their prospective masters, regardless of their sympathies with either the Rada or the Bolsheviks. Lenin and Trotsky were more perceptive in this regard, and they decided to build the Red Army from scratch by organizing special detachments of Red Guards. No systematic policy allowing for the creation of ideologically motivated military units dedicated to the Rada was

---

[16] Concerning the behavior of the Ukrainian peasants during the Revolution and Civil War, see N. Popov, *Ocherk istorii Vsesoiuznoi Kommunisticheskoi Partii, (Bolshevikov)* (Moscow, 1928), pp. 120–122, cited in Borys, p. 175. See also the report of the German Officer Celin Rose (Verbindungsoffizier der militärischen Stelle des Auswärtigen Amtes), "Eindrücke in der Ukraine," Deutsches Zentral Archiv Potsdam, Büro Dr. Helferich, Bd. 192993, fol. 191–98, cited in J. Pajewski, *Mitteleuropa, Studia z dziejów imperializmu niemieckiego, w dobie pierwszej wojny światowej* (Poznań, 1954), p. 338. Valuable observations on the peasants may be found in the memoirs of Y. Horlis-Horskyi, *Kholodnyi yar*, 2 vols. (2nd ed.; New York: "Hoverla" Publishing Co., 1961).

instituted. Party haggling, delays, and indecision concerning the nature and role of the military were all responsible for the inadequate forces that were committed to defend the Rada when the Bolshevik invasion and the Communist uprising in Kiev took place.[17]

The shift to the left, which inevitably led to the questioning of land ownership, influenced the relative passivity of the Rada toward the arbitrary seizure of land and undoubtedly alienated many of the so-called more "respectable" elements, who were also the most property conscious. The tensions emanating from this situation made many members of the Rada particularly sensitive to the dangers of "class enemies" and their relation to the Revolution. Since a number of the commanding officers at the Rada's service were conservatives who attached greater emphasis to military discipline than to the revolutionary zeal of the troops, something like a "Kornilov complex" developed between the Rada and its troops. Without doubt, this proved to be detrimental to military effectiveness and mutual trust and respect.

Even during the Rada's worst crisis, with Bolshevik troops rapidly approaching Kiev, the Ukrainian government made no attempt to win over the thousands of Russian officers who had escaped from areas dominated by the Bolsheviks, though they represented a well-trained cadre for military defense.[18] The Rada showed the same hesitation with regard to the Russian middle class, not to mention Ukrainians with conservative convictions or inclinations. It might be argued that even though many of these elements disagreed violently with the Rada's leftist policy, they would have preferred cooperation with it to an eventual Bolshevik take-over. The Bolshevik government, by using political commissars, a hostage system, and other methods of Red terror, made selective use of the professional skills of many "class enemies" during the Civil War. Being in possession of a vigilant and penetrating party and police system, and following the principle that all means are justified by the end, they could afford such uneasy cooperation with less risk than the Rada, which possessed neither the will to use mass terror nor a reliable apparatus at its command for the supervision of such tactics.

---

[17] Borys Martos, "M. S. Hrushevskyi, iakym ia ioho znav," *Ukrainskyi istoryk,* 1–2 (New York-Munich, 1966), p. 78.

[18] Doroshenko, Vol. I, pp. 279–281.

In spite of the many weaknesses of the Rada, the Communists in the Ukraine were probably not strong enough to overthrow it on their own. The Bolshevik march on Kiev, following the declaration of war on the Ukrainian People's Republic, was made possible, according to Soviet sources,[19] primarily because Red Guards were sent from Soviet Russia. This initiated the first military intervention in the internal affairs of the Ukraine after the October Revolution, thus setting a precedent for military intervention on the part of the Central Powers only two months later. Soviet interference was the first in a series of foreign interventions which made the consolidation of Ukrainian statehood impossible.

Taking into consideration the Rada's military weakness and a need for consolidation of its authority, it had little to gain from the continuation of war against the Central Powers. The precarious internal situation, the uncertain relations with the Bolshevik government in Petrograd, and the heavy burden of millions of combat troops stationed on its territory made the conclusion of an early peace increasingly urgent. However, having pledged in the Third Universal to continue the federation with Russia, and having accepted the view that a peace treaty had to be signed by a central All-Russian constitutional government, the Rada did place some self-imposed limitations on its initiative for a separate treaty. Yet, when the newly installed Bolshevik government appealed on November 26, 1917, for a truce and peace negotiations, the Rada had to reconsider its previous stand.

It was only after the actual meeting of Soviet representatives with spokesmen of the Central Powers and the agreement to initiate peace talks on December 5, 1917, that an exploratory delegation was sent by the Rada to Brest-Litovsk. This delegation arrived on December 16, one day after the truce was actually signed, and it was met in a friendly way by representatives of the Austrian and German governments, though obviously with certain reservations and no commitments.[20] After receiving the reports of some of the delegates returning from Brest-Litovsk on December 22, the Rada issued a proclamation to all nations concerned, informing them of

[19] *Ibid.*, p. 283.

[20] John S. Reshetar, *The Ukrainian Revolution, 1917–1922: A Study in Nationalism* (Princeton, N.J.: Princeton University Press, 1952), p. 103. See also Doroshenko, Vol. I, p. 240.

the Ukrainian government's intention to participate as a full-fledged party in the peace negotiations. Concurrently, it stated the reasons for this decision and the basic principles upon which peace was to be secured. A positive reply to this memorandum arrived from the German government on December 26, 1917. Two days later, the Rada decided to send a peace delegation with mandatory powers to sign the peace treaty. Hrushevskyi, who was regarded as an expert on Eastern and Central European politics, had a decisive voice in the selection of the delegates and was the only one who gave the delegation some detailed instructions before its departure.[21] Ironically, Hrushevskyi, frequently accused by his enemies as an "Austrophile" or "Germanophile,"[22] advised the delegation to ask for peace terms that from the standpoint of the Central Powers, were more demanding than those brought by Trotsky. While Trotsky, in the name of national self-determination and peace without annexations, demanded the evacuation of all territory previously held by the tsarist empire, Hrushevskyi went beyond the pre-war boundaries in his demands and, also in the name of the principle of self-determination, insisted that the Austro-Hungarian territories inhabited by Ukrainians—eastern Galicia, Bukovina, and Carpatho-Ukraine—should be transferred to the Ukrainian People's Republic. He regarded as a minimum concession the integration of Eastern Galicia and Bukovina into one Austrian crown land under a local Ukrainian administration.[23] These demands were actually submitted by the Ukrainian delegation, and they were not entirely unsuccessful.[24]

Documents from both the German and Austrian Foreign Offices indicate that, in an effort to weaken Russia, the creation of an independent Ukraine was considered a possibility in the early stages of the war, a time when the Central Powers expected an easy and

---

[21] "Mérey an das k.u.k. Min. d. Äussern: Über die Ankunft der Delegierten der Kiewer Zentralrada, sowie Bedenken gegen ihre Zulassung zur nachträglichen Unterzeichnung des Waffenstillstandsvertrages," Brest-Litovsk, Dec. 16, 1917, H-H-SA/PA, 1056 Kr. 70/6, Hornykiewicz, Vol. II, pp. 3–4. See also John W. Wheeler-Bennett, *Brest-Litovsk: The Forgotten Peace* (London: Macmillan and Co., 1956), p. 155.

[22] Doroshenko, Vol. I, p. 256.

[23] Lubomyr Wynar, "Chomu M. Hrushevskyi povernuvsia na Ukrainu," *Ukrainskyi istoryk,* IV, 3–4 (New York-Munich, 1967), pp. 106–108. See also Reshetar, p. 117.

[24] Doroshenko, Vol. I, p. 296.

decisive victory.[25] Still, the independence of the Ukraine was not one of the primary goals for which Germany and Austria entered the conflict, and both powers could afford to be flexible on this issue. As the war was prolonged and reached the critical point of exhaustion for the Central Powers, their ambitions in Eastern Europe were drastically reduced, while their interest in a separate peace with Russia increased proportionately. When, in November 1917, the new Russian government expressed its willingness to negotiate for peace, the Central Powers were eager to seize upon this opportunity, thinking primarily in terms of the liquidation of the eastern front. This priority was one of the factors that affected the new approach of official circles within Austria and Germany toward the Ukrainian problem.

It is significant that the Central Powers entered negotiations and concluded a truce with Soviet Russia, which claimed that, as the only representative of the All-Russian government, it was entitled to enforce a truce on all fronts. At this point, the Central Powers also ignored the *de facto* existence of an independent Ukraine. The arrival of the Ukrainian delegation after the truce was signed was regarded as a potential obstacle to the speedy progress of peace negotiations, particularly by Austria. This fear was aggravated by the challenge to the idea of "peace without annexations" then being voiced by the German High Command and the Pan-Germanic League. The idea of Ukrainian participation in the peace negotiations could not be dismissed lightly, because, as the Germans pointed out, other alternatives were even more dangerous. For instance, three days after signing the truce with Soviet Russia and only one day after the Soviet ultimatum to the Rada, France extended official recognition to the Ukraine. Therefore, it was conceivable that a Ukraine that was rejected by the Central Powers and attacked by Soviet Russia might be forced to join the Entente. At the time of the signing, it was known to the Central Powers that both the Russian southwestern and the Rumanian fronts were formally subordinated to the Rada and were recently reorganized as the so-called "Ukrainian Front." An influential German at Brest-Litovsk, General Hoffmann, apparently was not aware of the

---

[25] "Protokoll der allgemeinen vertraulichen Besprechung zwischen der deutschen und der ukrain. Delegation: Über die Grenzen des ukrain. Staates, den zukünftigen rechtlichen Status Ostgaliziens, sowie die Bildung dreier Verhandlungskommissionen für die Ausarbeitung der politischen, rechtlichen und wirtschaftlichen Friedensartikel," Brest-Litovsk, Jan. 13, 1918, H-H-SA/PA, Pr-L 325, in Hornykiewicz, Vol. II, pp. 90–96.

degree of weakness and demoralization of these troops, and he referred to them as "militarily not unimportant."[26] The Central Powers were also aware of the impact that the outcome of elections to the All-Russian Constituent Assembly might have had. The Soviet prospects for remaining in power would be substantially weakened after the creation of an All-Russian constitutional government and this situation might have permitted the establishment of a non-Bolshevik Russian regime that would be less inclined either to consider or to honor a peace with the Central Powers. To avoid such an eventuality, it appeared advantageous to create at least the prospects for a peace treaty with the Ukraine.

In this complicated situation, the German and Austrian Foreign Offices agreed that the peace negotiations should be conducted on the basis of the principle of national self-determination. This formula was justified by the argument of the Central Powers that the Soviet government was entitled to insist on the principles of national self-determination proclaimed by Lenin within the territory of the former tsarist empire. Such principles, however, were not applicable to the citizens of the Central Powers. The purpose of Germany and Austria was to abstain from any outright annexations and, wherever it seemed advantageous to them, simultaneously to press the Soviet government to grant independence to those non-Russian ethnic groups that inhabited territory located between Russian proper and the borders of Austria and Germany. These "buffer states" might then be brought within their sphere of influence. Specifically mentioned were Poland, Courland, Livonia, Estonia, and Lithuania, which in one way or another were to be "attached" either to Germany or to Austria.

During the initial stage of the negotiations, the Austrian Foreign Minister, Czernin, and the German Secretary of State, Kühlmann, stressed that even these concealed attempts at annexation should be abandoned if they endangered prospects for the conclusion of peace.[27] Czernin even went so far as to threaten a separate peace with Russia, should Germany become reluctant to give up the idea

---

[26] "Czernin an Kaiser Karl I: Über die unbedingte Notwendigkeit, den Krieg zu beenden," April 12, 1917, H-H-SA/PA, 504 G. L. XLVII/3–20, in Hornykiewicz, Vol. II, pp. 1–3.

[27] Mérey an das k.u.k. Min. d. Äussern: Über die Ankunft der Delegierten der Kiewer Zentralrada, sowie Bedenken gegen ihre Zulassung zur nachträglichen Unterzeichnung des Waffenstillstandsvertrages," Dec. 16, 1917, H-H-SA/PA, 1056 Kr. 70/6, in Hornykiewicz, Vol. II, p. 3. See also *ibid.*, pp. 119–120.

of annexations; he argued that Austria had formally agreed to go to war in order to preserve the integrity of the territory of its allies but not to guarantee the expansion of their territory.[28] With regard to the Ukraine, Czernin suggested (and Kühlmann endorsed the view) that the Ukrainian delegation should be admitted to the peace negotiations only if Soviet Russia would agree. In case of a Russian refusal, Czernin had already prepared a statement for the Ukraine explaining why its presence at Brest-Litovsk would not be admissible and why the Central Powers had to deal with the Soviets as the sole heirs of the former Russian government.[29]

It is a significant but often overlooked fact that it was actually the Soviet government that recognized the Rada as an independent political agent in international affairs, thus allowing it to participate in the peace negotiations.[30] According to the evidence available, this recognition did not stop the Soviet invasion of the Ukraine. Neither did it change the Soviet intention to give the appearance of holding the sovereign rights of the Ukrainian people in high esteem, while in reality helping the Communists of the Ukraine to overthrow the Rada government. The Bolshevik "double game," as well as Trotsky's tactics of delaying the negotiations, initially strengthened the position of the Ukrainian government in relation to the Central Powers. In the end, however, it undermined that position and endangered the security and welfare of the Ukrainian people, while simultaneously exposing Soviet Russia to a formidable danger by inducing German and Austrian troops to march eastward.

Various sources indicate that the Rada turned to the Central Powers for military assistance only after considerable hesitation. Even though the Soviet invasion started in the second half of December 1917, and such important Ukrainian cities as Kharkiv, Chernihiv, Poltava, and Katerynoslav (Dnipropetrovsk) fell to the Red Guards within a month after the initiation of military opera-

---

[28] "Czernin an Hohenlohe: Über den Stand der Friedensverhandlungen in Brest-Litovsk, die Dringlichkeit des Friedensschlusses, sowie die Misstimmung der deutschen Obersten Heeresleitung gegenüber dem Ballhausplatz," Vienna, Jan. 2, 1918, H-H-SA/PA, 1056, Kr. 70/6, in Hornykiewicz, Vol. II, pp. 9–13.

[29] *Ibid.*

[30] "Czernin an Mérey: Stellungnahme zum Auftreten der ukrain. Delegierten als Mitglieder einer separaten Friedensdelegation," Vienna, Dec. 17, 1917, H-H-SA/PA, 1056 Kr. 70/6, in Hornykiewicz, Vol. II, p. 5.

tions, it was not until February 12, 1918, that the Ukrainian delegation in Brest-Litovsk presented an official request to Germany for
military help. There is an indication, however, that before issuing
an official request to Germany the Ukrainian government tried to
secure military assistance from Austria.[31] It seems that for a brief
period certain Austrian officials, anxious to keep their German
allies away from the Ukraine, tried to convince the Ukrainian
representatives to limit themselves to Austrian military aid.[32] The
delay and hesitation of Vienna, as well as the rapidly deteriorating
military situation in the Ukraine, motivated the Ukrainian delegation eventually to accept military aid from Germany. Even then,
every precaution was taken by the Ukrainian representatives to
qualify and circumscribe German assistance. Well before the
peace treaty was signed, Hrushevskyi sent to Brest-Litovsk a representative of the Union for the Liberation of the Ukraine, Skoropys-
Ioltukhovskyi, in order to determine whether the Germans would
be willing to release Ukrainian prisoners of war held in Germany
to fight on the Rada's side.[33] When this proved unfeasible, and
regular German troops had to be accepted instead, the Ukrainian
representatives tried to limit German military operations to the
Russian-Ukrainian border districts.[34] Also, the German High Command was confronted with a Ukrainian request to sign a written
agreement that would oblige them to withdraw troops from the
Ukraine immediately after the conclusion of military operations.[35]
These stipulations met with little success.

Though there is no doubt that German troops entered the
Ukraine upon the official invitation of the Ukrainian government,
certain questions remain unresolved. How many members of the
Cabinet were involved in submitting the final request, and did
Hrushevskyi himself know or approve of it? Many circumstances
indicate that a number of Rada members were taken by surprise
and had mixed reactions when they learned that German troops

---

[31] Doroshenko, Vol. I, p. 322.

[32] *Ibid.,* p. 322.

[33] "Wiesners Notiz über eine Besprechung mit der ukrain. Delegation
über die militär-politische Lage in der Ukraine sowie die Frage einer
eventuellen Waffenhilfe der Mittelmächte zugunsten der Ukraine," Brest-
Litovsk, Feb., 1918, H-H-SA/PA, 153, Russl. XId, in Hornykiewicz, Vol.
II, pp. 276–277.

[34] Doroshenko, Vol. I, pp. 37–38.

[35] Reshetar, p. 117.

had entered the country. The German documents indicated, at least initially, that the Rada failed to inform the Ukrainian population that the troops were coming upon the invitation of the Ukrainian government; those who knew reported that the German entry into Kiev was regarded as the arrival of new occupation forces rather than of friendly allies.[36] All in all, the Rada members considered the intervention of German troops an unexpected, unwelcome event and, at best, a necessary evil.

The presence of German and later Austrian troops represented risks and opportunities for both the Rada and the Central Powers. Throughout the war, the population of the Ukraine had viewed the Austrians and Germans as enemies. On this basis alone, a sudden military alliance with the protagonists was psychologically unsound. Furthermore, the Rada considered Germany and Austria reactionary states. Indeed, these powers were undoubtedly determined to expel Bolshevik troops from the Ukraine, but the Rada was at the same time afraid that the extended presence of foreign troops might hamper its own socialist program. On the other hand, military aid provided the Rada with a new lease on life and an opportunity to rebuild those parts of its administration and transportation system that were indispensable for effective control of its territory and trade relations.

For Germany, the intervention delayed the transfer of troops from the eastern to the western fronts, but it kept alive the original plan for an independent Ukraine to balance the strength of Russia. It also provided the opportunity for stronger and more immediate economic ties with the Ukraine and the strategic advantage of controlling the Crimea for the duration of the war. For Austria, military involvement in the Ukraine represented more problems than advantages. The unfavorable image of new involvements in the East after the widely publicized Treaty of Brest-Litovsk, the uncomfortable proximity of German troops along Austria's eastern frontiers, and the lack of sympathy toward the socialist and irredentist Ukrainian government, hardly provided sufficient motivation for a wholehearted intervention. Why should Vienna exert its own military resources on behalf of a state whose existence only contributed to an increase of Austrian internal problems? When it did so, it was because other alternatives were potentially more

---

[36] Dmytro Doroshenko, *Moi spomyny pro nedavne-mynule, 1914–1918 roky,* Vol. II (Lviv, 1923–24), p. 75.

dangerous. The possible existence of a Soviet state bordering on Austria was even less acceptable. Moreover, only Austrian intervention might counterbalance German influence in the Ukraine, and finally, it appeared that badly needed food and supplies could be secured only if Austria followed the German example and sent its own troops into the Ukraine.[37]

Whatever the conflicting long-range policies of the German, Austrian, and Ukrainian governments, they shared one common goal at the beginning of the intervention: to restore the Rada's authority and to enable it to control the people and resources of the Ukraine with only a minimal involvement of foreign troops.[38] The Rada, in turn, was concerned with achieving the earliest possible withdrawal of Austrian and German forces. The new Ukrainian allies originally overestimated the strength of the Rada's appeal to the masses and its influence on the sizeable remnants of the former tsarist army stationed on Ukrainian territory.[39] They thought that after the expulsion of the Bolsheviks the Rada would be in a position to operate a more or less normal state apparatus, maintaining order and carrying out immediately the stipulated conditions of the treaty concerning the delivery of goods. The first instructions issued by the German and Austrian High Command to their troops strictly limited their role to military assistance.[40]

Faced with the unanticipated weaknesses of an emerging nation attempting to establish itself among the turmoils of revolution and the stresses of civil war, both Germany and Austria decided to modify their policy toward the Ukraine. Two approaches appeared

---

[37] Wheeler-Bennett, p. 313.

[38] "Direktiven für die Unterstützung der ukrainischen Regierung bei der Verwaltung," Baden, March 10, 1918, H-H-SA/PA, 152 P.A.X. Russland, XId (Ukraine), Nr. 27.612, entry 2820. See also "German Ambassador in Kiev, Mumm, to Ausw. Amt," Kiew, March 20, 1918, Auswärtiges Amt, Bonn, Kommissionsakte Brest-Litovsk, Bukarest 41, Ukraine Polit. 1, Allgemeine, IA 1233, Nr. 33.

[39] Hornykiewicz, Vol. I, pp. 271–274, and Vol. II, p. 3.

[40] "Direktiven für die Unterstützung der ukrainischen Regierung bei der Verwaltung. Das k.u.k. Armee-Oberkommando, Quartiermeisterabteilung," Baden, March 10, 1918, H-H-SA, 152 P.A.X. Russland XId (Ukraine), Nr. 27.612, entry 2820. See also Wilhelm Groener, *Lebenserinnerungen* (Göttingen: Vandenhoeck & Ruprecht, 1957), diary entry for February 19, 1918.

to be feasible. They could assist the Rada in gaining the confidence and cooperation of the masses by providing a framework for a reliable administration and a supply of manufactured goods in exchange for the food which they needed, upholding at the same time the indispensable aspects of the Rada's land reform. Failing this, they might strive to undermine further the Ukrainian government and transform the country into a colonial protectorate rather than a future ally.

Following the entry of Austrian troops into the Ukraine, Viennese policy endorsed to a considerable degree Prince Hohenlohe's recommendation to exploit the territory economically, but not make any commitments concerning its political future. Hohenlohe was concerned that Berlin's support of the Ukraine would prejudice the Central Powers' relations "with the remaining part of Russia."[41] Under the new circumstances, it took longer for the Germans to clarify their policy, and as late as March 22, 1918, General Groener complained about the lack of instructions from Berlin.[42]

The German military tended to accept the Austrian view, at least with regard to the ruthless exploitation of the Ukraine. Concerning the implementation of the treaty's economic stipulations, neither Austria nor Germany was inclined to negotiate with the Rada. Rather, they began to favor the idea of a government that would be subservient to the Central Powers' interests, regardless of how it affected the majority of the Ukrainian population.

German policy toward the Ukraine crystallized along the following lines. The German Foreign Office, represented in Kiev by Ambassador Mumm, strove to attain two somewhat incompatible objectives. While trying to strengthen Ukrainian nationalism in order to keep the country independent from Russia, it also made an independent Ukrainian state both the target of German colonial exploitation and a transit route to East Asia.[43] Some German military circles, particularly those of General Ludendorff and Field

---

[41] "Hohenlohe an Czernin: Österreichische Interessen in bezug auf die Ukraine und die deutsche Politik gegenüber den östlichen Randstaaten," Berlin, March 25, 1918, H-H-SA/PA, 154 Russl. XIg. Ausfertigungsauszug Nr. 32/P.A., in Hornykiewicz, Vol. I, p. 328.

[42] *Ibid.*, p. 329.

[43] "Forgách an das k.u.k. Min. d. Äussern: Haltung österreichischer und deutscher Militärbehörden in der Ukraine der Zentralada gegenüber," Kiev, March 22, 1918, H-H-SA, 152 Russl. XId, in Hornykiewicz, Vol. I, pp. 326–27.

Marshal von Eichhorn, were interested in establishing a military base on the Crimean Peninsula. Both leaders were also sympathizers of the Pan-Germanic League and concerned with securing privileges for German colonists in the Ukraine and subordinating various aspects of Ukrainian sovereignty to what they thought were the national interests of the German state. Thus, the Supreme German Command in the Ukraine supported the plans of the former Secretary of Colonial Affairs, Friedrich von Lindequist, and the German Pastor, Winkler, for the establishment of racial German colonial states in both the Crimea and in Tauria. The Ukrainian state was supposed to act as a protector for these German states, but because this project was connected with the cession of Ukrainian territory to the German ethnic group, and because the Ukraine itself was supposed to be penetrated by German businessmen and political and military advisors, such a proposal could hardly have been acceptable to any self-respecting and popularly elected government.[44] General Groener, who was more of a military technician and transport organizer than a foreseeing politician, sympathized with the Austrian-type short-range objectives of ruthlessly exploiting the Ukraine, thus relying on force rather than on a policy aimed at securing a certain degree of popular support. This attitude was reflected in a letter from the Ukraine, dated April 15, 1918, in which he wrote: "I am now convinced . . . that we should rely exclusively on our military power and try to utilize Ukrainian resources to the utmost; should the current Ukrainian government fail to serve our interest, well, we must not hesitate to send it to the devil."[45]

The earliest suggestions (which came from Austrian official circles) for replacing the Rada by a more manageable Ukrainian government came approximately one month after German troops entered the Ukraine.[46] Toward the end of March and during the first days of April, the circles around Ludendorff, Groener, and the German Foreign Office also accepted this idea, although they disagreed with the Austrians, as well as among themselves, about

[44] "K.u.k. Armee Oberkommando: für den Chef des Generalstabes: Die Abtrennung Tauriens und der Bahn Charkow-Sewastopol als rein deutsche Interessenobjekte," April 2, 1918, H-H-SA 152 P.A.X. Russl. XId, Nr. Tel. 5174; see also "Auswärtiges Amt an den Grafen Forgách in Kiew," April 3, 1918, H-H-SA, 150 P.A.X. Russl. XIa Nr. 80.

[45] H-H-SA/PA 152 Russl. XId, Tel. Nr. 244.

[46] Groener, p. 568.

the methods, timing, and alternatives to be implemented should the Rada be overthrown.[47]

The Rada, which returned to Kiev with the advancing German troops, hoped to reestablish viable governmental authority. The determining factors in this situation were the Rada's relations with the Ukrainian peasant masses on the one hand, and with its new allies on the other. Both elements were closely interrelated. Unless the Rada came to terms with the peasantry, the food deliveries stipulated in the Treaty of Brest-Litovsk could not materialize. The Ukrainian government was convinced that the peasants, representing an overwhelming portion of the population, must be won over in order to assure the democratic type of government for which it was striving. It also expected that the troops of the Central Powers, which were clearing Ukrainian territory of Bolshevik forces, would withdraw as soon as possible after accomplishing their task, an expectation that appeared logical in view of the need for these troops on the western and Italian fronts.[48]

In order to secure the support of the Ukrainian peasant masses, the Rada promulgated a far-reaching land reform in its Fourth Universal of January 25, 1918. This document represented a declaration of independence for the Ukrainian People's Republic, including simultaneously the reform, which went so far as to abolish all land ownership and to approve the universal distribution of land belonging to the state, the church, and the large estates. At the time of its passage, the reform became of mere academic concern, since the authority of the Rada continued to decline with the rapid advance of Bolshevik troops. Following the German intervention and reestablishment of its authority in the Ukraine, the Rada needed more than words to assure the peasants that their revolutionary gains would be preserved. Not only did the legitimization of distributed land become more important, but assurances were needed for the well-to-do and middle-income peas-

---

[47] "Graf Forgách an das Auswärtige Amt: Berichte des Herrn von Wassilko über Zentralrada," March 28, 1918, H-H-SA 152 P.A.X. Russl. XId, Nr. Tel. 5174; see also "Auswärtiges Amt an den Grafen Forgách in Kiew," April 3, 1918, H-H-SA, 150 P.A.X. Russl. XIa, Nr. 80.

[48] Groener, Appendix, letter of April 15, 1918. See also "Pricing an das k.u.k. Min. d. Äussern: Besprechung beim General Groener über die politisch und militärisch sich immer mehr zuspitzende Lage in der Ukraine," Kiev, April 25, 1918, H-H-SA/PA 152 Russl. XId, Telegramm Nr. 244.

ants that their landholdings, old and new, would not become subject to arbitrary seizures by the government. No less important was the question of handling the agricultural surplus held by the peasants. An exchange of goods between state trading organizations or authorized private dealers could help the Rada to secure the confidence of the peasant masses under its authority, to provide goods that might be used for supplying Ukrainian cities, and to initiate in an orderly and peaceful way the promised food deliveries to the Central Powers.

The legitimization of landholdings and the modification of a complete abolition of property rights on land probably were among the less formidable obstacles now in the way of good relations between the Rada and the masses. In practice, the Rada's actual land expropriations did not affect the holdings of the peasants, not even the middle-sized and large landholdings. There were some indications that the radical land reform announced on January 22 was composed in a hasty fashion, and that Ukrainian Socialist-Revolutionaries were chiefly responsible for it. In any case, because of public opinion, the Rada was forced to consider a revision of the land reform. On April 29, 1918, the Rada changed the previous land law providing that landholdings not exceeding thirty *desiatynas* should not be subject to expropriation.[49]

The situation with regard to securing food supplies was different. Here the Rada could not easily avoid a direct confrontation with the peasantry and the demanding allies. Since Austria and Germany were determined to obtain food in the Ukraine without delivering the promised manufactured merchandise, compulsory food requisitioning was inevitable. There was little doubt that the defiant and well-armed Ukrainian peasants would resist, for they had already resisted the Bolshevik "flying detachment" during its first occupation of the Ukraine. The Rada's dilemma was clear; it had no power to hold off the arbitrary action of the Central Powers and it could not dissociate itself from the cause of the Ukrainian peasants. The situation that arose is well characterized by an outstanding contemporary, Friedrich Naumann, the well-known author, journalist, and member of the German Reichstag:

> It is undeniable that by military requisitions it is possible to secure the available food, if in this measure one disregards intentionally popular opinion. Then we will face the fact that neither

---

[49] Doroshenko, *Istoriia* . . . , Vol. II, p. 35.

a republican nor a Cossack government accountable to its people will be able to persist, and in this way, an occupation status will result, and the securing of grain will be connected with bloodshed at the present time as well as in the future; and above all, we could hardly count on a new harvest, because what would motivate a peasant to work, if we don't offer him more than a piece of paper which he does not value?[50]

Striving for support from the Ukrainian peasant masses, the Rada could partially avoid complicity with her allies by not participating in the requisitions and by using various technical excuses to make the arbitrary export of food supplies from the Ukraine difficult and slow. German and Austrian official reports were full of complaints indicating that the Rada made ample use of such tactics. By April 1918, policy-making circles in Germany agreed that further interference in Ukrainian internal affairs would be possible and even desirable. Now the ramifications of food requisitions took on a new political dimension, and the further existence of the Rada became increasingly problematic.

This applied particularly to the prevailing view within official German circles that the landowners and their large estates would be more productive and more accommodating than those of the Ukrainian peasants, who divided their land and equipment and who were not inclined to dispose of their surpluses on credit.[51] To restore the pre-revolutionary social-economic order in the Ukraine, the Central Powers needed a government that would rely on force rather than on popular support. From the Rada's point of view, such a policy was unacceptable and unrealistic. Its only chance of counteracting these measures was to gain nation-wide support by openly defying German and Austrian interference, by asserting its own jurisdiction and freedom of action, and by securing a popular mandate through elections. There are indications that the Rada used some of these methods in order to gain popular support. It attempted to bring about the withdrawal of Austrian troops[52] and

---

[50] Friedrich Naumann, "Wir und Russland," *Die Hilfe,* May 16, 1918, p. 244.

[51] "Mumm an Staatssekretär von Kühlmann," Bukarest, March 20, 1918, Auswärtiges Amt, Bonn, Kommissionsakte Brest-Litovsk/Bukarest 41, Ukraine Polit. Allgemeine, 122, SS, Berlin, Ausw. No. 940.

[52] "Graf Forgách an das Auswärtige Amt: Berichte des Herrn Wassilko über Zentralrada," March 28, 1918, H-H-SA, 152 P.A.X. Russl. XId, Nr. Tel. 5174. See also "Der K. Unterstaatssekretär Bussche an Staatssekretär von Kühlmann, Bukarest: Im Anschluss an das Telegramm Nr. 277 von

it protested the imposition of German military jurisdiction over Ukrainian citizens. Further, it publicly nullified Field Marshal von Eichhorn's legislation favoring compulsory cultivation of land and restoration of the large landed estates. It then requested the German government to recall Eichhorn, and, in spite of the resistance of the Central Powers, it planned on calling popular elections and a meeting of the Ukrainian Constituent Assembly in the near future.[53] The feeble manner in which these policies were carried out and the insufficient time that the Rada had at its disposal to implement such popular measures permitted the Germans to overthrow it at a moment when not much immediate risk was involved.

What is unusual about the Rada's one-year experiment in governing is the fact that amidst the unsettling circumstances of the Russian and Ukrainian Revolutions it was able to awaken the Ukrainian masses to the idea of national statehood. Its success in this effort compelled both Soviet Russia and the Central Powers, notwithstanding many hesitations and shifts in policy, to recognize Ukrainian statehood, at least in principle. Also remarkable is the Rada's consistent adherence to democratic methods and determination to preserve the basic democratic character of the Ukrainian state. The Rada was able to persevere, even though the masses were unprepared for such a sophisticated political system and many of its own members showed little understanding of practical politics. Considering the pressures exerted by the Provisional Government, the Soviet Russian government, and finally the Central Powers, this may be considered a remarkable feat. Although the Rada experienced serious internal weaknesses, the decisive factor in its fall proved to be not an internal uprising, or some other form of an internal cataclysm, but an intervention in Ukrainian internal affairs by foreign states—first Soviet Russia, and then Germany and Austria.

Of course, it would be possible to focus on the Rada's many

Bötschafter v. Mumm," March 28, 1918, Auswärtiges Amt, Bonn, Kommissionsakten Brest-Litovsk/Bukarest 41, Ukraine, Polit. Allgemeine. Fr. A. Rumän. 967 Nr. 325.

[53] "Der Vertreter des k.u.k. Minister des Äussern beim k.u.k. Armee-Oberkommando an das Auswärtige Amt: Politische Lage in der Ukraine," Baden, April 4, 1918, H-H-SA, 152 P.A.X. Russl. XId. Ausw. Amt, 3839, Nr. 28.287. See also "K.u.k. Armee-Oberkommando N.A. Nr. 7089: Lage in der Ukraine (Speziell Kiew)," March 30, 1918, Ausw. Amt No. 3686, p. 141, *ibid.*

shortcomings and conclude that even without intervention the Rada's internal disintegration would have been inevitable. One might also accept the theory that, without assistance from the Central Powers, the Rada would never have been able to assert itself. However, actual evidence validating such predictions has not been firmly established. German and Austrian documents, which have frequently been used to substantiate these assumptions, are not entirely reliable. They were written primarily by people who were antagonistically inclined to any socialist government and who tried to measure a fluid revolutionary situation by the standards of an orderly *Rechtsstaat*.[54]

It is easily forgotten that similar reports and estimates, frequently written by the same diplomats or officers, described the appalling chaos in Soviet Russia and predicted the imminent collapse of its government.[55] The German government itself was so strongly convinced that the Bolshevik authorities had little chance to assert themselves in the long run, that it decided not to overthrow them, fearing that another Russian government might be strong enough to resist Germany's plans for the economic exploitation in the east.[56]

These miscalculations concerning the durability of Soviet Russia do not imply that the Ukrainian Rada and the Soviet government were not "weak," but they do show that their "weakness" was relative. The Bolsheviks proved to be organizationally and militarily stronger than any other group competing for power. However, their ability to resist foreign invasions during their first year in power was more than questionable. Lenin's predictions in January 1918 that a renewed German advance against Soviet Russia would prove that neither the former Russian Imperial troops nor the Russian masses would rally to the cause of a "revolutionary war" proved to be correct.[57] Realizing his vulnerability, Lenin, in

---

54 Groener, Introduction.

55 K.u.k. Armee-Oberkommando, Chef des Generalstabes an das k.u.k. Ministerium d. Äussern: Verhältnisse in Russland und Ukraine," Baden, April 23, 1918, H-H-SA, P.A. 152 Russl. XId. Nr. 281–284. See also the reports of the German Ambassador in Moscow to the German Foreign Office, August 1, 1918, and August 5, 1918, cited in Fritz Fischer, *Griff nach der Weltmacht* (Düsseldorf, 1961).

56 Fischer, pp. 763–766.

57 After the Germans reopened their military operations against Soviet

the fashion of Hrushevskyi, was willing to use either German or Entente military aid in order to protect his political system from destruction by one of these belligerent powers. When in the end he abstained from calling on foreign "imperialist" troops, it was not because such a measure would have conflicted with his principles, but because he did not encounter such a sweeping invasion as the one that the Rada had to face in the case of the Red Guards.

Hrushevskyi, in his role as head of the Rada, certainly did not emerge as a strong executive leader of the caliber of Kemal Ataturk, Piłsudski, or Lenin. His deep respect for freedom and for the initiative of the masses, as well as his dedication to parliamentary practices in government, prevented him from using his popular appeal for the enhancement of personal power. After the intervention of the Central Powers, Hrushevskyi still was considered the most venerable personality in the Rada, but his rather limited authority continued to decline[58] because of the presence and policy of foreign military authorities, and because he preferred to abstain from partisan strife in the government. As a parliamentary leader in the legislative body, he remained unsurpassed during the brief period of Ukrainian independence, and his reputation was not marred by compromise or deviation from the idea of democracy.

The remaining members of the Rada, who were more inclined than Hrushevskyi to struggle for personal influence or for particular party programs, shared nevertheless his inexperience in many aspects of practical policy. In their disagreements, it was usually exaggerated partisan beliefs rather than personal gain or vested interests that prevailed. Neither career nor power could attract the majority of them to serve in Skoropadskyi's government, even

---

Russia on February 18, 1918, Lenin again voiced his skepticism with regard to the success of a revolutionary war: "A peasant does not wish to go to war and will not participate in it. Is it possible at the present time to order a peasant to fight? Yet if the continuation of war would have been desirable, then there was no sense in demobilizing our army. A permanent war is utopia. A revolutionary war should not be just a phase . . . a peasant not only would refuse to participate in a revolutionary war, he would overthrow those who openly defend it." N. Ovsianikova (ed.), *Lenin i Brestskii Mir (statti i rechi N. Lenina v 1918 g. o Brestskom Mire)*, Sostavleno po materialam IV toma *Sobraniia sochinenii N. Lenina* (Moscow: Gosizdat, n.d.), p. 16.

[58] "Trauttmansdorff an Czernin: Politische Lage in der Ukraine," Baden, April 4, 1918, H-H-SA, 152 Russl. XId, Nr. 199.

though many did receive invitations to assume leading positions in the new regime.[59]

The Rada tried to establish contact with the masses, but it displayed little skill in making its program operational. However, the interplay of innumerable crises and the extremely brief periods of respite did not allow the Rada to organize itself and to achieve greater stability. While it may be readily admitted that the Rada did not excel as an organized force, it was probably the most acceptable type of government, insofar as the majority of the Ukrainian people were concerned, that could have been founded under these particular circumstances.

[59] Doroshenko, *Istoriia* . . . , Vol. II, pp. 53–59. See also Martos, p. 75.

CHAPTER THREE

The Ukraine Under Hetman Pavlo Skoropadskyi

Taras Hunczak

BY VIRTUE OF the agreement between the Central Powers and the Ukraine concluded on February 9, 1918, at Brest-Litovsk,[1] the German and Austro-Hungarian armies advanced into the Ukraine to fight against the Bolshevik armies, which, by February 9, controlled not only a large portion of the country but also its capital—Kiev. Without encountering any serious resistance, the Austro-German armies, supported by some Ukrainian detachments, made very rapid progress. By March 2, Kiev was in German hands, and by the end of April almost all of the Ukraine was cleared of the Bolsheviks.[2]

To inform the population of the true meaning of German assistance, the Rada issued a declaration on February 23, 1918.

. . . . In order to put an immediate end to the pillaging of the Ukraine and to make possible, upon the conclusion of peace, immediate promulgation of laws to deal with the condition of workers, the Council of People's Ministers has accepted the military assistance of the friendly powers, Germany and Austria-Hungary. . . .

They are coming to the Ukraine to suppress disorder and anarchy and to establish peace and order. . . . They are coming purely to help our Cossacks who are staunchly defending our country, our land, and our freedom from the armed attacks of the Russian government, the Council of People's Commissars, which, like the old tsarist government, wishes to subject the Ukraine to the authority of Russian capitalists, and thus to enable the Russian people to live on the labor and wealth of the Ukraine.

---

[1] For a thorough account, see John W. Wheeler-Bennett, *The Forgotten Peace: Brest-Litovsk* (New York, W. Morrow and Co.: 1939).

[2] Xenia Joukoff Eudin, "The German Occupation of the Ukraine in 1918," *The Russian Review*, I, 1 (Stanford, Cal., 1941), p. 91.

. . . In helping the Ukrainian government in its fight against violators and plunderers, these troops have no hostile intentions toward us; it is in the interest of Germany and Austria-Hungary that order should be re-established and an opportunity for peaceful work to be given to the toilers of the Ukraine.[3]

It is really difficult to say whether the Ukrainians were optimistic about the entire arrangement or just anxious to save Ukrainian independence, hoping to work out some feasible plan after the first objective was achieved. It seems, however, that the exigency of the situation—saving the Ukrainian government from certain disaster—determined the political activity of the Rada.

The objectives of Germany and Austria-Hungary were much more clearly defined—they wanted food, raw materials, and, perhaps, manpower that could be used as a source of labor for Germany.[4] To achieve the above was no easy matter, since the Bolshevik invasion of the Ukraine released a strong undercurrent of socio-economic revolution, which had been previously averted by the revolutionary legislation of the Rada. This revolution precipitated the chaos that the Germans found upon entering the Ukraine.[5] In view of the existing situation, the Germans became skeptical of the Rada's ability to fulfill its treaty obligations. Commenting on the general conditions in the Ukraine, Colonel von Stolzenberg, in Kiev, telegraphed the German commander of the eastern front on March 9, 1918:

It is very doubtful whether this government, composed as it is exclusively of left opportunists, will be able to establish firm authority. Decisive and most difficult battles await us in the West. If it is impossible to do it any other way, then we must take by force what [food] is absolutely necessary for our life and fight.[6]

A similar view was held by von Bülow, the representative of the German Foreign Office at Brest-Litovsk. Describing the hostile attitude of the peasants toward the Germans in a report dated

---

[3] *Ibid.*, p. 92.

[4] Erich Ludendorff, *Meine Kriegserinnerungen, 1914–1918* (Berlin: Vlg. von E. S. Mittler und Sohn, 1922), p. 531.

[5] For an informative contemporary account of the actual conditions in the Ukraine, see "Doklad . . . o polozhenii del na Ukraine . . . ," in *Arkhiv russkoi revoliutsii*, Vol. I (Berlin, 1921), pp. 288–292.

[6] M. Kamianetskyi, *Nimtsi i Ukraina* (Winnipeg: Vyd. Ukrainsoi Vydavnychoi Spilky v Kanadi, 1940), p. 59.

March 10, he suggested that, if necessary, force should be used to obtain that which was essential to Germany's war effort.

A much more far-reaching recommendation was made to the Austro-Hungarian government by Field Marshal Langer. On April 3, 1918, he informed Vienna that:

> . . . A great quantity of food could be gotten from the Ukraine under the condition that: 1) the Ukrainian government will be substituted by some other one, which would not present such violent opposition, 2) enough soldiers will be sent into the country, and 3) enough energy and ruthlessness will be displayed in gathering products.[7]

For the Ukrainians it was indeed an irony of fate; they invited an ally to aid them and were in turn occupied by him. The man who signed the peace agreement with the Rada on February 9 approved its overthrow on April 3, 1918.[8]

Anticipating a reorientation of Berlin toward the existing regime, the supreme commander, Field Marshal von Eichhorn, decided to intervene directly in the internal affairs of the Ukraine. On April 6, he issued an order to his subordinates in which he not only accused the peasants of not sowing the fields, but also commanded his subordinates to see to it that the fields were sowed, even if the initiative of the military forces proved necessary. It stated, moreover, that the harvest was the possession of the person who sowed it and would be purchased at "suitable prices."[9]

The interference was extremely serious. Not only was the Rada's agrarian law completely ignored, but, in virtue of von Eichhorn's order, the occupation army usurped a legislative authority that legally belonged only to the Ukrainian parliament. Von Eichhorn's order was bitterly resented by the Rada, which on April 13 issued the following statement:

> The German troops have been invited to the Ukraine by the Ukrainian government to assist in the reestablishment of order, but the assistance was to be strictly within the limits indicated by the Government of the Ukrainian National Republic.
>
> Arbitary interference on the part of the German and Austro-Hun-

---

[7] *Ibid.*

[8] I. I. Mints and E. N. Gorodetskyi, *Dokumenty o razgrome german-skikh okupantov na Ukraine v 1918 godu* (Moscow, 1942), p. 64.

[9] Pavlo Khrystiuk, *Zamitky i materialy do istorii ukrainskoi revoliutsii, 1917–1920 rr.,* Vol. II (Vienna: J. N. Vernay, 1921–22), pp. 201 ff.

garian military commands in the social, political, and economic life of the Ukraine is completely unwarranted.

Any interference similar to Field Marshal von Eichhorn's order can only disorganize the national life of the Ukraine, complicate social-political relations, and, in addition, make the fulfillment of the economic agreement between the Ukrainian National Republic and the Central Powers impossible . . .[10]

The German military authorities did not pay any attention to the Rada's protests. On the contrary, they persisted in their policy of subversion. On April 18, Mumm, the German ambassador in Kiev, informed Berlin that the Chief of Staff in the Ukraine, General Groener, "insists even more energetically than before to overthrow the present government immediately after the [trade] agreement is signed."[11] Having lost all hope of workable cooperation with the Ukrainian government, the Germans decided either to establish a new government or to modify the existing one in such a way as to make it subservient to their interests.[12] On April 24, Mumm informed Berlin that:

> At the meetings which were held last night and today between General Groener, Count Forgach, the two military plenipotentiaries and myself, the following decisions were made concerning our policy and military activity in the Ukraine:
> Collaboration with the present government, considering its tendencies, is impossible. The establishment of a general governorship is for the time being not expedient. Until it is possible to preserve the Ukrainian government, it must in its activities depend on the German and Austrian supreme commanders. The Ukrainian government must not hinder the military and economic undertakings of the German authorities.[13]

---

[10] Eudin, pp. 93 ff.

[11] Kamianetskyi, p. 60.

[12] In his letter home dated April 21, Groener wrote: "Die Kiewer Regierung macht uns grosse Sorgen, mit den unreifen Leuten ist nichts zu arbeiten. Wir müssen eine andere Regierung haben, aber welche? Es gibt im Lande keine regierungsfähige Partei und keine rechten Männer—sie sind alle Schwätzer, die stets nur Ideen entwickeln und nicht auf realem Boden stehen." Wilhelm Groener, *Lebenserinnerungen* (Göttingen: Vandenhoeck und Ruprecht, 1957), p. 387.

[13] Haus-, Hof- und Staats-Archiv in Vienna (hereafter H-H-SA), 152 P.A.X.; XId. "Telegram des Herrn von Princig, Nr. 244," Kiew, 25 April 1918; also Kamianetskyi, p. 61.

In the meantime, the Germans found a suitable candidate to head the new government. He was the former commander of the 34th Army Corps, Lieutenant General Pavlo Skoropadskyi.[14]

In the evening of April 26, Skoropadskyi met with General Groener to discuss the conditions under which the Germans would support his regime. The conditions that he was presented with amounted, if accepted, to an outright surrender of sovereignty to the occupying powers. They included acceptance of the Peace Treaty of Brest-Litovsk, the dissolution of the Rada, and the abolition of the Ukrainian Constituent Assembly. The size and disposition of the Ukrainian army was to be determined by the German authorities. All limitations on the export of raw materials and manufactured goods were to be eliminated. In the agrarian sphere, the Germans demanded restoration of the right of ownership and payment for land received when holdings would be divided; large holdings were to remain intact. All cabinet appointees designated by Skoropadskyi had to be *personae gratae* to the occupation authorities.[15] In spite of great limitations on his freedom of action, Skoropadskyi accepted all of the important conditions. To create the impression that the planned coup was spontaneous and of Ukrainian initiative, the conspirators availed themselves of the Congress of the Landowners' Alliance, which was held on April 29.[16]

Upon examining the membership of the Alliance of Landowners, we find that it was composed of russified intermediate and large landowners who had little sympathy with the Ukrainian national movement. They met in Kiev to express their demands for the establishment of the principle of private ownership, the termina-

---

14 For the German evaluation of Skoropadskyi and his entourage, see "Zusammenfassender Bericht über die politische und wirtschaftliche Lage in der Ukraine" (Kiev, May 18, 1918), Papers of General Wilhelm Groener, File Microcopy No. 137, reel XXVII, folder 254-I, National Archives of the United States, Washington, D.C.

15 H-H-SA, 152 P.A.X.; XId. "Telegram des Herrn von Princig, Nr. 275," Kiev, 30 April 1918; also Groener, pp. 398–399.

16 For an excellent summary of the German plans and actions leading to the overthrow of the Rada and the establishment of the Hetmanate, see Basil Dmytryshyn, "German Occupation of the Ukraine, 1918: Some New Evidence," *Slavic and East European Studies*, X (Montreal, 1965–66), pp. 79–92; also Peter Borowsky, *Deutsche Ukrainepolitik 1918* (Lübeck und Hamburg: Matthiesen Verlag, 1970), pp. 102–116.

tion of social experimentation, and the dissolution of the Rada.[17] The Congress was attended by 6,432 delegates, who represented the following provinces: Kiev, Poltava, Chernihiv, Podillia, Volhynia, Kherson, and Kharkiv.[18] Under German protection the delegates met in the city circus. At about two o'clock a new guard appeared at the entrance—over 500 Russian officers armed with rifles. General Skoropadskyi arrived shortly thereafter. When, apparently by prearrangement, General Skoropadskyi appeared in the box, he was given an ovation. After the assembly quieted down a little, the president of the Congress, Mykhailo M. Voronovych, former tsarist governor of Bessarabia, called upon the landowners to confer upon Skoropadskyi the title of "Hetman." The suggestion was greeted by long ovations. The General rose, went to the stage and said:

> Gentlemen! I thank you for having conferred authority upon me. It is not for my own gain that I assume the burden of the provisional government. You all know that anarchy is rampant everywhere and that only firm authority can reestablish order. I shall rely for support upon you and upon the stable and prudent portions of the population, and I pray to God to grant me the strength and firmness to save the Ukraine.[19]

In order to give this election by acclamation greater significance, and to establish the legitimacy of the new regime, the landowners decided that a pontifical *moleben* (*Te Deum*) was to be held in the old cathedral of St. Sophia. Prior to this, the new Hetman, attired in a black Cossack uniform, was anointed by Bishop Nikodim.[20]

When these events were taking place, the Rada was still discussing the draft of the Ukrainian constitution. As the forces staging the coup advanced, the *Sich* Riflemen made an attempt to defend the building in which the Rada was holding its deliberations. In the skirmish that ensued three supporters of the Hetman were killed.

---

[17] John S. Reshetar, Jr., *The Ukrainian Revolution, 1917–1920: A Study in Nationalism* (Princeton, N.J.: Princeton University Press, 1952), p. 130.

[18] M. Pasika, M. Karpyshyn, and T. Kostruba, *Za velych natsii* (Lviv, 1938), p. 130.

[19] *Vistnyk* (Vienna), May 19, 1918, p. 282; also H-H-SA, 152 P.A.X.; XId. "Politische Vorgänge in Kiew II" (23. IV—30. IV), von C. Trauttmansdorf.

[20] D. Doroshenko, *Istoriia Ukrainy 1917–1923 rr.,* Vol. II (2nd ed.; New York: Bulava Publishing Corporation, 1954), pp. 37–38.

This was the only bloodshed in the coup. By the early hours of April 30, the Hetman's forces were in control of all government offices and the *Sich* Riflemen were disarmed. Thus, the Ukrainian State replaced the Ukrainian National Republic.

Professor Fedyshyn maintains that the *coup d'état* of April 29 was "the most critical stage in the Ukrainian Revolution."[21] Indeed, in the revolutionary epoch the coup can be viewed as a turning point, as a result of which some of the previously observable national elements receded into the background, thus permitting the social factors to play an increasingly important role. The Ukrainian socialists were profoundly shocked by this unexpected turn of events, not only because they were against the establishment of a monarchical form of government, but also because they regarded General Skoropadskyi as a reactionary in the social and national spheres. His wealth and social position in the Russian Empire made the Ukrainian leaders suspicious of his true intentions.

Pavlo Petrovych Skoropadskyi was born on May 16, 1873. A son of a nobleman,[22] he attended the Pages' School, from which he emerged as an officer. In 1897, he married a wealthy niece of P. N. Durnovo, a prominent Russian arch-conservative and Minister of the Interior. Having participated in the Russo-Japanese War, he was promoted to the rank of colonel; in 1910 he was placed in command of the 20th Finnish Regiment of dragoons. In 1912 Skoropadskyi was promoted to major general with the privilege of serving as an aide-de-camp to Nicholas II. From the First World War he emerged as a lieutenant general in command of the 34th Army Corps.[23] A career like this would hardly be conducive to his becoming a Ukrainian nationalist.

Skoropadskyi's interest in purely Ukrainian affairs dates back to the summer of 1917. With the agreement of the higher command and the General Secretariat, he began to Ukrainianize his 34th Corps, later known as the "First Ukrainian Corps." It is to the credit of Skoropadskyi that they saved the Rada from the disorganized Bolshevik troops moving from the front to Kiev.[24] Despite this invaluable service, Skoropadskyi did not gain favor in

---

[21] Oleh S. Fedyshyn, *Germany's Drive to the East and the Ukrainian Revolution, 1917–1918* (New Brunswick, N.J.: Rutgers University Press, 1971), p. 133.

[22] For a complete genealogy of the family, see Pasika *et al.*, pp. 50 ff.

[23] Doroshenko, Vol. II, pp. 25–26.

[24] *Ibid.*, p. 27.

the eyes of the Ukrainian leadership. Vynnychenko, whose view of Skoropadskyi was widely shared, referred to him as the "Russian general of Little-Russian extraction."[25] A similar view was held by George Cleinow:

> . . . We are dealing with Skoropadskyi as a representative of the old-minded monarchical circles of the court of Petersburg, who hope, with the help of the Germans and the riches of the Ukraine to establish again a Russian state. . . .[26]

But, of course, the soundest basis for evaluating General Skoropadskyi is to appraise his rule as Hetman of the Ukraine.

Immediately upon assuming office, Skoropadskyi issued an edict (*hramota*) on April 29, 1918, in which he proclaimed himself "Hetman of All Ukraine." In it he pointed out the inability of the Rada to bring about order and reconstruction. Furthermore, the Hetman declared, in accordance with the agreement which he had made with the Germans, the Rada, the *Mala Rada,* and all the land committees were to be dissolved. Likewise, all the ministers and their immediate aides were removed from their positions. All other civil servants were to remain working in the various ministries as before. The Hetman promised to issue an electoral law for the election of members to a Ukrainian parliament. In accordance with the wishes of his supporters and the German authorities, he also declared that "the right of private ownership, as the foundation of culture and civilization, is reinstated in total, and all the ordinances of the former Ukrainian government and of the Provisional Russian Government, so far as they affect property rights, are abrogated." In order not to alienate the small landowners, Skoropadskyi promised that the land would be transferred to them from large owners, but at the actual value. In conclusion, he promised to safeguard the interests of the working class and to improve working conditions of the railroad employees.[27]

On the same day, the Hetman issued a decree calling for a provisional government of the Ukraine, which was to operate until the convocation of the parliament. The form of government was to be

---

[25] Volodymyr Vynnychenko, *Vidrodzhennia natsii,* Vol. III (Vienna: Vyd. Dzvin, 1920), p. 16.

[26] George Cleinow, "Das Werdende Russland," *Die Grenzboten* (Berlin, 1918), p. 174; see also Henry Cord Meyer, "Germans in the Ukraine, 1918: Excerpts from Unpublished Letters," *The American Slavic and East European Review,* IX (1950), pp. 105–115.

[27] Doroshenko, Vol. II, pp. 49–50.

a dictatorship. The decree explicitly stated that the governing authority was to reside exclusively in the Hetman. He bestowed upon himself the power to make all cabinet appointments and the right of an absolute veto over all legislation. Furthermore, the Hetman was to be commander-in-chief of the army and navy. As for civil liberties, there was to be freedom of speech and assembly—however, "within the limits of the law." While freedom of worship was recognized, the leading state religion was to be Christian Orthodoxy.[28]

One of the most difficult and urgent tasks facing the new Hetman was the formation of a cabinet. It had to be a cabinet that was acceptable to the German authorities and, at the same time, that had the support of at least one of the major Ukrainian parties. With that in mind, he appointed Mykola Ustymovych as provisional premier and directed him to contact prominent Ukrainian leaders, especially the more moderate Socialist-Federalists, to whom he offered seven portfolios. Since Ustymovych did not succeed in forming a cabinet, because of the Socialist-Federalists' refusal to cooperate, he was replaced on April 30 by Mykola Vasylenko, a Constitutional Democrat (Kadet) and member of the law faculty of the University of Kiev. He was likewise unable to secure cooperation of the Socialist-Federalists.

The Social Democrats, Socialist-Revolutionaries, and Socialist-Federalists were willing to participate in the cabinet, but on those conditions which the delegates of those parties presented to General Groener on May 2:

> 1) a complete change in the government, 2) a change in the agrarian policy, 3) voluntary dissolution of the Rada, 4) establishment of a new provisional legislative body to be known as the *Derzhavna Rada* (State Council) representing all segments of the population, 5) convocation of the Ukrainian Constituent Assembly as soon as peace and order were established.[29]

General Groener informed the delegates that the Germans did not participate in the coup and that the presence of the Socialists in the cabinet was desirable; however, a return to the Rada was out of the question, since the Hetman was already accorded recognition by Berlin.[30]

Hoping to find a new solution to this problem, Oleksander

---

[28] *Ibid.*, pp. 50–53; also Vynnychenko, Vol. III, pp. 22–24.

[29] Dr. Paul Rohrbach, "Ukrainische Eindrücke," *Deutsche Politik*, III, pt. 1 (Weimar, 1918), p. 680.

[30] Doroshenko, Vol. II, p. 55.

Shulhyn and Serhii Iefremov, prominent Socialist-Federalists, sent a note to General Groener on May 3 in which they declared that they were willing to accept Skoropadskyi only as the provisional president of a Ukrainian republic under the Rada's constitution of April 29; later, the Constituent Assembly would elect a new Hetman who would be a titular executive. The Socialist-Federalists would participate only if the Ukrainian parties were given a majority of the portfolios, including the premiership, foreign affairs, agriculture, and education. Since, however, Vasylenko's cabinet was almost completed, Groener merely replied that the Ukrainian demands were presented too late. The Socialist parties decided that if any of their members wished to enter the cabinet they would have to resign from the party.[31]

When the cabinet was taking its final form, Vasylenko was succeeded by a dignified landowner from Chernihiv and Poltava, Fedir Lyzohub. Under his direction the cabinet took its final shape. From the Ukrainian point of view, the most constructive member of Lyzohub's cabinet was Dmytro Doroshenko. Indeed, it could be said without any reservation that in him the cabinet had one nationalist with an unimpeachable reputation. But what about the other members of the cabinet? By Doroshenko's own admission (and one should keep in mind that he is the principal apologist of the Hetman's regime) only five—Butenko, Doroshenko, Kistiakovskyi, Liubynskyi, and Rohozha—of Lyzohub's fifteen-member cabinet belonged to the group that supported the Ukrainian cause.[32]

Looking at the composition of the cabinet, one can well appreciate the feelings of the Ukrainian Socialists, who considered it to be foreign and hostile to the Ukrainian national idea. Skoropadskyi, however, does not seem to have been disturbed by the ill-advised combination of which he was the principal architect, i.e., a Ukrainian state occupied by the Germans and run by a govern-

---

[31] *Ibid.*, pp. 56 ff.

[32] *Ibid.*, p. 64. Reporting on their mission to the Ukraine, Axel Schmidt and Paul Rohrbach stated: "The present [Hetman] cabinet is of Great Russian orientation and is endeavoring to lead the Ukraine back to Moscow. It simply cannot be trusted, since it is composed mainly of the Kadets. These people have clearly shown themselves enemies of the Ukraine not only during the tsarist regime but after the Revolution as well." Fedyshyn, pp. 220–221.

ment composed of persons who were "Ukrainian by blood but Muscovite in spirit."[33] Even Skoropadskyi's appointee as chief of the press bureau at the Hetman's headquarters was a declared anti-Ukrainian, A. Maliarevskyi.[34]

With the establishment of the Hetman's regime, the Germans achieved their immediate objective—a free hand in the internal affairs of the Ukraine. Henceforth, they conducted themselves as a power occupying the country.[35] The Germans almost completely disregarded the fact that there was a Ukrainian government in existence. They issued decrees in different provinces of the country that abrogated civil liberties, yet the Hetman did not protest. Already on May 1, 1918, a commander of the German corps in Kharkiv, Mengelbir, issued an order forbidding all public meetings and work stoppages.[36] Furthermore, any information concerning the German army had to pass through censorship and be approved before being published. In a report to Berlin, dated May 19, regarding the political situation in the Ukraine, Baron von Mumm stated:

> I consider it necessary to support in the Ukraine the fiction of an independent ally state as long as it serves our interests. . . . Such a policy is motivated by many reasons . . . it is necessary to consider the authority of the Ukrainian government among the population, which we shall undermine if it should clearly show that it [the government] is only a puppet [nur Puppe] in our hands, and the government's decrees serve exclusively our interests.[37]

In their new position as masters of the Ukraine, the Germans found full support among the large landowners, who from the very beginning identified their interests with those of the occupying powers. As soon as the coup was carried out and the Hetman revoked the land decrees of the Rada, they began to feel that the old order was returning. To get back some of the property that had been taken from them, they organized punitive expeditions,

---

[33] Doroshenko, Vol. II, p. 110.

[34] For Maliarevskyi's views, see A. Maliarevskyi (A. Sumskoi), "Na pereekzamenovke P. P. Skoropadskyi i ego vremia," *Arkhiv grazhdanskoi voiny,* Pt. 2 (Berlin, n.d.), p. 111.

[35] Mints and Gorodetskyi, p. 80.

[36] Oblt. Dr. Joh. Kavčič: "Bericht über die Ukraine," Kriegsarchiv, Vienna.

[37] *Ibid.,* p. 83.

undertaken by adventurers and former Russian soldiers, who usually went about their business in a very cruel way.[38]

As a result of these harsh acts and the Hetman's complete lack of interest in the fate of the peasants, widespread opposition to Skoropadskyi's regime and the German troops developed throughout the country.[39] This dissatisfaction and opposition manifested itself already on May 8–10, during the Ukrainian Peasant Congress. The Germans, aware of the peasants' attitude, acted resolutely. Their troops invaded the first session and arrested the members of the presidium and the credentials committee. As a result of this repressive act, the Congress left the city, and the deliberations were held in the Holosivskyi Forest on the outskirts of Kiev. The Congress, which consisted of approximately 12,000 delegates, resolved:

> To reject with contempt the Hetman's self-styled authority, which was created by the nobles, large estate owners, village kulaks, and capitalists, and which has no support or recognition from the democratic groups of the Ukraine, and to call the peasants to a decisive and uncompromising armed struggle against the Hetman's regime. . . .
>
> To insist that the Central Powers refrain from interfering in the economic and political affairs of the Ukrainian National Republic, and to protest against and to condemn strongly the active interference by means of military superiority of representatives of foreign powers in the class struggle in the Ukraine, the dispersion of the Ukrainian parliament, and the establishment of the Hetmanate in the Ukraine, which can only appeal to a small group of landowners and capitalists hostile to the Ukrainian National Republic and to all the achievements of the revolution.[40]

Two days later, on May 12, the Second All-Ukrainian Workers' Congress met secretly to demand a Ukrainian National Republic, the convocation of a constituent assembly, transfer of all land into the hands of the toiling people without compensation, reestablishment of the eight-hour day, worker control of industry, and freedom of speech and of the press.[41] In mid-May, the Ukrainian Social Democratic Labor Party held its fifth congress and came forth with

---

[38] For details see Isaak Mazepa, *Ukraina v ohni i buri revoliutsii, 1917–1921*, Vol. I (Prague: Proboiem, 1942), pp. 45–55.

[39] Kavčič, pp. 6–7.

[40] Eudin, p. 98.

[41] Doroshenko, Vol. II, pp. 42–43.

resolutions similar to those of the Workers' Congress. At the same time, the Socialist Revolutionary Party held its fourth congress. At this congress a split occurred, separating the members into leftists, who were advocating a social revolution in the Ukraine, and rightists, who wanted a return to the conditions that existed under the Rada.

As opposition to the Hetman's regime crystallized, the nationalists organized, in mid-May, the Ukrainian National State Union (*Ukrainskyi Natsionalno-Derzhavnyi Soiuz*), whose objective was to save the threatened Ukrainian statehood and to consolidate all forces for the purpose of creating an independent Ukrainian state. The Union was composed of the Socialist-Federalists, Socialist-Independentists, Democratic-Agrarians, and the postal, telegraph, and railroad workers.[42] The Social Democrats and Socialist-Revolutionaries joined the Union in a consultative capacity only.[43]

The formation of the Union was of monumental significance, for it became the center of the opposition and the voice of the people. It began to act very energetically. As early as May 24 it presented a memorandum to the Hetman in which it charged that the cabinet was non-Ukrainian in its composition and political orientation.[44] The presence of the Russian Kadets and Octobrists in the government, it was claimed, and their anti-Ukrainian policy, made it impossible for the new government to enjoy the confidence of the masses. The memorandum also criticized the recent bans of the workers' and peasants' congresses as well as of the zemstvo congress, acting as if the revolution did not occur at all. The spread of disorder and Bolshevism was ascribed to the Hetman's regime, and the Union maintained at the same time that the only solution was to form a Ukrainian national government.[45]

Similar demands and charges against the Hetman were made on June 16 by the All-Ukrainian Alliance of Zemstvos, which was as important as the Ukrainian National State Union. Without receiving any answer from Skoropadskyi, Symon Petliura, the leader of the Alliance of Zemstvos, appealed to Ambassador Mumm, but the Germans preferred not to take any position in the matter.[46]

---

[42] Khrystiuk, Vol. III, p. 63.

[43] Doroshenko, Vol. II, p. 103.

[44] A similar opinion was expressed by Graf Forgách on June 28, 1918. See H-H-SA, 152 P.A.X.; XId. Telegram Nr. 618.

[45] Doroshenko, Vol. II, pp. 103–107.

[46] *Ibid.*, p. 111.

In the light of these demands, complaints, and charges against the Hetman's regime, one might form an erroneous opinion that during Skoropadskyi's rule no constructive contribution was made to Ukrainian statehood. Nothing could be further from the truth, for it was precisely during his reign that the Ukrainians made considerable progress in education, in foreign affairs, and in the organization of the Ukrainian army.[47] After Skoropadskyi's fall, the Directory inherited not only a well-organized army and supply service, but also a good military administration, which greatly increased its fighting ability against the Bolsheviks.

Skoropadskyi even showed some interest in the all-important land question. His ultimate objective seems to have been to create a strong class of intermediate peasants who would obtain land with the help of the government. For that purpose, a State Land Bank was to be established. Skoropadskyi's attitude toward land reform was stated most clearly during a reception on June 25 for the delegates of agriculturalists from the provinces of Kharkiv, Kherson, Poltava, and Volhynia. He said that a land law in preparation would provide for the following:

> There will be no more large land estates; the land will be given over to the land toiling people; however, not more than 25 *desiatyns* for one person, also one person may not buy land in different localities. . . .[48]

Unfortunately, the plan never became a reality. Indeed, a land law, similar in its provisions to the ideas expressed by the Hetman, was prepared under the new Minister of Agriculture, V. M. Leontovych, at the beginning of November 1918. But it came too late to be implemented or to produce any results. Therefore, in reality, nothing was done to replace the reforms that the Hetman had revoked already on the first day of his regime.

However far-reaching and constructive Skoropadskyi's plans might have been, they were overshadowed by two more significant considerations—immediate agrarian reform and the Ukrainianization of his government. Without a satisfactory settlement of these questions, the anti-Hetman opposition, which in many areas

---

[47] For the details on the organization of the Ukrainian army under the Hetman, see Doroshenko, Vol. II, pp. 235–248; Zenon Stefaniv, *Ukrainski zbroini syly v 1917–1921 rr.* (Ulm, Germany: Biblioteka Ukrainskoho Kombatanta, 1947), pp. 99–110.

[48] Doroshenko, Vol. II, p. 283.

turned into open rebellion, could not possibly have been stopped. Since June the peasant rebellion began to assume threatening proportions. Reporting to Vienna on June 9, 1918, Count Forgách wrote:

> In the southeastern part of Kiev province, especially in Zvenyhorod, strong peasant insurrections occurred. Several German units were cut off. For the suppression of the insurrection the Germans have undertaken energetic measures and many troops were sent from Kiev. . . .[49]

As time progressed, the popular movement gained in intensity, until entire provinces were under the control of the rebels.[50]

The Germans soon began to see the fruits of their policy of violence. The fields were not cultivated, the crops were not harvested, and people refused to work in the mines and the factories and on the railroads. Despite their policy of requisitioning, the Germans were getting even less—"not even Germans could make bayonets serve as ploughshares."[51] These considerations, plus the fear of a Ukrainian union with Russia, prompted Baron Mumm to inform Premier Lyzohub on June 29 that it would be desirable to bring a few Ukrainians into the cabinet. The Germans thought that perhaps the government would gain the confidence of the broad masses if it were more representative of the people.

Skoropadskyi was likewise anxious to do something in order to change the existing situation. On July 8, he sent a letter to Premier Lyzohub, who concurrently held the interior portfolio, complaining that the local officials were acting contrary to the policy in Kiev and that the agrarian program was being widely misinterpreted, thus encouraging anti-government agitation. Unable to cope with the problem, Lyzohub resigned. He was succeeded by Ihor Kistiakovskyi, who previously held the position of Secretary General.[52] The latter's policy of arresting numerous Ukrainian leaders on grounds of their being "Bolsheviks" was largely instrumental in increasing the tension that developed during July and in further discrediting the government in nationalist circles.

To remedy the situation, Skoropadskyi instructed Dmytro Doro-

---

[49] Mints and Gorodetskyi, p. 144.

[50] For a contemporary account, see N. M. Mohylianskyi, "Tragediia Ukrainy," in *Arkhiv russkoi revoliutsii*, Vol. XI (Berlin, 1923), p. 97.

[51] Gerald Freund, *Unholy Alliance* (London, 1957), p. 12.

[52] Doroshenko, Vol. II, p. 337.

shenko in July to negotiate secretly with prominent Ukrainians about the possibility of their entering the cabinet. Among the persons consulted, Professor D. Bahalii, the former Rector of Kharkiv University, E. Shrah, and P. Doroshenko refused to accept the premiership.[53] The Ukrainianization of the cabinet was also hindered by the arrest of Petliura on July 12. He was released only upon promising not to engage in any conspiratorial activity. Also, the plan to Ukrainianize the government had to be postponed, since the assassination on July 30 of Field Marshal von Eichhorn produced an atmosphere in which it was almost impossible to carry on any constructive work.[54]

During July, the National State Union was transformed into the Ukrainian National Union (*Ukrainskyi Natsionalyni Soiuz*), with the Social Democrats and the moderate Socialist-Revolutionaries entering the new organization. Its purpose was to exert pressure on the government and to prepare the way for the take-over by the Ukrainian national parties. The Union was composed not only of political parties, but also of peasants, professional, labor and cultural organizations, and student groups.[55] Because it was a broad-based organization, the Union became truly representative of the Ukrainian people.

Skoropadskyi, aware of the Union's power, hastened to get its support in another attempt to Ukrainianize the government. It was toward this end that on October 5, Vynnychenko, Andrii Nikovskyi, and Fedir Shvets went secretly to the Hetman's residence and presented him with a list of ministerial candidates. It was decided that Lyzohub was to remain as premier, but no agreement could be reached on the number of portfolios to be assigned Ukrainians nor on the choice of candidates. As a result, the formation of a new cabinet was delayed for two weeks. In the meantime, the position of the Union improved, when on November 10 Baron von Mumm was ordered to direct Hetman Skoropadskyi to Ukrainianize the cabinet.[56]

---

[53] *Ibid.*, p. 380.

[54] *Ibid.*, p. 125.

[55] *Ibid.*, pp. 386–387.

[56] Mints and Gorodetskyi, p. 136. Also the Austrians tried to impress upon Skoropadskyi the necessity to Ukrainianize the cabinet in order to give it a wider representative basis with a national and democratic character. See H-H-SA, 152 P.A.X.; XId, Telegram No. 1111, Prince Fürstenberg, Kiev, 16 October 1918.

In order to understand the Hetman's policies, they must be viewed within the context of a complex international situation. On September 29, 1918, Bulgaria concluded an armistice with the Entente, and soon after Turkey followed. In the West, the German armies started retreating, while the Austro-Hungarian Empire was beginning to disintegrate. The defeat of the Central Powers was imminent. It was, therefore, imperative for the Hetman's government to reach an understanding on internal affairs and then enter into relations with the Entente. The Ukrainian Ministry of Foreign Affairs was especially anxious to have the Entente recognize the Ukraine as an independent state.

The Minister of Foreign Affairs, Dmytro Doroshenko, thought it essential to explain to the other members of the cabinet the nature of the Ukraine's relations with the Central Powers, the neutral states, and the Entente. The discussion that followed revealed that a number of ministers did not approve of Doroshenko's policy because of its "nationalistic course."[57] This precipitated a cabinet crisis in mid-October. Aware of the negotiations that the Hetman was conducting with the National Union, several cabinet members (Vasylenko, Minister of Education; Gerbel, Minister of Supply; Vagner, Minister of Labor; Kokoltsov, Minister of Agriculture; Zinkivskyi, Minister of Cults; Afanasev, State Controller; and Rzhepetskyi, Minister of Finance) discussed with Premier Lyzohub the role that the Ukraine should play at the forthcoming peace conference. According to them, the Ukraine was to serve only as a base of operations in a war against the Bolsheviks in order to establish a reunited Russia.[58]

The National Union came to the rescue of the Hetmanate, and on October 24 a coalition cabinet was formed.[59] Lyzohub retained the post of Premier. Hutnyk was succeeded by a landowner and sugar refiner, Sergei F. Mering. Likewise, Gerbel and Rzhepetskyi retained their positions in spite of their strong anti-Ukrainian sentiments. Originally, Vynnychenko demanded eight portfolios; in the end, however, the Union accepted the following five: Petro Stebnyt-

---

[57] Doroshenko, Vol. II, p. 393.

[58] Reshetar, pp. 193–194.

[59] Prince Fürstenberg explained the October cabinet crisis as an intrigue of conservative Russophile groups, who had hidden themselves behind the Hetman to prevent at all costs the Ukrainianization of the government. See H-H-SA, 152 P.A.X.; XId, Telegram No. 1136, Prinz Fürstenberg, Kiev, 23 Oktober 1918.

skyi, Education; Oleksander Lototskyi, Cults; Volodymyr Leontovych, Agriculture; Andrii Viazlov, Justice; and Slyvinskyi, Labor.[60]
Since the Alliance had members in the cabinet, it would seem that
Skoropadskyi would finally obtain the support he sought. However,
cooperation did not materialize, for soon after the cabinet was
formed the National Union disavowed it and refused to accept any
responsibility for its actions. Instead, the leaders of the National
Union started a more intensive preparation for an uprising against
Skoropadskyi.

Meanwhile, other forces were working to overthrow the Hetmanate. The Bolsheviks, who were industriously preparing themselves against the Hetman, conducted their activities in two direc-
tions. Their first objective was to gain the support of the peasants;
their second, to reach an understanding with the German soldiers,
whose power kept Skoropadskyi in his position. With regard to
the peasants, the Bolsheviks had little success.[61] Their propaganda,
however, found fertile ground among the war-weary German
soldiers, who simply wanted to go home. By November 17, there
were actual soviets formed among German soldiers, who discussed
with the local Bolsheviks the question of overthrowing the Hetman's government and substituting in its place a government of
soviets.[62]

Hoping to save his regime from the impending crisis, Skoropadskyi embarked upon a most radical course: a second *coup d'état*,
which would cast aside all the previous trappings of independence
and openly espouse the cause of federation with Russia. As the
first step in that direction, he dissolved the old cabinet in order to
remove from important governmental positions those who stood
for Ukrainian independence. Then he appointed a new cabinet,
headed by a former tsarist minister, Gerbel, which "consisted mostly
of Russian monarchists."[63] Finally, on November 14, Skoropadskyi
issued an edict:

---

[60] Doroshenko, Vol. II, p. 397.

[61] V. Antonov-Ovseenko, *Zapiski o grazhdanskoi voine*, Vol. III (Moscow, 1924), p. 12.

[62] *Die deutsche Okkupation der Ukraine: Geheimdokumente* (Stras-
bourg: Ed. Prométhée, 1937), p. 225.

[63] James Bunyan, *Intervention, Civil War, and Communism in Russia,
April–December* 1918 (Baltimore, Md.: The Johns Hopkins Press, 1936),
p. 29.

When compared with other remaining parts of long-suffering Russia, the Ukraine has had the most fortunate fate. The Ukraine was the first to establish a basis for law and order. With friendly support of the Central Powers she has maintained internal peace until the present. Being sympathetic to Great Russia and all its sufferings, the Ukraine has attempted with all its strength to aid its brethren, tendering them broad hospitality and supporting them in the struggle to restore firm political order in Russia.

Before us now stands a new political task. The Allies have long been the friends of the former great and united Russian State. Now . . . the conditions of its future existence have definitely changed. The former vigor and strength of the All-Russian State must be restored on the basis of the federative principle. In this federation, the Ukraine deserves to play one of the leading roles, because from the Ukraine law and order spread throughout the country, and within her borders for the first time the citizens of former Russia, humiliated and oppressed by Bolshevik despotism, were freely encouraged. . . . The Ukraine must take the lead in the matter of the establishment of an All-Russian federation, the final goal of which will be the restoration of Great Russia. . . .

Deeply convinced that any other policy would mean the destruction of the Ukraine, I appeal to all who cherish her future to unite around me and stand in defense of the Ukraine and Russia. I believe that in this sacred, patriotic cause, you, citizens and Cossacks of the Ukraine and the remainder of the population, will render sincere and strong support.

I hereby commission the newly formed cabinet to undertake the execution of this great historic task in the very near future.[64]

The die was cast. There was now no way in which the Hetman could possibly negotiate with the Ukrainian nationalists. On November 13, Vynnychenko presided over a small group of conspirators, informing them that Skoropadskyi was preparing to issue an edict proclaiming a federation with Russia. To head the insurrectionary government, a Directory of five was established: Vynnychenko, Symon Petliura, Fedir Shvets, Opanas Andriievskyi, and Andrii Makarenko.[65]

The Directory commenced its work by issuing a proclamation, which appeared in the streets of Kiev during the night of Novem-

---

[64] Khrystiuk, Vol. III, pp. 120 ff.

[65] Arnold D. Margolin, *From a Political Diary: Russia, the Ukraine, and America, 1905–1945* (New York: Columbia University Press, 1946), p. 33.

ber 14–15,[66] accusing the Hetman of being "a coercionist and usurper of popular authority. His whole government is declared to be inactive because it is anti-popular and anti-national."[67] All Russian officers were told to surrender their arms and leave the country. Skoropadskyi and his ministers were advised to resign in order to preserve peace and avoid bloodshed. Within a day the three members of the Directory were at Bila Tserkva, from which they, with the support of the *Sich* Riflemen, began to march toward Kiev on November 18. The struggle of the loyal supporters of the Hetman became quite hopeless because entire units were going over to the forces of the Directory. In addition to the many smaller units, two entire divisions, the Zaporozhian and Sirozhupan, defected to the revolutionaries.[68]

As the forces of the Directory advanced closer to Kiev, the German army decided to defend the capital. The Directory halted the advance to prevent any unnecessary bloodshed. Thus, under the protection of German troops and Russian officer detachments, Skoropadskyi continued to hold the office of Hetman. During this temporary halt of the Directory forces at Kiev, the insurrectionists occupied other provinces and by the end of November they were the real masters of the entire territory.[69] The stalemate was resolved when, on December 12, the German Command made an agreement with the Directory to remain neutral and to withdraw from Kiev. Now Petliura had a free hand to attack the city. The Directory's army, led by Colonel Ievhen Konovalets, entered Kiev on December 14, and after a few skirmishes with the Russian officers, established a military government.

Just before the Directory's forces entered Kiev, Skoropadskyi, seeing the futility of any further resistance, signed the following declaration of abdication:

> I, Hetman of all the Ukraine, have employed all my energies during the past seven and one-half months in an effort to extricate the Ukraine from the difficult situation in which she finds herself. God has not given me the strength to deal with this problem, and now,

---

[66] Elias Hurwicz, *Geschichte des russischen Bürgerkrieges* (Berlin: E. Laubsche Verlagsbuchhandlung Gm. b. H., 1927), p. 123.

[67] Khrystiuk, Vol. III, p. 131.

[68] Doroshenko, Vol. II, p. 421.

[69] *Die deutsche Okkupation der Ukraine*, p. 15.

in the light of conditions which have arisen and acting solely for the good of the Ukraine, I abdicate all authority.[70]

For a few more days General Skoropadskyi lived hiding in Kiev. Then, disguising himself in a German uniform, he left for Germany, together with his wife, who had disguised herself as a nurse.

Skoropadskyi came to power relying on the Germans. Having alienated all the nationally conscious elements in the Ukraine, he left with the Germans when their support was no longer forthcoming.

---

[70] Reshetar, pp. 203–204.

CHAPTER FOUR

The Directory of the Ukrainian National Republic

Martha Bohachevsky-Chomiak

THE UPRISING LED by the Directory of the Ukrainian National Republic against the regime of Hetman Pavlo Skoropadskyi came as a surprise not only to the non-participants, but also to members of the Directory itself.[1] The Directory raised the standard of revolt on the night of November 14–15, 1918. Within a month it was swept triumphantly into Kiev by a largely spontaneous peasant movement, kept in line by military formations of the *Sich* Riflemen, the Zaporozhian Corps and the *Serdiuky*. Although it could not hold Kiev, the Directory and its successor managed to keep up active military and political operations in the Ukraine until October 1921, and after that to continue political activity as an émigré government that long survived its original participants.

The idea of revolt against the Hetman matured slowly. Skoropadskyi was unpopular among the majority of the radical Ukrainian intelligentsia, who regarded him as a representative of the conservative bourgeoisie and who detested his reliance on the propertied classes and his willingness to use Russian conservatives in the Ukrainian government. They were also wary because of the Hetman's collaboration with the Germans. The moderates supported the Hetman as long as his government pursued a steadfast policy of Ukrainian national independence.[2]

The crisis in the Hetman government began in the middle of

---

[1] The influx of the conservative non-Ukrainians into the cities of the Ukraine must be noted. See A. I. Denikin, *Ocherki russkoi smuty*, Vol. IV (Berlin, 1925), pp. 184–187; Roman Gulia, "Kievskaia epopeia," *Arkhiv russkoi revoliutsii*, Vol. II (Berlin, 1921), p. 60; A. D. Margolin, *Ukraina i politika Antanty* (Berlin, 1922), p. 77.

[2] Dmytro Doroshenko, *Istoriia Ukrainy, 1917–1923 rr.*, Vol. II, (Uzhhorod: Svoboda 1930), pp. 407–409; Denkin, Vol. IV, p. 182.

October, when certain ministers suggested that Skoropadskyi make the reconstruction of a unified Russian state his primary objective. Other ministers resigned in protest, with the result that the Hetman turned to Vynnychenko with the proposal to form a new government.

Volodymyr Vynnychenko, a flamboyant if erratic mainstay of the Ukrainian Social Democratic Labor Party, firmly believed in socialism and nationalism and felt that the Ukrainians supported both. He was also convinced that the Hetman was an enemy of progress and of the Ukrainian people, and toyed with the possibility of an armed insurrection against the regime as early as the summer of 1918.[3] His own party considered the idea of revolt at the time dangerous and treasonable,[4] so Vynnychenko, instead of advocating revolution, became the elected head of a legal party of opposition, the Ukrainian National Union. He turned down Skoropadskyi's offer but proposed some candidates for the new coalition government, and the Hetman accepted his suggestions.[5] The coalition was strained and ineffective, and the Hetman seemed to lean more heavily on the bourgeoisie and the Russians. As a result, the idea of a coup gained popular support.[6]

Active preparations for the uprising began in the last days of October. Coordinating efforts were masked under the activity of the Ukrainian National Union, where Vynnychenko at times publicly disclaimed any thought of an uprising.[7] He and Mykyta Shapoval convinced various disaffected Ukrainians to join the cause, and the movement gained momentum.

To overcome the Hetman's small armed forces, the leaders knew they would need the support of the Central Powers and of the *Sich* Riflemen.[8] The neutrality of the first was desirable; the support of the latter was essential. At first the *Sich* Riflemen tried to avoid

---

[3] Volodymyr Vynnychenko, *Vidrodzhennia natsii*, Vol. III (Kiev-Vienna: Vyd. Dzvin, 1920), p. 494.

[4] Mykyta Shapoval shared Vynnychenko's views at the time. Vynnychenko, Vol. III, p. 88; M. Shapoval, *Hetmanshchyna i dyrektoriia* (New York, 1958) mimeograph; and Margolin, p. 74.

[5] Pavlo Khrystiuk, *Zamitky i materialy do istorii ukrainskoi revoliutsii 1917–1920, Vol. III* (reprint of 1921–22 edition; New York, 1969), p. 114.

[6] The Russians did not support the Hetman either. Khrystiuk, Vol. III, p. 124; Denikin, Vol. IV, pp. 186–197.

[7] Margolin, p. 75; Khrystiuk, Vol. III, p. 129; Shapoval, p. 48.

[8] Ievhen Konovalets, *Prychynky do istorii ukrainskoi revoliutsii* (Prague, 1928), pp. 11–12; and Doroshenko, Vol. II, pp. 412–413.

political involvement. Later on, however, their leader, Colonel Ievhen Konovalets, agreed to support the uprising; Konovalets' aides, Andrii Melnyk and Fedir Chernyk, then attended a meeting of the National Union.[9] The *Sich* Riflemen were instrumental in persuading the German and Austro-Hungarian armies and their soldiers' councils to remain neutral during the uprising.[10]

The final meeting of the revolutionaries took place on the night of November 13, 1918, at the Ministry of Communications in Kiev.[11] They agreed only on a general program—to re-establish the republic, to reinstate democratic liberties and self-government, to grant land to the peasants, and to guarantee basic labor rights to workers.[12] It was assumed that final policy decisions would be made by an elected representative body.

Summoning all his eloquence, the volatile Vynnychenko pleaded for a dramatic uprising, a direct march on Kiev (presumably from the city itself), and an assertion of national and social ideals, even at the cost of predictable suppression by the German garrison. He was outvoted, and an alternative plan was accepted. This called for beginning operations from the town of Bila Tserkva, head-quarters of the *Sich* Riflemen, where it was hoped that the people would be organized into military formations.[13] That night, as the Hetman prepared his manifesto, the opposition elected the Direc-tory—a provisional revolutionary organ whose purpose was to lead the uprising. Vynnychenko became its chairman. Other members included Makarenko, the leader of the railroad workers, Opanas Andriievskyi, a Socialist-Independent and a political moderate (almost a rightist), and Fedir Shvets, a professor of geography.[14] Symon Petliura, the man who proved to be the most tenacious and eventually the most powerful figure in the Directory, was not even

---

[9] *Ibid.*, p. 406; Oleksandr Udovychenko, *Ukraina u viini za derzhavnist: istoriia orhanizatsii i boiovykh dii ukrainskykh zbroinykh syl, 1917–1921* (Winnipeg: D. Mykytiuk, 1954), pp. 41–43.

[10] Arkhivnoe Upravlenie pri Sovete Ministrov Ukrainskoi SSR, *Grazh-danskaia voina*, Vol. II, book 3 (Kiev, 1967), pp. 434, 437; Denikin, Vol. IV, 197.

[11] Vynnychenko, Vol. III, p. 91; Shapoval, p. 59; Khrystiuk, Vol. III, p. 129

[12] *Ibid.*, Vol. IV, p. 14; Vynnychenko, Vol. III, p. 132.

[13] *Ibid.*, p. 122.

[14] Khrystiuk, Vol. III, p. 131; Shapoval, pp. 59–64, later said he pre-dicted the failure of the Directory and hence would have nothing to do with it.

present at the meeting, but he had previously agreed to coordinate military action.

Petliura, a Social Democrat with a service background during the Rada government, had become prominent as an organizer of Ukrainian military detachments. He enjoyed the support of the *Sich* Riflemen, had been arrested by the Hetman for his pro-Entente views, and had served as the chairman of the Kiev zemstvo. The meeting authorized the Directory to leave for Bila Tserkva and named a separate Revolutionary Committee to coordinate activity in Kiev.[15]

The manifesto of the Directory discussed that night was drafted by Vynnychenko, and it reflected his views and his dynamism as well as his lack of precision. Throughout his political career, Vynnychenko remained the consummate writer he primarily was. The appeal of the manifesto was emotional, and that was what the Directory needed at the time. It attacked the regime of "the general of the Russian army, P. Skoropadskyi ... whose rule destroyed the rights of the people and who engaged in unheard-of prosecution of democracy in the Ukraine." Vynnychenko warned Skoropadskyi not to oppose the movement and urged the Germans to maintain their neutrality. He also enjoined the population "to rally with us in an armed force ... to bring back all social and political gains of revolutionary democracy." The manifesto promised that the Ukrainian Constituent Assembly would enforce these rights. At the same time, Vynnychenko, Petliura, Shvets, and Andriievskyi, who signed the document on behalf of the Directory, called on "all warriors to maintain order and to prevent looting firmly and ruthlessly."[16]

While this document was being posted on the streets of Kiev, Petliura, as Supreme Commander of the Armed Forces, issued his own universal calling on soldiers, Cossacks, and the population to support the cause of an independent Ukraine against "the Hetman and the unemployed Russian officers."[17]

Later Vynnychenko viewed the publication of Petliura's universal

---

[15] Among its members were M. Avdiienko, V. Chekhivskyi, A. Pisotskyi, Z. Vysotskyi, M. Halahan, N. Zahorodnyi, M. Marchenko and many Socialist-Revolutionaries.

[16] Since Petliura was already at Bila Tserkva, it is very doubtful that he personally saw the document. Texts in Khrystiuk, Vol. III, pp. 131–132 and Vynnychenko, Vol. III, pp. 110–114.

[17] Text in Khrystiuk, Vol. III, p. 133.

as a personal affront and as proof of the heroic ambitions of the Supreme *Otaman,* as Petliura came to be known.[18] It seemed inconceivable to the popular and brilliant writer that the quiet Petliura—erstwhile journalist, bookkeeper, editor, and essayist of second-rate literary criticism with a patriotic bent—could have appeared as a spokesman of a national and social movement that Vynnychenko considered his preserve. Yet, because of Petliura's activity in the army during the Rada period and because of his eloquence, slightly tinged with histrionics, Petliura proved to be the man capable of boosting the morale of the soldiers and of convincing others to join the cause.[19]

The Directory came closest to exercising full power in the Ukraine during the first two months of its existence. The revolt against the Hetman regime spread so rapidly among the peasants that the *Sich* Riflemen, in charge of the universal mobilization, could barely cope with the task. The inability of the Directory to discipline these peasant-volunteers, its most numerous supporters, was a fatal flaw in the movement.[20]

The leadership, including at first even Petliura, failed to realize the importance of a professionally organized, disciplined army. They were willing, as true classic intelligentsia, to see in the peasants a selfless, dedicated, and disciplined force, with no need for added military and administrative control. At best, some of them, including Vynnychenko, argued for the establishment of a political commissariat to control not the men, but the officers.

When the Directory began its revolution, the strongest organized force on which it could rely was the corps of the *Sich* Riflemen. Since this unit also possessed an effective internal administrative apparatus, it was often burdened with administrative as well as military tasks.[21] The elite corps of the Hetman army, the *Serdiuky,*

---

[18] Vynnychenko, Vol. III, pp. 132–137.

[19] For favorable impressions of Petliura, see Margolin, p. 191; I. Kedrovskyi, "Pochatky natsionalnoho viiska," in *Zbirnyk pamiati Symona Petliury 1879–1926* (Prague, 1930), pp. 216–220; Oleksander Dotsenko, *Litopys ukrainskoi revoliutsii,* Vol. II, book 4 (Lviv, 1923–24), p. 13. For a more balanced account see Isaak Mazepa, *Ukraina v ohni i buri revoliutsii, 1917–1921,* Vol. I (2nd ed.; n.p., 1950), pp. 116–117.

[20] Vynnychenko, Vol. III, p. 130; Khrystiuk, Vol. IV, p. 9; Mazepa, Vol. I, pp. 31, 59; Udovychenko, p. 49.

[21] The Riflemen, for instance, did not want to command Kiev. Konovalets, pp. 19–21.

made up of landed peasants, sided with the Directory, as did the efficient Zaporozhian Corps. But the Directory was unable to preserve discipline and maintain the battle capacity of either these groups or the rest of its forces. The peasants, war-weary at the beginning of the struggle, were interested in acquiring land and were rarely concerned with broader considerations of policy or tactics, once the Hetman and his grain-requisition squads were removed.

In an attempt to organize a popular army quickly, Petliura assigned funds to persons who were willing to organize local detachments. Money was often simply handed out and no separate accounts were kept. The leaders were expected to feed, clothe, and arm their detachments, and to coordinate strategy with the center; in practice, however, they usually acted on their own. Moreover, as the central authority of the Hetman state disintegrated, it was often the military that provided basic civilian services. For these reasons, the individual *otamans,* as the local commanders were known, acted in the old Cossack lordly tradition—making, interpreting, and enforcing policy.[22]

Various *otamans* appeared throughout the Ukraine. Some were sanctioned by the Directory and some operated alone. A few of the more powerful ones, by shifting loyalties, critically altered the political configuration in the country.[23] The *otamans* not only compromised the emerging government through their activities but actually endangered it. Most damaging to the Directory was the fact that some *otamans* were anti-Semitic, while others were incapable of coping with anti-Semitic outbreaks. The Directory denounced anti-Semitism, periodically punished perpetrators of anti-

---

[22] Vynnychenko, Vol. III, p. 352.

[23] Particularly significant were the activities of Petro Bolbochan, Matvii Hryhoriiv, and Nestor Makhno. Bolbochan pursued conservative policies and eventually conspired against Petliura. See Mazepa, Vol. I, p. 76; Vynnychenko, Vol. III, pp. 145–147, 295–297. Hryhoriiv, a former staff captain of the tsarist army, was assassinated by Makhno. Makhno, the anarchist, pursued an independent line, although he was allied sometimes with the Directory and sometimes with the Bolsheviks. The best available secondary account in English that deals with Hryhoriiv is Arthur Adams, *Bolsheviks in the Ukraine: The Second Campaign, 1918–1919* (New Haven, Conn.: Yale University Press, 1963); on Makhno, see David Footman, *Civil War in Russia* (New York: Praeger, 1962), as well as most of the contemporary sources cited in this study.

Semitic outbreaks, appropriated large sums of money to reimburse victims of pogroms, reactivated the national-personal autonomy law of the Rada for national minorities, and created a special ministry for Jewish affairs, headed by a Jew. But it was unable to enforce its policies. This caused a loss of popularity at home and abroad.[24] As was the case with other contenders in the area, the Directory was unable to establish effective control even over the military, to whom it had delegated authority.[25]

The uprising led by the Directory took by surprise the other powers interested in the Ukraine. Deprived of German support, the Hetman regime disintegrated, although Skoropadskyi, with the help of a German unit, managed to hold Kiev for a full month after the proclamation of the uprising. The Russian Whites retreated to the south, concentrating in Odessa, where they hoped to receive help from the Allies. For a time the Directory did not come into conflict with them.

The local Bolsheviks, previously expelled from the Ukraine, did not have Moscow's support to launch a new effective offensive and had to rely on clandestine organization and limited action, often in contradiction to the policies of the center.[26] Vynnychenko thought that the Soviet government had assured him of benevolent neutrality in return for the legalization of the Bolshevik Party in the Ukraine. The Moscow Soviet promised to recognize the Ukrainian government and not interfere in its affairs.[27] However,

---

[24] To this day, the false impression lingers that the movement in which Petliura participated was anti-Semitic. When Vynnychenko wrote his memoirs he accused Petliura of unconscious anti-Semitism. Vynnychenko, Vol. III, pp. 365–367. For a recent analysis, see Taras Hunczak, "A Reappraisal of Symon Petliura and Ukrainian Jewish Relations, 1917–1921," *Jewish Social Studies*, XXXI, 3 (New York, 1969). Limitations of space prevent a full discussion of the issue, but it is worthwhile to remember that neither the Soviets nor Denikin could prevent anti-Jewish outbreaks. See Margolin, *passim;* Denikin, Vol. V. pp. 148–150; A. A. Goldenweyzer, "Iz kievskikh vospominanii," *Arkhiv russkoi revoliutsii,* VI (Berlin, 1922).

[25] Denikin argued that dictatorship was essential, but he was ineffective himself. Denikin, Vol. IV, p. 201. The Bolsheviks had to contend with the willful actions of local guerrillas.

[26] Most convenient account in Adams, *Bolsheviks in the Ukraine;* see also *Gosudarstvennaia voina,* Vol. I, book 3, pp. 465–469, 562–567; Sergei Mazlakh, "Oktiabrskaia revoliutsiia na Poltavshchine," *Letopis revoliutsii,* No. 1 (Kharkiv, 1922), pp. 127–142; Denikin, Vol. IV, p. 180.

[27] Vynnychenko, Vol. III, p. 158.

as the success and the popularity of the anti-Hetman revolt spread, the Bolsheviks attacked the new Ukrainian government, although Moscow disclaimed responsibility.

It was not until January 16, 1919, that the Directory reconciled itself to the unpleasant and, for some, inconceivable fact that it was engaged in a war with Soviet Russia.

According to Vynnychenko, it was he who prepared the uprising and led the Directory from November 15, 1918, to February 10, 1919, although he realized the futility of the venture and his own lack of power *vis-à-vis* Petliura and the military. Yet he also argued that his resignation from the Directory was a supreme personal sacrifice undertaken to placate the Entente powers and to gain their good will. Vynnychenko dated the end of the Directory with his own resignation. The subsequent regime he considered to be merely the reign of various *otamans*.[28] But a close analysis of the policies of the Directory after Vynnychenko's resignation shows no drastic changes in the government.

The Directory had to make two basic decisions. The first concerned the type of government to be instituted in the Ukraine— a parliamentary democracy or a more socialistic workers' state. The other decision, closely connected to the first, was whether an alliance should be concluded with the Entente or with the Soviets. Neither the Entente nor the Soviets were really interested in Ukrainian independence, but the Ukraine needed the good will, or at least the neutrality, of one of these parties in order to survive.

The fact that the Directory, even though it enjoyed military and political superiority, was concerned with external forces must not be construed only as a weakness of the national movement. Rather, this was a reflection of the psychological and intellectual traditions of the intelligentsia participating in the uprising of the Directory. These traditions included the manifold repercussions of the tsarist system of government, the exclusiveness of the political opposition movement in Russia, and the inordinate idealization of the West by the progressive intelligentsia of Eastern Europe. It is only in this light that one can fully grasp the dilemma and the tragedy with which these men were faced. They were fighting for principles rather than for land; they could not envision hostility in forces that they idealized.

The situation was further complicated by the fact that the Galician Ukrainians, of the former Austro-Hungarian Empire, had

---

[28] *Ibid.*, p. 264.

succeeded, albeit temporarily, in asserting their independence. The two branches of the Ukrainians agreed to unite, by means of a decision reached on December 1, 1918, in Fastiv and solemnized formally in Kiev on January 22, 1919. But the Galicians maintained their own army and their autonomy, hoping that their chances of gaining international recognition would be better than those of the Ukraine proper. By July 15, however, the Galician Ukrainian government and army sought refuge in the eastern Ukraine before the advancing Polish forces.[29]

Throughout November and December 1918, the armies of the Directory took district after district, including Odessa.[30] Its victories culminated on December 14 in a grand entry into Kiev, yet peace did not follow. In the north the Bolsheviks were openly hostile, and in the south the reputed voice of France, Consul Henno, threatened the Directory with imminent French intervention.[31] The double threat loomed over all discussions of policy.

The Directory has been accused of failing to provide a program, of compromising with its internal and external enemies, even "of being afraid to . . . formulate the will of the people."[32] These failings stemmed from its democratic character and the unwillingness of any one group to exert sufficient pressure to have its program adopted.

When it became clear that other "elder statesmen," like Hrushevskyi, would not be called to power, Vynnychenko became the most obvious person to provide a comprehensive program. In the early

---

[29] The Polish victory over the Ukrainians was facilitated by help from the French, who thought the Poles were waging a war against the Bolsheviks. See Vynnychenko, Vol. III, pp. 242–243; Mazepa, Vol. I, p. 87; and a favorable account by the Galician Ukrainian, Sydir Yaroslavyn (Isidore Sokhotsky), *Vyzvolna borotba na ukrainskykh zemliakh u 1918–1923rr.* (Philadelphia, 1956).

[30] Odessa was taken on December 12, although the Ukrainians honored the French request to leave an international zone as a refuge for the Russian White émigrés who did not have the strength to control the area; Denikin, Vol. V., p. 10.

[31] No one at the time could realize that the French threats were empty gestures. See John Bradley, *Allied Intervention in Russia* (New York, 1968).

[32] Panas Fedenko, "Povstannia natsii," in *Zbirnyk pamiati Symona Petliury (1879–1926)* (Prague, 1930), p. 79; also Khrystiuk, Vol. IV, *passim;* Mazepa, Vol. I, p. 76.

days of December, he suggested the *rada* principle, by which he meant vesting power only in the representatives of the working classes; his proposal should not be confused with the democratic Rada government that preceded the Hetman regime. He argued that the loss of "moderate, petit bourgeois, national elements" would be more than offset by the support "of the city and village proletariat," the basis of the Ukrainian nation.[33]

Vynnychenko's plan was roundly rejected by the Directory and the party leaders. To salvage some of it, he, in his own words, "cunningly ... proposed ... the acceptance of a system of 'toilers' councils' composed of representatives of all those elements of society which do not exploit the labor of others."[34] This proposal was accepted, but the Toilers' Congress that was to implement the plan was not convened until the end of January 1919, when Kiev was already threatened by the Bolsheviks.

Meanwhile, on December 26 the Directory issued a comprehensive statement of policy known as the Declaration of the Directory.[35] This compromise document was too brief to be a constitutional draft and too long to be effective propaganda. It tried to strike a balance between revolution and order, thereby leaving the Directory open to charges of both Bolshevism and reaction. It promised expropriation of state, church, and large private landholdings and the distribution of land particularly to those peasants who had rallied to the republican cause. It left "all small peasant households and all labor households" intact. Special Peoples' Land Administrations were organized to carry out the reform.[36] Control of industry by the workers was also promised.

The most interesting part of the Declaration vested power in the new government in the workers, the peasants, and the "toiling intelligentsia" and tried to convince "the so-called ruling classes, the classes of the landed and industrial bourgeoisie," of their inability to govern and to persuade them of the justice of their disenfranchisement. The workers, peasants, and toiling intelligentsia could choose representatives for a Toilers' Congress, to which

---

[33] Vynnychenko, Vol. III, p. 134, 140

[34] *Ibid.*, p. 141.

[35] Text in Vynnychenko, Vol. III, pp. 168–176; Khrystiuk, Vol. IV, pp. 15–18.

[36] Later individual landholdings were limited to fifteen *desiatyns*, Mazepa, Vol. I, p. 75.

the Directory "as a temporary supreme power acting in a revolutionary period" would hand over the reins. Until the convocation of this assembly, the Directory would try to avoid bloodshed and to solve the problems facing the country by taking into account existing historical and political conditions in line with the progress made by the more advanced West. The Directory charged the government, especially the Council of Ministers, with carrying out this program.

The Council of Ministers, also appointed by the Directory on December 26, was a coalition cabinet headed by V. M. Chekhivskyi. It reflected not only the differences between the parties but the intra-party disagreements; the latter were serious enough to lead to an outright secession of the leftist factions from both the Ukrainian Social Democratic and Socialist Revolutionary parties. Meetings with peasants, workers, and different interest groups continued throughout January. Accusations were hurled and tempers grew short. When decisions were reached, minority opinions often supplemented the documents.[37] Despite accusations that the Directory was nationalist in orientation, these initial discussions, which occurred during a time of spontaneous and unified national uprising, revealed the strength of an almost exclusively socialist ideological commitment.[38]

There was some talk of establishing a dictatorship for the duration of the war. The *Sich* Riflemen supported this proposal, and Konovalets suggested that Vynnychenko assume the dictatorship. When he refused, the Riflemen proposed the establishment of a triumvirate of Petliura, Konovalets, and Melnyk. Petliura declined, but countered with a proposal that Konovalets join the Directory. The council of the Riflemen refused to give permission for this move.[39]

The convocation of the Toilers' Congress was postponed by the

---

[37] See Khrystiuk, Vol. IV, *passim;* Mazepa, Vol. I, pp. 76–84; Vynnychenko, Vol. III, *passim;* Fedenko, in *Zbirnyk,* pp. 81–82.

[38] Such disparate critics as Khrystiuk, Denikin, the Soviets, even Adams, accuse the Directory of nationalism. Yet Matthew Stakhiv—who could hardly be accused of lacking Ukrainian patriotism—concluded that the major reason for the Directory's failure to institute control over the territory was the low level of development of national consciousness in the Ukraine. M. Stakhiv, *Ukraina v dobi dyrektorii,* Vol. VI (Scranton, Pa.: Ukrainska naukovo-istorychna biblioteka, 1962–66), p. 137.

[39] Konovalets, pp. 20–22; Vynnychenko, Vol. III, p. 233.

festivities of January 22, 1919, proclaiming the unification of Western Ukraine (Galicia) and the Ukrainian National Republic, ruled by the Directory. When the Congress did meet, it was under the shadow of the Soviet advance. Elections by *curiae* of peasants, workers, and intelligentsia were held under the shadow of news of military reverses. As a result, only some 300 of the 593 elected deputies could attend. Of these, the strongest group was the central faction of the Social Democrats and the solid Galician bloc.[40] The Socialist-Revolutionaries were so badly split that their numerical advantage in the Peasants' Union could not be exploited. Moreover, their insistence on the immediate implementation of the *rada* principle was so unpopular that the Congress was more often chaired by a Galician radical than by a Socialist-Revolutionary.[41]

After three days of open deliberations and closed party sessions, the Congress authorized the Directory to rule the country until the next session of the Toilers' Congress,[42] and provided for the establishment of new elective organs for local government or for the appointment of commissars, where local self-government was not feasible. After organizing its own commissions with governmental functions, the Congress adjourned, to the sound of rumbling Soviet cannons. On February 2, the Directory and the government left Kiev for Vynnytsia. Soviet forces took the capital three days later.

The Directory's failure to arrange peace with Soviet Russia strengthened the moderate elements within the Directory and precipitated the resignation of Chekhivskyi and Vynnychenko.[43] The

---

[40] Sixty-five Galicians attended; for the best account see Mazepa, Vol. I, pp. 88–95; Khrystiuk, Vol. IV, pp. 57–68; also Vynnychenko, Vol. III, p. 243; Fedenko, in *Zbirnyk,* pp. 80–83. Non-Ukrainians did not pool their resources to elect a representative. Goldenweyzer, "Iz kievskikh vospominanii."

[41] Two Galician radicals, Semen Vityk and Teofil Starukh, and the Socialist-Revolutionary Dmytro Odryna made up the presidium; the place reserved for the leftist bloc remained unfilled because the parties could not agree on a candidate. Chekhivskyi reported the failure of negotiations with the Bolsheviks; General Oleksander Grekov's exposé of the weakness of the armed forces of the Directory (Mazepa, Vol. I, p. 92; Denikin, Vol. V, p. 13) did not seem to have much effect.

[42] This Congress was to be convened as soon as possible either by its own Presidium or by the Directory.

[43] Vynnychenko and particularly Chekhivskyi were convinced that the natural ally for the Ukrainian National Republic was the Russian Soviet

Social Democratic Party withdraw its support from the Directory, but permitted some of its members, like Petliura, to suspend membership in the Party so that they could continue to serve in the government. The way was now cleared, at least on the Ukrainian side, for an acceleration of the negotiations with France, which was serving as spokesman for the Entente. The Directory had begun these negotiations almost as soon as it came to power, and the cabinet headed by Ostapenko, who replaced Chekhivskyi, strove to achieve peace with the Entente and to implement moderate policies at home. These aims had to be genuine, since they survived the humiliation the Directory received from the French.

From the beginning, the Directory did everything it could to coax the Entente into recognizing Ukrainian independence.[44] The Entente's tortuous policy toward the former Russian province and its unwillingness to sanction efforts to "Balkanize" the Empire are now known. The Directory, however, felt that the Allies would be on its side, since the ideals of nationalism, liberalism, socialism, the concept of the rights of man, and the justification of revolution had

State. In numerous exchanges with the Russian representative Chicherin, the Directory wanted to believe that Georgii Piatakov, the leader of the invading Soviet armies, was acting independently of Moscow. Piatakov's relationship to Lenin is discussed in Adams, *Bolsheviks in the Ukraine*. For the Soviet version, see A. V. Likholat, *Razgrom burzhuaznonatsionalisticheskoi direktorii na Ukraine* (Moscow, 1949) and I. K. Rybalka, *Rozhrom burzhuaznonatsionalistychnoi dyrektorii na Ukraini* (Kharkiv: Vyd. Kharkivskoho derzhnavnoho universytetu, 1962). For the Ukrainian interpretation, see Khrystiuk, Vol. IV, pp. 29–40; Vynnychenko, Vol. III, *passim;* Mazepa, Vol. I, pp. 66–72; Fedenko, p. 84. Even in the face of an obvious Soviet advance, the Directory sent its final mission, headed by Iurii Mazurenko, to Moscow on January 11. They were not aware that five days before Mazurenko left Kiev, Piatakov established a Ukrainian Soviet Socialist Republic, and the Russian Chief of Staff agreed to a separate Ukrainian Front; *Grazhdanskaia voina,* Vol. I, book 3, pp. 542–543.

[44] The Directory sent mission after mission to various European capitals; it tried to get its representatives into Paris; it carried on a propaganda campaign that emphasized the historical rights of the Ukraine and the anti-Bolshevik nature of its government. See especially Margolin, pp. 102–106; Khrystiuk, Vols. III and IV, *passim;* Mazepa, Vol. I, p. 105; Vynnychenko, Vol. III, pp. 419–426. Stakhiv, Vol. III, p. 236, reports (according to information given him personally by Mykhailo Korchynskyi) that Chekhivskyi, foreseeing a period of war, had a plan to save the Ukrainian intelligentsia by getting as many of them abroad as possible.

all come from the West. Petliura, on whose resignation the Entente insisted, had been imprisoned for his pro-Allied stand. The Directory rejected social revolution, and it had no imperialistic ambitions. What then could stand in the way of an understanding?

The Directory obstinately sent missions to the French, appealing to the conscience of the nations of the world, arguing, pleading, waiting for aid from day to day. France's intervention in Odessa made the Directory willing to accede to most of that country's demands, except the resignation of Petliura. Negotiations continued, but no aid was received.[45]

In the last analysis, the Directory lost out because of its reliance on France. The radical intelligentsia in the Ukraine felt justified in seeking an understanding with the Soviets because of what they considered to be the lack of patriotism and the reactionary policies of the government. Also, the government's insistence on pursuing very moderate social policies fostered apathy among the peasants, which sometimes turned into open hostility. *Otaman* Hryhoriiv, one of the government's most effective military leaders, was opposed to the French orientation and in protest turned with his army to the Soviets. It was Hryhoriiv, not the Soviets, who drove the French from Odessa in the first days of April 1919. This did not end the pro-Entente orientation, but it led to a new crisis in the government.[46]

What had originally began as one possible course of action—cooperation with the Entente—became a necessity in the face of the reverses suffered in the war with the Bolsheviks. A vicious circle developed: the more the Directory needed the aid of the Entente, the less the Entente showed any interest in the faltering government.

The Council of Ministers appointed after Vynnychenko's resignation in February 1919 has gone down in the annals of progressive Ukrainian historiography as a bourgeois cabinet. However, the most dramatic events during its tenure, from February 13 until April 9,

---

[45] Among the French demands were: the formation of a Ukrainian government that would exclude Vynnychenko or Petliura and that would be approved by the French; French control of the army, the railroads, and the finances; the freeing of some Hetman officials arrested by the Directory. See Mazepa, Vol. I, p. 129; Denikin, Vol. V, p. 37, accused the French of favoring the Ukrainians.

[46] Mazepa, Vol. I, p. 189; Adams, p. 201; also F. Anulov, "Soiuznyi desant na Ukraine," *Letopis revoliutsii,* Vol. VII (1924), pp. 28–38.

1919, demonstrated the weakness of bourgeois values. These two months were an unhappy period in the life of the Directory. Although the emigration of Vynnychenko removed for a brief time the personal frictions within the Directory, there was no unity between it and the cabinet, the armies, and often the peasants. There was no precise constitutional delineation of functions between the Directory and the Council of Ministers. The Directory lost the backing of its key military groups; various conventions of party representatives, peasant assemblies, and *ad hoc* committees bombarded it with demands to modify its policies.[47] By the middle of March, the Bolsheviks had forced the Directory even out of Vinnytsia and, by taking Zhmerynka, a key railroad point, had cut the front in half.

Meanwhile, the war with Poland waged by Galician Ukrainians was also going badly.

The Directory tried to tackle its problems in a democratic manner and during its peregrinations across the country held discussions with various interest groups. As a result of a consensus, reached in April, between the government and the opposition, a new Council of Ministers was formed under Borys Martos. It was a cabinet composed exclusively of members of the Social Democratic and Socialist-Revolutionary Parties; later it was reinforced by Galician radicals.[48] Martos demanded that the Directory be subordinate to the government in political decisions, that there be a firm delineation of functions between these two bodies, that peace with the Soviets be concluded as soon as possible, and that local workers' councils be established.[49]

---

[47] Khrystiuk, Vol. IV, pp. 111–116; Mazepa, Vol. I, pp. 115–148.

[48] The list of cabinet members is in Vynnychenko, Vol. III, p. 289, and Khrystiuk, Vol. IV, pp. 119–120. The best presentation of the formation of the government is in Mazepa, Vol. I, pp. 158–159. Although Martos had originally been Petliura's choice, the latter was ambivalent about the appointment and tried to counter the doctrinaire and tactless young premier-designate with the appointment of moderates; Mazepa, Vol. II, pp. 52–53; Victor Andriievskyi, *Z mynuloho,* Vol. II (Berlin: "Ukrainske slovo," 1921), p. 12

[49] These demands reflected the results of talks between the Directory and the Social Democratic and Social Revolutionary parties, as well as by representatives of the Toilers' Congress; see Khrystiuk, Vol. IV, pp. 118–119.

A lengthy declaration by the government was issued one week later.[50] Socialist, Jacobin, and anti-Soviet in nature, its aim was to win over the peasants and workers of the Ukraine who were rebelling against the Soviet forces. The government stressed its adherence to democracy in general, to the control functions of the toilers' councils, to land reform, to a broad program of public workers, and in particular to strong trade unions. Promising to rid the Ukraine of all foreign forces, the Martos government pledged not to depend on any outside powers so as not to compromise Ukrainian sovereignty.

To stress its adherence to the principle of nationalism, the socialist government proceeded to integrate Galicia and its autonomous structure within the unified system of the Ukrainian National Republic. A Ministry of the Western Province of the Ukrainian National Republic (i.e., Galicia) was established on July 4.

Of all the Ukrainian governments, that of Martos, in both its political and its personal make-up, was least suited to tamper with the sensitive Galician issue. Forced together by the pressures of Soviet power and later also of White and Polish armies, the Ukrainians turned to the time-honored expedient of blaming political opponents for their own defeats. The professed socialism of Martos provided a ready-made scapegoat. The Leftists, on the other hand, were also dissatisfied with Martos' failure to pursue policies of *rada* power and peace with the Soviets, particularly since hopes for a reversal in the struggle against the Bolsheviks were buoyed by reports of peasant dissatisfaction and resistance in Bolshevik-controlled territory. Expectations were further stimulated when several strong *otamans* changed their support to the Directory and when delegations from several local Ukrainian anti-Bolshevik revolutionary committees come to discuss terms for cooperation.[51]

Still, tension was heightened by the economic crisis, exacerbated by the Entente's blockade of the Ukraine (including Poland and Rumania), by continued shifts in the location of the government, and by talk of fiscal mismanagement.[52] The Galicians had endowed

---

[50] For text, see *ibid.,* pp. 120–122.

[51] Vynnychenko, Vol. III, pp. 439–440; Khrystiuk, Vol. IV, pp. 130–139; Fedenko in *Zbirnyk,* pp. 92–96.

[52] Mazepa, Vol. II, p. 22; M. Dobrylovskyi, "Z istorii hospodarskoi polityky nezalezhnoi Ukrainy, 1919–1920," in *Zbirnyk,* pp. 150–158.

their president, Petrushevych, with dictatorial powers, despite the formal unity of the Republic.[53]

The critical situation within the Directory was reflected in the tensions between Petliura and Andriievskyi, a rightist who was often supported by Petrushevych. After an unsuccessful coup headed by *Otaman* Oskilko, Andriievskyi, according to a personal letter to Petliura, seemed to have resigned from the Directory and was no longer invited to its meetings. Yet in June he still urged Petliura to resign in an attempt to meet the demands of the Entente. Petrushevych remained a member of the Directory but, as a sign of opposition to Martos, he no longer attended meetings.[54]

To resolve these difficulties, Martos was replaced by a coalition headed by the reasonable Isaak Mazepa, a compromise Social Democratic candidate. Despite "virtually superhuman efforts," Mazepa could not marshal forces to maintain power in the Ukraine, while parties spent untold energy battling each other.[55]

Meanwhile, in other parts of the Ukraine, the Bolsheviks could not hold power, and many territories were taken over by Denikin, who fought to re-establish a united Russia. But Denikin did make some concessions to the "Little Russians" and ventured a few overtures to Petliura, although he had no intention of recognizing the latter's government.[56] The Entente insisted on cooperation with Denikin as a prerequisite for aid; the Galicians were inclined to negotiate with Denikin, while the eastern Ukrainians felt that such a course would be disastrous, since the Ukrainian population rose spontaneously against Denikin at the slightest provocation.

By July, the territory controlled by the Directory was limited to the Podillia area, north of present-day Moldavia.

Here, thanks to the military reforms begun in March and the military activities of the Ukrainian Galician Army and the insurgents against the Bolsheviks, the Directory was able to establish a fairly efficient administration. In early August, the Ukrainian armies began to advance once more.

As the armies of the Ukrainian People's Republic moved south-

---

[53] When Petrushevych became a dictator, some commentators considered him to have forfeited his seat on the Directory; see Khrystiuk, Vol. IV, p. 147, also Mazepa, Vol. I, p. 146.

[54] Mazepa, Vol. II, p. 6; also Mazepa, Vol. I, pp. 192–194.

[55] Phrase quoted in Vynnychenko, Vol. III, p. 477; see also Mazepa, Vol. II, pp. 39–62.

[56] Fedenko, in *Zbirnyk*, pp. 104–105, gives some pertinent texts.

west, General Denikin pressed north. There was no actual state of war between the two powers. The Directory and the Galicians wanted to preserve peace with Denikin despite his policies. Since the Ukrainian People's Republic deployed the bulk of its forces against the Bolsheviks, it had no reserves left to use against the Whites. Konovalets and some other military leaders urged the taking of Odessa, even at the cost of sacrificing Kiev, in order to have an outlet to the outside world, but national fervor was so strong that the taking of Kiev seemed imperative.[57]

The city was taken by the end of August after a struggle with the Reds, but no specific instructions had been given for dealing with Denikin's Volunteer Army, which entered over a bridge that the Ukrainians had for some reason failed to destroy. A clash resulted, although the politically inexperienced Galician officer in charge of the detachment that came into contact with the Russians tried to avoid it even at the cost of national honor and arrest by the Volunteer Army.[58] The Galicians were roundly taken to task for their inapportune actions, but even after the Kievan incident they argued for cooperation with Denikin. The leaders of the Ukrainian National Republic, however, maintained that delay in declaring war against Denikin threatened the loss of the great revolutionary potential of the Ukrainian masses. Nevertheless, some attempts at negotiation were made. After they failed, the Directory declared war on Denikin on September 24, 1919. Petrushevych, the Galician leader, participated in this decision.[59]

By its procrastination, the Ukrainian government had again failed to hold the masses. Exhausted by the war with the Soviets, the Ukrainian forces finally succumbed to the third enemy—typhus. Petliura and Mazepa predicted that Denikin would not be able to hold the Ukraine because his lines were overextended and there was opposition in the rear.[60] Realizing this, they made another

---

[57] Mazepa, Vol. II, pp. 63–66; Konovalets, p. 30; Dotsenko, Vol. II, book 4, pp. 128–133. On discussions about policy toward Denikin, see *ibid.*, pp. 159–257; Mazepa, Vol. II, pp. 78–82; and Denikin, Vol. V, pp. 253–257.

[58] Mazepa, Vol. II, pp. 67–70; Vynnychenko, Vol. III, pp. 447–455; Dotsenko, Vol. II, book 4, pp. 25–28, 151.

[59] Text in Dotsenko, Vol. II, book 4, pp. 255–256; see also Mazepa, Vol. II, p. 82.

[60] Dotsenko, Vol. II, book 4, p. 288; see also Denikin, Vol. V, pp. 219, 232, 274, and 312–314.

effort to reach some agreement with the Soviets.[61] They also intensified their search for an alternate policy. On the other hand, the Ukrainian Galician Army, decimated by typhus and in danger of complete disintegration, pressed, against the wishes of Petrushevych, for an immediate agreement with Denikin. By the beginning of November, the situation was so tense that General Myron Tarnavskyi, the commander of the Ukrainian Galician Army, stopped attending joint government-military conferences. The military leaders of the Ukrainian National Republic began to talk of the possibility of an imminent collapse at the front.[62]

Warned by dire predictions, the Directory agreed to join the Ukrainian Galacian Army in sending a delegation to Denikin. But, before the Directory's delegation was able to reach the Ukrainian Galician Army, General Tarnavskyi, obsessed by the need to save at least the remnants of his forces, signed on his own authority an alliance with Denikin on November 15, 1919. Tarnavskyi left loopholes in the agreement in order to nullify it in the future.[63] According to the terms of the agreement, the Galician Army subordinated itself to Denikin's Volunteer Army, with the provision that it would not be used against Petliura's forces. The Galicians were also to receive food and medicine during a period of rest and reorganization. Petrushevych, who had not been consulted by Tarnavskyi, immediately rescinded the agreement, removed the general, and placed him before a military court.[64] Nonetheless, two weeks later Tarnavskyi's successor was forced to conclude a similar agreement with Denikin.[65]

The Ukrainian Galician Army was accused of giving the Republic a fatal "stab in the back" and of causing the November

---

[61] Mazepa, Vol. II, p. 121; also Dotsenko, Vol. II, book 4, p. 104. Neither the Soviets nor the Galicians showed much interest in this venture, which was organized by a Western European socialist.

[62] Mazepa, Vol. II, pp. 115–135; Dotsenko, Vol. II, book 4, pp. 268–275.

[63] For a defense of Tarnavskyi, see Osyp Levytskyi, "Viiskovyi dohovir Ukrainskoi Halytskoi Armii z Dobrarmiieiu Generala Denikina," *Ukrainska halytska armiia* (Winnipeg: Vyd. Khorunzhyi USS Dmytro Mykytiuk, 1958), pp. 484–514. The author, a signatory of the convention, also wrote *Halytska armiia na velykii Ukraini* (Vienna, 1921), which has not been available to me.

[64] Dotsenko, Vol. II, book 4, pp. 276–286; Denikin, Vol. V, p. 258; Mazepa, Vol. II, pp. 122–138 and Fedenko, in *Zbirnyk,* p. 103.

[65] Dotsenko, Vol. II, book 4, pp. 289–291.

catastrophe.[66] Indeed, the willful actions of the Galician Army underscored what may be considered the final crisis within the government of the Directory. There had never been full agreement among the members of the government. The critical situation of November exacerbated that lack of unity. Apparently, Petliura had always been skeptical that the Ukraine could preserve its independence without some support by at least one of its neighbors.[67] Soviet successes in the Ukraine in November and December 1919 forced the Directory to move, both figuratively and literally. Mazepa and most of the military leaders suggested that the Republic change its tactics, go underground, and prepare an insurrection against the Soviets, but these suggestions were only partially accepted by the Directory. Petliura vacillated between expressions of hope, a profound sense of history and feeling of accomplishment, and "some unknown malaise"[68] that made him despondent. He thought seriously of resigning.[69] Unable to exercise effective control even in better times, he was now faced with insubordination, intrigue, theft, and a complete collapse of authority.[70]

The last full meeting of the Directory was held on November 15, 1919. At that session Makarenko and Shvets received broad plenipotentiary powers and went abroad. (The following year both were ejected from the Directory for misconduct.) Petrushevych received safe passage from the Ukraine through Rumania.[71] Petliura was given the powers of chief of state.

Hope was buttressed at this time by a new turn in Ukrainian

---

[66] Phrase used by Oleksandr Lototskyi, *Derzhavnyi provid Symona Petliury* (Paris, 1930), p. 7; see also Mazepa, Vol. II, p. 111, and Dotsenko, Vol. II, book 4, *passim*. The Galician army lacked supplies and medicines. After it broke with the rapidly disintegrating Denikin forces, some of its detachments came to an agreement with the Soviets. Finally, the remains of the army were handed by Petliura to Poland, where the soldiers were interned. For an account by a participant, see Nykyfor Hirniak, "Ukrainska Halytska Armiia v soiuzi z chervonymy," in *Ukrainska Halytska Armiia*, pp. 513–533. See also Mazepa, Vol. II, pp. 171–184.

[67] Lototskyi, p. ii.

[68] Dotsenko, Vol. II, book 4, p. 269; Mazepa, Vol. II, pp. 154–156. This mood is evident in his public statements; see the speech delivered in Starokonstantyniv on November 26, 1919, in Fedenko, in *Zbirnyk*, pp. 101–102.

[69] Dotsenko, Vol. II, book 4, p. 337; Mazepa, Vol. II, p. 157.

[70] *Ibid.*, pp. 157–159; Fedenko, in *Zbirnyk*, pp. 102–103.

[71] Mazepa, Vol. II, pp. 144–145.

foreign policy towards Poland. There had been intermittent attempts to establish contact between Poland and the Ukrainian People's Republic, beginning in January 1919. These attempts were plagued by Poland's unwillingness to write off eastern Galicia, where the majority of the population was Ukrainian, and to agree to expropriation of large estates belonging to Polish nobility in the Ukraine. Eventually, after numerous Ukrainian missions, Andrii Livytskyi, on behalf of Petliura but without the specific authorization of the government,[72] signed an agreement with the Poles in early December. This agreement, which was rather humiliating in tone, gave in to almost all of Warsaw's demands in return for Polish help in the reconquest of the eastern Ukraine from the Soviets. It served as a basis for a definitive agreement concluded in April between Petliura and Piłsudski. This pact recognized Polish control of Galicia and gave in to some Polish claims in the administration of the Ukraine and its armies.[73]

With the aid of the Poles, Petliura began preparations for a new advance into the eastern Ukraine. The joint Ukrainian-Polish operation had all the characteristics of a successful campaign. In the end, however, the Soviets, after initial reversals, proved to be the stronger power. In October 1920 Poland entered into peace talks with the Soviets in Riga, and the final peace agreement was signed the following month. Petliura was excluded from these negotiations. His armies continued to operate in the Ukraine, but they again failed to hold it. Their retreat lasted only three weeks. By November 26, the forces of the Ukrainian People's Republic, some thirty thousand strong, had crossed the river Zbruch into what was now Polish territory. The following week, Makhno, who had turned anti-Soviet, was defeated.

On the diplomatic front, the Ukraine also suffered final defeat. Galicia was awarded as a temporary mandate to Poland on June 25, 1919, and by the end of December 1920 Petliura's request for membership in the League of Nations was tabled. Moreover, his

---

[72] Mazepa knew nothing of this move, but he and Petrushevych had agreed to preliminary discussions with the Poles in September. Mazepa, Vol. II, pp. 86, 107, 188, and Vol. III, pp. 8–19.

[73] Accounts and texts in Dotsenko, Vol. II, book 5; I. A. Khrenov and N. Gasiorovska-Grabovska (eds.), *Dokumenty i materiialy po istorii sovetsko-polskikh otnoshenii,* Vol. II (Moscow: AN SSSR, 1964), pp. 656–663, and Serhii Shelukhin, *Varshavskyi dohovir mizh poliakamy i S. Petliuroiu* (Prague: Vyd. Nova Ukraina, 1926).

alliance with Piłsudski alienated even those European progressives who had supported the Ukrainian cause.[74]

Within the ranks of his own government, Petliura was unable to prevent the subsequent crisis. Mazepa resigned as premier on July 26 and then left the government altogether because he did not consider the policies of his successor, Viacheslav Prokopovych, progressive. By October Prokopovych also resigned. Livytskyi, who replaced him, did not enjoy the support of the many Ukrainian parties. Petliura set up his government-in-exile in Tarnów, Poland, where he made plans for one final attempt at regaining the Ukraine.

To placate the parties that had meanwhile organized an All-Ukrainian National Council in Vienna, Petliura set up a Council of the Republic, hoping to rally all émigrés to his cause. But the major parties did not support Petliura's Council, and he disbanded it in the summer of 1921. At the same time he appointed P. Pylypchuk as head of a new government. Petliura also considered joining the Russian ex-terrorist Boris Savinkov in a march against the Soviets. This venture was not realized, but the idea of an armed struggle against the Bolsheviks did strike a sympathetic chord among Petliura's advisers. Preparations were made for a second Winter Campaign.

The efforts of General Iurii Tiutiunnyk to repeat the Winter Campaign of the previous year were doomed from the start. The Poles sabotaged the action, permitting only one thousand Ukrainians to participate, and the Soviets had advance knowledge of the plan.[75]

The failure of armed intervention in the Ukraine convinced Petliura of the need to change his policies. He left Poland and settled in Paris, where he continued to promote the cause of what he considered to be the continuation of the Ukrainian National Republic. His death at the hands of an assassin in 1926 helped endow him with the aura of national greatness.

---

[74] For example, the British Labour Party; Margolin, pp. 216, 252–256.

[75] Udovychenko, p. 162; Mazepa, Vol. III, pp. 99–107; Konovalets, pp. 38–39.

CHAPTER FIVE

The Communist Take-over of the Ukraine

Yaroslav Bilinsky

> The Soviet regime has gained victory in the Ukraine not by its internal forces but only with the help of a strengthened Soviet Russia at the moment when the German Army began to disintegrate.   E. Kviring[1]

IN DECEMBER 1967 the Ukrainian Soviet Socialist Republic celebrated its fiftieth anniversary. Time and the proverbial victors' effect may make it appear as if its establishment had been preordained and smooth. In fact, it took the Communists three campaigns before the Ukraine was finally subjugated in the summer of 1920; twice the Soviet forces had to retreat. A perusal of some contemporary memoirs and later studies turns up some unexpected weaknesses of the ultimate victors. The nationalist victims were weaker still, but they were nevertheless strong enough to offer determined resistance and to wrest some concessions from the enemy.

On the eve of the October Revolution[2] there was no unified Bolshevik organization in the Ukraine, and some of the local groups were quite weak. At the Sixth Congress of the Russian Social Democratic Labor Party (Bolshevik) or RSDLP(b) in August 1917, there

---

[1] E. Kviring, "Nashi raznoglasiia," in M. Ravich-Cherkasskii (ed.), *Pervyi sezd Kommunisticheskoi Partii (bolshevikov) Ukrainy: 5–12 iiulia 1918 goda* (Kharkov: Komissia po istorii Oktiabrskoi revoliutsii, 1923), p. 13. Henceforth cited as *I sezd KP(b)U.*

[2] All dates in this article are according to the New Style, though the Bolshevik take-over will be referred to as the October, not the November, Revolution.

were, in fact, as many as three Bolshevik delegations from the Ukraine: the Donets-Kryvyi Rih-Kharkiv group (15,000 members), the "South-Western *Krai*" or Kiev group (about 5,000 members), and the Rumanian front or Odessa group. Altogether, the Bolshevik Party in the Ukraine numbered close to 22,000 members.[3] The Iuzivka (Donets)-Kryvyi Rih Bolshevik *Krai* Committee included such prominent leaders as Artem (Sergeev) from Kharkiv, and E. Kviring and Iakovlev (Epshtein) from Katerynoslav (Dnipropetrovsk). The most outstanding leaders of the Kiev Bolsheviks were Evgeniia Bosh and Georgii Piatakov (not to be confused with Leonid Piatakov). Odessa remained on the sidelines.

The reason for the essential bifurcation of Bolshevik organization in the Ukraine in 1917 was twofold. As Borys points out, the Central Committee (CC) of the RSDLP(b) had authorized the convening of separate regional conferences in Kiev and Katerynoslav but dragged its feet on establishing an all-Ukrainian organization.[4] Second, and more important, was the fact that many prominent Bolshevik leaders in the Ukraine, with the exception of Mykola Skrypnyk and a few others who became prominent after the October Revolution, were Russian patriots first and Ukrainian residents second. As Georgii Piatakov declared at the meeting of the Kiev Committee of the RSDLP(b) on June 17, 1917:

> Generally we should not support the Ukrainians. . . . Russia cannot exist without the Ukrainian sugar industry; the same can be said about coal (the Donets Basin), grain (the Black Earth belt), etc. These branches of industry are closely connected with the whole remaining industry of Russia. Moreover, the Ukraine does not form a distinct economic region, for it possesses no banking centres, like Finland. . . .[5]

In her revealing post-mortem of the first period of Soviet rule in the Ukraine, Evgeniia Bosh admits that it was not until Decem-

---

[3] M. M. Popov, *Narys istorii Komunistychnoi Partii* (*bilshovykiv*) *Ukrainy* (Kharkiv, 1928), p. 108. According to Jurij Borys, *The Russian Communist Party and the Sovietization of Ukraine: A Study in the Communist Doctrine of the Self-Determination of Nations* (Stockholm, 1960), p. 134 n., who consulted the proceedings of the Sixth Congress, the Donets-Kryvyi Rih center numbered about 16,000 members; all the Bolsheviks in the Ukraine, 22,402.

[4] Borys, pp. 134–136.

[5] *Ibid.*, p. 129.

ber 1917 that the Bolsheviks started an energetic and insistent struggle against Ukrainian nationalists.[6] One of her collaborators, I. Iu. Kulyk, adds the precious detail that *Golos sotsial-demokrata,* the organ of the Kievan [sic] Bolshevik Committee between February and October 1917, did not publish a single editorial on the Ukrainian question, though it managed to expound on the Moslem problem in Russia.[7] As late as 1923, Kviring, of the Katerynoslav organization, defended the regional separatism of the Kharkiv-Donets-Kryvyi Rih group by stating that in 1917 his region was threatened by the White Don Cossacks and that only Red Russian troops from the North could protect it. "Under these circumstances the leadership of our struggle gravitated toward Kharkiv and Moscow. . . . Kiev could not help us, and we could not help Kiev." Furthermore, a united Soviet Ukraine did not really exist at that time.[8] Even more telling is an introductory sentence in one of Kviring's earlier articles: "Katerynoslav is a major workers' center of South Russia [sic]."[9]

The deeper cause of local Bolshevik alienation from any kind of Ukrainian national movement—whether of the yellow-blue (nationalist) or red (Communist) type—was to be found in the composition of the party. As frankly admitted by Nikolai N. Popov, the foremost historian of the Communist Party (Bolshevik) of the Ukraine, the Bolsheviks in the Ukraine were recruited "predominantly from the Russian or the Russified proletariat."[10] The proletariat, however, constituted only a small minority. No precise data on the national composition of the Bolsheviks in 1917 is available, for the Party was not formally organized until July 1918. But at the end of 1920 it included only 19.0 percent Ukrainians, and in April 1922 only 23.3 percent Ukrainians, compared with 53.6 percent Russians and 13.6 percent Jews,[11] even though the Ukrainians formed about 80 percent of the total population.

---

[6] Evgeniia Bosh, *Natsionalnoe pravitelstvo i sovetskaia vlast na Ukraine* (Moscow, 1919), p. 23. The phamphlet was written in August 1918.

[7] I. Iu. Kulyk, "Kievskaia organizatsiia ot fevralia do oktiabria 1917 goda," *Letopis revoliutsii,* No. 6 (Kharkiv, 1924), p. 197.

[8] Kviring, in *I sezd KP(b)U,* pp. 4, 5.

[9] E. Kviring, "Ekaterinoslavskii sovet i Oktiabrskaia revoliutsiia," *Letopis revoliutsii,* No. 1 (Kharkiv, 1922), p. 63.

[10] Popov, p. 9.

[11] For 1920, see Vsevolod Holubnychy, "Outline History of the Communist Party of Ukraine," *The Ukrainian Review,* No. 6 (Munich, 1958), p. 124. For the 1922 figures, see Borys, p. 155.

Conversely, the Ukrainian nationalist parties relied on a small group of intelligentsia, and, at least initially, they captured the imagination of the peasants and the soldiers. In Vynnychenko's memoirs there is an inimitable description of the Ukrainian peasant delegates at the All-Russian and the First Ukrainian Peasant Congresses (both in early June 1917), who vociferously insisted on the transformation of the former Russian Empire into a federal state.[12] More tangible are the results of the elections in the Ukraine to the All-Russian Constituent Assembly held in late November 1917. According to Lenin, the Ukrainian Socialist-Revolutionaries (SR's) obtained almost four million out of a total of 7.6 million votes.[13] If the Ukrainian peasants had been motivated solely by economic and social concerns, they might easily have voted for the Russian SR's, whose economic program was quite similar. The Ukrainian nationalist parties were, initially, also very popular with Ukrainian front soldiers. A Bolshevik source notes that the Central Rada exercised a "rather significant influence" on the soldiers and that the Rada-sponsored Soldiers' Congresses in Kiev represented hundreds of thousands and sometimes more than a million soldiers who were ethnic Ukrainians.[14] It is true, as Popov implies, that during the following years the anarchic emotions of the land-hungry Ukrainian peasantry—and peasant-soldiers, too, for that matter—would prove more compatible with the utopian promises and extraordinary disciplinary powers of the Bolsheviks, but in 1917 the latter did not pay sufficient attention to either the Ukrainian peasants or the soldiers.[15]

Under these circumstances, and considering the weakness and

---

[12] Volodymyr Vynnychenko, *Vidrodzhennia natsii*, Vol. I (Kiev-Vienna: Dzvin, 1920), pp. 174–179.

[13] Borys, pp. 159–161. Partly for polemical purposes and partly under the impact of the second Soviet defeat in the Ukraine, Lenin described the results of the elections in December 1919 in his important article, "Vybory v uchreditelnoe sobranie i diktatura proletariata," *Sobranie sochinenii*, Vol. XVI (2nd ed.; Moscow, 1923), pp. 439–459. See also the judgment by Oliver H. Radkey, *The Election to the Russian Constituent Assembly of 1917* (Cambridge, Mass.: Harvard University Press, 1950), pp. 19, 30.

[14] I. [Iu.] Kulyk, "Kievskaia organizatsiia bolshevikov v oktiabrskie dni (Opyt kratkoi kharakteristiki)," *Letopis revoliutsii*, Nos. 5–6 (Kharkiv, 1927), pp. 222–223.

[15] M. M. Popov, *Zhovten na Ukraini* (Kiev, 1934), pp. 29–34. See also his *Narys*, p. 120.

political obtuseness of the Bolshevik organizations in the Ukraine, particularly in Kiev, there is small wonder that an attempt to stage a Bolshevik coup on December 12, 1917, ended in failure: loyal Ukrainian troops disarmed the pro-Bolshevik soldiers and sent them home.[16] More painful was the failure of the Bolsheviks to seize power in Kiev by quasi-legal means. They convoked an All-Ukrainian Congress of Soviets for December 17. The Rada, how-ever, flooded the Congress with its adherents from the Ukrainian peasantry, a move that seemed just enough, given the Bolshevik attempt to grossly over-represent the workers, who were mostly Russified. Nor was the Bolshevik cause at the Congress helped by the ultimatum of the Soviet Russian Council of People's Com-missars to the Rada, which the Council issued at that very moment, without having bothered even to inform the Ukrainian Bolsheviks in advance.[17]

Almost inevitably the Bolshevik delegates left the Congress with-out achieving any success. Clandestinely, they moved to Kharkiv, outside the limits of effective Rada control, where a congress of soviets from the Donets and Kryvyi Rih Basins was taking place. The Kievan Bolsheviks renamed it the First All-Ukrainian Congress of Soviets of Workers', Soldiers' and Peasants' Deputies, which then elected a Central Executive Committee of the Ukraine (TsIKU). In turn, the Committee formed on December 26, 1917, the People's Secretariat—i.e., the first Soviet government of the Ukraine. But the TsIKU was merely being tolerated by the representatives of the Donets and Kryvyi Rih Soviets and was completely boycotted by the Katerynoslav group.[18] Most humiliating also was the attitude of the Kharkiv hosts toward their fellow party members from Kiev. As Iurii Lapchynskyi, the General Secretary (i.e., Prime Minister) of the first Soviet government in the Ukraine, complained later, the

---

[16] Bosh, p. 20; Iakiv Zozulja (ed.), *Velyka ukrainska revoliutsiia: Kalendar istorychnykh podii za liutyi 1917—berezen 1918 roku* (2nd rev. ed.; New York: Ukrainian Academy of Arts and Sciences in the U.S., 1967), p. 37.

[17] Bosh, pp. 20–21; Georg Lapchynskyi, "Z pershykh dniv vse-ukrainskoi radianskoi vlady," *Letopis revoliutsii*, Nos. 5–6 (Kharkiv, 1927), pp. 63–64; Borys, pp. 169–176; *Peremoha velykoi Zhovtnevoi revoliutsii na Ukraini*, Vol. I (Kiev: Akademiia Nauk URSS, Instytut Istorii, 1967), pp. 250 ff. (henceforth cited as *Peremoha*).

[18] Borys, pp. 179–180.

Kharkiv Soviet forced the Kievan delegates to sleep in their meeting rooms after having offered them the hospitality of one of the town's jails.[19]

As Borys further indicates, the attitude of the Bolsheviks in the Ukraine concerning the creation of a Ukrainian Soviet center was far from unanimous. The so-called "Kievans," Piatakov, Bosh and Kreisberg, and the "Ekaterinoslavians," Kviring and Epshtein, considered the Ukraine a part of Russia. They reasoned that the Ukrainians might well be a separate people, but from the point of view of the proletarian revolution, when considering the economic resources and strength of Russia, the secession of the Ukraine was counterrevolutionary and would mean the downfall of the Revolution. Some "Kievans" admitted a political federation for the Ukraine, but they would hear no talk of economic antonomy. Another current was formed by the federalists, who, in the question of nationalities, adhered to the view that the Ukraine had to be a part of the RSFSR built on federal principles and had to have its own government and also its own Communist Party. To this group belonged Skrypnyk, Lapchynskyi, and Zatonskyi. The third group considered the Ukraine to be an independent, though Soviet, republic, which had to be in political alliance with Soviet Russia, but on the basis of equality. To this group belonged, at that time, Vasyl Shakhrai, Serhii Mazlakh, and Neronovych. The latter then joined the Ukrainian Social Democrats *nezalezhnyky* (independents), who tended to support the Soviets.[20] The first Soviet Ukrainian government was as alien as were the Bolsheviks in the Ukraine. Of its thirteen members, only four (Zatonskyi, Skrypnyk, Shakhrai, and Martianov) had a good command of the local language.[21] But all this did not really matter, for the function of that government was merely to lend "its name [and] its banner to cover up the occupation policy of Soviet Russia in the Ukraine."[22] The real power

---

[19] Writes Lapchynskyi: "[As] is known, the Kharkiv Soviet offered us to stay in the jail near the railroad station and gave us several cells. But it was so cold and damp there, and [the cells] smelled so much of disinfectant that we fled after our first night." Georg Lapchynskyi, "Pershyi period radianskoi vlady na Ukraini: TsVKU ta narodnii sekretariat (Spohady)," *Letopis revoliutsii*, No. 1 (Kharkiv, 1928), p. 160.

[20] Borys, pp. 180–181.

[21] Lapchynskyi, p. 165.

[22] Khrystiuk, as quoted in Borys, p. 180.

in Kharkiv rested in the hands of Lenin's freewheeling military plenipotentiary, Antonov-Ovseenko.[23]

Considerable controversy surrounds the question of whether or not Antonov's forces were composed of Russians. At present, Soviet historians freely admit the considerable aid of both arms and personnel given by Soviet Russia to the less well-disciplined and centrally uncoordinated Red Guard detachments in various Ukrainian cities—notably in the industrial South—while they remain silent on the national composition of Antonov's troops, which by February 1918 defeated the Rada.[24] Though Antonov has been rather circumspect in his memoirs, he does admit that the core of his troops was Russian and that he regarded his Ukrainian detachments as political window dressing.[25] Most revealing, however, is the complaint of V. M. Shakhrai, the First Soviet Ukrainian Commissar of War, who apparently said in December 1917:

> The only military support which we possess for our struggle with the Central Rada is the army that Antonov has brought into the Ukraine from Russia and which looks down upon everything Ukrainian as something hostile and counterrevolutionary.[26]

Also controversial is the size of Antonov's invading force. Though a recent non-Soviet Ukrainian source put it at 30,000 men,[27] a

---

[23] The *locus classicus* on the relations between Antonov and the (Soviet) People's Secretariat is probably Lenin's telegram and follow-up letter of February 2, 1918 (following a complaint by Bosh), ordering Antonov to use "consummate national tact (*natsionalnyi arkhitakt*)" and to recognize "all kinds of sovereignty (*vsiacheskii suverenitet*)" of the Kharkiv TsIKU. See V. A. Antonov-Ovseenko, *Zapiski o grazhdanskoi voine*, Vol. I (Moscow, 1924), p. 182.

[24] Clearest is Mykhailo N. Kulichenko, *Komunistychna partiia Ukrainy v borotbi za utvorennia URSR* (Kiev, 1962), pp. 18–19, 26–29. For a more contemporary source, see Kviring, "Ekaterinoslavskii," p. 69. For the number of Red Guards, see *Peremoha*, Vol. I, p. 279.

[25] He explained his delay in attacking the Rada by the absence of purely Ukrainian combat troops—they were necessary before he would proceed. Antonov-Ovseenko, Vol. I, p. 133, See also other detailed evidence culled by Borys, p. 179. For a more general and guarded statement, see Popov, *Narys*, p. 135, and his *Zhovten*, p. 78.

[26] As cited in Lapchynskyi, pp. 171–172. The situation was improved a little by the recruitment of the Red Ukrainian Cossacks under Primakov.

[27] Zozulia, p. 44.

Soviet source suggests fewer than 6,500 men.[28] Beyond any doubt, however, the Rada fell easily, despite its popularity with Ukrainian peasants and peasant-soldiers prior to November 1917.

Until the October Revolution the Ukrainian peasants supported the Rada in its efforts to wrest greater autonomy from the Provisional Government. It is difficult to avoid the impression that in their preoccupation with defining the legal and political status of their country and with Ukrainianizing certain detachments in the former Imperial Army, the Rada neglected the peasant concern for more land. Friction with the Bolsheviks immediately after November 7 also tempted the Rada to further inaction. Furthermore, the democratic Ukrainian politicians fell into the same political trap that had closed in on Kerensky: they felt that the agricultural reform should be debated and passed by a Ukrainian Constituent Assembly, which was to be elected on January 10, 1918, and to be convened on January 22, 1918.[29] But the peasants did not want to wait any longer. Possibly under the impact of Lenin's sweeping land decree of November 8, 1917, they started expropriating the lands themselves.[30] The Rada vainly tried to pass a provisional land reform measure during December 27–30. In the very last days of its stay in Kiev, January 31, 1918, it finally did pass a radical-sounding bill,[31] but it was too little and too late; the Bolsheviks could always outpromise the democratically responsible Rada in their dealings with the land-hungry peasantry.[32]

The desire to Ukrainianize the army prompted, according to a former Ukrainian officer, two demands: the consolidation of front units with a high proportion of Ukrainians into distinct units without impairing the combat effectiveness of the army, and secondly, the transfer of Ukrainians in the reserve units to stations in the Ukraine. For political reasons, the Russian Provisional Government sabotaged the process with all conceivable means, creating sharp disappointment and frustration among the Ukrainian soldiers, who initially had enthusiastically supported Ukrainianization. The

[28] *Peremoha*, Vol. I, p. 290.

[29] Illia Vytanovych, "Agrarna polityka ukrainskykh uriadiv rokiv revoliutsii i vyzvolnykh zmahan (1917–20)," *Ukrainskyi istoryk*, IV, 3–4 (New York–Munich, 1967), p. 31.

[30] *Ibid.*, pp. 34, 40; Kulichenko, p. 18.

[31] Zozulia, pp. 42–43, 50, 87–90 (text of law). Vytanovych, pp. 33 ff.

[32] For a brief scholarly treatment of Bolshevik policy, see Borys, pp. 266–280.

result was that even already Ukrainianized detachments dissolved before Antonov's Bolshevik offensive.[33]

One of the deeper reasons for the defeat of the Rada in January 1918, however, has been noted by the not always impartial but occasionally perspicacious Vynnychenko. As he saw it, the war in December and January was a struggle for influence over the popular masses, since neither the Rada nor Antonov had a strong, disciplined army.[34] The prevailing *Zeitgeist* was profoundly radical, at least in the economic and social sense, but the democratic and moderate Rada failed to grasp it.[35] The Ukrainian soldier did not see in the Ukrainian nationalist government "the desire to take once and for all the side of the toilers, did not see in its camp any tendency to do anything radical in that direction."[36] The Ukrainian peasant troops, infected by Bolshevik demagogy, literally disintegrated, leaving the defense of the nation's capital to college and *gymnasium* students and the few nationally conscious workers.[37]

Under these circumstances, the Bolshevik victory of January 1918 is less surprising than the fact that as a result of their food requisitions[38] and the bloody persecution of nationally conscious Ukrainians[39] they soon managed to incur the anger of the volatile Ukrainian peasant masses, who only a short while before had become disillusioned with the Rada. Describing the 1918 retreat of the "badly armed and completely undisciplined" Soviet Red Army in the face of the Germans and Austrians, Bosh concluded that "the feeling and the sympathies [of the Ukrainian population] were not on the side of the Soviet detachments."[40]

---

[33] Volodymyr Kedrovskyi, "Ukrainizatsiia v rosiiskii armii," *Ukrainskyi istoryk,* IV, 3–4 (New York–Munich, 1967), pp. 67–68, 73–77.

[34] Vynnychenko, Vol. II, p. 151.

[35] *Ibid.,* pp. 90 ff., 111–115, 219.

[36] *Ibid.,* p. 158.

[37] *Ibid.,* pp. 156, 216–217.

[38] Borys, pp. 269–270; also Antonov-Ovseenko, Vol. I, p. 184; *I sezd KP(b)U,* p. 69.

[39] Vynnychenko, Vol. II, pp. 271–272; Michael Hrushevskyi, *A History of Ukraine* (New Haven, Conn.: Yale University Press, 1941), p. 543. Faint echoes of Muravev's misdeeds in Kiev appear in Antonov-Ovseenko, Vol. I, pp. 87, 89, 160, and in Mariia Skrypnik, *Vospominaniia ob Iliche, 1917–1918* (Moscow-Leningrad, 1928), pp. 72–73, 82 (showing Lenin's attitude to Muravev).

[40] Bosh, p. 35.

An account of how the Central Powers and the Rada delegation outmaneuvered the incredibly inept Soviet representatives at Brest-Litovsk or a discussion of the White (landowners') terror under Hetman Skoropadskyi,[41] which contributed to a renewed radicalization of the Ukrainian countryside, is outside the scope of this study. It would be more pertinent to comment on two other significant events of 1918: the attempted partition of Ukrainian territory and the establishment, in exile, of the Communist Party (Bolshevik) of the Ukraine (CP(b)U).

In its Third Universal of November 20, 1917, the Rada claimed as Ukrainian territory, among others, the Kharkiv, Katerynoslav, Kherson, and Tauria gubernias, excluding the Crimea.[42] On December 7, 1917, Stalin wrote an article in *Pravda* on behalf of the Soviet Council of People's Commissars, which rejected the Ukrainian claims. This was possibly done with the secret encouragement of Lenin,[43] though Soviet sources are very reticent on the subject. The local Bolsheviks tried to establish as many as four independent Soviet republics in the South: the Donets-Kryvyi Rih, Odessa, Tauria, and Don Republics,[44] the most important being that of Donets-Kryvyi Rih, the Ukrainian equivalent of the Ruhr Basin. Despite strong opposition from Skrypnyk, the formal establishment of the Donets-Kryvyi Rih Soviet Republic was ratified at the Congress of Soviet deputies from that region, which met in Kharkiv on January 27–30, 1918. The Kharkiv and Katerynoslav (Dnipropetrovsk) Bolsheviks apparently obtained clearance from the People's Commissars in Petrograd.[45] Skrypnyk continued protesting and, more importantly perhaps, the German occupation forces refused to acknowledge the separation of the industrial regions from the predominantly agricultural Right-Bank Ukraine. By March 15, 1918, Lenin reversed his stand and told the Donets Bolsheviks to join with Skrypnyk and his group.[46] Thus he pre-

---

[41] For a brief description of this, see Vytanovych, p. 49.

[42] See the universal reprinted in Zozulia, p. 71.

[43] Borys, pp. 182–183.

[44] Jurij Lawrynenko, *Ukrainian Communism and Soviet Russian Policy toward the Ukraine: An Annotated Bibliography, 1917–1953* (New York: Research Program on the USSR, 1953), p. 76.

[45] Antonov-Ovseenko, Vol. I, p. 188; also Popov, *Narys*, pp. 140, 143–144. For a somewhat censored but recent Soviet account see *Peremoha*, Vol. II, pp. 142–145.

[46] *Peremoha*, Vol. II, p. 145.

vented a potential amputation of Ukrainian territory, and the way was cleared for the establishment of a single Communist Party of the Ukraine.

During the evacuation from the Ukraine, about seventy participants met at the Taganrog Conference on April 19–20, 1918, and decided to replace the TsIKU and the People's Secretariat with the so-called "insurgence nine," and to establish the Communist Party (Bolshevik) of the Ukraine (CP(b)U). Some leftist Kievan delegates, joining forces with some of the more nationalistic Bolsheviks from Poltava against the opposition of the Katerynoslav group, carried Skrypnyk's resolution to establish an independent Ukrainian Communist Party that would be joined with the Russian Communist Party (RCP) only through the Third International. Somehow the Central Committee (CC) of the RCP approved the Taganrog resolution on May 18, 1918.[47] The Katerynoslav group, under Kviring, preferred "an autonomous party with its own Central Committee and Congresses but subordinated to the common Central Committee and to the Congresses of the Russian Communist Party."[48] But, since the Taganrog Conference was a more or less accidental meeting, it was decided to convene a Party congress in Moscow on June 20, 1918. The Taganrog Conference merely elected an Organization Bureau, which included among others Skrypnyk, Piatakov, Zatonskyi, and S. Kosior.

At the stormy First CP(b)U Congress in Moscow, which took place from July 5–12, the Katerynoslav group, in a secret session and with the support of the CC RCP, won the adoption of a resolution cancelling the Taganrog resolution on independence. Furthermore, another resolution was passed in favor of uniting the Ukraine with Russia "within the confines of the Russian Soviet Socialist Republic." Most of the initially secret thirteen-member CC elected at the First Congress represented the Russophile Katerynoslav group.[49] The newly established party, as a whole, had 4,364 members represented at the Congress.[50] Shortly before the Congress, however, the CP(b)U was joined by a small group of leftist

---

[47] Popov, *Narys*, pp. 150–151; Holubnychy, p. 72; Borys, pp. 138–140. Holubnychy states that the crucial Taganrog resolution was carried by a vote of 35 to 21; Borys reports that it won by 26 to 21 votes.

[48] As cited in Borys, pp. 138–139.

[49] *I sezd KP(b)U*, p. 136 and *passim;* Popov, *Narys*, pp. 161–166; Holubnychy, pp. 73–74; Borys, pp. 140–142.

[50] See *I sezd KP(b)U*, p. 146 for the breakdown.

Ukrainian Social Democrats, who strengthened the Ukrainian element in the party.[51]

Given the murky situation in the Ukraine and perhaps also the sharp controversies at the First Party Congress, it was decided to convene the Second Congress within two months. It actually took place October 17–22, 1918, again in Moscow and again with the Russophile Katerynoslav group in the ascendance. This time Stalin was elected as one of the members of the Ukrainian CC.[52] The limits of Ukrainian Party autonomy were finally "nailed down" at the Eighth Congress of the RCP in March 1919, only a few weeks after the Third Congress of the CP(b)U held in Kharkiv.[53] With one exception, the CP(b)U became a more or less docile regional organization of the RCP.

To a surprising extent, the second Communist occupation of the Ukraine in the first half of 1919 resembled their first attempt in 1917–1918. With the collapse of Germany and Austria-Hungary and the resulting confusion among the Austro-German occupation troops in the Ukraine, the days of the unpopular Hetman Skoropadskyi were numbered. Nationalists organized in the Ukrainian National Union (Vynnychenko, Petliura, and others), not the relatively weak local Bolsheviks, took the initiative in overthrowing the Hetman.[54] It may be that the Bolsheviks had less influence after the promulgation of the ill-fated Order No. 1 of August 6, 1918, which called for a general uprising.[55] Admittedly, the Bolsheviks had concluded an agreement with Vynnychenko to support the nationalist insurgents in return for a future legalization of the Communist party,[56] but they certainly would not have cooperated with the Directory had they felt strong enough to overthrow the

---

[51] Popov, *Narys*, p. 161.

[52] *Ibid.*, pp. 166–168; Holubnychy, p. 74; Borys, pp. 143–145. See also M. Pohrebinskyi, *Druhyi zizd KP(b)U* (Kiev: Derzhavpolitvydav URSR, 1958), *passim*, esp. pp. 123 ff.

[53] Popov, *Narys*, pp. 186–190; Holubnychy, pp. 75–76; Borys, pp. 145–146.

[54] Even Professor Carr, who, on the whole, is rather critical of Ukrainian nationalists, points out the weakness of the local Bolshevik organization. Edward H. Carr, *The Bolshevik Revolution, 1917–1923,* Vol. I (New York: Macmillan, 1951), p. 300.

[55] Pohrebinskyi, pp. 65–70.

[56] Arthur E. Adams, *Bolsheviks in the Ukraine: The Second Campaign* (New Haven, Conn.: Yale University Press, 1963), p. 44.

Hetman by themselves. As in 1917, the Communists decided to grasp by force of arms what they could not achieve with popular support. On November 12, 1918, two days before the National Union's insurrection against the Hetman, Antonov was ordered by Lenin's Council of People's Commissars to prepare for a military invasion of the Ukraine within ten days. Even the redoubtable Antonov, whose former associate Muravev had been killed several months earlier after getting himself involved in the SR's challenge to Lenin, could not act fast enough, regardless of the extensive co-operation he had received.[57] Nonetheless, by the end of December, Antonov's forces moved again and they took Kiev on February 5, 1919.

Once more, the initial strength of the Ukrainian nationalists dissipated before the onslaught of the better-disciplined Bolshevik troops. Petliura, soon to become the leading member of the Directory and Commander in Chief of the nationalist forces, started the anti-Hetman uprising in early December with about 8,000 men.[58] At the end of the month he commanded a comparatively regular force of somewhere between 100,000 and 127,000.[59] But within half a year Petliura's army dwindled to about 50,000 soldiers,[60] and by September 11, 1919, he had only 9,000 infantrymen.[61] There was also a shortage of arms, supplies, and trained officers.[62] Both political reasons and an outbreak of typhoid fever in the fall of 1919 contributed to the decline of Petliura's forces.[63]

As in 1917, the peasants were fired with a demand for land. To attract more soldiers, the Directory promised its veterans an allotment of seven *desiatynas* (nineteen acres) each and on January 7, 1919,

---

[57] *Ibid.*, pp. 25–44 *passim.*

[58] *Ibid.*, p. 78. John S. Reshetar, Jr., *The Ukrainian Revolution: A Study in Nationalism* (Princeton, N.J.: Princeton University Press, 1952), p. 257.

[59] The higher estimate, with detailed breakdown, is given in V. Prokhoda, "Vozhd ta viisko," in *Zbirnyk pamiaty Symona Petliury (1879–1926)* (Prague: Mizhorhanizatsiinyi komitet dlia vshanuvannia pamiaty Symona Petliury, 1930), pp. 133–136. Reshetar, p. 257, gives an estimate of 120,000.

[60] Prokhoda, p. 141.

[61] Isaak Mazepa, "Tvorena derzhava (Borotba 1919 roku)," in *Zbirnyk pamiaty*, p. 38.

[62] *Ibid.*

[63] Prokhoda, p. 142.

enacted a land reform, though this came too late to be effective.[64] Once more the Ukrainian masses and a few political leaders became infatuated with the idea of the Soviet form of government. To stem the tide, the Directory refrained from convening the Rada, but called a Congress of Toilers for the second half of January 1919. It supported the Directory, but was not able to prevent the Soviet occupation of Kiev two weeks later.[65]

There were additional complicating factors. The left wing of the Ukrainian SR Party and the Ukrainian Social Democratic (SD) Party split off from the main body of nationalists but still (from the end of 1918 through January 1919) did not join the Bolsheviks.[66] There were also personality conflicts in the Directory, especially between Petliura and Vynnychenko, which the latter laid bare in his memoirs with more than a drop of vitriol. Despite his unquestionable patriotism, steadfastness, and political common sense, Petliura was not a good military administrator. He did not succeed in welding the numerous, initially enthusiastic peasant bands and their warlords (*otamans*) into a single disciplined regular army.[67]

In 1919, the Bolsheviks in the Ukraine, like the proverbial Bourbons, had neither forgotten anything old nor learned anything new. Both their agricultural policy and their treatment of the nationally conscious Ukrainian intelligentsia were as ill-considered in 1919 as they had been a year before. On November 20, 1918, a provisional Soviet Ukrainian government was secretly established under the Russophile Piatakov. Within about six weeks he was replaced by Khristiian Rakovskii, who in 1919 was even more Russophile than his predecessor.[68] But real power lay in the hands of Antonov, the commander of the Red Army in the Ukraine, and in those plenipotentiaries for food supply, who in turn were backed by the notorious *Cheka,* the semi-secret political police.

The historian Popov sharply criticizes the second Soviet government for pursuing an agricultural policy which resulted "in the alienation [*vidkhid*] of broad peasant masses" from the regime.[69] The herding of peasants into communes, which had been endorsed in March 1919 by the Third Congress of the CP(b)U, was a drastic

---

[64] Reshetar, p. 257; Adams, pp. 90–92.

[65] Reshetar, pp. 231–233, 258–259.

[66] *Ibid.,* pp. 227–229.

[67] Prokhoda, p. 137; Adams, p. 79.

[68] Borys, pp. 206 ff.; Adams, p. 55.

[69] Popov, *Narys,* pp. 184–186; quotation from p. 186.

mistake.[70] In his memoirs, A. Shlikhter reveals exactly what was wrong with the Bolshevik supply policy that he implemented: the food needs of Russia were given absolute priority,[71] some 2,700 Russians were dispatched to the Ukraine as procurement agents to help collect the food,[72] and numerous local and not-so-local peasant uprisings flared up as a result.[73]

The second Soviet government's shortcomings in the cultural field were also pronounced. In the first declaration of that government, which Rakovskii made at a meeting of the Kharkiv Soviet of Workers' Deputies in January 1919, the national question was virtually ignored. Only in passing did he mention that it might be a good idea to educate children in the native tongue. Similarly, at the first meeting of the Kiev Soviet in February 1919, Rakovskii refused to consider Ukrainian as the state language and subsequently made no efforts to Ukrainianize the state apparatus, i.e., to introduce the Ukrainian language.[74] In Rakovskii's government, Ukrainians were given subordinate positions: Zatonskyi became Commissar of Education; Khmelnytskyi, Commissar of Justice; Skrypnyk was relegated to state control; Zharko was put in charge of communications; while Kotsiubynskyi and Shchadenko were made decorative members of Antonov's Revolutionary Military Council. The real power, insofar as any had been delegated by Lenin, was held by the Rumano-Bulgarian Rakovskii, the Head of the Council and Commissar of Foreign Affairs; by Piatakov, Kviring, and Rukhimovich, commissars for the national economy; by Shlikhter and Bubnov, commissars for food supply; and by Antonov himself.[75] Despite these potentially negative similarities between the first and second Soviet governments, the Directory also encountered complications during the course of 1919. These were the Galician

---

[70] *Ibid.*, pp. 188–189. On the other hand, a later Soviet source, N. N. Suprunenko, *Ocherki istorii grazhdanskoi voiny i inostrannoi interventsii na Ukraine, 1918–1920* (Moscow: Nauka, 1966), p. 196, approves of that resolution because it ran parallel to the one passed by the Russian Party [sic].

[71] A. Shlikhter, "Borba za khleb na Ukraine v 1919 godu," *Letopis revoliutsii*, No. 2 (Kharkiv, 1928), pp. 101–104.

[72] *Ibid.*, pp. 117, 135.

[73] *Ibid.*, pp. 106 (with statistics), 133, 135. See also Antonov-Ovseenko, Vol. III, pp. 338–341.

[74] Popov, *Narys*, p. 185 n.

[75] Borys, p. 208.

question, the French intervention in Odessa, Jewish pogroms, and the Voluntary Army of General Denikin.

Eastern Galicia, which had been under Austrian rule since the late eighteenth century, was an ethnically mixed territory with a Ukrainian majority virtually everywhere but in the cities, of which Lviv was the most important one. Making good use of the opportunities offered by the more liberal Austrian regime, and with some assistance from eastern Ukrainians, notably Hrushevskyi, the Galician Ukrainians developed a firm network of Ukrainian language schools, adult education societies, rural cooperatives, and even political parties. They were both more effectively organized and more conscious of their nationality than the Ukrainians under tsarist rule. Since the winter of 1917–1918, a detachment of Galician *Sich* Riflemen (*Sichovi Striltsi*) under Ievhen Konovalets and Andrii Melnyk proved to be the most reliable and effective unit of both the Rada and the Directory. When the Galicians rose in November 1918 to establish the West Ukrainian Republic, they were able to mobilize, by April 1919, between 225,000 and 240,000 men, a feat that the Directory could hardly approach, despite its claims to a larger territory and population.[76] On January 22, 1919, a union between the East and West Ukrainian Republics was solemnly proclaimed in Kiev.

But strain soon developed between the two governments, particularly when the Galicians met a determined and ultimately successful Polish resistance during their effort to take over eastern Galicia. The strain could ultimately be reduced to a conflict of priorities; the majority of the Galicians believed that their province—the piedmont of the Ukraine—should be liberated first and, if necessary, at the expense of the eastern Ukraine. The eastern Ukrainians argued that theirs was the larger, richer, and politically more important territory; they believed in the primacy of the struggle in the East and hoped for a speedy liquidation of the conflict with the Poles. The disagreement between eastern and western Ukrainians became particularly acute when the Galician Army command concluded a treaty with Denikin's troops on November 6, 1919.[77] One of their motives appears to have been the desire to persuade the

---

[76] Figures in Wasyl Kutschabsky, *Die Westukraine im Kampfe mit Polen und dem Bolschewismus in den Jahren 1918–1923* (Berlin: Junker und Dünnhaupt, 1934), p. 233.

[77] Mazepa, pp. 54–55; Reshetar, pp. 288–291.

Entente, specifically France, to exert a restraining influence on the Poles, for both Denikin and Piłsudski were *personae gratae* in Paris. The eastern Ukrainians retaliated by concluding a military agreement with Poland on April 21, 1920, ceding Galicia in return for Polish and indirectly Allied (particularly French) military aid.[78] The East-West Ukrainian disagreements, though not decisive, obviously helped the Bolsheviks in their struggle against the Directory.

One of the themes of Petliura's foreign policy was the attempt to gain the support of the victorious Entente. If the Allied powers had defeated Germany and were known to be hostile to the Bolsheviks, what more natural approach could there have been than to appeal for their help? Unfortunately, the somewhat insensitive and offensive treatment of the Directory's emissaries at the hands of the French Colonel Freydenberg,[79] who insisted on the dismissal of Petliura and Vynnychenko, coupled with the touching faith of the French in Denikin, rudely shattered the Directory's illusions. The Bolsheviks, of course, tried to make political capital out of the Directory's alleged subservience to Western imperialism, casting themselves in the role of defenders of Ukrainian territory against foreign intervention. The Directory continued to negotiate with the French, but to no avail. On March 6, 1919, when the French left Odessa, they relinquished the city not even to regular Soviet troops but to Hryhoriiv's Red partisans.[80]

The question of Jewish pogroms, in which Petliura's troops did take part, is an extremely controversial one, and to do it justice would lead beyond the scope of this study. In the author's judgment, Petliura was unable rather than unwilling to discipline his heterogeneous forces sufficiently to prevent them from engaging in those orgies of lawlessness, which, incidentally, were also common under Denikin.[81] No matter who was to blame for the pogroms, they

[78] Reshetar, pp. 300–305.

[79] *Ibid.*, pp. 234–244, esp. pp. 241–242; Borys, pp. 216–218; Adams, pp. 104–105.

[80] Adams, pp. 186–214.

[81] The reader may consult two contemporary books on this matter: Elias Heifetz, *The Slaughter of Jews in the Ukraine in 1919* (New York: Seltzer, 1921), which is anti-Petliura, and Arnold D. Margolin, *Ukraina i politika Antanty* (Berlin: Efron, 1921), which is basically friendly to Petliura. Popov, *Narys*, p. 211, writes that Denikin's pogroms "exceeded by far even those of Petliura." See also Solomon Goldelman, *Zhydivska natsionalna avtonomiia na Ukraini* (Munich, 1963) and Taras Hunczak,

poisoned the atmosphere between the nationalists and the second largest minority in the Ukraine, and they drove many Jews into the arms of Bolshevism.

Finally, there was the Russian monarchist, General Denikin. In the summer of 1919, with Allied help and the aid of the combined East and West Ukrainian Armies, Denikin swept the Bolsheviks out of the Ukraine. But his reactionary outlook precluded any cooperation with the anti-Bolshevik Ukrainians and prevented him from obtaining the popular support necessary for permanently defeating the Bolsheviks. The importance of the Denikin episode during the second half of 1919 is that it placed the Directory in a very difficult political position. If it did not declare war on Denikin, it would lose the rest of its popular support; if it declared war (as finally happened) and tried to keep aloof from Denikin's theater of operations, it would be punished by the Entente, which supplied Denikin with arms, materiel, and drugs but refused similar aid to Petliura—that "Bolshevik" who was somehow inexplicably fighting the Bolsheviks.

The forced Soviet withdrawal from the Ukraine in 1919 led to a re-evaluation of Lenin's policy toward the country. First of all, on orders of the CC RCP, the CC CP(b)U, which had been elected at the Third Ukrainian Party Congress in March 1919, was dissolved toward the end of July, and its power passed to a Rearguard Bureau composed of Kossior, Drobnis, and Rafail-Farbman.[82]

In November 1919, a few Ukrainian Bolshevik leaders, secretly and against the wishes of the CC RCP, met at Gomel. Those represented included Communists from Volhynia, the Chernihiv district, and other important leaders like Lapchynskyi, Zatonskyi, Kosior, Manuilskyi, and Kotsiubynskyi. It was not an official party conference, but it served, nevertheless, as a good opposition platform for Lapchynskyi's group of so-called "Federalists," who insisted on greater autonomy for the Ukraine as well as for the CP(b)U. Lapchynskyi's theses included, among others, the following points:

1) The Ukraine, throughout the whole extent of its territory, must be a Soviet Socialist Republic, ruled exclusively by its own Soviet power, the supreme organ of which is the All-Ukrainian Congress of Soviets.

"A Reappraisal of Symon Petliura and Ukrainian-Jewish Relations, 1917–1921," *Jewish Social Studies*, XXXI, 3 (New York, 1969).

[82] Holubnychy, pp. 76–77; Borys, p. 146.

2) The uniting of the Ukraine with other Socialist Republics, independent *of whether they have been or will be created on the territory of the former Russian Empire or outside this territory,* may take place only on genuinely federative principles, namely, so that the organs of administration common to all federated states should consist of the representatives of all members of the federation, and that within the Ukraine such organs should function through the local, Ukrainian, organs of Soviet power.

3) In particular, when certain branches of the administration and of the economy of the Ukraine are united with those of Russia and other Soviet Republics, the common federative organs controlling these branches must not, on any account, be identical with the corresponding administrative organs of Great Russia proper.[83]

With respect to the CP(b)U, Lapchynskyi's theses demanded:

1) This Party had to be a completely independent section of the International. . . . [Its] supreme organ was to be the All-Party Congress; the Party had at its disposal all the Party workers who were within the boundaries of the Ukraine.

2) The CP(b)U united all Communists who were working in the Ukraine, regardless of their nationality.

3) The CP(b)U was to unite all parties which worked in the Ukraine and shared the principles of the Communist International. . . .[84]

But the attitude of the critics is perhaps best expressed by a colleague of Lapchynskyi's whom Borys identifies as *Pavlo* Popov (not to be confused with the historian, N. N. Popov). In a detailed memorandum addressed to the CC RCP, Popov complained:

. . . That centre [of CP(b)U leadership] which exists has not been able to master this task [i.e., to give an answer to any question offered by life], not because of the composition of its personnel but because . . . it has considered everything from the viewpoint of narrow centralism, completely disregarding the fact that the course of the Revolution in Russia has not been at all uniform, that the Ukraine cannot accept as ready-made the forms of life which have been worked out in Russia during a year and a half of Soviet construction in circumstances completely different from those in the Ukraine.

. . . .

It has come about that, as a rule, the Party also had no influence in

---

[83] As cited by Borys, p. 239.

[84] As cited in *ibid.,* p. 147. The first quotation (note 84) is apparently *verbatim,* the second (note 85) is a paraphrase.

the countryside which is Ukrainian in its composition, it has done nothing in order to attract the poorer elements to its side, but instead it has gladly admitted to its membership the petty-bourgeois elements from among the Russian and Jewish craftsmen whose attitude is more or less Russophile . . . the Ukraine has been regarded merely as an object from which to extract material resources, and moreover the interests of class struggle in the Ukraine have been completely ignored.[85]

The Ukrainian "Federalists" were not the only critics. Greater weight was probably given by Lenin to Ordzhonikidze, a close associate of Stalin's. Ordzhonikidze wrote to Lenin on November 19, 1919, that the struggle with the insurgents was already rather difficult.

But all this is nothing compared with the tremendously important question of our actual relations with the Ukrainian peasant. Here, it is my deep conviction [that] the policy of dragging him into the commune is senseless and disastrous. This time we must find a common language with the Ukrainian peasant at all costs . . . Many of the functionaries in the Ukraine must not be returned there. Best of all, the greatest possible number of local personnel is to be attracted; from the Centre are to be sent those who are most responsible and with them a great number of workers from Petrograd and Moscow.[86]

In any case, under the pressure of complaints from Ukrainians, from such neutral observers as Ordzhonikidze, and possibly on the insistence of such centrist Ukrainian Bolsheviks as Manuilskyi, H. Petrovskyi, and Zatonskyi, Lenin pushed through a resolution at several high-level meetings (an RCP Politburo meeting on November 21, 1919, a plenary session of the CC RCP on November 29, and at the Eighth All-Russian Conference of the RCP) that was rather conciliatory toward the Ukrainians. It was done just in time to gain more popular support for the third Soviet invasion of the Ukraine, which started in December 1919 and was essentially completed by early February 1920. This was the final Communist occupation, for only limited parts of the Ukraine were temporarily ceded again during the joint Petliura-Piłsudski spring campaign of 1920. It was Lenin's resolution of December 3, 1919, that guided Soviet policy in the Ukraine throughout most of the 1920's. In view

---

[85] As cited in *ibid.,* p. 238. On the conference, see also Holubnychy, p. 77.

[86] As cited by Borys, p. 240.

of its fundamental importance, both as a critique of Soviet policies in 1918 and 1919 and as a preview of change, it would be useful to quote some of the resolution's more important provisions:

1) Undeviatingly following the principle of self-determination of nations, the Central Committee considers it essential to confirm once more that it is the policy of the Russian Communist Party to grant independence to the Ukrainian SSR.

. . . .

3) At the present time, the relations between the Ukrainian SSR and the RSFSR are determined by a federal connection. . . .

4) Taking into consideration that Ukrainian culture (language, education, etc.) has been for centuries suppressed by tsarism and the exploiting classes of Russia, the Central Committee of the Russian Communist Party charges every party member to act with all means available against any obstacles to the free development of the Ukrainian language and culture.

. . . .

Measures must be taken immediately to ensure that all government offices possess a sufficient number of Ukrainian speaking personnel and that in the future all personnel have some grasp of the Ukrainian language.

. . . .

7) The agricultural policy should be carried out with special consideration of the agricultural interests of poor and medium peasants.

. . . .

(ii) *Sovkhozes* should be established only in the exact sizes needed, taking into consideration the vital interests of the surrounding peasants.

(iii) As to the union of peasants in communes, *artils,* etc., the party policy is to be diligently carried out, which does not permit in this matter any compulsion.[87]

Lack of space does not permit an analysis of the fascinating events of the years 1920–1923, when the Soviet regime finally took a firm hold in the Ukraine. Four developments, however, may be mentioned in brief. At its Fourth Conference (the more dignified term, Congress, was not permitted), held in March 1920, the CP(b)U was humiliated once more by Moscow. The RCP dissolved the Central Committee elected at the Conference. This time the reason was not occasioned by specifically Ukrainian events; rather, it was

---

[87] Popov, *Narys,* pp. 212 ff. Partly translated in Holubnychy, pp. 78–79, from which points 1, 3, and 4 were taken.

attributed to the spreading of the so-called workers' opposition in Russia to the CP(b)U.[88] A more positive development was the selective incorporation of the Ukrainian SD's (Independents), and more importantly, of the Ukrainian SR's (*Borotbists*) into the CP(b)U, the latter in 1920.[89] As noted by Popov, the influx of *Borotbists* into the CP(b)U achieved two things: it furnished the Party with "considerable cadres of party workers who could speak Ukrainian," and it provided individuals who were in touch with the peasantry.[90]

Outside the scope of this study is also the very complex constitutional maneuvering, which gave the Soviet republics—at least on paper—greater rights than Stalin was prepared to grant them. Ukrainian Bolsheviks were prominent in the so-called struggle against "autonomization."[91] Finally, Borys rightly points out that the struggle for the Ukraine was not completely over even in 1921. In late 1920, Moscow had to dispatch Molotov to head the CP(b)U, and Frunze was made a Deputy Chairman of the Council of People's Commissars of the Ukraine in order to coordinate the military struggle against the peasant insurgents. The party also decided to grant amnesty to all the insurgents, which resulted in the surrender of over 10,000 peasant guerrillas in 1921 alone.[92] In drawing further conclusions from this study, it seems appropriate to cite the observations of Richard Pipes concerning the struggle between the Bolsheviks and the nationalist movements:

Whereas the Bolsheviks had long prepared for a revolution and knew what to do with power once they had attained it, the nationalists did not. They had lacked the opportunities to evolve an ideology, or to secure disciplined political cadres. The nationalist movements after 1917 suffered from profound cleavages among conservative, liberal, and radical tendencies, which prevented them from attaining the unity necessary for effective action. In critical movements, the national governments which had sprung up in the borderlands were weakened

---

[88] Holubnychy, pp. 79–80; Borys, pp. 147–151.

[89] See the analysis in Borys, pp. 246–266.

[90] Popov, *Narys*, p. 219.

[91] Richard Pipes, *The Formation of the Soviet Union: Communism and Nationalism, 1917–1923* (Cambridge, Mass.: Harvard University Press, 1954), chapter VI, esp. pp. 250–251, 280–282; Borys, chapter IV. A good recent Soviet book is Kulichenko, *Komunistychna partiia*.

[92] Borys, pp. 280–281.

from within, torn by dissensions among the divergent groups combined under the banners of nationalism. Another weakness of the nationalists was their inability, and, in some instances, their unwillingness, to win over the predominantly Russian and Russified urban population of the borderlands. They were also far too dependent on the politically immature and ineffective rural population.[93]

For the Ukraine the statement has to be slightly modified. The rightist Bolshevik, Kviring, who stressed the need for help from Soviet Russia, had his own political reasons for not exaggerating the effectiveness of the Bolsheviks in the Ukraine. Yet he still was historically correct: the CP(b)U was a sorry lot composed chiefly of minority nationals who were incapable of winning the upper hand even at a Soviet Congress without the support of Red divisions from outside the Ukraine. On the other hand, Lenin as a statesman was more than a match for Hrushevskyi, Vynnychenko, and Petliura. It must be emphasized, however, that personalities were not decisive; neither Alexander the Great nor even Napoleon could have helped the Rada in 1918.[94] Indeed, the Ukrainian governments were too much at the mercy of volatile popular passions (*narodnia stykhiia*), or, as Pipes concluded, "too dependent on the politically immature and ineffective rural population." After decades of hard work, the Ukrainians created a strong, well-organized national movement in Galicia, but even this succumbed to the onslaught of the better organized and stronger Poles, who were moveover backed by France. To create within three years a national movement and a new state out of the chaos caused by two large-scale and countless smaller revolutions in the eastern Ukraine, while at the same time suffering from diplomatic isolation and being deprived of any access to arms, clothing, and drugs, would have called for superhuman efforts on the part of any democrat. Not surprisingly, the struggle was won by Lenin's Bolsheviks, the party that had built chaos into its political program.

Nonetheless, the seemingly futile struggle of Ukrainian nationalists and national Communists such as Skrypnyk had three far-reaching consequences. Under their pressure, which ultimately was generated by the nationally conscious if politically immature popular masses in the eastern Ukraine, Lenin revised his policy in three respects. In the party declaration of December 1919 he promised

---

[93] Pipes, pp. 283–284.
[94] Vynnychenko, Vol. II, p. 219.

Ukrainians cultural autonomy—a pledge that was more or less honored by Stalin throughout the 1920's, the period of so-called *korenizatsiia*. Lenin also disregarded the idea of detaching the industrial Donets-Kryvyi Rih Basin from the Ukraine, which, if successful, would have "pastoralized" the republic for decades to come. Thirdly, the Russian Communists granted the Ukraine full Soviet Republican status, including the constitutional right to secession. Thus far, this status has brought the Ukraine a modicum of cultural autonomy and a limited influence on All-Union domestic politics, no more. But in view of the rapid transformation in Eastern Europe, the observer of the current scene would be rash to conclude that the arrangement of 1924 must remain immutable forever. Was the Communist take-over of the Ukraine a complete success by 1920, or was it rather a Pyrrhic victory? In another fifty years historians might be able to provide a more definitive answer, but fifty years after the Ukrainian Revolution the question remains moot.

CHAPTER SIX

Political Parties
in the Ukraine

Jurij Borys

THIS STUDY IS devoted to all political parties active in the
Ukraine.[1] A Ukrainian party is one that represents various Ukrainian ethnic elements and has, in a qualitative sense, a positive attitude toward the Ukrainian national idea. These parties can be
regarded as the nationalist parties of the liberation movement.

Nationalism was the most important movement in Central and
Eastern Europe during the late nineteenth and early twentieth
centuries. In that part of the world national identity was not
acquired by birth or citizenship. Rather, an individual more or less
freely determined his own nationality. For instance, one might be
a citizen of the Russian or Austro-Hungarian Empires but be of
Russian, Ukrainian, Armenian, or Estonian nationality.

A similar situation existed with regard to political affiliation.
Thus, a Ukrainian or Polish worker with radical political leanings
had to decide, on the one hand, whether he would support a Social
Democratic or Socialist-Revolutionary party, and, on the other,
whether it would be a Russian, Ukrainian, or Polish Social Democratic or Socialist-Revolutionary party. The electoral campaign was,
therefore, two-dimensional, divided between different political
parties and different ethnic affiliations within the same political
party. As will be shown later, it was partly the prospect of fighting
against the fraternal Ukrainian or Georgian parties that prompted
Lenin to demand an integrated and united Social Democratic Party
for the whole of Russia. Of course, this ideal was valid assuming
the Russian Empire would remain intact; as soon as non-Russian

---

[1] This study derives much of its material from **Jurij Borys**, *The Russian
Communist Party and the Sovietizaiton of Ukraine: A Study in the Communist Doctrine of the Self-Determination of Nations* (Stockholm, 1960),
especially Chapter II.

areas separated and created *de facto* independent states, or whenever the Russian state became a federation of republics, the existence of distinct national parties of any kind was inevitable.

The national differentiation of political life was possible only under a political system that recognized freedom of assembly and organization. Neither the tsarist nor the Soviet government was favorably disposed to political pluralism. Thus, nationality parties flourished only during the short liberal period just after the Russian Revolution of 1905 and from the February Revolution of 1917 to the final victory of Bolshevism in Russia and its borderlands. Ukrainian political parties should be classified as revolutionary parties during the first period, and as semi-governing parties during the second. After the final establishment of the Bolshevik government in the Ukraine, Ukrainian national parties were abolished. They continued to exist only in exile, where they indulged in forceful ideological and propagandistic campaigns against each other and especially against the Russian political parties.

Another characteristic of parties in the Ukraine and in other regions of the Russian Empire, such as Finland and the Baltic region, was that nationality often coincided with social stratification. In the Ukraine, the majority of the Ukrainian ethnic population belonged to the lower strata of society and was composed not only of poor and middle-class peasants and dispossessed agricultural workers, but also the lower strata of the rural intelligentsia—clerks, school teachers, and priests. In the urban areas, the Ukrainian element was found among industrial workers, servants, police, and military officers of lower rank. There were very few Ukrainians among the higher echelons of society. Such individuals as Tereshchenko, a sugar magnate and later Foreign Minister in the Russian Provisional Government, and Savenko, the Russian chauvinist from the newspaper *Kievlianin,* can hardly be considered Ukrainians.

Consequently, there were no rightist or conservative Ukrainian parties, and most political groups bearing the epithet Ukrainian were—in fact or in name—socialist. Some were more socialist than nationalist, others expressed a nationalistic zeal that in most cases took precedence over class solidarity. Because these two aspects of Ukrainian politics were so closely interwoven, most parties had to navigate carefully between nationalism and socialism. Non-socialist political parties in the Ukraine were rare.

Political parties active in the Ukraine between 1917 and 1920 were influenced by the Ukrainian national movement as formulated in the late nineteenth and early twentieth centuries. This had been a protest movement, struggling not so much for political power within the framework of existing institutions as against national oppression. In positive terms, the goal was self-determination for the Ukrainian nation. The abolition of national autonomy, guaranteed in 1654 by the Treaty of Pereiaslav, forced the Ukrainian political movement to concern itself largely with problems of cultural renaissance and the re-emergence of national consciousness. In a sense, the Ukrainophile movement remained apolitical and indifferent to social reforms. Beyond protest against russification, the Ukrainophiles raised no objections to the tsarist regime[2] and continued to flourish long after the Russian Revolution of 1905. Their organization, *Stara Hromada* (Old Society), attracted most of the moderate intellectuals, who cherished a strong sentiment for the country's romantic past but who never advocated anti-Russian separatist action. Their maximal political demand was confined to autonomy for the Ukraine. The *Stara Hromada,* together with the *Zahalna Ukrainska Organizatsiia,* had an important influence on the future national struggle, fostering national feeling among the masses and educating the national cadres that played such an important role in the Ukrainian movement of 1917. These organizations also influenced Russian liberals to take a more positive attitude toward the Ukrainian question in the Duma and in the press.[3]

In opposition to this "non-political" movement, a more radical political party came into being, the Ukrainian Radical Democratic Party (URDP). Ideologically, this party was influenced by Mykhailo Drahomanov, a learned historian and sociologist from the University of Kiev. Like his contemporaries, Ziber, Podolianskyi, and Antonovych, Drahomanov was a moderate socialist who was influenced by Proudhon and Saint-Simon as well as by Bakunin, and who considered the political struggle a waste of time and energy. The preponderance of his thought was given to economic and social reforms and to the education of the masses. His ideology

---

[2] S. Iefremov, *Z hromadskoho zhyttia* (St. Petersburg, 1909), pp. 34–35; also the Ukrainian Marxist historian M. Iavorskyi, *Korotka istoriia Ukrainy* (Kharkiv, 1927), pp. 90–91.

[3] Iefremov, p. 42; Ie. Chykalenko, *Spohady (1861–1907),* Vol. III (Lviv: Dilo, 1925–26), pp. 6 ff; D. Doroshenko, *Ievhen Chykalenko, ioho zhyttia i hromadska diialnist* (Prague: Vyd. Fondu im. Ie. Chykalenka pry Ukrainskomu akademichnomu komiteti 1934), pp. 34 ff.

was a mixture of syndicalist socialism and conventional liberalism. With regard to the Ukraine, Drahomanov claimed political freedom and the re-emergence of the Ukrainian nation as a member of the family of civilized nations.[4]

The Ukrainian Radical Democratic Party, in many respects the most influential party in the Ukraine, was a non-socialist, liberal party that resembled the Russian Constitutional Democrats (Kadets). The middle peasants, the lower and middle bourgeoisie of the cities, and a significant number of the intelligentsia provided the social basis for the Ukrainian Radicals. They demanded constitutional monarchy in Russia, a federalist structure for the Empire, and autonomy for the Ukraine. In the Second Imperial Duma more than thirty of the forty Ukrainian deputies represented this party.

In 1908, a moderate element of the URDP formed a non-party organization, the Ukrainian Progressivist Association (TUP— *Tovarystvo Ukrainskykh Progresystiv*). Most prominent among its leaders were the historian and later President of the Ukrainian Republic, Mykhailo Hrushevskyi, Professor Serhii Iefremov, and Ievhen Chykalenko. The TUP demanded autonomy for the Ukraine and concentrated mainly on combatting aggressive Russian nationalism.[5]

The Revolutionary Ukrainian Party (RUP), founded in Kharkiv in 1900, was the embryonic organization of the future socialist party. Most of the social-democratic leaders of 1917 received their political training in this party, which, ideologically, was a conglomeration of Ukrainian nationalism, Drahomanivism, and Marxism. Originally, it was a "bloc of very heterogeneous elements" with members of "different political shades, from liberals and nationalists to socialists." One contemporary, Natalia Romanovich-Tkachenko, described how the RUP was on the one hand composed of intelligentsia, students, and peasants urging that "the workers of the world unite," while on the other it also included a right wing that dreamed of purely nationalist goals.[6]

---

[4] M. Drahamanov, *Volnyi Soiuz-Vilna Spilka: opyt ukrainskoi politiko-sotsialnoi programmy* (Russian ed.; Genève, 1884), pp. 7 ff.; D. Doroshenko, "Mykhajlo Drahomanov and the Ukrainian Movement," *Slavonic and East European Review*, No. 48 (London, 1938), pp. 662 ff.

[5] H. Lototskyi, *Storinky mynuloho*, Vol. III (Warsaw: Ukrainskyi naukovyi instytut, 1932–34), p. 91; Chykalenko, Vol. III, p. 30.

[6] N. Romanovich-Tkachenko, "Na dorozi do revoliutsii," *Ukraina*, Book 4, p. 108.

After the right wing broke away, the RUP inclined toward social-democratic ideals. In 1903, the Kievan Committee of the RUP adopted a radical Marxist program that appeared as a kind of Ukrainian variant of the Russian Social Democratic Party. However, this program was bitterly criticized by the nationalist and socialist factions of the Party. Although the RUP was obviously inclined toward Marxism, its national aspirations antagonized the Russian Social Democrats. This antagonism became more acute when the RUP claimed to represent not only the Ukrainian agricultural proletariat but also the industrial workers. The most prominent leaders in the RUP were M. O. Rusov, O. V. Antonovych, P. P. Kanivets, V. Vynnychenko, B. P. Tkachenko, O. Skoropys-Ioltukhovskyi, and M. Porsh. Many subsequently became leaders of the Ukrainian Social Democratic Party.[7]

Very soon the RUP was split into different factions. Its right wing, under the leadership and ideological influence of Mikhnovskyi, formed in 1902 the Ukrainian People's Party (*Ukrainska Narodna Partiia*). This new party adopted Mikhnovskyi's nationalistic program, slightly camouflaged by a small dose of socialism. The Party became the most nationalistic of all Ukrainian parties, demanding an independent, though socialist, Ukraine. During the period of the Ukrainian Republic, 1917–1919, it adopted the label of socialism, renaming itself the Ukrainian Party of the Socialist-Independentists.[8]

The leftist elements of the RUP formed the Ukrainian Social Democratic Union, generally known as the *Spilka,* which accepted the Russian Social Democratic platform *vis-à-vis* the nationalities and the unity of the movement for the whole of Russia. The *Spilka* entered the Russian Social Democratic Party as an autonomous organization, accepted *Iskra*'s principle that in the provinces there should be unified organizations without regard for national differences, and recognized the Russian Party program of "complete equality for all citizens regardless of sex, religion, race and nationality."[9] The nihilistic approach of certain Russian Social Democrats toward the nationality question forced many *Spilkists,* such as Tkachenko, Vikul, Dovzhenko, and others, to return "to

[7] Borys, p. 72.

[8] *Ibid.,* pp. 70–71.

[9] M. Popov, *Narys istorii kommunistychnoi partii (bilshovykiv) Ukrainy* (5th ed.; Kharkiv, 1931), p. 61; also Borys, p. 75.

the bosom of the national-socialistic Ukrainian Social Democratic Labor Party."[10]

In 1908, members of the *Spilka*, under the leadership of Basok-Melenevskyi, started the newspaper *Pravda*, in which Leon Trotsky cooperated. At first, *Pravda* was published in the name of the *Spilka* and in Ukrainian, but soon it became the organ of the Trotsky group and appeared in Russian. On the editorial board were, in addition to Trotsky, Basok-Melenevskyi, Skobelev, Semkovskyi, and Joffe.[11] The *Spilka* was one of the strongest organizations in the social-democratic movement. In the 1907 elections to the Second Imperial Duma, it won fourteen seats, while the Ukrainian Social Democratic Party received only one. At the London congress of the Russian Social Democratic Party, in 1907, the *Spilka* was represented by ten delegates, who sided with the Menshevik faction and were quite hostile toward Lenin's Bolsheviks. That same year the organization ceased to exist. Its decline was due mainly to the fact that it was unable to compete with the Russian Party for hegemony in the large urban areas, where the Russians had firm control. Thus, isolated from the peasants and unable to win over the industrial workers, the *Spilka* lost the social basis of its existence.[12]

The Ukrainian Social Democratic Labor Party (USDLP) was formally constituted at a congress of the Revolutionary Ukrainian Party held in 1905. The party represented a kind of synthesis embodying the varying demands put forth by Ukrainian socialists. They wanted their Russian colleagues to recognize them as the sole representatives of the Ukrainian proletariat, either as an independent section of the international socialist movement or as an autonomous section of the Russian Party. But their demand to receive a status similar to that of the Jewish *Bund,* the Latvian Social Democracy, or Polish Social Democracy was rejected.[13]

In principle, the Ukrainian Social Democrats supported the idea of an independent Ukrainian state, but they had for tactical reasons

---

[10] M. Ravich-Cherkasskii, *Istoriia kommunisticheskoi partii* (*b-kov*) *Ukrainy* (Kharkiv, 1923), p. 40.; Lev Iurkevych [L. Rubalka], "Rosiiski marksysty i ukrainskyi robitnychyi rukh," *Dzvin*, Nos. 7–8 (1913), p. 89.

[11] Popov, p. 76; Ravich-Cherkasskii, p. 40.

[12] I. Mazepa, *Ukraina v ohni i buri revoliutsii*, Vol. I (Prague, 1942), p. 10.

[13] Borys, p. 74, n. 30.

temporarily accepted autonomy within the Russian federation as their minimum demand. Ideologically, the Party stood close to the Russian Mensheviks and adopted a Ukrainian variant of the Erfurt Program of German Social Democracy. Its short-term objectives were the education of the Ukrainian workers in the spirit of class solidarity and national consciousness, and the creation of a strong Ukrainian socialist movement as a counterpoise to Russian centralist ambitions.

The USDLP differed from the Russian Party on two main points: it rejected the dictatorship of the proletariat, and it demanded recognition of the nationality principle in the organization of socialist parties. After the reactionary government of Stolypin was installed, the Social Democrats emigrated to Galicia, where under Austro-Hungarian rule the Ukrainian national movement developed freely. The Party published a monthly journal, *Our Voice,* which served as the organ of Ukrainian Social Democrats from Russia and Austria. In exile, they waged a severe struggle against attempts by Russian and Polish socialists to monopolize activity and ignore a separate Ukrainian socialist movement.[14] A heated dialogue developed between Lenin and Iurkevych, a Ukrainian Social Democrat who accused the Russian socialists of "nationalistic intolerance" and demanded "complete organizational freedom for the labour movement of the subjugated nations."[15] Lenin, on the other hand, accused Iurkevych of all sins, fighting him because "this scabby, foul, nationalistic bourgeois . . . , under the banner of Marxism, had prophesized the division of the workers according to nationality, [and] a *separate* national organization of the Ukrainian workers."[16] Lenin was disturbed by the activity of the Ukrainian socialists, who intruded into his revolutionary plans for Russia and only complicated the entire problem by adding unpleasant, disintegrative elements to the general confusion. But the Ukrainian Social Democratic Party persisted, writing to the Second International Congress in Stuttgart in 1907, and again to the Kienthal Conference, appealing to the international proletariat to support its demand for Ukrainian national autonomy.[17] Its leaders, M. Porsh, V. Sadovskyi,

---

[14] *Ibid.*

[15] Iurkevych, p. 93.

[16] V. I. Lenin, *Sochineniia,* Vol. XXXV (4th ed.; Moscow, 1941–50), pp. 100–101.

[17] *L'Ukraine et la Guerre: Lettre ouverte adressée à la 2ème conférence socialiste internationale tenue en Hollande en mai 1916* (Lausanne, 1916).

S. Petliura, M. Tkachenko, V. Vynnychenko, and others, played an important role in the Ukrainian Republic, 1917–1920.[18]

When Russian armies captured Galicia during the First World War, most of the Ukrainian Social Democrats fled to the West. Some of them, like Iurkevych, continued propaganda activity from Switzerland. There they published a newspaper, *Borotba* (The Struggle), criticizing both pro-Russian elements and other organizations like the Union for the Liberation of the Ukraine, which acted on the assumption that the defeat of the tsarist armies was the only hope for Ukrainian liberation.

The Ukrainian Socialist Revolutionary Party was one of the last to emancipate itself from association with its Russian counterpart. Several semi-independent organizations of Ukrainian Socialist Revolutionaries (SR's) existed, but not until 1907 was an all-Ukrainian party founded. Even after its formation, this party did not demonstrate the same vitality as the Social Democrats. During the First World War, Ukrainian SR's published an illegal journal in Kiev, *Borotba,* which, even after the liberation of Russia from tsarist rule, continued to exist as an official organ of the Party. Ukrainian SR's ideologically resembled their Russian equivalent, but differed in their commitment to the national movement. They supported the idea of a federal Russian republic and free development for the Ukrainian language.[19]

Ukrainian political parties in the period before the fall of the tsarist regime could be characterized as revolutionary parties proposing different political ideologies but representing, nevertheless, a single national liberation movement. Only after assuming *de facto* political power in the middle of 1917 did they begin to transform themselves into national governmental parties. However, the abnormal circumstances caused by the social and political struggle in the Russian Empire affected both the character and the structure of the parties.

On the eve of the Russian Revolution of 1917, the Ukrainian national movement was either unknown or ignored. The Russian

---

See also K. Zalevskii, "Natsionalnye partii v Rossii," in L. Martov *et al.* (eds.), *Obshchestvennoe dvizhenie v Rossii,* Vol. III, bk. 5 (St. Petersburg, 1914), pp. 297–298.

18 Mazepa, Vol. II, pp. 123–135.

19 P. Fedenko, *Sotsializm davnii i novochasnyi* (London: Vyd. Nashe slovo, 1968), pp. 202–204.

government, political organizations, and public opinion persistently neglected to recognize openly the Ukrainian question. Most reactionary circles ascribed the Ukrainian movement to a German-Austrian intrigue against Russia, while more liberal Russians attributed it to the fanatic activity of a small number of intellectuals. Only the tenacity and energy of individual political and cultural leaders kept the movement alive. The reaction after the 1905 revolution had driven most Ukrainian national parties and organizations either underground or into exile, and, until the Russian occupation of Galicia in 1916 Lviv, remained the sole center of Ukrainian political and cultural life.

Only after the fall of the tsarist regime did a more favorable perspective open for free political activities among the non-Russian nationalities. The Provisional Government, having abolished the restrictive legislation, also opened the avenue for national self-assertion to Ukrainians. Numerous cultural and political organizations, which began to organize soon after the change in the regime, manifested in different ways the basic national aspirations of their people. Ukrainian self-determination was complicated by the fact that almost twenty-five percent of its population belonged to non-Ukrainian minorities—predominantly Russian, Polish, and Jewish. These national groups exhibited more political influence than might have been expected from their number. Being predominantly urbanites, on a higher level of social stratification, and having, further, the support of official policy and governmental bureaucracy, they exercised an enormous challenge to any radical movement that proclaimed liberation for the Ukraine.

A specific phenomenon of the political life in the Ukraine was that, as a rule, parties organized not only according to ideological or socio-economic criteria but also according to nationality.

Ukrainian political parties, representing the largest nationality in the Ukraine (approximately seventy-five to eighty percent of the entire population), exhibited solid political power, both individually and as a block. They received seventy-five percent of all votes cast in the Ukraine during the elections to the All-Russian Constituent Assembly in December 1917. As in the Russian part of the Empire, the Socialist-Revolutionaries proved to be the strongest party, while the Ukrainian Social Democrats and other socialist groups received far fewer votes.[20]

---

[20] For the election results, see Borys, pp. 157–161.

The following review embraces all political parties and organizations of some significance in the period between the February Revolution and the final victory of Bolshevism.

The Ukrainian Party of the Socialist-Revolutionaries (SR's) was founded in April 1917. There was very little ideological difference between this party and the Russian Socialist-Revolutionaries. It was a kind of agrarian socialist party, similar to the Russian *Narodnik* movement in the late nineteenth century. The socialization of land and its distribution among the peasants solely for their own use represented in reality the abolition of private ownership. Nevertheless, this prospect attracted more peasants than any other political program available at that time. In a resolution, the SR's called for the creation of a Ukrainian Land Foundation, which was to carry out the distribution of land to the peasants. At this early stage, they demanded autonomy for the Ukraine, called for the immediate convocation of a territorial Ukrainian Constituent Council, and proposed that a federal-democratic republic would be the best form of state for Russia. By the end of 1917, its policy regarding the nationality question had gradually evolved from the demand for limited autonomy to that of complete independence for the Ukraine.

The Ukrainian SR's derived their support from lower and middle-class peasants and partly from the rural proletariat. Urban elements were a rarity. In a bloc with the Social Democratic Union (the *Spilka*), the SR's carried over sixty percent of all votes in the Ukraine in the election to the All-Russian Constituent Assembly. The weight of the Party was felt in all spheres of political life during the entire period of the Ukrainian People's Republic. In the Rada, they played an important role, especially after the President of the Republic, Hrushevskyi, joined them. The Ukrainian SR's formed the first government in January 1918, when their representative, Holubovych, formed a cabinet. This cabinet was shortlived, however, for the German military authorities soon initiated a *coup d'état*, and authority was transferred to the conservative Hetman Skoropadskyi. The Ukrainian SR's remained opposed to the Russian Provisional Government as it tried to postpone recognition of Ukrainian autonomy, and they were also helpful during the critical period in January 1918, when the Rada proclaimed the independence of the Ukraine. With regard to independent statehood, they expressed the old socialistic dream of federation for all countries. The Party organ, *Narodna volia*, emphasized that: "[By] satisfying the demand for independence, Ukrainian democracy has not deviated an inch from the idea of world brotherhood, from plans for a free union of all countries."[21]

During the rule of the Directory, the Ukrainian SR's joined the opposition, though for a short period they did form a cabinet. The Party's influence over the policy of the Directory gradually declined, however, because of a split within its ranks. Already in January 1918 there were signs of internal conflict,[22] and by April the Party suffered its first split. The left internationalist faction, later called the *Borotbists*, unexpectedly took over the Party's Central Committee, while the right wing formed its own faction, the so-called *Centre*. Since the right wing continued to support the Directory in its struggle against the Bolsheviks, the left wing refused to do so. The leaders of the right and *Centre* wings went into exile in 1920, where they continued to split into factions while simultaneously waging a propaganda war against the Soviet system in the Ukraine. Subsequently, most of its leaders, including Professor Hrushevskyi, Khrystiuk, Shrah, Chechel, and others, returned to the Soviet Ukraine. There they continued literary or scholarly activities until the beginning of the Stalin era, when they were tried for anti-Communist and nationalistic activity and liquidated. Other Ukrainian SR leaders included M. Kovalevskyi, O. Sevriuk, M. Shapoval, and M. Zalizniak.

The left wing of the Party, the *Borotbists*, occupied an uncertain position between the Rada and Soviet power, moving to the left or returning again to the right according to the moods of the peasantry. In spite of their leftist position, they disagreed basically with Bolshevism on the peasant issue and, being a peasant party, they could not become one hundred percent Communist. On the other hand, their "nationalism" antagonized Lenin's party. They also refused the dictatorship of the proletariat, which from the Bolshevik point of view was a most horrible sin. The *Borotbists*, as well as other leftist

---

[21] For the history of this party, see A. Zhyvotko, "Do istorii Ukrainskoi Partii Sotsialistiv Revolutsioneriv," *Vilna spilka*, No. 3 (Prague-Lviv, 1927–29), pp. 128–132; V. Andriievskyi, *Z mynuloho*, 3 vols. (Berlin: Ukrainske slovo, 1921–23); *Le parti socialiste revolutionnaire ukrainien* (Prague, 1919); P. Khrystiuk, *Zamitky i materialy do istorii ukrainskoi revolutsii, 1917–1920 rr.,* Vol. III (Vienna: Dzvin, 1921–22) pp. 19 ff.

[22] For the history of the factionalism in this party see: Borys, pp. 251–266; Iwan Majstrenko, *Borotbism: A Chapter in the History of Ukrainian Communism* (New York: Research Program on the USSR, 1954); Khrystiuk, Vol. III, pp. 23–24.

parties standing on the Soviet platform, were disillusioned with the irreconcilable attitude of the Bolsheviks in the matter of the sharing of power. In the end, they were driven into open conflict with the Bolsheviks, whereupon they formed their own government and controlled a considerable portion of the Ukraine. The partisans of their government, under the command of *Otaman* Hryhoriiv, seized Odessa from the French occupation forces. However, increased pressure from the anti-Communist front drew the *Borotbists* "on this [the Soviet] side of the barricades."[23]

As the Ninth Congress of the Russian Communist Party declared in March 1920, the main reason for the antagonism of the Bolsheviks toward the *Borotbists* was the fact that the latter "had not broken with their chauvinist past"—in other words, with their defense of Ukrainian independence.[24] The *Borotbists* made several attempts to receive recognition from the Executive Committee of the Comintern, as the only representatives of the Ukrainian working masses, the only real Communist Party. The Comintern cynically proposed that the *Borotbists* liquidate their party and join the Communist Party (Bolsheviks) of the Ukraine (CP[b]U).[25] After the consolidation of Soviet power in Russia and the Ukraine, the *Borotbists* decided to amalgamate with the CP(b)U from within and, perhaps, even nursed the idea of taking over its leadership.[26] The influence of the *Borotbists* upon the CP(b)U was recognized even by the Premier Minister of the Soviet Ukraine, Khristiian Rakovskii: "The two parties, the CPU and the UCP . . . met each other half way, the one rectifying its Communist line, the other adapting itself to the peculiarities and specific conditions of the social, economic, national, and cultural life in the Ukraine."[27]

Although the dreams of the *Borotbists* did not materialize, their activity did pressure the centralist Bolsheviks into making considerable concessions to Ukrainian national aspirations, at least in the cultural field. Without the existence of this party and the Ukrainian Communist Party (Independentists) it may be doubted whether the Bolsheviks would have recognized even the formal existence of the

---

[23] Popov, pp. 192.

[24] *Deviatyi sezd RKP(B), mart-aprel 1920 g.* (Moscow, 1934), pp. 96–97, 142–143.

[25] *Kommunisticheskii internatsional,* Nos. 7–8 (Moscow, 1920), cols. 1125–26; see also Maistrenko, pp. 184–186.

[26] Borys, p. 261.

[27] Ravich-Cherkasskii, pp. 148–149.

Ukrainian Soviet Republic. Most of the leaders of the *Borotbists,* such as M. Poloz, M. Liubchenko, V. Ielanskyi, and I. Lyzanivskyi, continued their "nationalistic" activity within the CP(b)U and the Russian Communist Party until they disappeared as victims of Stalin's terrorist activities.

The Ukrainian Social Democratic Party was a continuation of the party with the same name discussed above. Ideologically, it was similar to the Russian Mensheviks or any other Western European socialist party that advocated democratic processes and moderate revolutionary activities. In principle, it was a Marxist party, but it was very different from the Communist variant of Marxism. It adhered to the parliamentary system of government and rejected the principle of the dictatorship of the proletariat and especially of its party. Its agrarian policy was similar to that of the SR's, advocating the expropriation of the large estates and the distribution of land among the poor peasants.[28]

In one respect the Social Democrats differed from the Mensheviks, and that was on the nationality question. The Mensheviks did not extend their liberalism beyond the recognition of limited autonomy to non-Russian nationalities, and this included the Ukraine. The Ukrainian Social Democrats progressively adopted the idea of an independent Ukrainian state. The Party, under the leadership of the successful writer Vynnychenko and a devoted Ukrainian patriot Petliura, had an enormous influence on the development of the Rada. While in March 1917 the Social Democrats expressed Ukrainian national ambitions in only a very limited form, by January 1918 the Party assumed the role of a fully independent government within the framework of the Ukrainian People's Republic. As Vynnychenko has indicated, the Ukrainian Social Democratic Party was prepared to "abandon its Social Democratic purity" for the sake of national unity. National liberation became the first priority, while "the solution of social problems had been postponed until the future."[29] It was never a popular mass party, but it did have talented leaders, among whom were Vynnychenko, Petliura, M. Porsh, V. Sadovskyi, I. Mazepa, V. Chekhivskyi, B. Martos, D. Antonovych, and P. Fedenko.

---

[28] For the history of this party, see Mazepa, Vol. I; V. Vynnychenko, *Vidrodzhennia natsii,* Vol. III (Vienna: Vernay, 1920); Khrystiuk, Vol. III, pp. 19 ff.

[29] Vynnychenko, Vol. III, pp. 82 ff.

The social base of the organization was a conglomeration of Ukrainian workers and radical-minded intelligentsia. It was not as successful as the SR's at the elections, and it elected only two deputies to the All-Russian Constituent Assembly. Its official organ was *Robitnycha Hazeta* (The Workers' Newspaper). After the defeat of Ukrainian independence in 1920, the majority of leaders as well as many of the rank and file members went into exile—first to Poland, then to Czechoslovakia—where they pursued propaganda activity and organized émigré workers and youth into the socialist movement. The former Premier, Vynnychenko, made an attempt to collaborate with the Ukrainian Soviet regime and was even appointed to that government in the early twenties, but he soon became disillusioned by the hegemonistic attitude of Russian leadership, returned to Vienna, and engaged in energetic criticism of Soviet rule in the Ukraine.[30]

The Ukrainian Social Democratic Party, however, was affected by radical waverings within its own leadership. Already in January 1918 its left wing had pronounced itself in favor of the Soviet system. Its local leader in Kharkiv, Medvediev, even became the Chairman of the Central Executive Committee of the Ukraine for a short period. Another left-wing Social Democrat, Neronovych, became for a short time People's Secretary (Minister) for War in the Soviet government. At the First Congress of the CP(b)U in 1918, this group brought for a time the first truly Ukrainian contingent into the Communist Party. One of them, Butsenko, was even elected to the Central Committee of the CP(b)U.

However, the real split in the Ukrainian Social Democratic Party did not occur until the end of 1918, during the war between the Directory and Soviet Russia.[31] A new organization was founded with an entirely "independent" position on most questions. The issue of disagreement between the moderate and right wing of the Party and the Independentists was concerned with the system of government in the Ukrainian Republic and the relationship with the Russian Soviet government. The Independentists believed that the Ukraine could survive as an independent state only under a Soviet system. This was obviously a mere stratagem which, they

---

[30] On Vynnychenko's Canossa, see his "Povorot tov. Vynnychenka z Ukrainy," *Nova doba,* No. 34 (Vienna, 1920).

[31] On this split, see A. Butsenko, "O raskole U.S.-D.R.P. 1917–18 god," *Letopis revoliutsii,* No. 4 (Kharkiv, 1922–23), pp. 121–122.

thought, would have deprived the Russian Bolsheviks of the claim
that they were fighting for a Soviet Ukraine; such a government
would already have been in existence.[32] Apart from this argument,
an important influence on the evolution of the Ukrainian Social
Democrats toward Communism resulted from the general drift to
the left in Europe, especially in Germany and Hungary.

The right wing argued that the introduction of the dictatorship
of the proletariat in the Ukraine, where there was a complete
absence of a Ukrainian working class, would mean dictatorship by
the Russian Bolsheviks. As Vynnychenko put it, "we shall have
here the dictatorship of the Piatakovs, Antonovs, etc."[33] The Independentists tried their program, but it did not prove successful;
neither the Russian Bolsheviks, their emissaries in the Ukraine,
nor the Soviet Premier, Rakovskii, was willing to recognize the
"bourgeois nationalist" elements in their government. At the end of
the Civil War, when the Russian Bolsheviks made their third
attempt to Sovietize the Ukraine, the Independentists cooperated
with the Soviet authorities. Their representative, Hrynko, entered
the Military Committee created in Moscow in December 1919,
which subsequently conquered the Ukraine. The Independentists
soon changed their name to the Ukrainian Communist Party or
Ukapists. The organization was legally recognized, but after the
consolidation of Bolshevik power the *Ukapists* were ordered to dis-
band and join the CP(b)U. The *Ukapists* applied for membership
in the Comintern, but membership was refused and they were
branded as typical Ukrainian "nationalist-separatists."[34] The Independentists published a newspaper, *Chervonyi prapor* (The Red
Banner), and their most prominent leaders included M. Tkachenko,
J. Mazurenko, Ie. Neronovych, and M. Drahomiretskyi.

The Ukrainian Party of Socialist-Federalists[35] was formed in
March 1917 by members of the Ukrainian Progressivist Association
(TUP). In composition as well as in ideology the Socialist-Federal-
ists resembled the Russian Kadets, although they stressed the need

---

[32] Mazepa, Vol. I, pp. 76–78.

[33] Khrystiuk, Vol. IV, pp. 50–52.

[34] Popov, p. 274.

[35] D. Doroshenko, *Istoriia Ukrainy 1917–1923*, Vol. I (Uzhhorod: Svoboda, 1930–32), pp. 11 ff; P. Haidalemivskyi, *Ukrainski politychni partii,
ikh rozvytok i prohramy* (Salzwedel, Germany, 1923); Andriievskyi, *Z mynuloho*.

for Ukrainian cultural autonomy. The party was socialist in name only. In fact, it was a typical petty-bourgeois, liberal party advocating the transformation of Russia into a federation of free states with the Ukraine as an equal member. As a long-range goal, the Socialist-Federalists advocated the formation of a world federation. However, after the decline of democratic government in Russia it supported the Rada's claims for independence.

During the Skoropadskyi regime, the Ukrainian Socialist-Federalists progressed rapidly toward the idea of an independent Ukraine. When leftist, pro-Soviet tendencies arose among other Ukrainian parties in 1919, this party stood firmly for the preservation of liberal democracy. As a party, it must be pointed out, it did not attract any mass membership, nor did it collect a considerable number of votes in the 1917 elections. In spite of this, the Party played a very important role in the political life, supplying a large number of highly qualified functionaries to the Rada as well as to the Skoropadskyi government and the Directory. The leading Socialist-Federalists were A. Nikovskyi, S. Iefremov, V. Leontovych, D. Doroshenko, V. Prokopovych, and O. Shulhyn. They were influential figures within the Ukrainian national movement, men with polished manners and rather "civilized," moderate inclinations—perhaps too moderate to be useful in the political situation that developed in the Ukraine and elsewhere in Eastern Europe after the First World War.

The Ukrainian Party of Socialist-Independentists[36] was composed mainly of Ukrainian patriots who either had a military background or who were still in active service. Genetically this was a direct continuation of the Ukrainian People's Party, and it should not be confused with the Independentists, a left-wing faction of the Ukrainian Social-Democrats. The Socialist-Independentists were determined separatists, the only party that worked from the beginning for an independent, sovereign Ukrainian state. Mykola Mikhnovskyi exercised a decisive influence over this little group of fanatical nationalists, and his pamphlet, *Independent Ukraine,* became a kind of bible for the increasing number of nationalistic youth. In spite of its "socialist" label, the party had very few socialistic ideas in its program, being almost exclusively a petty-bourgeois nationalistic party. It placed its policy priorities on the formation of a strong patriotic Ukrainian army, the only effective instrument for the

---

[36] Doroshenko, Vol. I; Haidalemivskyi, *Ukrainski politychni partii.*

implementation of national sovereignty. The stubborn opposition of most Russian parties and the Provisional Government to Ukrainian national demands provided a favorable atmosphere for the Independentists. The Independentist political program almost totally neglected the social and agrarian issues, and its influence on the electorate was minimal. In addition to Mikhnovskyi, other active leaders were A. Makarenko, P. Andriievskyi, O. Stepanenko, and Ivan Lutsenko.

The Ukrainian Democratic-Agrarian Party[37] was perhaps the most conservative of all Ukrainian parties. It was founded in the summer of 1917 at Lubny, in connection with a congress of landowners in Poltava. In a sense, it adhered to the well-known thesis of Stolypin, who initiated a program to support strong, independent farmers and thus stabilize the countryside. Its program was written by the well-known historian Viacheslav Lypynskyi, whose ideal was a Ukraine dominated by the landed Cossack aristocracy. According to Lypynskyi, the Ukraine should be organized as an independent monarchy ruled by a Hetman. His and the Party's position regarding the minorities was determined by the latter's attitude toward Ukrainian independence: "Every alien that recognizes our right to full independence is our ally, even if he has a different view on other political questions."[38] The "separatist" position distinguished the Democratic-Agrarians from the Union of Landowners, which contributed much to the successful *coup d'état* that in April 1918 elevated General Skoropadskyi to the position of Hetman. Dmytro Dontsov, the brothers Shemet, and M. Boiarskyi were the most important party members.

The Ukrainian Federalist-Democratic Party was founded in December 1917 by the moderate Ukrainian intellectuals B. Berenkovych, V. Naumenko, I. Kviatkovskyi, Professor I. Luchytskyi, and others. It was another conservative party with a very cautious social program that sought to transform Russia into a federal state. The Federalist-Democrats played a minimal role in Ukrainian political life.

Several Russian political parties existed in the Ukraine during

---

[37] S. Shemet, "Do istorii Ukrainskoi Demokratychno-Khliborobskoi Partii," *Khliborobska Ukraina*, Vol. II (Vienna, 1920), pp. 56 ff; V. Andriievskyi, *Do kharakterystyky ukrainskykh pravykh partii* (Berlin: Hoffmann and Salzwedelie, 1921), pp. 13 ff.

[38] Shemet, p. 13.

the period under consideration. Indeed, there were fundamental differences in the motivations of the Russian and the non-Russian political organizations. The Russian elements did not have any national liberation goals; on the contrary, they represented political objectives that conflicted with those of the Ukrainian parties. Most important was their tendency to keep the Ukraine within the orbit of the Russian Empire. As central power disintegrated in Moscow, the Russian parties assumed a watchdog function and became the sole representatives of centripetal, integrative tendencies in the Ukraine. Regardless of ideological and social differences, the Russian parties that still functioned after the declaration of an independent Ukrainian state acted in unison in one particular issue— opposition to Ukrainian self-determination.

Beginning at the extreme left, the Communist Party of the Ukraine (CP(b)U) should be mentioned first. Treating this party with other Russian parties may raise some justifiable objections. There are indeed methodological difficulties in classification. If we consider this party from the structural and organizational point of view, we may well be justified in calling it Russian. The same can be said about its composition during the period under study. Yet, in spite of the seemingly positive attitude of the Bolsheviks, and Lenin in particular, toward the self-determination of nationalities, their position concerning national parties was strictly negative.

Lenin held that the proletariat of all nationalities in the Russian Empire should be organized into a single united party organization. The Bolsheviks not only rejected the independent existence of the nationality parties but even refused to recognize the autonomous existence of any nationality organization.[39] It is interesting to note that Lenin's animosity toward the prospect of independent existence for national parties was far more categorical *vis-à-vis* Ukrainian social democracy than, for instance, the Jewish *Bund;* he did not question the latter's existence but merely fought its demand for autonomy within the Russian party, a move that would have created a precedent for other national parties. Favoring a strictly centralized party, Lenin demanded the complete subordination of local organizations. This principle was reiterated in a resolution adopted by the Eighth Party Congress in March 1919: "At the present time, the Ukraine, Latvia, Lithuania and Belorussia exist as separate Soviet Republics... But this does not mean

---

[39] Lenin, Vol. XXXV, pp. 100–102.

that the Russian Communist Party ought, in its turn, to organize itself on the basis of a federation of independent Communist Parties." On the contrary, "*one* centralized Communist Party with one Central Committee guiding all the work of the Party in all parts of the RSFSR is imperative.... Central Committees of the Ukrainian, Latvian, and Lithuanian Communists have the rights of regional committees of the Party and are completely subordinated to the CC RCP."[40]

In accordance with the attitude of the Russian Bolshevik leadership, the social-democratic organizations of the Bolshevik faction did not, at the beginning, attempt to organize a separate party or a separate center for its organizations on Ukrainian territory. In spite of the fact that the first Soviet government in the Ukraine was set up in December 1917, the Communist Party of the Ukraine was officially created only in July 1918—i.e., only after the end of that regime, when most of its leaders went into exile in Moscow. Its relationship with the Russian center in Moscow caused a great deal of friction among the leaders of CP(b)U, which divided into two factions, the integralists and the independentists.

Apparently, the more nationalistic members of the Bolshevik faction in the Ukraine approached the idea of a separate organization soon after it became evident that this territory was achieving a kind of autonomous status within the Russian Empire. These attempts were hampered by two forces—the Bolsheviks in the Ukraine with centralistic tendencies, such as Evgeniia Bosh and Georgii Piatakov, and, naturally, the Russian Communist Party (RCP) in Moscow. On behalf of the Politburo, Sverdlov wrote: "*The creation of a separate, Ukrainian Party,* whatever it might be called, whatever program it might adopt, *is considered undesirable.*"[41] Soon, however, more positive voices were heard from Moscow, and in late December 1917 an independent social democratic organization "with the same rights as an independent region" was recognized.[42] The Communist Party of the Ukraine was created at a congress held in Moscow, in July 1918. It was independent in name though

---

[40] *Vosmoi sezd RKP (b)* (Moscow, 1919), p. 367.

[41] *Protokoly Tsentralnogo Komiteta RSDRP, august 1917–fevral 1918* (Moscow, 1929), p. 39.

[42] U. Riadnina, *Pershyi sezd KP(b)U* (Kiev: Derzhpolitvydav URSR, 1958), p. 136.

actually subordinate to Moscow, a status that reflected the position of the centralist elements in the CP(b)U (the so-called "Ekaterinoslavs"). It also reflected the general position of the RCP regarding the Ukraine, which considered it an integral part of Russia and the CP(b)U "part of a single Russian Communist Party." After stormy debates, the resolution presented by the "nationalist," Skrypnyk, demanding the creation of "a separate Communist Party (Bolshevik) of the Ukraine [to be] formally tied with the Russian Communist Party through the International Commission of the Third International," was rejected.[43]

In brief, the position of the two different factions of the CP(b)U regarding its status reflected the ethnic composition of the party. The Russian and russified elements were inclined toward a centralized party for all of Russia, while the Ukrainian elements defended the idea of an autonomous or independent existence. The creation of the CP(b)U was, however, the result of general political circumstances, and it was considered a kind of necessary compromise with growing Ukrainian nationalism. From the very beginning, the Russian Communist leadership adopted a negative position based on the decisions of the congresses and the rules of the party. Even after the creation of the CP(b)U, Moscow exercised close control of the Ukrainian organization, and special emissaries of the Central Committee were sent to every Congress of the CP(b)U in order to protect the interests of the center. Such a role was played by Kamenev at the Second Congress, Sverdlov at the Third, Stalin at the Fourth, and Zinoviev at the Fifth. In addition, the central offices of the CP(b)U were consistently occupied by faithful centralists, for the most part Russians. Thus, Piatakov, Kviring, Molotov, and later Kosior, Kaganovich, and Postyshev, all non-Ukrainians, held the position of the First Secretary of the Party. Even the Central Committee was predominantly non-Ukrainian.[44]

There are no reliable statistics on the ethnic composition of the CP(b)U for the early period. However, the figures from 1922 and 1926 are quite illustrative. The composition of the CP(b)U according to nationality was:[45]

---

[43] *Istoriia CP(b)U v materiialakh ta dokumentakh, 1917–1920 rr.* (2nd ed.; Kharkiv, 1934), pp. 29–30, n. 1, p. 356; Popov, p. 165.

[44] Borys, pp. 142–153.

[45] *Ibid.,* p. 155.

	1922	1926
Russians	53.6%	37.4%
Ukrainians	23.3	43.9
Jews	13.6	11.2
Others	9.5	7.5

Only after nine years of the existence of the Ukrainian Soviet Republic did the Ukrainian elements constitute the largest group in the party. Small wonder that Bukharin, at the Twelfth Party Congress (in 1925), admitted that "in the Ukraine ... the composition of the party is Russian-Jewish."

The figures published by Radkey and Lenin reveal the precarious position of the Bolsheviks. At the elections to the Kiev City Council on August 7, 1917, they received six seats out of a total of ninety-eight, and in the elections to the All-Russian Constituent Assembly held at the end of the year, they received only ten percent of the vote. With regard to party membership, the picture was even less encouraging. Bolshevik sources reveal that in Kiev their organization had by March 1917 about 200 members, and these chiefly craftsmen.[46] At the Sixth Congress of the Russian Boleshevik Party in August 1917, the Bolsheviks of the Ukraine represented about 23,000 members, while the Petrograd organization alone had 40,095 members.[47] There is much evidence of the weakness of the Bolsheviks in the Ukraine during the struggle against the Rada and later during the Directory.

The Party's final success must be attributed to the external conditions in Eastern Europe, the general disintegration of anti-Bolshevik forces, and the indecisiveness of the Western powers, conditions in which such organizational geniuses as Lenin and Trotsky most certainly prospered. Had it not been for the Russian military intervention in the Ukraine, the local Bolsheviks would have had to wait for better times. However, they constituted a compact, determined organization and a considerable propagandist instrument in the struggle against the idea of an independent Ukrainian state. This movement, assisted by the gigantic force concentrated in Soviet Russia, succeeded in neutralizing, for the time being, the nationalistic aspirations of the Ukrainian people.

---

[46] Ravich-Cherkasskii, p. 43.

[47] *Shestoi sezd RSDRP(b): august, 1917 g.* (Moscow, 1934), pp. 194–195.

The Russian Party of Socialist-Revolutionaries (SR's)[48] ideologically resembled its Ukrainian counterpart and in most cases was identical to the SR's in Russia proper. It was separated from the mother organization merely by political or administrative borders. The relationship between the Russian and the Ukrainian SR's was not clarified until the Provisional Government made its first concessions on the Ukrainian question, accepting *de facto* the autonomous government of the Rada. Subsequently, the minority parties accepted the idea of participating in the autonomous Ukrainian government. The minorities (Russian, Jewish, and Polish) asked for forty percent of the seats in the provisional representative council (the Rada), but they were alloted only thirty percent. The Russian SR's received four seats in the *Mala Rada,* and one of its leaders, A. Zarubin, was appointed Minister for Post and Telegraph. After the declaration of the independence of the Ukrainian Republic on January 25, 1918, Zarubin resigned. The SR's supported the idea of an autonomous Ukraine within the Russian federation, but they were negatively disposed toward the idea of an independent Ukraine. In the competition against their Ukrainian counterparts the Russian SR's lost most of their influence among the electorate during the elections to the All-Russian Constituent Assembly. The party disappeared from the Ukrainian political scene at the end of 1919, partly because members emigrated to Russia or abroad, and partly because of transfers to the Russian Communist Party. The most prominent leaders among the Russian SR's were A. M. Zarubin, Sklovskii, Sukhovykh, and Zaluzhnyi.[49]

The Russian Social Democratic Party (Mensheviks)[50] formed the Ukrainian section of the all-Russian Menshevik Party, competing on the one side against the Russian Bolsheviks and on the other against the Ukrainian Social Democrats. During the first period of liberalism in Russia after the March Revolution, the Mensheviks predominated among the industrial workers and radical intelligentsia. In the elections of 1917 the Party obtained an insignificant number of votes, 2.5 percent in the whole of Russia and less than

---

[48] O. H. Radkey, *The Agrarian Foes of Bolshevism* (New York: Columbia University Press, 1958), pp. 269–270; Doroshenko, Vol. I, p. 120; Popov, pp. 142 ff.

[49] Borys, p. 95.

[50] Khrystiuk, Vol. I, pp. 145 ff. and Vol. II, p. 18; Doroshenko, Vol. I, pp. 120 ff.

one percent in the Ukraine. By the end of 1918 many of their supporters had joined the Bolshevik Party. The Menshevik attitude toward Ukrainian national aspirations resembled that of the *Bund*. Without much enthusiasm, they accepted the autonomous status of the Ukraine, but they voted against the Fourth Universal. They participated in the Rada government with the prime intention of averting the tendency toward separation of the Ukraine from Russia. A joint resolution of the Mensheviks and the *Bund* ridiculed the idea of a separate Ukrainian state, which "assists the plans of the Austro-German imperialists..., the independence of the Ukraine... means victory not for the revolution, but for imperialism, and is bound to weaken Russia and international democracy..." They voted against the Universal in order to "show the international proletariat its loyalty to the proletarian ideal."[51] One could hardly expect a more absurd motivation than the one provided in this resolution. Balabanov and Kononenko were among the foremost leaders of the Mensheviks in the Ukraine.

The Russian People's Socialists,[52] together with its left wing, the *trudoviki,* represented petty-bourgeois groups that leaned toward a liberal democratic ideology. In many cases they cooperated with the Ukrainian Party of Socialist-Federalists and other bourgeois groups. With regard to Ukrainian national demands, this party was favorably inclined; it did not call for the creation of a fully sovereign, independent state, but rather envisioned a federalist Russia. It was one of the marginal political organizations with very little influence and hardly any power. In the elections of 1917 it was unable to elect a single representative from the Ukraine and it elected only four from the whole of Russia. Its leaders, A. S. Zarudnyi and Arnold Margolin, played a significant role in bringing Ukrainian and minority interests together.

The Russian Constitutional Democrats,[53] widely known as the Kadets, did not differ ideologically or socially from the All-Russian Party led by Miliukov. This rather conservative liberal party, which

---

[51] Borys, p. 120. See also S. Goldelman, *Lysty zhydivskoho sotsial-demokrata pro Ukrainu* (Vienna: Zhydivs'ke vyd. Hamoin, 1921), pp. 3–4.

[52] A. Margolin, *Ukraina i politika Antanty: zapiski ievreia i grazhdanina* (Berlin, 1922), pp. 40 ff.

[53] P. Miliukov, *Istoriia vtoroi russkoi revoliutsii*, Vol. I (Sofia: Rossiisko-Bolgarskoe knigoizd., 1921) and his *Rossiia na perelome*, Vol. II (Paris, 1927); Khrystiuk, Vol. III, pp. 26 ff.

defended human rights and fought for constitutional rule in Russia, categorically denied the demands for Ukrainian national self-determination, going so far as to reject autonomy even within the Russian federation. Instead, it recommended a kind of local autonomy with some concessions in cultural matters. In this respect, the Ukrainian branch of the Kadets resembled the Party's metropolitan leadership. It should be remembered that the Kadets caused a major crisis in Moscow, in July 1917, when they withdrew their ministers from the coalition in protest against the Provisional Government's recognition of the Ukrainian General Secretariat as the *de facto* government of the Ukraine. During the elections of 1917 the Kadets collected 2.4 percent of the votes in the Ukraine, which roughly corresponded to its strength on the all-Russian scale. The following year some Kadets participated in Hetman Skoropadskyi's government. The leading Kadets in the Ukraine were Krupnov, Steingel, Vasylenko, Rzhepetskyi, and Hutnyk.

The Russian Monarchists in the Ukraine[54] often appeared under the designation "The Bloc of the Non-Partisan Russians," representing extreme Russian chauvinism and reaction. They flocked around the well-known newspaper, *Kievlianin,* which was published by the Russian nationalist and Ukrainophobe, Vasilii Shulgin. This political group was highly inimical to the idea of a Ukrainian state, opposing even moderate demands for cultural autonomy. They even refused to recognize the existence of a Ukrainian nationality, maintaining that there existed only one Russian nation from the Carpathian Mountains to Vladivostok. For example, in the November 17, 1911 issue of *Kievlianin,* Savenko wrote that "the Polish, Armenian, Finnish and other problems are peripheral, i.e., secondary. The Mazepist [the Ukrainian separatist] problem injures Russia at the foundation of its existence as a great power. Poland, Finland and other borderlands did not give Russia its greatness." Consequently, the monarchists and reactionary Russian nationalists did everything to obstruct the realization of Ukrainian national emancipation. During the Skoropadskyi regime they attempted to turn the Ukraine into a base for restoring the unity of the Russian Empire, and during the Civil War they supported such reactionary military leaders as Denikin, Vrangel, and Iudenich.

Besides the above-mentioned local groups, there were a number

---

[54] A. Denikin, *Ocherki russkoi smuty,* Vol. I (Berlin, 1924–25), pp. 179 ff.

of reactionary groups organized by Russian immigrants in the Ukraine after the Bolshevik seizure of power in Russia. Their common interest was to fight against the Bolshevik regime and to restore a one and indivisible Russia. Among the most important should be mentioned the Conference of the Members of the Legislative Chamber, a pro-German monarchist group headed by Baron von Muller-Zakomelskii, V. Gurko, and Krzhizhanovskii. Even the Kadet Professor Pavel Miliukov participated for a time in this organization. The group was later reorganized and renamed the Council of State Union (*Soviet Gosudarstvennogo Obedineniia*) and included men like Krivoshein and Tretiakov. The struggle against Ukrainian independence was one of its political priorities.

At the same time, the Kiev National Center was organized, whose aim was to unite the "representatives of all non-Socialist parties, except for the extreme right, as well as representatives of all citizens' groups and organizations under a slogan [stressing] 'the need to reinstate one, indivisible Russia, fight against Bolshevism, fight against Germany, and keep faith with the Entente'." The foremost duty of the National Center was to "fight against Ukrainian independence," since the Ukrainians were not a nation but rather "a political party organized by Austria and Germany." The major personalities in this group were M. Fedorov, Volkov, Salazkin, Shulgin, and Professor Novgorodtsev.[55]

If the existence of Russian political parties in the Ukraine can be considered unique, the existence of Jewish and Polish political organizations was typical for ethnically diverse countries that recognized personal nationality autonomy. The theory, which was advocated by the Austrian socialists Otto Bauer and Karl Renner, proposed cultural autonomy not only for nationalities occupying a distinct territory but even for those scattered through the country. In order to guarantee this right, special institutions had to be created. Even political parties, including social-democratic ones, should be organized according to nationality principles. The Ukrainian Republic can be considered the first state in modern times to have implemented these principles, admitting the representatives of the minority parties to its parliament, the Rada, as well as to its government, the General Secretariat.

The Jewish political community took advantage of the situation and missed no opportunity to have its voice heard and its influence

---

[55] Borys, pp. 96–97.

felt. There was a slight tactical difference between the Jewish parties in the Ukraine and those in other parts of Russia. The dilemma faced by Jewish parties was twofold: on the one hand, they were heavily involved in the struggle for the emancipation of their fellowmen from national, religious, and social suppression; on the other hand, they opposed in principle the idea of the disintegration of the Empire and the creation of a number of independent national states. In this sense, they seem to have contradicted their own political purpose. The Jews were unique in that they did not inhabit any specific territory. Hence, they had no desire to have any particular lands separated from the rest of the Empire. On the whole, the Jews in the Ukraine, as in the other borderlands, sided with the dominant nation, first with the Poles and then with the Russians, and, tending to consider themselves superior to the surrounding peasants, they "continued to speak their German dialect . . . or adopting the superior, dominant culture of ruling Great-Russia."[56] Bertram Wolfe concludes that "almost unconsciously, most of the Jews of the cities of Poland, Lithuania and the Ukraine tended to become opponents of the national separation movements that arose during the break-up of the empire in 1917."[57]

In principle, Jewish political parties sought a solution to the nationality problem within the framework of a general liberal democratic system that would guarantee the greatest personal and group freedom in economic, cultural, and religious activity. Even an extreme Jewish nationalist organization like the Zionists did not aspire to more than the right of the Jews to preserve their national traditions. Thus, it was not the principle of national self-determination that they professed, but rather general humanitarian emancipation and the establishment of individual freedoms and social justice. This tendency can partly provide an explanation for the fact that only a small segment of the Jewish political community organized in their own national parties. In most cases, Jewish elements were found in all parties, but especially in radical ones like the Menshevik and the Bolshevik factions of the Russian Social-Democratic Party.

The General Jewish Workers' League, the *Bund*, was originally organized to represent the Jewish radical intelligentsia, artisans,

---

[56] B. Wolfe, *Three Who Made a Revolution* (New York: Dial Press, 1948), p. 183.

[57] *Ibid.*

and semi-proletariat in the territories of Lithuania, Poland, and Russia. The *Bund* was the first social-democratic organization on Russian soil with a definite program and organization. It had a great impact not only on the Jewish community in Eastern Europe, but also on the Russian social-democratic movement as a whole.[58] At the time of the February Revolution, the Ukrainian branch of the *Bund* had 175 local organizations. The Ukrainian section was subordinated to the all-Russian *Bund,* which in turn was closely allied to the Russian Social Democratic Party, the Mensheviks. In the Ukraine, the *Bund* fought for the national autonomy of the Jews and, consequently, supported Ukrainian demands for autonomy. On the other hand, it strongly opposed the creation of an independent Ukrainian state.[59] However, it was the only minority party that, during the entire period, cooperated with the Ukrainian parties and took an active part in the Rada government.

As Ukrainian nationalism gained in strength and anti-Semitic outbreaks took place, the *Bund* showed strong pro-Communist leanings, a sign of drastic political wavering. There soon appeared an inner conflict within the *Bund* leadership, leading to a split, from which three factions emerged: a right wing, led by Liber; a center, headed by Rafes; and a left wing, under Heifez. The Heifez group joined the Russian Communist Party, and shortly thereafter the center followed in its footsteps. In May 1918 the *Bund,* together with the United Jewish Socialist Party, formed a Jewish Communist Union, which soon joined the Russian Communist Party.[60]

The Jewish People's Party[61] was a petty-bourgeois group without the slightest trace of the socialism that was so popular at the time. It had no great influence and drew its support mainly from Jewish intellectuals and professionals.

The United Jewish Socialist Party[62] belonged to the bloc of

---

[58] S. Schwarz, *The Jews in the Soviet Union* (Syracuse, N.Y.: Syracuse University Press, 1951), p. 49.

[59] The representative of the *Bund* and three Mensheviks were the only votes put against the Fourth Universal. Borys, p. 120.

[60] *Ibid.,* pp. 97–98; M. Rafes, *Natsionalnye voprosy* (Moscow, 1921) and his *Dva goda revoliutsii na Ukraine: evoliutsiia i raskol Bunda* (Moscow: Gos. izd.; 1920), pp. 74 ff.

[61] Rafes, *Dva goda,* pp. 9 ff.

[62] *Ibid.,* pp. 10 ff.; Doroshenko, Vol. I, p. 120.

Socialist-Revolutionaries, but it soon came into conflict with the Russian SR's, basically because of the great emphasis that the Jewish section placed on the nationality question. That circumstance, however, drew this party closer to the Ukrainian SR's. The Jewish SR's supported the Ukrainian demand for autonomy and participated in the Rada. After a split in 1918, its left wing, together with the *Bund,* formed the above-mentioned Jewish Communist Union. The Jewish SR's were led by M. Litvakov, Gutman, Dubinskii, Silberfarb, Sehaz-Anin, Chugrin, and others.

The Jewish Social Democratic Workers Party *(Paolei-Zion)*[63] stood farthest to the right of all the socialist groups. It did not have a great number of adherents, since the radical Jewish elements as a rule joined the *Bund* or the Mensheviks; and, though it was close to the Ukrainian Social Democratic Party, it did not favor Ukrainian independence or separation from Russia. Like other political parties, the *Paolei-Zion* split during the Civil War, whereupon its left wing formed a new organization called the Social Democratic Party, *Paolei-Zion.* The party's leading figures included Goldelman, Menchkovskii, and Revutskii.

The Zionist Party[64] in the Ukraine was perhaps the most conservative and nationalistic of all Jewish parties, and it devoted much energy to promoting the idea of a separate autonomous Jewish unit. Therefore, it understood, more than any other minority party, Ukrainian political aspirations, and, because of its position on the national question, it could cooperate with the Rada. The Zionists energetically propagated the use of Hebrew and the preservation of orthodox Judaism. The leading figures in the Ukraine were Zangwil, Mandelstam, Paperin, Sirkin, and Sheltman.

The Polish minority resembled, in a sense, the Russians, except that their continued imperialist ambitions deprived them of a sense of reality. This was especially evident among the more conservative elements of the landowning class, which had difficulty accepting the idea that the *chłopy,* or lower class peasants as they customarily called the Ukrainian peasants, could raise themselves to the level of an independent nation equal to the Polish one. More moderate Polish elements approached the problem realistically, considering Ukrainians a natural ally against Russian imperialism,

---

[63] Rafes, *Dva goda,* pp. 10 ff.; Doroshenko, Vol. I, p. 120.
[64] Margolin, pp. 44 ff.; Khrystiuk, Vol. II, pp. 143 ff.

and, in most cases, cooperating with the Ukrainian national movement. There were only two significant political parties in the Ukraine that represented Poles.

The Polish Socialist Party (PPS-center)[65] was the Polish equivalent of the Russian Mensheviks or the Ukrainian Social Democrats. On the nationality issue, it was similar to those Ukrainian socialists who supported the declaration of an independent Ukrainian Republic. During the Piłsudski-Petliura alliance against Soviet Russia, the party was closely associated with the Ukrainian Social Democrats. Its leaders were K. Domosławski, W. Korsar, and I. Libkind. In 1919, the latter formed a pro-Bolshevik wing.

The Polish Socialist Party (PPS-left)[66] stood close to the Russian Social Democratic Party, differing from it only on the nationality question. The PPS-left agitated for an independent Polish Republic and, consequently, supported the Ukrainian demand for independence. However, when the Bolsheviks entered the Ukraine in early 1918, the majority of its leaders went over to their camp. Among its most prominent leaders were Witold Matuszewski and Bolesław Iwinski.

The Polish Democratic Center Party[67] represented Polish landowners in the Ukrainian countryside and inevitably was opposed to the more radical agrarian policy of the Rada. The party avidly promoted the idea of an independent Poland, but was indecisive with regard to Ukrainian self-determination. When the Third Universal was adopted, the Polish representative in the Rada, W. Rudnicki, declared that its political content was implicitly directed against the interests of the Polish minority. On the other hand, he expressed joy that "the Ukrainians were entering the European community of nations." Besides Rudnicki, who served as Under Secretary for Polish Affairs in the Rada cabinet, the party leadership included M. Mickiewicz, S. Stempkowski, R. Knoll, I. Ursin-Zamaraev, and M. Baraniecki.

The Polish Executive Committee[68] was a conservative Polish organization that provided moral and material support for the liberation movement in Poland and that pretended to be a non-

---

[65] H. Jabłoński, *Polska autonomia narodowa na Ukrainie, 1917–1918* (Warsaw: Towarzystwo miłośników historii, 1948), pp. 25 ff.

[66] *Ibid.*

[67] *Ibid.*

[68] *Ibid.;* Doroshenko, Vol. I.

partisan organ for all Poles residing in the Ukraine. These preten-
sions were energetically challenged by other Polish political parties.
The Committee was favorably disposed toward the idea of an independent Ukrainian state. Its president was Joachim Bartoszew-
icz, and among other leaders were M. Baraniecki and Zygmund
Chojecki.

Political parties in the Ukraine reflected the complexity of social
and ethnic problems and the diversity of their political orientation.
The four major nationalities (Ukrainians, Russians, Poles, and
Jews) organized their own national political groups. The pre-emi-
nence of the national idea and the consequent fragmentation of
political life was reflected even in the working class, which, con-
tradicting Marx's thesis about class solidarity, formed political
parties according to nationality divisions. Thus, in the Ukraine
there were Ukrainian, Russian, Polish, and Jewish social-democratic parties.

However, the major distinction between the Ukrainian and
minority parties was in their attitude toward self-determination.
Whereas the Ukrainian parties emphasized national liberation as
the first step toward the solution of other problems, the minority
parties were decidedly more cautious. The Russian parties, being
merely remnants of the national Russian parties before the *de
facto* separation of the Ukraine, became the principal custodians
of Russian imperial interests and strove to prevent Ukrainian self-
determination. The Polish political parties recognized in principle
the demand for an independent Ukrainian state; however, in matters concerning Ukrainian-Polish borders they adhered to the traditional Polish position. Almost all Jewish political parties and
some of the Russian socialist parties (Mensheviks, SR's and *trudoviki*) agreed to the demand for Ukrainian autonomy with a
federal Russian Empire, but categorically rejected the idea of
Ukrainian independence. On the other hand, the bourgeois and
reactionary Russian parties adopted a firm, integralist position,
considering the Ukrainian liberation movement as a German in-
vention.

The Russian Bolsheviks in Moscow and their agent, the CP(b)U,
were very ambiguous; they recognized the "abstract right of the
Ukrainian people to self-determination," but they still considered
it the duty of the Russian state to neutralize this right. The creation
of the Soviet Ukrainian state, headed by Rakovskii's puppet gov-

ernment, reflected this political line. The intense struggle of the Ukrainian political parties, the national liberation government, and the army, and the continuing activity of the Ukrainian leftist parties, the *Ukapists,* and the *Borotbists* after the defeat of the Directory, all contributed immensely to the Bolsheviks' recognition of Ukrainian pseudo-nationhood.

CHAPTER SEVEN

The Communist Party of the Ukraine and Its Role in the Ukrainian Revolution

John S. Reshetar, Jr.

THE UKRAINIAN REVOLUTION burst forth so unexpectedly in 1917 that it caught the future leaders of the Communist Party of the Ukraine completely unprepared. Indeed, in that year there was no such party, but only a collection of unrelated local organizations in the more important cities of the eastern Ukraine which were associated with Lenin's All-Russian Social Democratic Labor Party. A Communist Party of the Ukraine did not emerge until 1918 and then only in a semi-Ukrainian form with very little Ukrainian content. This state of affairs was the result of a particular development experienced by Marxist organizations in that part of the Ukraine located within the Russian Empire.

Socialist organizations began to appear in the Ukraine in the 1890's, and the first such group, more intellectual than political in nature, included such prominent figures as Lesia Ukrainka and Mykhailo Kotsiubynskyi. At the founding congress of the All-Russian Social Democratic Labor Party, which met in Minsk in 1898, three of the five organizations represented were functioning in Kiev and Katerynoslav, but they were not related to the Ukrainian national movement. As a consequence, a distinctly Ukrainian Socialist Party emerged in 1900 under the leadership of a group of Ukrainians who had ceased identifying with Polish culture. Because of tsarist Russian censorship, this party had to publish its organ, *Dobra novyna,* in Lviv; it advocated an independent Ukrainian Republic and a social revolution.

Probably the most active and promising Ukrainian political organization prior to 1905 was the Revolutionary Ukrainian Party

(RUP), founded in 1900 by students at Kharkiv. Its activities helped promote peasant unrest and strikes in 1902; its work was conducted in the Ukrainian language, in contrast to other parties, who used Russian. However, the RUP suffered from the dilemma of attempting to fuse the national and social revolutions at a time when socialists were frequently ignoring nationality matters and were naively predicting the elimination of national differences in the interests of class solidarity. In January 1905 a division occurred within the RUP when a minority splinter group led by Mariian Melenevskyi and Oleksander Skoropys-Ioltukhovskyi seceded to form the so-called *Spilka,* a Ukrainian branch of the All-Russian (*Rossiiskaia*) Social Democratic Labor Party (RSDLP).

The *Spilka* professed a proletarian orientation and claimed that the RUP's advocacy of Ukrainian national independence would weaken the socialist cause. The splinter group joined the All-Russian Social Democratic Labor Party (RSDLP) without obtaining any significant concessions regarding its status, although it did retain a separate identity as the "Ukrainian *Spilka.*" However, the *Spilka's* position became untenable because it was not permitted to become the RSDLP's sole organization functioning on Ukrainian territory. Russian Marxists living in the Ukraine usually retained their own urban party organizations, because the *Spilka* was regarded primarily as a means of attracting Ukrainian peasant support. Jewish Marxists tended to affiliate with the Jewish Social Democratic *Bund.* Thus the *Spilka* was not able to obtain for itself the recognition within the RSDLP that would have assured its future growth, although it did succeed in electing fourteen deputies to the ill-fated Second State Duma in 1907. The repressive policies of the tsarist government during the period of reaction beginning in 1907 and the lack of support within the RSDLP doomed the *Spilka.* Nor could the *Spilka* compete effectively with the RUP, which in December 1905 had renamed itself the Ukrainian Social Democratic Labor Party.[1]

The *Spilka* had no future in Lenin's Bolshevik scheme of party organization, which denied the right of national units—apart from

---

[1] For a brief survey of the early development of Ukrainian socialist groups and parties, see Panas Fedenko, *Ukrainskyi rukh u 20-omu stolitti* (London: 'Nashe Slovo,' 1959), pp. 18–64, 68–73. Data on the RUP, the *Spilka,* and the USDLP can be found in M. Ravich-Cherkasskii (ed.), *Revoliutsiia i KP(b)U v materialakh i dokumentakh (khrestomatiia),* Vol. I (Kharkiv: 'Proletarii,' 1926), pp. 301–322, 508–538.

that of the Russians—to function within the RSDLP. By 1909, a group of Russian and Jewish Mensheviks attempted to utilize what remained of the *Spilka*. As the latter was Ukrainian in name only, it could not obtain support from Ukrainians whom it was supposed to attract. By 1914 it had expired, and, ironically, two of the *Spilka*'s founders, Melenevskyi and Skoropys-Ioltukhovskyi, soon joined the Union for the Liberation of the Ukraine, which functioned in Vienna during the First World War and strove to help bring down Imperial Russia and establish Ukrainian national independence.

Nationally conscious Ukrainian socialists were attracted to the Ukrainian Social Democratic Labor Party (USDLP), which had several thousand members in 1907. Despite the oppressive conditions imposed by the Russian regime after 1907, the USDLP continued to publish materials, particularly in Lviv, which was under Austrian rule. The activities of the USDLP were very disturbing to Lenin, who feared that nationally conscious Ukrainian industrial workers would not be attracted to the RSDLP and to his Bolshevik faction.[2] Lenin was especially annoyed by the writings of the USDLP leader and Central Committee member, Lev Iurkevych, who wrote under the pen name L. Rybalka, and by those of other Ukrainian socialists that appeared in the Kiev monthly, *Dzvin*, published by Iurkevych, Volodymyr Vynnychenko, and Iu. Tyshchenko.

Lenin attacked Iurkevych repeatedly in his *Critical Notes on the Nationality Question,* written in the autumn of 1913. This work is important because it reflects Lenin's arrogance and his condescending attitude toward the Ukrainians. After denouncing Iurkevych as a "Ukrainian national-socialist," Lenin issued the following revealing dictum: "With the single action (*pri edinom deistvii*) of the Great Russian and Ukrainian proletarians a free Ukraine *is possible;* without such unity there cannot even be any talk of it."[3] He also introduced the invidious concept of "bourgeois national-

---

[2] The lack of Ukrainian support for Lenin's *Iskra* is evident in the remarkable absence of Ukrainian family names among the newspaper's agents and collaborators in the Ukraine. See S. O. Ktytarev, *Leninska "Iskra" i pidnesennia revoliutsiinoho rukhu na Ukraini* (Kiev: Vyd. Akademii Nauk URSR, 1959). The chief *Iskra* agent in the Ukraine was Fridrikh Vilgelmovich Lengnik. The non-Ukrainian nature of Bolshevism is confirmed in I. D. Remezovskii, *Revoliutsionnaia i obshchestvenno-politicheskaia deiatelnost Ulianovykh na Ukraine* (Kiev: Izd. Kievskogo universiteta, 1963).

[3] V. I. Lenin, *Polnoe sobranie sochinenii*, Vol. XXIV (5th ed.; Moscow: Gospolitizdat, 1961), p. 128, italics in original.

ism" and applied it to socialists who defended their right of national self-determination against those who would violate this right
in the name of "the proletariat." Lenin warned: "If the Ukrainian
Marxist permits himself to be carried away by the *fully legitimate
and natural* hatred for Great-Russian oppressors to the *point* that
he transfers even a minute part *(chastichku)* of the hatred, even if
only [in the form of] alienation, to the proletarian culture and the
proletarian cause of the Great Russian workers, then that Marxist,
in so doing, slides into the morass of bourgeois nationalism."[4]

Iurkevych offered a powerful (but since neglected) rejoinder,
which was published in Geneva in 1917. He dared to call Lenin's
views on the nationality question hypocritical, for the Bolshevik
leader had granted a right and then denounced its use in practice;
and, in so doing, he was actually advocating the unity of the Russian Empire. Iurkevych noted that Russian revolutionaries operating in the Ukraine never condemned the national oppression of
Ukrainians by Russians and actually encouraged it through their
assimilatory practices and by their opposition to "separatism" and
"chauvinism."[5] He stated that Lenin, in practice, advocated the
fusion of nations, because he did not recognize the right of self-
determination in party organization and insisted that the members
of an oppressed nation accept their "voluntary" attachment to the
oppressing nation. Iurkevych asserted that Lenin was not advo-

---

[4] *Ibid.,* p. 130, italics in original. On April 26, 1914, Lenin is said to
have added a terse one-sentence postscript to a letter sent by Zinoviev
from Cracow to the editors of *Dzvin* in which he indicated that he was
"profoundly indignant" *(vozmushchen gluboko)* over the advocacy of a
separate Ukrainian Social Democratic organization. *Ibid.,* Vol. XLVIII, p.
283 and p. 411, n. 318. In the fourth edition of Lenin's *Works*—in contrast
to the fifth edition cited here—the sentence is represented simply as a
statement sent by Lenin to the journal; presumably this is to be explained
by the fact that in 1950 Zinoviev was a total "unperson," and it was
necessary to distort the text. In the fourth edition the sentence is said
to have been written in March 1914. See V. I. Lenin, *Sochineniia,* Vol.
XXXV (4th ed.; Moscow: Gospolitizdat, 1950), p. 99.

[5] The work by Lev Iurkevych [L. Rybalka], *Russkie sotsial-demokraty
i natsionalnyi vopros* (Geneva, 1917) is discussed in Ivan Maistrenko,
Storinky z istorii Komunistychnoi Partii Ukrainy, Pt. 1 (New York: Prolog,
1967), pp. 12–24, 28, 32. Also see the discussion in Jurij Borys, *The
Russian Communist Party and the Sovietization of Ukraine* (Stockholm,
1960), pp. 86–90.

cating internationalism, but great power centralism and assimila-
tionism, which he had adopted for purposes of his own brand of
socialism.

Viewed in the perspective of subsequent developments, Lenin's
dichotomy between a progressive proletarian culture and reactionary bourgeois national oppression proved to be specious. Lenin assumed, incorrectly, that the behavior and cultural traits of the
oppressing nationality would somehow miraculously change or be
abandoned with the proclamation of the "dictatorship of the proletariat." He assumed naively (or dishonestly, for purposes of organizational unity) that the Russian "proletariat" was incapable of
oppressing other nationalities and of employing discriminatory
practices. Lenin's "theory" also broke down when he denied *in practice* the existence of a progressive national culture among the
"proletarians" of the non-Russian nationalities while claiming this
for the Russians. If "proletarian" culture *per se* were "progressive,"
then Lenin should not have denounced the efforts of non-Russians
to establish their own socialist party organizations.

Not many Ukrainian socialists accepted Lenin's sophistic reasoning, which would have doomed the cause of Ukrainian national
liberation in the name of the organizational unity of socialism.
Consequently, there were very few Ukrainian Old Bolsheviks, and
they were often immersed in non-Ukrainian affairs. Thus, Mykola
Skrypnyk, who joined the RSDLP in 1891 and who was to play an
unparalleled role in Ukrainian Communism, was fulfilling Bolshevik Party assignments in such cities as Petrograd, Tsaritsyn, Samara,
Riga, and Iaroslavl. In 1917, he was a delegate to the Sixth Congress
of the RSDLP from the Petrograd organization. Only in 1903–1905
—and after 1917—was Skrypnyk active in the Ukraine. One of the
few Ukrainian Bolsheviks who defended Ukrainian interests prior to
1917 was Hryhorii Petrovskyi, an industrial worker who joined the
Social Democratic movement in 1897. Petrovskyi was elected to the
Fourth Duma in 1912 from the workers' *curia* in the Katerynoslav
Province; he used his position to denounce the tsarist government's
oppression of the Ukrainian nation in a Duma speech calculatingly
inspired by Lenin and delivered on May 20 (June 2), 1913. Yet
Petrovskyi also carried out numerous assignments for the Party that
in no way furthered the Ukrainian cause.

Bolshevik Party membership in the Ukraine in 1917 was mostly
non-Ukrainian—consisting primarily of Russians and Jews—and
was either hostile or indifferent to the Ukrainian national move-

ment. It blithely ignored Lenin's tactical advice in 1917 to utilize national grievances against the Provisional Government in Petrograd. The Bolsheviks in the Ukraine made no effort to publish in the Ukrainian language and confined their appeal largely to the cities and to the military units in which Russians tended to predominate. In the smaller cities, the opportunities for Bolshevik agitators were very limited. For example, an account of Party activities in Zhytomyr, conducted by one Borisov, indicates that "the Bolshevik press hardly ever got to Zhytomyr; there were no Bolsheviks (party members), and the workers, scattered throughout small enterprises, were unorganized..."[6] Borisov states that he arrived in Zhytomyr in May 1917 and agitated alone for some time until he managed to convert one Menshevik to Bolshevism; by July, he claimed to have recruited twenty-five members, largely from among workers and soldiers. He ignored the numerous Ukrainian peasantry, and when the Zhytomyr garrison was "Ukrainianized," the local Bolsheviks had no military force at their disposal. Pitifully small, their sole salvation was to rely on external support.[7]

The Kiev "Social Democratic [Bolshevik] organization" is reported to have had only 200 members in March 1917, and these were mostly young people.[8] The non-Ukrainian nature of the Kiev Bolshevik organization was evident in the membership of the city committee elected at a conference held in May 1917.[9] Of the fifteen members, only one, Volodymyr Zatonskyi, was an ethnic Ukrainian. The Kiev Bolsheviks were so weak that they were unable to collect

---

[6] Borisov, "Ocherki revoliutsii na Volyni," *Letopis revoliutsii,* No. 3 [8] (Kharkiv, 1924), p. 50.

[7] *Ibid.,* pp. 60–61. For evidence regarding the weakness of the Bolsheviks among Ukrainians in the Vinnytsia party organization, see I. Miller (Birshtein), "Iz istorii Vinnitskoi organizatsii bolshevikov (1917 god)," *ibid.,* Nos. 3–4 [18–19] (1926), pp. 91–105. In February 1917, the Chernihiv Bolshevik organization had no more than fifty or sixty members. See Iu. Kotsiubynskyi "Chernigovskaia organizatsiia bolshevikov vo vremia voiny," *ibid.,* No. 2 [23] (1927), p. 185.

[8] I. Tu. Kulik, "Kievskaia organizatsiia ot fevralia do oktiabria 1917 goda," *ibid.,* No. 1 (1924), p. 189.

[9] *Ibid.,* p. 191. The committee consisted of: G. Piatakov, A. Horvits, M. Zarnitsyn, E. Bosh, I. Kreisberg, R. Farbman, V. Zatonskyi, M. Kugel, Liber, Nusbaum, V. Primakov, Loginov (Pavel), S. Shreiber, M. Reut, and Dovnar-Zapolskii.

sufficient funds to obtain a printing press for the publication of their newspaper, *Golos sotsial-demokrata*.[10] In the Kiev municipal elections, the Bolsheviks (listed as "revolutionary social democratic internationalists") received only 9,000 votes (five percent).[11]

The Kiev Bolshevik organization generally ignored the question of nationality and complacently assumed that elimination of "class oppression" would end national oppression and make the nation an "anachronism." Individual Bolsheviks were permitted to discuss the nationality question, but only as individuals and not on behalf of the Party. However, the presence of the Rada in Kiev continued to remind local Bolsheviks of the appeal of Ukrainian nationalism. They could no longer ignore this Ukrainian representative institution because its popularity was growing rapidly, especially after it had demonstrated that it could make demands of the Petrograd Provisional Government in the name of Ukrainian rights.

The Bolsheviks accepted ten seats in the Rada (which had a membership of more than 800), and, though they participated in that body from July until November 1917, they played a passive role. For a very brief period they also participated in the *Mala Rada,* a large committee that served as an interim legislative body. The Bolsheviks had little choice but to make common cause with the Rada in its demands against the Provisional Government. They protested the ineffective efforts of Kerensky and of the Russian Mensheviks in Kiev to prevent the convocation of the Second All-Ukrainian Military Congress in June. While opposing collaboration with the "national bourgeoisie" of any nation, the Kiev Bolsheviks paid lip service to the principles of full equality for nations and languages and "broad territorial autonomy" for the Ukraine.[12]

The seizure of power by Lenin's Bolsheviks in Petrograd on November 7, 1917, and the end of the Provisional Government brought the Kiev Bolsheviks and the Rada to a turning point in their relationship. However, it was still necessary to defeat the military units in the Kiev area and the Staff of the Kiev Military District, which was attempting to defend Kerensky's defunct regime. The Rada established a Committee for the Defense of the Revolution in the Ukraine, which the Kiev Bolsheviks, Leonid Piatakov

---

[10] *Ibid.,* p. 194. The editors of *Golos sotsial-demokrata* were N. N. Lebedev, R. V. Galperin, and M. Zarnitsyn.

[11] *Ibid.,* p. 201.

[12] *Ibid.,* pp. 198–199.

(already a member of the Rada), Volodymyr Zatonskyi, and Isaak Kreisberg, joined.[13] The Russian Socialist-Revolutionaries, the Kadets, and the Mensheviks who had seats in the Kiev city council supported the non-existent Provisional Government. When the Russian Military Staff arrested a number of Kiev Bolsheviks, representatives of the Rada succeeded in obtaining their release. Fighting in Kiev broke out and ended with victory for the Rada's forces when the Russian Military Staff withdrew from the city.[14]

The Bolsheviks had aided the Rada in its conflict with the hapless supporters of the Provisional Government. Once this enemy was defeated, the Kiev Bolsheviks launched a campaign against the Rada. Although they had never really approved of it, they did find it expedient to participate in the Rada.[15] The Bolshevik withdrawal was based on the pretext provided by a November 8 resolution of the *Mala Rada,* which condemned Lenin's seizure of power in Petrograd; this resolution was adopted largely at the insistence of representatives from the Russian and Jewish minorities.[16]

Yet the Kiev Bolsheviks, despite their influence in the Kiev Soviet of Workers' and Soldiers' Deputies, had to reckon with the fact that the Rada was in control of the city and enjoyed support. Thus, the Kiev Soviet recognized the Rada as the government of Ukrainian territory but on the condition that the city soviet be recognized as the municipal government of Kiev and that an All-Ukrainian Congress of Soviets be convened for the purpose of "reconstructing" the Rada.[17] But the Rada could not accept restructuring based upon workers' soviets in the cities of the Ukraine

---

[13] Pavlo Khrystiuk, *Zamitky i materialy do istorii ukrainskoi revoliutsii, 1917–1920 rr.,* Vol. II (Vienna, 1921; republished in photoreproduction in New York, 1969), p. 42.

[14] *Ibid.,* Vol. II, pp. 45, 192–194.

[15] On the attitude of many of the Kiev Bolsheviks toward the Rada, which contrasted with that of Lenin during most of 1917, see Borys, pp. 122–130. A Soviet collective work concedes that the Rada had strength among "significant" strata of the Ukrainian peasants, soldiers, intelligentsia, and artisans." *Narysy istorii Komunistychnoi Partii Ukrainy* (2nd ed.; Kiev: Derzhpolitvydav, 1964), p. 169.

[16] Khrystiuk, Vol. II, p. 44.

[17] S. Shreiber, "K protokolam pervogo vseukrainskogo soveshchaniia bolshevikov," *Letopis revoliutsii,* No. 5 [20] (Kharkiv, 1926), p. 58. Also, see Zatonskyi's statement in the minutes published on pp. 72–73 of the same issue.

which represented the interests of the Russian minority. The Kiev Bolsheviks did not want a Rada in which the Ukrainian majority (i.e., the peasantry) would predominate—hence the demand for restructuring the Rada's membership on the basis of Russian-dominated urban soviets.[18]

The Kiev Bolsheviks had the task of attempting to compete with the Rada or, failing that, to overthrow it. In order to do so, they would have to overcome the disadvantage of not having a separate Ukrainian Bolshevik Party organization and of being primarily a Russian organization that did not represent Ukrainian interests and that was subordinate to the Central Committee of the RSDLP. In order to appraise the situation and to develop appropriate tactics, a Bolshevik Regional Conference of the Southwestern Region was held in Kiev on December 16–18, 1917. It was attended by forty-seven voting delegates and seven non-voting delegates who represented twenty-four local Bolshevik organizations in the Kiev, Katerynoslav (Dnipropetrovsk), Kherson, Chernihiv, Poltava, Podillia (Podolia), and Volhynia regions. However, sixteen of the delegates were from the city of Kiev and another seven were from the Kiev region; together they comprised half of the voting delegates. The Bolshevik organizations represented at this conference claimed a total membership of 18,021, of which the Kiev city membership was said to be 5,000. The norms of representation varied markedly. Not represented were the heavily Russian Kharkiv, Odessa, and Donets Basin Bolshevik organizations.

Although the Kiev Conference of Bolsheviks in December 1917 had few practical consequences, the debate and the resolutions adopted reflected weakness, certain disagreements within the Bolshevik ranks, and the need to develop more effective methods of struggle. Three important issues confronted the Conference: the question of whether or not to rename the party; the tactics to be employed at the All-Ukrainian Congress of Soviets, which was to convene in Kiev on December 17; and the position to be adopted regarding Lenin's ultimatum to the Rada. On the question of nomenclature, there was no thought of establishing a Ukrainian Social Democratic Labor Party, for such a party existed and was represented in the Rada. Alternative names were proposed by Vasyl Shakhrai: "the RSDLP of Bolsheviks in the Ukraine"; by Lapchyn-

---

[18] The Kiev Bolsheviks were acting on the basis of instructions from the Russian Bolshevik leadership in Petrograd. See Borys, p. 171.

skyi: "the RSDLP, Ukrainian Union of Communists"; and by Aleksander Horvits: "the RSDLP of Bolsheviks, Social Democracy of the Ukraine."

The Conference favored the name "the RSDLP of Bolsheviks, Social Democracy of the Ukraine," although it recognized that any change would have to be approved by Lenin's Central Committee in Petrograd. The debate over nomenclature reflected the dilemma of the Bolsheviks: a change in name was essential if they were to win some converts from among the Ukrainians, but it also entailed the risk of weakening their ties with the Bolshevik center in Petrograd. Kogan, the delegate from Zhytomyr, stated that "it is imperative to create a social democracy of the Ukraine, otherwise the masses will not follow us."[19] Leonid Piatakov of the Kiev organization, who was soon to pay with his life for his Bolshevism, noted: "To conduct work under the name of the Russian Bolsheviks is very difficult—it repels the masses from us. If we retain the old name we will always be Russians (*rossiiany*)."[20] Halaida, who was not a voting delegate, favored the renaming and advocated appealing to the peasantry and publishing in the Ukrainian language.

Some of the Bolshevik delegates were not convinced. Kulyk declared that "it is impossible to call our territorial organization Ukrainian, because that is chauvinism [sic] and it would lead to our being confused with other Ukrainian parties."[21] Evgeniia Bogdanovna (Gotlibovna) Bosh of the Kiev organization, an ultracentralist, opposed Lenin's slogan regarding the right of national self-determination and insisted that it was being used by the "imperialistic bourgeoisie" of Europe. Vasyl Shakhrai refuted her reasoning:

> That the bourgeoisie conceals its policies by means of the national flag is entirely natural not only for the imperialistic bourgeoisie. The bourgeoisie always utilizes the protective coloration not only of nationalism but of socialism. But that does not give us grounds for saying that socialism is nonsense and is a bourgeois trend. We need to knock out of the hands of the bourgeoisie the weapon of the national struggle which can yet be revolutionary.

---

[19] "Protokoly oblastnogo sezda bolshevikov (pervoe vseukrainskoe soveshchanie 1917 g.," *Letopis revoliutsii*, No. 5 [20] (Kharkiv, 1926), p. 75.
[20] *Ibid.*, p. 80.
[21] *Ibid.*, p. 81.

Bosh was not to abandon her simplistic and doctrinaire standard. With incredible obtuseness she stated that "in the Ukraine there is not a national struggle but a class struggle, and there is only a national cover (*pokryvalo*) with which the bourgeoisie conceals the class movement."[22] Yet Bosh and the less flexible Bolsheviks were in a minority.

Those who constituted the majority and who voted for a new name were not, for the most part, in favor of a Ukrainian national Bolshevik organization. Horvits, whose formula was adopted, stated that it would be a "territorial" and not a national party organization and likened it to those of the Latvian and Polish Social Democrats. Horvits reassured Bosh and others that "the Social Democracy of the Ukraine will be a regional (*raionnaia*) organization of the RSDLP."[23] Lapchynskyi, a Ukrainian, spoke of the Ukrainian Party organization being admitted to a new and as yet non-existent Third Communist International as a separate section despite its remaining within the RSDLP. Thus, while there was recognition of the need to overcome Bolshevik weakness in the Ukraine by means of some Ukrainian coloration, the issue remained unresolved.

The Kiev Conference of Bolsheviks also had the task of determining the tactics to be employed in the All-Ukrainian Congress of Workers', Soldiers' and Peasants' Deputies that convened on December 17. There was general agreement that the Bolsheviks would be in a minority at the Congress (whose convocation they themselves had initiated) and would be at a disadvantage in dealing with the Rada. Bobko, a delegate from Chernihiv, noted that "we have no real strength for a struggle against the Rada."[24] Leonid Piatakov predicted that they would fail to split the Congress of Soviets. Vladimir Aussem of the Poltava Bolshevik organization proposed that they question the credentials of the delegates to the Congress and declare it to be "incompetent." He noted that "we will without doubt not obtain a majority, but we can effect a split (*raskol*)."[25] Although this is the tactic the Bolsheviks adopted, the split was not effective at the Congress itself, but it did provide a pretext for Russian intervention in Ukrainian affairs.

The Bolsheviks at the All-Ukrainian Congress of Workers', Sol-

---

[22] *Ibid.*, pp. 76–78.

[23] *Ibid.*, p. 81.

[24] *Ibid.*, p. 75.

[25] *Ibid.*, p. 71.

diers' and Peasants' Deputies were heavily outnumbered, and their efforts to influence the deliberations of the 2,500 delegates were doomed to fail. Their position became utterly untenable when the Congress was told of Lenin's December 16 ultimatum to the Rada threatening immediate war unless the Ukrainian government ceased permitting anti-Bolshevik Russian military units to cross Ukrainian territory on their way to join General Kaledin's forces in the Don Region. The hostility of the delegates could not be assuaged by Zatonskyi and Shakhrai, two of the few Kiev Bolsheviks who could speak Ukrainian and who addressed the Congress. At the Bolshevik Party conference, Zatonskyi had warned his fellow Bolsheviks that Lenin's ultimatum came close to foreign intervention and that it would lead to a conflict between the two nationalities. He said that Petrograd was poorly informed and expressed the fear that "it will be necessary to wage war against the Ukrainian people, and the Bolsheviks are but few in number (*nebolshaia kuchka*)."[26] Since Lenin had not consulted the Kiev Bolsheviks before issuing the ultimatum, Shakhrai endeavored to improvise at the Congress. He tried to defend Lenin and claimed that it was all a "misunderstanding," but he also criticized the Rada because the Bolshevik Conference had adopted a resolution in support of the ultimatum.[27]

Thus, the small Bolshevik minority had little alternative but to walk out of the All-Ukrainian Congress of Soviets. The Bolshevik delegates, joined by some fellow travelers, met to discuss their next move. Two delegates from Kharkiv proposed that the group go to that city, where a Congress of Soviets of the Donets-Kryvyi Rih *oblast* was being held. Most of the Bolsheviks decided to make the journey, although some returned to their homes and others had to borrow money for their railroad tickets. The Bolsheviks proceeded to the railroad station in "small groups in a semi-conspiratorial manner" because they feared that the Rada authorities would arrest them. On the night of December 20-21, 1917, the initiators of the future Soviet Ukrainian government left Kiev, Iurii Lapchynskyi tells us that when the group arrived in Kharkiv they saw in

---

[26] *Ibid.*, p. 83. Another delegate, Aleksandrov, stated that the ultimatum should have been issued five weeks earlier because "now the Rada has dropped deep roots. . . . We will have to fight against almost the entire Ukrainian people and not against the Rada" (p. 84).

[27] *Ibid.*, p. 88. Shakhrai's speech is quoted in Khrystiuk, Vol. II, pp. 70–71.

the station Russian troops from Petrograd under the command of Rudolf Sivers, a twenty-five-year-old recruit to Bolshevism.[28] These troops and others that followed were to provide the principal means by which the Bolsheviks would attempt to govern the Ukraine.

Although the Kiev Bolsheviks were not greeted warmly in Kharkiv, they nevertheless formed a new General Secretariat—a "workers' and peasants' government" of the Ukrainian People's Republic. They joined the Donets-Kryvyi Rih *oblast* congress of soviets and renamed it the "First All-Ukrainian Congress of Soviets of Workers', Peasants' and Soldiers' Deputies"—conveniently ignoring the much larger and more representative Kiev Congress from which they had withdrawn.[29] Not many of the Bolshevik hosts in Kharkiv were receptive to the idea of a Ukrainian Republic. Instead, the policy was to establish several republics on Ukrainian territory. In addition to a Ukrainian Republic (limited to the Right Bank and to the Poltava and Katerynoslav regions), there were to be separate republics for the Donets Basin and Kryvyi Rih area, the Odessa Region, the Crimea, and the Don Region.

The Ukrainian Soviet Government proclaimed at Kharkiv included a Central Executive Committee (TsIKU) of forty-one members, of whom twenty-eight were identified as Bolsheviks and only a few were ethnic Ukrainians.[30] All administration heads were Bolsheviks, except for one left-wing Socialist Revolutionary, Evgenii Terletskii. The "People's Secretariat" included Shakhrai (military affairs), Skrypnyk (labor), Zatonskyi (education), and Lapchynskyi. When Shakhrai was sent to Brest-Litovsk as a Ukrainian delegate to challenge the Rada's delegation, he was succeeded by Iurii Kotsiubynskyi, son of the talented writer Mykhailo Kotsiubynskyi. Although Kotsiubynskyi was nominally responsible for military affairs and named "supreme commander," the invasion of the Ukraine by exter-

[28] Georg [sic] Lapchynskyi, "Z pershykh dniv vseukrainskoi radianskoi vlady (spohady)," *Litopys revoliutsii,* Nos. 5–6 [26–27] (Kharkiv, 1927), pp. 65–66.

[29] It is revealing that the collective Soviet work, *Narysy istorii Komunistychnoi Partii Ukrainy* (2nd ed.; Kiev, 1964), a study of nearly 700 pages, makes no mention of the Kiev Congress of Soviets or of the journey to Kharkiv (pp. 201–202).

[30] S. Sh., "Iz istorii Sovvlasti na Ukraine," *Letopis revoliutsii,* No. 4 [9] (Kharkiv, 1924), p. 173, note 1. This account is of special importance because it is based on oral data provided by Skrypnyk, Aussem, Kulyk, and others within a month after the establishment of the Kharkiv government.

nal forces was under the actual command of V.A. Antonov-Ovseenko. Thus Kotsiubynskyi, a Ukrainian with a prominent surname, provided a modest amount of needed coloration, which was hardly sufficient to conceal the fact of invasion.

The Kharkiv "People's Secretariat of the Ukrainian People's Republic" published a newspaper that was only partly in the Ukrainian language. This "all-Ukrainian government" was for several weeks a "center without peripheries, a staff without an army, for it had neither territory, nor a population over which to rule, nor armed forces."[31] The "victorious army of Soviet Russia" made it possible for the Kharkiv government to extend its limited territory.[32] All of the regime's declarations and pronouncements reflected utter dependence on Lenin's government, which even had to provide it with funds.[33] The Kharkiv Secretariat regarded itself part of Lenin's government, as evidenced by the appointment of Zatonskyi (its Secretary of Education) to the post of "People's Secretary of the Ukrainian Republic attached to the Workers' and Peasants' Government of the All-Russia (*Rossiiskoi*) Federation."[34] In addition, Mykola Skrypnyk was ordered to Kharkiv as an "agent" of the RSDLP Central Committee.[35]

The fact that the Ukraine, as represented by the Kharkiv "People's Secretariat," was not really independent of Russia was hardly surprising in view of the absence of a separate Ukrainian Bolshevik party organization. Reliance was to be placed not on the possible appeal of a Ukrainian Communist Party but on military force. Although Lenin's regime had been insisting during December 1917 that General Kaledin's forces in the Don Region were the greater danger, in mid-January the Bolshevik military forces were directed against the Rada and the Ukrainian People's Republic.

The main Russian Bolshevik force that moved against Kiev was commanded by Colonel Mikhail Muravev, a Russian monarchist who had joined the Socialist Revolutionary Party in 1917. He insisted that Revolutionary Committees be established in the towns

---

[31] *Ibid.*, p. 175.

[32] *Ibid.*, p. 176.

[33] P. V. Zamkovoi *et al.* (compilers), *Bolshevitskie organizatsii Ukrainy v period ustanovleniia i ukrepleniia sovetskoi vlasti (noiabr 1917-aprel 1918 gg.); sbornik dokumentov i materialov* (Kiev: Gospolitizdat USSR, 1962), pp. 23–24, document No. 14.

[34] *Ibid.*, pp. 35–36, documents Nos. 25 and 26.

[35] *Ibid.*, p. 29, document No. 17.

taken by his troops. This in itself provided eloquent testimony to the lack of Bolshevik strength in the local soviets. In Poltava, the arrogant and cruel Muravev threatened to arrest the entire executive committee of the local soviet unless it "elected" a revolutionary committee consisting exclusively of Bolsheviks and Left Socialist-Revolutionaries. He also threatened to destroy physically the city.[36]

The Bolsheviks who remained in Kiev attempted an armed uprising to overthrow the Rada in late January 1918. Basing themselves primarily on the Kiev Arsenal, the local Bolsheviks succeeded in waging street warfare against the forces of the Rada from January 29 to February 2. Aided principally by Russian railroad workers, the Kiev Bolsheviks were unable to overthrow the Rada. The Rada's forces in the city, which included many students, numbered six to eight thousand, while the Bolsheviks claimed that they had four to five thousand. The Rada retained control of the telephone system, had greater mobility, and had the services of many trained army officers as well as the aid of Ukrainian sailors from the Black Sea fleet.[37] By February 2 and 3, the Bolshevik insurgents were besieged in the Arsenal and were compelled to surrender when Ukrainian forces under the command of Symon Petliura arrived in the city and deployed artillery. Petliura's forces had retreated from the area northeast of Kiev, where they had been resisting the advancing Russian forces. It is evident that the local Bolsheviks could not themselves have overthrown the Rada, but their uprising in Kiev did weaken the defense of the city and aid the Russian invader.[38] On February 7, after several days of fighting, Muravev's forces succeeded in establishing themselves in Kiev, although sporadic fighting continued for several days.[39]

Muravev, whose conduct had acquired a psychopathic character,

---

[36] Smetanich, "Poltava pered 'Oktiabrem'," *Letopis revoliutsii*, No. 3 [8] (Kharkiv, 1924), pp. 69–70. For a first-hand description of Muravev's personality and conduct, see G. Lapchynskyi, "Borotba za Kyiv, sichen 1918 r.," *ibid.*, No. 2 [29] (1928), pp. 209–219.

[37] S. Mishchenko, "Ianvarskoe vosstanie v Kieve," *ibid.*, No. 3 [8] (1924), pp. 27–32. The author commanded forces in the Arsenal during part of the uprising.

[38] Concerning the essentially Russian nature of these forces, see Borys, p. 179. Muravev's Order No. 14, issued prior to the taking of Kiev, states that he was bringing freedom "from the distant north" on sharp bayonets. See M. G. Rafes, *Dva goda revoliutsii na Ukraine* (Moscow: Gosizdat, 1920), pp. 81–82.

[39] Zamkovoi *et al.*, pp. 53–54, document No. 50.

sought to extirpate every vestige of Ukrainian rule and national consciousness in Kiev. The government of the Ukrainian People's Republic (the Rada) retreated to Zhytomyr and to Sarny and on February 9, 1918, concluded the Treaty of Brest-Litovsk with the Central Powers, which brought it diplomatic recognition. The Ukrainian delegates of the Kharkiv Bolshevik "People's Secretariat" sent to Brest-Litovsk (Shakhrai and Medvediev) failed to gain recognition from the Central Powers and, characteristically, became part of the Russian delegation representing Lenin's government. The Kharkiv "People's Secretariat" arrived in Kiev on February 11, 1918, but within seventeen days had to abandon the city to the Rada's forces and to the Germans.

The "People's Secretariat" took refuge in Poltava, where Skrypnyk, who had become head of the retreating government, issued an appeal on March 8 (in the name of the Central Executive Committee of the Ukraine) calling for the establishment of a "military-political union (*soiuz*) of the soviet republics of the South of Russia." As if the pressure of the Rada's return and the advance of the Germans were not sufficient to prompt a unity effort in the face of the Bolshevik debacle, Skrypnyk sought to reassure the Russian leaders of the other four soviet republics. He stated that the Central Executive Committee of the Ukraine had "never viewed the Ukrainian Soviet Republic [sic] as a national republic but exclusively as a soviet republic on the territory of the Ukraine" and that it had "never stood for the total independence of the Ukrainian People's Republic [sic], viewing it as a more or less independent entity related by federal ties to the All-Russian Workers'–Peasants' Republic."[40] Skrypnyk pointed out that the Rada was now claiming—in accordance with its Third and Fourth Universals—the territories of the Don, Donets, Crimean, and Odessa soviet republics and that a mutual Bolshevik front was imperative.

Thus it was military defeat in March 1918 that provided the impetus for a merger of Bolshevik cadres in the Ukraine into a single organization. Lenin, too, saw the need for a single front and for Ukrainian coloration as well. In a letter dated March 14, 1918, to G. K. Ordzhonikidze, one of the leading Bolsheviks sent to the Ukraine to requisition food supplies for the Russian cities, Lenin said that it was necessary to undertake the "decisive and unqualified remaking (*perelitsovka*) in a Ukrainian manner (*na*

---

[40] *Ibid.,* pp. 61–62, document No. 56.

Ukrainskii lad) of all our [military] units in the Ukraine." Lenin also advised: "It is necessary to forbid [sic] Antonov to call himself Antonov-Ovseenko,—he must call himself simply Ovseenko. The same should be said of Muravev (if he remains at his post) and others."[41] The pathetic, dishonest, and transparent effort to conceal the Russian intervention by adopting Ukrainian names could not save the situation.

Skrypnyk's Ukrainian soviet government retreated to Katerynoslav. On March 15, the Central Committee of the All-Russian Communist Party—after hearing Shakhrai and Zatonskyi—decided that the Donets Soviet Republic should send representatives to a new All-Ukrainian Congress of Soviets and that the Donets Basin was part of the Ukraine.[42] At the Second Ukrainian Congress of Soviets, which met at Katerynoslav on March 17–19, the Bolsheviks barely received a majority. The Congress declared the Ukraine to be an independent soviet federated republic, since Lenin's government had agreed to recognize Ukrainian independence in the Brest-Litovsk Treaty.

However, the Bolshevik military units were in full retreat, and it was necessary for the Central Executive Committee to take refuge in Taganrog. There, at a meeting of Bolsheviks on April 19–20, 1918, a number of decisions were taken. It was decided, by a vote of thirty-five to twenty-one, with one abstention, to establish an independent Communist Party (of Bolsheviks) of the Ukraine with its own Central Committee and congresses; it was to be related to the Russian Communist Party through the Third International.[43] Thirty-four persons voted for the name change, which was proposed by Skrypnyk. A resolution proposed by E. Kviring was rejected; it provided that the Party call itself the "Russian Communist Party in the Ukraine" and be autonomous, having its own Central Committee and congresses, but being subordinate to the Russian Party's congresses and Central Committee.

The Central Executive Committee decided to dissolve itself as well as the "People's Secretariat" and to liquidate the first Ukrainian Soviet Republic. In place of the Bolshevik government there was established the "Revolutionary Nine," a bureau to conduct insurrectionary operations against the occupying Central Powers. It

---

[41] *Ibid.*, p. 65.

[42] The resolution is quoted in *Narysy*, pp. 212–213.

[43] Zamkovoi *et al.*, p. 83, document No. 68.

consisted of four Bolsheviks, four Left Socialist-Revolutionaries and one Left Ukrainian Social Democrat, but it was ineffective. Since the entire Bolshevik venture in the Ukraine had collapsed and the small Soviet military forces were in full retreat, it was decided to take refuge in Russia and to convene a Party congress in Moscow.

The First Congress met in Moscow July 5–12, 1918, with approximately fifty-five voting delegates, who claimed to represent Party organizations having a total of 4,364 members. Although the Kiev and Taganrog meetings had set precedents, the Communist Party (Bolshevik) of the Ukraine (CP(b)U) was formally founded in exile at the Moscow congress. The CP(b)U was to have its own congresses and Central Committee, but was to be a part of the Russian Communist Party (RCP) and be subordinate in programmatic matters to the latter's congresses and in matters of general policy to the Central Committee in Moscow. The CP(b)U was to have autonomy only in local matters and was made completely dependent on the Russian Communist Party. One resolution provided for the "revolutionary unification of the Ukraine and Russia on the basis of proletarian centralism within the confines of the Russian Soviet Socialist Republic on the way to the establishment of a universal (*vsemirnoi*) proletarian commune."[44] Thus did Lenin dispose of the Taganrog resolution. Yet the establishment of a single Ukrainian Party center, to which the various regional (*oblast*) party organizations were subordinate, was a step of great importance.

However, questions of tactics divided the CP(b)U at its First Congress. It was agreed that "the final victory of Soviet authority in the Ukraine is possible only on the condition of a victory of the workers in the West"; nevertheless, the organization of uprisings against the Germans and Hetman Skoropadskyi's regime in the Ukraine was approved.[45] The "left wing" at the Congress, led by G. Piatakov, A. Bubnov, and Zatonskyi from the Kiev organization, favored an uprising, but the "right wing," led by E. Kviring and Ia. Epshtein (Iakovlev), regarded this as "adventurism." The "right wing" distrusted the Ukrainian peasantry, especially the

---

[44] *Kommunisticheskaia Partiia Ukrainy v rezoliutsiiakh i resheniiakh sezdov i konferentsii, 1918–1956* (Kiev: Gospolitizdat, 1958), p. 17. Hereafter cited as *KPU v rezoliutsiiakh.*

[45] *Ibid.,* p. 12.

numerous middle peasants, and favored concentrating on the recruitment of industrial workers by the CP(b)U.[46]

The Congress met under Lenin's watchful eye, but Ukrainian developments were baffling to the RCP leadership. Béla Kun addressed the Congress in his capacity as head of a "federation of international groups," which was recruiting prisoners of war to communism.[47] The Congress elected a Central Committee of fifteen members and six candidate-members. Significantly, Skrypnyk was not included in the CP(b)U Central Committee because of his "errors" on the question of the relationship of the CP(b)U to the RCP at the Taganrog Conference.[48] Zatonskyi, who had been a physics instructor at the Kiev Polytechnical Institute, became Secretary of the Central Committee and began operations in Orel.[49] On August 5, 1918, the All-Ukrainian Central Military Revolutionary Committee, headed by A. Bubnov, issued order No. 1, calling for a general uprising in the Ukraine. This order was issued without the approval of the RCP,[50] and when only sporadic and isolated local risings occurred in the northern Chernihiv region, Bubnov and Piatakov were blamed.

As a result of this fiasco—the second experienced by the CP(b)U within six months since its expulsion from Kiev—a Second Congress was held in Moscow on October 17–22, 1918. It had 125 delegates, who claimed to represent more than 5,000 members; many delegates employed pseudonyms (the identity of all has not been established), since the Congress was conducted in a conspiratorial manner.[51] Lenin and Karl Liebknecht were elected honorary chairmen. Yet the CP(b)U was weak in membership; Kiev had but 348 members and Kharkiv about 300, while in the Donets Region and in Odessa the Party had more members.[52] The failure of the August rising prompted much criticism from the "Right" against the "Left"

---

[46] *Spohady pro pershyi zizd KP(b)U* (Kiev: Derzhpolitvydav, 1958), pp. 14–15, 27, 48–50.

[47] *Ibid.*, p. 37.

[48] *Ibid.*, p. 39.

[49] *Ibid.*, p. 20.

[50] *Ibid.*, p. 39.

[51] M. Pohrebinskyi, *Druhyi zizd KP(b)U* (Kiev: Derzhpolitvydav, 1958), p. 95.

[52] *Ibid.*, pp. 105–107.

(Kievan) majority in the Central Committee. The Congress adopted a resolution censuring the Central Committee and criticized it for inadequate preparation of the uprising and for its failures in organizational activity. However, the Congress failed to deal with the question of nationality policy.[53] Nor had the discredited "Left" been in agreement on the matter; both Bubnov and Piatakov were Russians who generally opposed concessions to Ukrainian nationalism. The Second CP(b)U Congress met under the supervision of Secretary of the RCP, Iakov Sverdlov, and Lev Kamenev; its subordination to the RCP soon became evident.

A new Central Committee was chosen—one in which the Katerynoslav "Right" enjoyed predominance; Stalin, who had never had any experience in Ukrainian affairs, was elected a member. The Kievan group did receive positions but decided to boycott the Committee. Kviring, who had no contact with the Ukraine prior to 1914, became Party Secretary. In November 1918 Georgii Piatakov and Zatonskyi proceeded to Kursk, where they sought to establish a nucleus for a new Ukrainian Bolshevik government. However, permission to proclaim the establishment of such a government was not given by Stalin. Piatakov pleaded for permission to form a "Provisional Workers' and Peasants' Government of the Ukraine" and to send military forces, because the Hetmanate of General Skoropadskyi was collapsing, and in its place the Ukrainian People's Republic, led by Symon Petliura and the Directory had emerged once again. Unless the Bolsheviks acted soon, they would lose the opportunity to influence events.

Moscow hesitated to open a Ukrainian front because it was overcommitted on existing military fronts in the Don Region and in Estonia and Latvia. Chicherin, the Russian Commissar for Foreign Affairs, was even prepared to deal with the Directory in Kiev—much to the annoyance of Zatonskyi and Piatakov.[54] In an effort to forestall such a move, the handful of Ukrainian Bolsheviks in Kursk kept bombarding Moscow with telegrams. The second Bolshevik "government" of the Ukraine was proclaimed on November 28, 1918; it was housed in a single railroad car in the Kursk station and was not even located on Ukrainian territory.[55] Only five per-

---

[53] *Ibid.*, p. 153.

[54] V. Zatonskyi, "Iz spohadiv pro Ukrainsku revoliutsiiu," *Litopys revoliutsii,* No. 5 (44) (Kharkiv, 1930), pp. 157, 162.

[55] *Ibid.*, p. 156. This fact is all the more ironic in view of the Soviet

sons were present at the "government's" first meeting: Antonov-Ovseenko, Artem, Zatonskyi, Kviring, and Piatakov.[56] Piatakov was to head the "government," whose seat was to be the small town of Sudzha, located southwest of Kursk along the Ukrainian-Russian ethnographic frontier. The editor of the government newspaper was to come from Moscow, and the finances were to be resolved in that city.[57] Since the "government's" future was dependent on military operations, Kursk remained its real center.

The immediate task was to move on Bilhorod and to take Kharkiv. Although the Directory's forces held Kharkiv in November and December, Zatonskyi and his colleagues succeeded in dealing with the German occupation forces there. In this way Antonov's military units were able to move on Kharkiv from Kursk, and it was also possible to obtain weapons (including machine guns and artillery) from the Germans, who were interested primarily in returning to Germany.[58] By means of various stratagems and an active propaganda campaign among German troops, the Bolshevik military force was able to take Kharkiv on January 3, 1919. As in January of the preceding year, Russian troops played a key role; a Moscow workers' division, the Ninth Division, a brigade, and two armored trains were sent by the "fraternal Russian people."[59]

Although the Bolsheviks were able to take Kiev by February 5, Vinnytsia was not taken until March 18, and the Directory's hard-pressed forces remained in the western Ukraine. The CP(b)U leadership, while enjoying some apparent success, nevertheless faced serious problems that were soon to send it again into Russian exile. Its condition was evident at the Third Congress, held in Kharkiv on March 1–6, 1919. It was attended by 216 voting delegates, but neither the Volhynia and Podillia regions nor the city of Odessa was represented. Again, as at the Second Congress, the Central Committee was criticized for having lost contact with most local Bolshevik groups, for failing to issue directives, and for not making Party literature available; its tactics were judged to have

---

disparagement of the Ukrainian Directory because it was housed in railroad cars during periods of military evacuation.

[56] M. Rubach, "K istorii grazhdanskoi borby na Ukraine," *Letopis revoliutsii,* No. 4 [9] (Kharkiv, 1924), p. 162.

[57] *Ibid.,* p. 164.

[58] Zatonskyi, pp. 160–161, 167.

[59] Pohrebinskyi, p. 205.

been "incorrect," and the Central Committee was termed "incapable."[60]

The conflict between the Kievan "Left" and the Katerynoslav "Right" persisted at the Congress as the former group attacked the latter's record in the Central Committee.[61] Sverdlov, who again represented the RCP, had to appeal for unity and discipline, and a reconstituted Central Committee undertook to deal with the many problems confronting the infant regime. The French were in control of part of the northern shore of the Black Sea, including Odessa, and the Third Congress recognized that it might be necessary to agree to "tactical concessions (*ustupki*)" as a "means of strategic maneuver" in dealing with the Entente.[62] Ironically, this position on concessions was adopted at a time when the Bolsheviks were falsely accusing the Directory and Petliura of "selling" the Ukraine to the Entente.

Probably the CP(b)U's weakness was its greatest problem. Although it claimed to have nearly 36,000 members by May 1919, 10,000 of these were in the Donets Region, 5,000 were in the Kharkiv and Katerynoslav Regions, 4,500 in the Kherson Region, 4,000 in the Kiev Region, 1,000 in Podillia, and only 500 in Volhynia.[63] Consequently, the Party's influence was confined largely to the Left Bank and weakened as it moved westward. Its ethnically Ukrainian membership was a small minority despite the fact that Ukrainians constituted an overwhelming majority of at least three-quarters of the population. Yet the CP(b)U Third Congress again ignored the nationality problem, and many Party members and officials manifested Russian "great power chauvinism" in their behavior, engaging in the most reprehensible forms of discrimination against Ukrainian language and culture.[64]

Moscow's utter lack of sensitivity to Ukrainian national aspirations and to the requirements of the situation was revealed by the appointment, late in January 1919, of Khristiian Rakovskii to replace Piatakov as head of the new Soviet government in the

---

[60] *KPU v rezoliutsiiakh*, pp. 33–34. The resolution criticizing the Central Committee was adopted by a vote of 99 to 92.

[61] O. Slutskyi, *Tretii zizd KP(b)U* (Kiev: Derzhpolitvydav, 1958), pp. 60–66.

[62] *KPU v rezoliutsiiakh*, p. 43.

[63] Slutskyi, p. 154.

[64] *Ibid.*, pp. 140–142.

Ukraine. The *déraciné* Rakovskii—a French-educated physician of Bulgarian origin, and a Rumanian subject who had become a Russian Bolshevik—was hardly qualified to deal with Ukrainian problems. His derogatory remarks at the Third Ukrainian Congress of Soviets regarding Ukrainian as an official language of the Republic showed that he was just another "Russian" official sent to rule over Ukrainians.[65] Lenin assumed that Rakovskii would create unity in the quarreling CP(b)U, but his appointment presaged still another and even more traumatic Bolshevik failure in the Ukraine.

While on the surface it appeared in 1919 that the Bolsheviks were consolidating their regime, they were actually repeating most of the errors of the previous year. Among the more important of these was the effort to develop agricultural communes and state farms on the former estates, rather than dividing the land, and the practice of requisitioning grain from the middle peasants. In January 1919 Lenin sent Aleksander Shlikhter to the Ukraine as commissar of supply. It was hoped that 50 million *poods* of grain could be collected by June 1, 1919, in order to feed Russia's cities and the Red Army. Shlikhter was aided by some 2,700 persons from Petrograd and Moscow, sent especially to requisition grain.[66] Relatively little was obtained, however, because by April and May the Ukraine was seething with peasant rebellion. While the Bolsheviks were able to retain their hold on many of the cities, they had lost the countryside. Large bands of peasants cut telegraph and telephone lines, seized sections of railroad right-of-way, and prevented Bolshevik officials from functioning. One such group, led by Hryhoriiv, was able to capture a number of cities, including Odessa, Kherson, Mykolaiv, Katerynoslav, and Cherkasy.[67]

During the summer of 1919 Denikin's forces moved into the Ukraine from the southeast and those of the Directory moved eastward to Kiev. The CP(b)U and its regime once again had to retreat into Russian exile as Denikin proceeded to threaten Moscow itself

---

[65] *Ibid.*, p. 141.

[66] A. Shlikhter, "Borba za khleb na Ukraine v 1919 godu," *Litopys revoliutsii*, No. 2 [29] (Kharkiv, 1928), pp. 117, 135.

[67] Slutskyi, pp. 94–95, 177–181. The failure of Bolshevik policy and the various uprisings of Ukrainian peasants are discussed in Arthur E. Adams, *Bolsheviks in the Ukraine: The Second Campaign, 1918–1919* (New Haven, Conn.: Yale University Press, 1963).

in the autumn of 1919. The demoralized nature of the CP(b)U is evident in the fact that on October 2, 1919, the Ukrainian Soviet Republic dissolved itself in Chernihiv and its members went to Moscow, where they placed themselves at the disposal of the RCP Central Committee. In the CP(b)U a conflict raged between those who wanted the Ukraine to have equal rights with the Russian Republic and those (largely non-Ukrainians) who desired the maximum subordination of the Ukraine to Russia and who wanted the CP(b)U to be nothing more than an *oblast* organization of the RCP.[68] This conflict prompted the convocation of an unofficial gathering of CP(b)U leaders held at Gomel in Belorussia for two days late in November 1919. The Gomel Conference was initiated by the Volhynian Regional Party Committee without the approval of the CP(b)U Central Committee; the latter sent Zatonskyi and S. V. Kosior to Gomel to dissolve the Conference, but they declined to do so. Although disagreement persisted at Gomel over the question of an independent Ukrainian Communist Party of Bolsheviks holding membership at the Comintern (as advocated by Lapchynskyi), the conference did register dissatisfaction with the RCP policy in the Ukraine and with the CP(b)U leadership.

The Gomel Conference reflected the need for a more realistic policy if an effort was to be made to win Ukrainian support for the regime. The demoralized condition of the CP(b)U in 1919 was reflected in a published statement by D. Z. Manuilskyi, who participated in the Gomel Conference: "Each spring we equip a successive troupe for the Ukraine which, after making a tour

---

[68] The reduction of the CP(b)U to *oblast* status was accomplished by the Eighth Congress of the RCP, which met in Moscow on March 18–23, 1919, shortly after the Third Congress of the CP(b)U. The RCP Congress explicitly rejected the federal principle for Party organization and declared that the "Central Committees of the Ukrainian, Latvian, [and] Lithuanian Communists enjoy the rights of province (*oblast*) committees of the Party and are completely subordinate to the Central Committee of the Russian Communist Party." *VKP(b) v rezoliutsiiakh i resheniiakh sezdov, konferentsii i plenumov Ts. K.,* Vol. I (7th ed; Moscow: Gospolitizdat, 1953), p. 443. As a consequence, the Fourth CP(b)U Congress had to be termed a "Conference." The action of the Eighth RCP Congress occurred despite the fact that the CP(b)U was a founder of the Comintern or Third International and a participating party (with its own delegation) at the First Comintern Congress that met early in March 1919. See *KPU v rezoliutsiiakh,* pp. 32, 40.

there, returns to Moscow in the autumn."[69] Manuilskyi also wrote critically of the Ukrainian "notables" whom Moscow included in the Ukrainian Soviet government, likening the practice to that of the colonial powers, who included prominent natives in colonial governments but to whom they assigned purely decorative roles.

The bankruptcy of Moscow's Ukrainian policy and the non-Ukrainian nature of the CP(b)U were amply demonstrated in the work, *Do Khvyli* (On the Current Situation), written between December 1918 and January 1919 by Serhii Mazlakh and Vasyl Shakhrai and published in Saratov.[70] The authors dared to state that national self-determination, as practiced by Moscow, involved no choice, and that the persons who called themselves Communists in the Ukraine were, for the most part, in support of the same "one and indivisible" Russia advocated by the Russian bourgeois parties. Mazlakh and Shakhrai demonstrated that the "internationalism" of the Bolsheviks was really just another version of Russian nationalism.[71] They were particularly critical of the "Katerynoslav

---

[69] Quoted in G. Lapchynskyi, "Gomelskoe soveshchanie (vospominiia)," *Letopis revoliutsii,* No. 6 [21] (Kharkiv, 1926), p. 40.

[70] Serhii Mazlakh and Vasyl Shakhrai, *Do khvyli; Shcho diietsia na Ukraini i z Ukrainoiu* (Saratov, 1919; 2nd ed., New York: Prolog Research and Publishing Assn., 1967). Mazlakh was a Jewish Ukrainian journalist who later headed the Central Statistical Administration of the Ukrainian SSR and disappeared during the purges in the late 1930's. Shakhrai was a *gymnasium* teacher who possessed considerable erudition and knowledge of European languages; he was a man of subtle thought and a talented and witty polemicist. Shakhrai was shot late in 1919 by the forces of General Denikin during their occupation of the Kuban Region. Their study is now available in an English translation, *On the Current Situation in the Ukraine,* edited by Peter J. Potichnyj with an introduction by Michael M. Luther (Ann Arbor, Mich.: University of Michigan Press, 1970).

[71] Shakhrai's disillusionment apparently began in December 1917, when he was appointed Secretary for Military Affairs in the first Soviet government in Kharkiv. G. Lapchynskyi quotes Shakhrai as asking at that time: "What kind of Ukrainian government is it that its members do not know and do not wish to know the Ukrainian language? [One] that not only does not enjoy any influence among the Ukrainian public, but never even heard their names before? What kind of 'Ukrainian Minister of Military Affairs' am I when all of the Ukrainianized units in Kharkiv have to be disarmed by me because they do not want to follow me in the defense of Soviet rule? As our sole military support in our struggle against the

Group" and demanded that the RCP drastically modify its entire policy, abandon outmoded attitudes, and rectify its errors and abuses. They also warned that the Ukraine would neither die nor accept national bondage. The authors noted that they wrote their work primarily for Comrade Lenin who, in their opinion, had lost sight of his most important writings on the nationality problem and who could, if he wished, restore Bolshevik policy to a course that allowed for an independent Soviet Ukraine with its own government and party.

The record of the CP(b)U in the Ukrainian Revolution was for the most part that of an appendage of the RCP; its subordinate status, its abject imitation of Russian Bolshevik resolutions and policies, and its repetition of RCP slogans were patently evident. Its creation was agreed to with considerable reluctance because of the fear that it would weaken the unity of the RCP and end Russia's hold on the Ukraine. The CP(b)U provided an indispensable means by which Lenin's regime could camouflage—albeit with only limited effectiveness—its conquest of the Ukraine. Indeed, the CP(b)U can be said to have served as the Trojan horse without which the pursuit of old Russian goals in the new, if transparent, garb of "revolutionary internationalism" would not have been possible.

While claiming to be Ukrainian, the CP(b)U was accustomed to denigrate the Ukrainian national movement, especially when the latter adopted national independence as its goal. By the use of the simplest and crudest kind of rhetorical and demagogical devices, the CP(b)U denounced the Ukrainian People's Republic, the Rada, the Directory, and their leaders as "chauvinists," as the "yellow and azure counterrevolution," or as a "dictatorship of the wealthy peasants." Not only was class warfare used to divide the Ukrainian nation, but the national movement and the national republic were referred to as the *Petliurovshchina*, and Ukrainian nationalists were termed disparagingly as *haidamaks* or as "Petliura-ites." While it was standard Bolshevik practice to denounce as "counterrevolutionary" all who disagreed with the RCP in any way, the purpose of this

---

Central Rada we have only the troops which Antonov brought to the Ukraine from Russia and who regard everything Ukrainian as inimical and counterrevolutionary?" Quoted in G. Lapchynskyi, "Pershyi period radianskoi vlady na Ukraini: TsVKU ta narodnii sekretariiat (spohady)," *Litopys revoliutsii*, No. 1 [28] (Kharkiv, 1928), pp. 171–172.

tactic in the Ukraine was to claim that the conflict was not a Russian-Ukrainian war but a Ukrainian "civil war."

Ukrainian independence—though recognized by Moscow during 1918—was denounced as a screen for foreign occupation. Echoing its masters, the CP(b)U repeated the canard that the Rada and the Directory had "sold" the Ukraine to "West European and American imperialists" or to France, Poland, and Rumania. By the same brand of logic, Lenin "sold" Russia to the Central Powers when he signed the Treaty of Brest-Litovsk. In practice, the CP(b)U also revealed a double standard; despite the reassuring claims made in the name of emancipation, what were its own activities if not a screen for alien occupation?

Yet one can question whether the CP (b)U—with its overwhelmingly non-Ukrainian membership during the revolutionary period— really served the interests of the RCP effectively. Had it done so, the RCP leadership would have been better informed regarding the Ukraine, and the two Bolshevik parties would not have experienced such failures, even though Russian military force was ultimately to triumph. In the end, the CP(b)U had to learn from its defeats, although the obtuseness and intolerance of much of its membership made that a slow and laborious process. The many conflicts within the CP(b)U meant that it was often functioning at cross-purposes, and that only part of its membership had an understanding of the Ukrainian Revolution. Its principal problem—one that could not be fully resolved despite the valiant efforts of the ethnically Ukrainian Communists—was that of identifying with Ukrainian interests. Such identification was possible only to the extent that it became a Ukrainian party in fact as well as in name.

CHAPTER EIGHT

The Fourth Universal and Its Ideological Antecedents

Ivan L. Rudnytsky

THE FOURTH UNIVERSAL adopted on January 25, 1918,[1] by the revolutionary parliament of the Ukraine, the Central Rada, contained the following solemn and memorable words: "From this day forth, the Ukrainian People's Republic becomes independent, subject to no one, a free, sovereign state of the Ukrainian people."[2]

The purpose of this paper is to study the Fourth Universal as a document of social thought, placing it within the framework of

---

[1] The vote on the Fourth Universal took place in the *Mala Rada* (the executive committee of the Central Rada) during the night meeting of January 24–25, 1918 (New Style), and the bill was passed in the early hours of January 25. The document was, however, antedated to January 22, as this was the date previously set for convening the Ukrainian Constituent Assembly. The Assembly had been unable to meet because of the outbreak of military hostilities between Soviet Russia and the Ukrainian People's Republic. See Pavlo Khrystiuk, *Zamitky i materiialy do istorii ukrainskoi revoliutsii,* Vol. II (Vienna: Ukrainskyi sotsiologichnyi instytut, 1921), p. 106. The incorrect date, January 22, became traditionally associated with the event, and Ukrainians outside the USSR still celebrate it as their national Independence Day.

The term "universal" applied originally to the proclamations of the hetmans and other high-ranking Cossack officers in the seventeenth and eighteenth centuries. The archaic term was revived by the Central Rada for its solemn manifestoes, which were addressed to the entire people of the Ukraine and which contained major policy statements and decisions of constitutional importance.

[2] The Fourth Universal, as printed in various works dealing with the history of the Ukrainian Revolution, shows slight textual variations. This study follows the full text of the Universals, which appear in the appendix of this book.

Ukrainian intellectual history and the political circumstances of the time. The discussion will focus on the essential aspect of the Fourth Universal, the declaration of Ukrainian independence. Other concepts, such as the constitutional structure and the social organization of the Ukrainian state, will be touched upon only incidentally.

First of all, it is necessary to keep in mind that the Fourth Universal was not the act by which a Ukrainian state was called into existence. This had been done two months earlier, on November 20, 1917, by the Third Universal, which stated: "From this day forth, the Ukraine is the Ukrainian People's Republic." At the same time, however, the Third Universal preserved a federative link between the Ukraine and the other lands of the former Russian Empire, and it even pledged to "stand firmly on our own soil, in order that our efforts may aid all of Russia, so that the whole Russian Republic may become a federation of equal and free peoples."[3] In contrast, the Fourth Universal proclaimed the complete political separation of the Ukraine from Russia.

The Third and Fourth Universals represent two progressive stages in the building of a Ukrainian state. But they can also be viewed as expressions of two alternative concepts of Ukrainian statehood—federalist and separatist. At the time of the adoption of the Third Universal, an all-Russian central government no longer existed. Thus, the federalist tendency of that act was not imposed from the outside; rather, it was quite voluntary. However, in the short span of time that separated the two Universals, there occurred a radical shift in the thinking of the Rada's leaders. To appreciate fully the meaning of this epoch-making change of views, it is necessary to survey briefly the origins of the ideas of federalism and state independence (*samostiinytstvo*)[4] in Ukrainian political thought.

---

[3] See appendix below.

[4] The Ukrainian terms are: *samostiinist*—the political independence of a country, its status of sovereign statehood; *samostiinytstvo*—the ideology, or mental attitude, aimed at the achievement of independent national statehood; *samostiinyk* (pl., *samostiinyky*)—a supporter of the program of *samostiinist*. English seems to lack precise equivalents. "Nationalism" is too broad, as it covers any striving towards national self-assertion, even without full political sovereignty. "Independence" may be somewhat confusing, because it does not only refer to the political status of a country but may have other connotations. For instance, a Ukrainian Party of Socialist-Independentists (*Ukrainska Partiia samostiinykiv-sotsiialistiv*) ex-

The federalist concept can be traced back to ideas prevalent among certain branches of the Decembrist movement which were active in the Ukraine during the early 1820's—especially in the Society of United Slavs.[5] In a more mature form one finds the same concept in the programmatic documents of the Cyril and Methodius Brotherhood of the late 1840's.[6] The Brotherhood's ideological legacy had a determining impact on the outlook of the Ukrainian national liberation movement during the second half of the nineteenth and the beginning of the twentieth centuries. The doctrine of federalism found its classical theoretical formulation in the writings of the outstanding pre-Revolutionary Ukrainian political thinker, Mykhailo Drahomanov (1841–1895).[7] On the eve of

---

isted during the Revolution. It would be quite misleading to refer to this party as one of independent socialists; what the party's name really implied was "supporters of an independent Ukraine, with a socialist internal structure." To avoid redundance, I shall use, depending on the context, any one of several terms as more or less synonymous: "independence," "sovereignty," "nationalism," as well as the original Ukrainian *samostiinist* and its derivatives.

There is also a need to clarify one other point of semantics. The English term "autonomy" denotes a country's self-government, which may or may not include its complete independence. In Ukrainian, as in other Slavic languages, "autonomy" means home-rule, short of full state sovereignty.

[5] See M. V. Nechkina, *Obshchestvo soedynennykh slavian* (Moscow-Leningrad: Gosudarstvennoe izd., 1927), and Georges Luciani, *La Société des Slaves unis (1823–1825)* (Paris: Université de Bordeaux, 1963). Luciani asserts (p. 66) that "the United Slavs . . . lacked the idea of a Ukrainian nationality distinct from the Great Russian nationality." Without entering into a detailed discussion, the opinion can be registered here that the United Slavs, despite the underdeveloped stage of their national consciousness, belong to the tradition of Ukrainian social thought; they had a considerable impact on the elaboration of later nineteenth-century Ukrainian political programs. See Osyp Hermaize, "Rukh dekabrystiv i ukrainstvo," *Ukraina,* No. 6 [15] (Kiev, 1925), pp. 25–38.

[6] See Georges Luciani, *Le Livre de la Genèse du peuple ukrainien* (Paris: Institut d'études slaves, 1956); P. A. Zaionchkovskii, *Kirillo-Mefodievskoe obshchestvo* (Moscow: Izd. Moskovskogo universiteta, 1959.)

[7] The fullest presentation of Drahomanov's federalist program is to be found in his *Volnyi soiuz—Vilna spilka: Opyt ukrainskoi politiko-sotsialnoi programmy* (Geneva, 1884), reprinted in *Sobranie politicheskikh sochinenii M. P. Dragomanova,* Vol. II (Paris: Osvobozhdenie, 1905–1906).

the First World War, this concept was upheld by the two main political groupings in the Russian Ukraine: the Social Democrats, whose ideologist was Mykola Porsh (1877–1944);[8] and the liberal populists, whose chief spokesman was the eminent historian Mykhailo Hrushevskyi (1866–1934). In the pamphlet *The Kind of Autonomy and Federation We Desire,* published in Kiev at the very beginning of the Revolution, Hrushevskyi wrote:

> The political goal of the Ukrainians is a broad national-territorial autonomy for the Ukraine within a federated Russian Republic. . . . The Ukrainians demand that one region, one national territory be formed from all Ukrainian lands . . . of the Russian state. . . . The Ukrainian territory ought to be organized on the basis of a broad democratic civic self-government, and representation must not be by *curiae.* This system of self-government ought to extend from the bottom—the "small zemstvo unit"—to the top—the Ukrainian Diet [*soim*]. The Ukrainian territory ought to be able to settle at home its own economic, cultural and political issues; it ought to keep its own armed forces, and dispose of its roads, revenue, land, and natural resources; it ought to possess its own legislation, administration, and judiciary. Only in certain matters, common to the entire Russian state, should the Ukraine accept the decisions of the central parliament, in which the proportion of Ukrainian representatives ought to be the same as that of the Ukrainian population to that of the population of the whole Russian Republic.[9]

See also Ivan L. Rudnytsky, "Drahomanov as a Political Theorist," in *Mykhailo Drahomanov: A Symposium and Selected Writings,* a special issue of the *Annals of the Ukrainian Academy of Arts and Sciences in the United States,* II, 1[3] (New York, 1952), pp. 70–130.

[8] On this distinguished Ukrainian interpreter of Marxism, see Andrii Zhuk, "Pamiati Mykoly Porsha (1877–1944)," *Suchasnist,* No. 1 [13] (Munich, 1962), pp. 52–64. Porsh attempted to prove in his writings that the centralistic structure of the Russian state impeded the growth of the Ukrainian economy, and that the fiscal and budgetary policies of the Russian government toward the Ukraine amounted to colonial exploitation. "Porsh's book, *On the Autonomy of the Ukraine* [Kiev, 1909], was in its time the only publication which offered, within the limits set by censorship, a broad interpretation of the national-political side of the Ukrainian movement. His book exercised a great influence on the political thinking not only of the [Ukrainian Social Democratic Labor] Party, but also of the Ukrainian community at large" (p. 61).

[9] *Iakoi my khochemo avtonomii i federatsii* (Kiev, 1917); excerpts reprinted in Mykhailo S. Hrushevskyi, *Vybrani pratsi* (New York: Associa-

During the first period of its existence, the actual policies of the Central Rada fully corresponded to this program.

With regard to the separatist concept, its earliest literary expressions are to be found in the pamphlets *Ukraina Irredenta* (1895)[10] by Iuliian Bachynskyi (1870–1934), and *An Independent Ukraine* (1900)[11] by Mykola Mikhnovskyi (1873–1924). Starting from different premises, each author reached the idea of Ukrainian statehood independently. Bachynskyi employed economic arguments within a Marxist frame of reference, while Mikhnovskyi reasoned from an historical and legal standpoint. The prominent Galician writer and scholar Ivan Franko (1856–1916) also became an early supporter of the *samostiinist* concept, as seen in his article, "Beyond the Limits of the Possible" (1900).[12] Somewhat later, in the years preceding the outbreak of the war, the separatist program found gifted advocates in the historian and sociologist Viacheslav Lypynskyi (1882–1931) and the publicist and literary critic Dmytro Dontsov (1883–1973).[13]

The two leading Ukrainian politcal parties in Galicia, the National Democrats and the Radicals, included the slogan of *samostiinist* in their respective programs. The platform of the National Democratic Party, adopted in 1899, stated: "The final goal of our

---

tion of Ukrainians of Revolutionary-Democratic Persuasion in the U.S.A., 1960), pp. 142–149.

[10] (1st ed.; Lviv, 1895); (3rd ed., with an historical introduction by Volodymyr Doroshenko and an appendix containing the correspondence between Iu. Bachynskyi and M. Drahomanov; Berlin, 1924).

[11] *Samostiina Ukraina* (Lviv, 1900), appeared anonymously; the latest edition: (London: Wolferhampton Branch of the Association of Ukrainians in Great Britain, 1967). See also Petro Mirchuk, *Mykola Mikhnovskyi: apostol ukrainskoi derzhavnosty* (Philadelphia: Tovarystvo ukrainskoi studiuiuchoi molodi im. M. Mikhnovskoho, 1960).

[12] "Poza mezhamy mozhlyvoho," *Literaturno-naukovyi vistnyk,* No. 10 (Lviv, 1900); reprinted in Bohdan Kravtsiv (ed.), *Vyvid prav Ukrainy: dokumenty i materiialy do istorii ukrainskoi politychnoi dumky* (New York: Prolog, 1964), pp. 134–153.

[13] See the articles on Dontsov (by V. Ianiv) and Lypynskyi (by I. L. Rudnytsky) in *Entsyklopediia Ukrainoznavstva: slovnykova chastyna,* Vols. II and IV (Paris-New York: Shevchenko Scientific Society, 1955–62), pp. 375–376 and 1292–1293. It is to be noted that both Dontsov and Lypynskyi achieved their full stature as political thinkers only after the Revolution.

striving is the achievement of cultural, economic and political independence by the entire Ukrainian-Ruthenian nation, and its future unification in one body politic."[14] This postulate had at first a declaratory rather than a practical political significance. But the worsening of the international situation, especially the growth of Russo-Austrian tension after 1908, moved it nearer to the sphere of political reality. The separatist concept found a striking expression in the manifesto issued on August 3, 1914, by the Supreme Ukrainian Council (*Holovna Ukrainska Rada*), a representative body founded at the outbreak of the war by the leaders of all Ukrainian parties in Galicia:

> The Russian tsars violated the Treaty of Pereiaslav [1654] by which they undertook the obligation to respect the independence of the Ukraine—and they enslaved the free Ukraine. For three hundred years the policy of the tsarist empire was to rob the subjugated Ukraine of her national soul, to make the Ukrainian people a part of the Russian people. The tsarist government has deprived the Ukrainian people of their most sacred right—the right of the native language. In contemporary tsarist Russia the most oppressed people are the Ukrainians. . . . Therefore, our path is clear. . . . The victory of the Austro-Hungarian Monarchy shall be our own victory. And the greater Russia's defeat, the sooner shall strike the hour of liberation for the Ukraine. . . . May the sun of a free Ukraine rise over the ruins of the tsarist empire![15]

In trying to assess the respective influence of the federalist and separatist alternatives in pre-Revolutionary Ukrainian political thinking, one must admit that the former was by far the more important. Not only did federalism enjoy chronological priority, but its theories were more impressively elaborated. The *samostiinyks* did not produce a theorist who could measure up to Drahomanov in intellectual stature or in the weightiness and sheer volume of his writings. As far as popular support is concerned, the idea of independent statehood had made headway only in Galicia prior to 1914. It is true that among the literary exponents of the separatist trend we find several natives of the Dnieper Ukraine: Mykola Mikhnovskyi, Viacheslav Lypynskyi, and Dmytro Dontsov. But they were unable to recruit more than a handful of followers among their

---

[14] Kost Levytskyi, *Istoriia politychnoi dumky halytskykh ukrainstsiv 1848–1914* (Lviv, 1926), p. 327.

[15] *Ibid.*, pp. 720–722.

compatriots in the Russian Empire. Mikhnovskyi's attempt, in 1902, to organize a Ukrainian People's Party (*Ukrainska Narodna Partiia*), with a nationalist-separatist program, proved stillborn. The bulk of the Ukrainian intelligentsia in the Russian Ukraine—and let us keep in mind that some four-fifths of the Ukrainian people lived within the borders of the Russian Empire—continued to adhere to the federalist platform. The only notable separatist political organization, whose members were central and eastern Ukrainians, was the Union for the Liberation of the Ukraine (*Soiuz Vyzvolennia Ukrainy*). But this was an émigré group, formed at the outbreak of the war by political exiles from the Dnieper Ukraine who resided in Austria. The Union owed its existence to the impact of the Galician-Ukrainian environment, and the organization's activities during war years took place wholly outside the Ukraine and within the camp of the Central Powers.[16]

The separatist, anti-Russian policy of the Union for the Liberation of the Ukraine was definitely rejected by the representative spokesmen of the Ukrainian national movement in Russia, Mykhailo Hrushevskyi and Symon Petliura (1879–1926). Hrushevkyi was spending the summer vacation of 1914 in the Carpathian Mountains, and the beginning of the war caught him on Austrian territory. The leaders of the newly founded Union approached him with the suggestion that he should move to Switzerland for the duration of the war and act on neutral soil as an authoritative representative of Ukrainian interests before world opinion. Hrushevskyi refused, and against considerable odds returned voluntarily through Italy to Russia. Upon his arrival in Kiev in November 1914, he was immediately arrested as a dangerous Ukrainian nationalist and spent the years before the fall of the tsarist regime in enforced residence in Kazan and Moscow.[17]

---

[16] On the Union for the Liberation of the Ukraine, see Dmytro Doroshenko, *Istoriia Ukrainy 1917–1923 rr.*, Vol. I (Uzhhorod, 1930–32), pp. 31–39; a selection of documents from the Austrian State Archives dealing with the Union, in Theophil Hornykiewicz (ed.), *Ereignisse in der Ukraine 1914–1922*, Vol. I (Horn, Austria: Verlag F. Berger for the W. K. Lypynsky East European Research Institute, Philadelphia, 1966), pp. 160–246; Wolfdieter Bihl, "Österreich-Ungarn und der 'Bund zur Befreiung der Ukraine'," in *Österreich und Europa: Festgabe für Hugo Hantsch zum 70. Geburtstag* (1965), pp. 505–526.

[17] See Liubomyr Vynar, "Chomu Mykhailo Hrushevskyi povernuvsia na

Petliura's political attitude is reflected in his letter (dated December 18, 1914) to Osyp Nazaruk (1883–1940), a prominent Galician journalist and politician sent to Stockholm by the Union for the Liberation of the Ukraine in order to re-establish contacts with the leaders of the Ukrainian movement in Russia. Petliura wrote: "Every step, word, or deed, which tends toward creating in the Russian Ukraine conditions subversive to the unity of the Russian state, or toward a weakening of that state at the present time [of war], is severely condemned in the Ukraine [by public opinion], because it is considered harmful also to Ukrainian interests."[18] Petliura roundly deprecated the orientation toward the Central Powers of the Galician Ukrainians and the émigré Union, and he expressed his conviction of Russia's invincibility. He also predicted that the war would lead to Russia's annexation of Galicia and Bukovina, an event he was willing to welcome as desirable from the viewpoint of Ukrainian interests. Hrushevskyi's and Petliura's demonstrations of loyalty to Russia in 1914 are, indeed, remarkable in view of the fact that only three years later they were to be counted among the founding fathers of an independent Ukrainian People's Republic. One of them, Petliura, was also to emerge soon

---

Ukrainu v 1914 rotsi?," *Ukrainskyi istoryk*, IV, 3–4 (New York-Munich, 1967), pp. 103–108. Vynar stresses Hrushevskyi's wish to refute, by his voluntary return, the charge frequently raised in the Russian reactionary press that the Ukrainian movement was allegedly pro-Austrian. Thus, Hrushevskyi hoped to deter persecution against his political friends. One need not deny that this motive played a part in Hrushevskyi's decision, but it may still be asserted that the primary motive derived from his general political philosophy.

[18] Symon Petliura, *Statti, lysty, dokumenty* (New York: Ukrainian Academy of Arts and Sciences, 1956), pp. 188–190. One has to take into account that Petliura was probably trying to provide an alibi for himself and his political friends in case his letter should fall into the hands of the Russian authorities. This would explain the almost exaggerated phrasing of the letter. Still, there is no reason to doubt that the expressed opinions corresponded with his basic convictions, which can be corroborated also from other sources. In a conversation with a friend, held at the beginning of the war, Petliura defined his political creed in the following manner: "In this critical moment we must make a clear decision. Our decision is the logical consequence of our old principles: to build the future of our people together with the peoples of Russia, and with their support." See Oleksander Lototskyi, *Storinky mynuloho*, Vol. III (Warsaw: Ukrainskyi Naukovyi Instytut, 1932–39), p. 264.

afterward as the standard bearer and living symbol of the Ukraine's armed struggle against the Russia of both Lenin and Denikin.

One wonders, then, why the federalist concept predominated in pre-Revolutionary Ukrainian political thought. First, we must take into account that the Ukraine had belonged to the Russian Empire for about 250 years (although for the first century, it is true, she enjoyed an autonomous status), and that this prolonged connection had formed a pronounced material and psychological bond between the Ukraine and Russia proper. Despite their grievances against the centralism of St. Petersburg, the Ukrainians did not feel themselves strangers in an empire to whose development many individuals of Ukrainian origin had made significant contributions. However, the acceptance of the empire, which appeared as an overwhelming and unshakable reality, could, and did, co-exist in Ukrainian minds with an awareness of a distinct Ukrainian ethnic identity and an allegiance to the special political and cultural interests of the homeland.

Two currents can be distinguished among the educated classes of the Ukraine in the second half of the nineteenth and early twentieth centuries: the "Little Russian" trend, whose supporters affirmed the merger of their people with Russia to the point of complete assimilation; and the Ukrainian nationalist trend, which attempted, with varying degrees of intensity, to preserve and strengthen a Ukrainian cultural and to some extent political identity. Not only the "Little Russians" but also the so-called "conscious Ukrainians" experienced the strong impact of Russian imperial civilization and, so to speak, stood with one foot in the all-Russian world. Prominent Ukrainian civil figures often belonged simultaneously to various Russian revolutionary and oppositional groups or made their living as Russian civil servants or zemstvo functionaries. Many eminent Ukrainian writers—from Hryhorii Kvitka-Osnovianenko (1778–1843) to Volodymyr Vynnychenko (1880–1951)—were bilingual. Outstanding Ukrainian scholars— such as the historians Mykola Kostomarov (1817–1885), Volodymyr Antonovych (1834–1908), Dmytro Bahalii (1857–1932), the linguist Oleksandr Potebnia (1835–1892), the sociologist Bohdan Kistiakovskyi (1868–1920), the economist Mykhailo Tugan-Baranovskyi (1865–1919)—occupied chairs at Russian universities and published their works in Russian. And one cannot forget, of course, the ecclesiastical unity between the Ukrainian and Russian peoples and the close economic links between the Empire's Great Russian North and the Ukrainian South.[19]

An astute Polish student of Russia's nationality problems, Leon Wasilewski, wrote on the eve of the First World War:

A Ukrainian intellectual always remains a Russian. Educated in Russian schools, and raised on Russian literature, in his public life —as a civil servant, lawyer, teacher, physician, scientist, etc.—he constantly uses the Russian language. . . . This symbiosis with the Russian element has created among the Ukrainian intelligentsia a feeling of complete national unity with Russia.[20]

Wasilewski's observations call for some critical comments. The fact that educated Ukrainians had experienced the strong impact of Russian imperial civilization did not mean that they had been turned into true Russians in the ethnic sense of the world. Moreover, the existence of an irreducible Ukrainian ethnic identity generated an awareness—if sometimes only in rudimentary form— of a separate cultural and political tradition. The extreme case of the "Little Russians" is particularly instructive. Close scrutiny shows that although they wished to identify completely with Russia, they retained certain specifically Ukrainian traits in their mental make-up.[21] Under favorable circumstances, this repressed "Ukrainian

---

[19] This statement, though essentially correct, needs to be qualified. While most Ukrainians belonged to the Russian Orthodox Church, the religious situation of the Ukrainian and the Russian peoples showed some significant divergent features. Also, the fact that the Ukraine was economically integrated in the Russian Empire did not preclude the fact that the economic interests of the Ukrainian South were often opposed to those of the Great Russian North. Limitations of space prevent the discussion of these important and highly complex issues, but the existence of the problems can be signaled and two works mentioned which, though by no means exhaustive, may provide a preliminary orientation. For the religious problem: Eduard Winter, *Byzanz und Rom im Kampfe um die Ukraine, 955–1939* (Leipzig: Otto Harrassowitz, 1942); for the economic problem: Konstantyn Kononenko, *Ukraine and Russia: A History of the Economic Relations Between Ukraine and Russia (1654–1917)* (Milwaukee, Wisconsin: Marquette University Press, 1958).

[20] Leon Wasilewski, *Ukraina i sprawa ukraińska* (Cracow: Książka, 1911), p. 194–195.

[21] A study of the problem would have to begin with an investigation of Russian writers of Ukrainian origin. The best-known case is Nikolai

complex" broke through with a force comparable to that of a religious conversion. In 1917, when the spell of the Empire was broken, thousands of former "Little Russians" almost overnight rediscovered themselves as nationally conscious Ukrainian patriots and potential separatists. While correctly assessing the extent of the russification of the Ukraine on the eve of the First World War, Wasilewski underestimated the potential strength of deep-seated Ukrainian nationalism.

A student of history must be sparing in the use of analogies. Nevertheless, a judicious application of comparisons may contribute to the illumination of a specific problem. If we search for cases paralleling that of pre-Revolutionary Ukraine, we will have to look toward other nationalities submerged under great empires and struggling for survival against the pressures and lures of a prestigious imperial civilization. The great historian and "Father of the Czech Nation," František Palacký, declared in 1848: "Certainly, if the Austrian Empire had not existed for ages, we would be obliged in the interests of Europe and even of mankind to create it as fast as possible."[22] Throughout the nineteenth century, Czech spokesmen continued to view the future of their nation within the framework of the Austrian Empire, which they wished to reorganize as a federation of nationalities, among whom the Czechs would inevitably play a distinguished role. This view was shared prior to 1914 by Thomas Masaryk, the future founder of the Czechoslovak Republic. It was the frustration of the hopes for Austria's constitutional reform, particularly after the Austro-Hungarian Compromise of 1867, which undermined this original loyalty of the Czechs to the Habsburg Monarchy. But, despite the growing political disaffection and the acrimonious ethnic rivalry between the Czechs and the Germans in Bohemia, the impact of Austrian mores on Czech society was very deep, and its marks are still clearly visible today.

Gogol, but other numerous, if less illustrious, examples could be adduced. A brilliant treatment is found in the essay of Evhen Malaniuk, "Malorosiistvo," *Knyha sposterezhen,* Vol. II (Toronto: Homin Ukrainy, 1962–66), pp. 229–241.

[22] Palacký's letter of April 11, 1848, addressed to the Preparatory Committee of the German National Assembly at Frankfurt; quoted from Hans Kohn, *Pan-Slavism: Its History and Ideology* (2nd rev. ed.; New York: Vintage, 1960), p. 77.

The fate of the nationalities of the "Celtic fringe" of the British Islands may also be considered. The emergence of a worldwide British Empire in the eighteenth century weakened the national identity of Scotland and Ireland by providing their traditional leading classes and the most energetic elements of the common people with new outlets: participation in Britain's economic enterprise and colonial expansion. Still, the Celtic nations of Great Britain, which seemed moribund a century ago, did not perish. Ireland, despite terrible population losses and the virtual extinction of the native language, regained political independence after the First World War. In our own times, we have witnessed a resurgence of Welsh and Scottish nationalism—a trend certainly connected with the passing of the old British Empire.[23]

We must not forget, of course, that the case of the Ukraine in certain essential aspects differs from the examples mentioned above. For instance, linguistically the Ukrainians certainly are closer to the Russians than the Czechs are to the Germans; nor are the Ukrainians differentiated from the Russians by religion, as the Irish are from the English. The most important difference, however, was of a political nature. The Ukrainian national movement was hampered by the Russian Empire's absolutist structure, which did not exist either in liberal England or even in conservative-constitutional Austria.

With these factors in mind, we are perhaps better prepared to understand the meaning of the prevalence of the federalist concept in pre-Revolutionary Ukrainian political thought: it was an attempt to strike a balance between national and imperial interests. Ukrainian patriots connected the prospects of national liberation with hopes for a future democratic and decentralized Russia. As their final goal, they envisaged the transformation of the centralistic

---

[23] It might be interesting to note that the example of Wales has been recently referred to by a Soviet Ukrainian publicist, writing in defense of Ukrainian linguistic and cultural rights in the USSR: "The Welsh language, which was considered to be on the point of extinction and which in 1921 was spoken in Britain by 930,000 people, is to become an official language in Wales, since it is now used by 3,000,000! All over the world nations are not dying out but, on the contrary, are developing and growing stronger, in order to offer as much as possible to humanity, to contribute as much as possible to the creation of the universal human race." Ivan Dziuba, *Internationalism or Russification?: A Study in the Soviet Nationalities Problem* (London: Weidenfield and Nicolson, 1968), p. 207.

Russian Empire into a commonwealth of free and equal peoples, within which the Ukraine would enjoy not only free cultural development but also political self-government. This ideal was already clearly formulated in the basic programmatic document of the Brotherhood of SS. Cyril and Methodius, *The Book of the Genesis of the Ukrainian People,* composed by Mykola Kostomarov in 1846: "And the Ukraine shall be an independent republic within the Slavic Union."[24] The ideology of the Brotherhood was colored by romantic Pan-Slavism.

The spokesman of the next, positivist generation, Mykhailo Drahomanov, restated the same ideal in more sober terms in 1882: "The independence of a given country and nation can be achieved either by its secession into a separate state (separatism), or by the securing of its self-government, without such separation (federalism)."[25] Of these two alternatives, Drahomanov definitely preferred the latter. It is noteworthy, however, that both Kostomarov and Drahomanov considered federalism not as an abdication from national independence but rather as the most rational and convenient form of achieving independence. This explains how it was possible, once faith in the feasibility of federalism collapsed, for Ukrainian political thought to turn quickly toward the concept of *samostiinist.*

The strength of the federalist concept lay in its correspondence to the objective conditions of the Ukrainian people prior to 1917. It was obvious that the progress of the Ukrainian national cause depended on the evolution of Russia as a whole. But federalism had also certain weak spots, which, if not fully visible to contemporaries, are easily identifiable in retrospect.

The fate of the federalist idea depended on the presence of forces within the dominant Russian nation that were willing to back this program.[26] The prospects were not encouraging. Since the Muscovite period, the Russian state had been highly centralized; a transition to federalism would have implied a break with the national past and the abandonment of a deeply ingrained tradition. Moreover, it was with regard to the question of the Ukraine that the Russians

---

[24] Luciani, *Le Livre,* p. 142.

[25] "Istoricheskaia Polsha i velikorusskaia demokratsiia," in *Sobranie,* Vol. II, p. 253.

[26] For a general discussion of this problem, see Georg von Rauch, *Russland: Staatliche Einheit und nationale Vielheit, Föderalistische Kräfte und Ideen in der russischen Geschichte* (München: Isar Vlg., 1953).

displayed a particularly defensive and intransigent attitude. Many Russians were willing to recognize that Poland, Finland, and perhaps the Baltic provinces possessed national identities that could never be fully assimilated, and thus these areas possibly merited a more or less autonomous status. Caucasia and Central Asia, whatever their strategic and economic importance, were recent colonial acquisitions, profoundly alien by race and culture, and their position in the Empire was obviously marginal.

The case of the Ukraine was altogether different. The emergence of the modern Russian Empire was based on the absorption of the Ukraine in the course of the second half of the seventeenth and the eighteenth centuries. The undoing of the work of Peter I and Catherine II appeared to threaten Russia's position as a great European power. The idea that the Ukraine was a distinct nation, and not a regional subdivision of an all-Russian nation, was unpalatable to Russian public opinion. The distinguished Russian historian and social philosopher, Georgii Fedotov, wrote in 1947:

> The awakening of the Ukraine, and especially the separatist character of the Ukrainian movement, surprised the Russian intelligentsia, and remained incomprehensible to them to the very end. We loved the Ukraine, its land, its people, its songs—and considered all this our very own.[27]

A full generation after the Revolution, Fedotov did not yet realize that the separatist character of the Ukrainian movement appeared only at a later stage and that its appearance was a result precisely of the Russians' peculiar "love of the Ukraine," which amounted to a denial of the Ukrainians' right to a national identity of their own.

The policy of the tsarist regime toward the Ukrainian national movement was, despite some minor tactical shifts, fully consistent: it was one of relentless repression. It was no wonder that Ukrainian patriots in their search for potential Russian allies pinned their hopes only on Russian radical and revolutionary forces. There were a few Russian revolutionary leaders—for example, Herzen—who showed an understanding of the plight of the Empire's oppressed nationalities and who leaned toward federalism. But, unfortunately, they were by far outweighed by the intellectual descendants of

---

[27] G. P. Fedotov, *Novyi grad* (New York: Izd. imeni Chekhova, 1952), p. 191.

Pestel, partisans of a centralized revolutionary dictatorship, whose attitude toward the claims of the non-Russian nationalities was one of indifference at best, and who met all federalist schemes with an undisguised hostility. It was by no means a fortuitous personal bias that made the celebrated leader of Russian radical thought, Belinskii, attack with savage scorn the Ukrainian literary revival of the 1830's and the 1840's.[28] Drahomanov was hardly mistaken in his conviction that the "Jacobin" proclivities of the Russian revolutionaries (he was referring to the Populists of the 1870's and the 1880's) constituted a grave potential threat to the cause of liberty of all peoples in the Russian Empire: "[The Russian revolutionaries] do not desire to shake the idea of a centralized and autocratic state, but only to transfer power into other hands."[29] And elsewhere:

> These mores . . . make the [Russian] revolutionary circles similar to the governmental circles: consequently, the future political system, founded by the revolutionaries, would be similar to the one existing now [i.e., to the system of tsarist autocracy].[30]

It should be remembered that these words were pronounced by a man who always believed in the necessity for Ukrainian-Russian cooperation, one based on genuine freedom and equality for both sides. Shortly before his death, Drahomanov responded to a right-wing Ukrainian critic:

> If we were to concede that the policy of Russification is an outflow of the "spirit," the "character," etc., of the Great Russian people, then only the choice between two alternatives would be left to us. The first alternative: resolutely to embrace separatism, either by forming an independent state, or by seceding to another state. The other alternative would be to fold our hands and to look forward to

---

[28] Belinskii's attitude toward the Ukraine has been scrutinized by Drahomanov in the preface to his publication of "Pismo V. G. Belinskogo k N. V. Gogoliu" (1880), reprinted in *Sobranie*, Vol. II, pp. 231–250. For a recent discussion of this problem, see Victor Swoboda, "Shevchenko and Belinsky," *The Slavonic and East European Review*, XXXIX, 2 (London, 1961), pp. 168–183. A sophistic attempt by a Soviet literary historian to clear Belinskii from the charge of Ukrainophobia is found in I. I. Bass, *V. H. Belinskyi i ukrainska literatura 30–40-kh rokiv XIX st.* (Kiev: Derzhavne vyd. khudozhnoi literatury, 1963).

[29] *Sobranie*, Vol. I, p. 220.

[30] *Ibid.*, Vol. II, p. 386.

our death, if we were to decide that separatism is beyond our will and strength.[31]

Drahomanov rejected the premises of this reasoning, and, therefore, he refused to accept the dilemma as genuine. Despite his skepticism regarding Russian revolutionaries, he continued to uphold to the last the program of an alliance between Ukrainian and Russian progressive forces. But the day was not too distant when Drahomanov's intellectual descendants, taught by bitter experience, were to reach the conclusion that a complete break-up of the Russian imperial state was a more realistic goal than its democratization and federalization, and that for the Ukraine the alternatives were, indeed, either independent statehood or national annihilation.

The second major drawback of the federalist concept was that it exercised, to some extent, a debilitating effect on the morale of Ukrainian society. Renunciation of the ideal of sovereign statehood dampened the energy of the national movement and lessened its militancy and fervor. The historian of Ukrainian political ideologies, Iuliian Okhrymovych (1893–1921), made a critical observation about Drahomanov, which could be applied also to the entire Ukrainian national movement of the second half of the nineteenth century: "He did not appreciate sufficiently the educational importance of maximal demands."[32] The fact that the basis of the federalist program was a compromise between Ukrainian and all-Russian interests gave it a lukewarm and timid air. This was at least one of the reasons why many young Ukrainians—an example being the heroic leader of the *Narodnaia Volia* (The People's Will Party), Andrei Zheliabov[33]—joined the ranks of the Russian revolutionaries and thus weakened the national movement.

---

[31] Mykhailo Drahomanov, *Chudatski dumky pro ukrainsku natsionalnu spravu* ([Vienna?]: Partiia Ukrainskykh Sotsiialistiv-Revoliutsioneriv, 1915), p. 94.

[32] Iuliian Okhrymovych, *Rozvytok ukrainskoi natsionalno-politychnoi dumky* (reprint of the 1922 ed.; New York: Vyd. Chartoryiskykh, 1965), p. 115.

[33] In a letter to Drahomanov on May 12, 1880, Zheliabov rationalized his leaving the Ukrainian national movement for Russian revolutionary activities in the following manner: "Where are our Fenians, where is our Parnell? The state of affairs is such that . . . while one sees salvation in the disintegration of the empire into autonomous parts, one is obliged to

It is instructive to compare the attitude of Drahomanov with that of his former disciple, Ivan Franko. The latter also believed that "the ideal of national independence lies for us at the present, from today's perspective, beyond the limits of the politically and culturally possible." But Franko continued:

> [*Samostiinist* belongs to the ideals] capable of inflaming the heart of the masses, of inducing people to the greatest efforts and the harshest sacrifices, and of giving them strength in the most severe trials and ordeals. . . . The thousand paths which lead to the realization [of the ideal of an independent Ukrainian state] are to be found directly under our feet. If we are aware of this ideal, and give our assent to it, we shall move along these paths, otherwise we may turn onto some very different roads.[34]

But pre-Revolutionary Ukrainian political thinking found it too difficult to take the bold step suggested by Franko. A great shock—the experience of 1917—was needed to effect a change in the mind of the Ukrainian community.

It was no accident that prior to the First World War the idea of *samostiinist* had found a mass following only in Galicia. The Galician Ukrainians, who lived under the rule of the Habsburg Monarchy, were directly exposed neither to Russian governmental pressure nor to the allure of Russian imperial civilization. The Russian impact, however, was also felt in Galicia, in the form of the so-called Muscophile, or Russophile, trend.[35] But the Galicians' separatism with regard to Russia had a reverse side—namely, their loyalty to Austria. It was true that the Austrian constitutional system had glaring shortcomings and that the Galician administration was controlled by the Poles, but the Austrian constitutional system assured the "Ruthenians" certain basic civil liberties and prere-

---

demand an [all-Russian] constituent assembly." The purpose of Zheliabov's letter was to offer to Drahomanov the position of the representative of *Narodnaia volia* in Western Europe. The text of Zheliabov's letter, with Drahomanov's comments, is to be found in *Sobranie*, Vol. II, pp. 413–435; the quoted passage is on p. 417.

[34] Ivan Franko, "Poza mezhamy mozhlyvoho," in *Vyvid prav Ukrainy*, p. 151–152.

[35] See Ivan L. Rudnytsky, "The Ukrainians in Galicia under Austrian Rule," *Austrian History Yearbook*, Vol. III, Pt. 2 (Houston, 1967), especially the section, "The Russian and the Ukrainian Idea in Galicia," pp. 408–416.

quisites for cultural and national-political advancement. The Dnieper Ukrainians, for their part, had no reason whatsoever to sympathize with Austria. This explains why anti-Russian separatism, in its specifically Galician version, failed to make many proselytes among the population of the central-eastern Ukraine.

At the outbreak of the war, the Galician Ukrainians pinned all their hopes on the final victory of Austria-Hungary and Germany.[36] As we have seen, this pro-Central Powers orientation was definitely rejected by the leaders of the Ukrainian movement in Russia. In their opinion, Vienna and Berlin intended to exploit the Ukrainian trump-card propagandistically, to use Ukrainian nationalism as a subversive force against Russia but without subscribing to any political commitments in favor of the Ukrainian cause.[37] A great danger existed in that the Central Powers, even in the event of a victorious outcome of the war, would finally come to an agreement with Russia, leaving most Ukrainian lands under the rule of the latter. Was it worthwhile, for the sake of dubious foreign aid, to compromise the Ukrainian national movement in Russia by provoking the Russian government and society into cruel reprisals?[38] Hrushevskyi and certain other Ukrainian leaders thought

---

[36] An exception to this pro-Austrian orientation of the Galician Ukrainians during the First World War was a small secret group of left-wing university and secondary school students. The group called itself the Drahomanov Organization (*Drahomanivka*), and adopted in the spring of 1918 the name of International Revolutionary Social Democratic Youth (*Internatsionalna revoliutsiina sotsiial-demokratychna molod*). Later it became the nucleus of the Communist Party of Western Ukraine. See Anonymous [Roman Rozdolskyi]. "Do istorii ukrainskoho livo-sotsiialistychnoho rukhu v Halychyni," *Vpered,* Nos. 3–4 (Munich, 1951).

[37] A glaring example of Austria's duplicity toward the Ukrainians was the imperial rescript of November 4, 1916, which extended the scope of Galicia's provincial autonomy and perpetuated Polish domination in the province, thus dashing Ukrainian hopes for the division of Galicia on ethnic lines. The rescript implied that at a later time an undivided Galicia would be united with a Polish Kingdom which the Central Powers had proclaimed on the territory they occupied in Russian Poland. If Vienna was willing to disregard so cavalierly the vital interests of its own loyal Ukrainian subjects, what could the Dnieper Ukrainians expect from it?

[38] The Russian jingoists persistently accused the Ukrainian movement of serving foreign, Austrian interests. For instance, the governor of Poltava province, Baggamut, reported on February 4, 1914, to the Minister of

in historical terms; they could not forget that the Cossack hetmans struggling against Muscovite encroachments tried to lean on the unreliable and often treacherous support of foreign powers—as in the case of Ivan Vyhovskyi (ruled 1657–1659) with Poland, Petro Doroshenko (1665–1675) with Turkey, and Ivan Mazepa (1687–1709) with Sweden. All these ventures brought great misfortunes to the Ukrainian people.

The formation of Ukrainian statehood passed through two distinct stages during the era of the Central Rada. The first lasted from spring to late fall, 1917; the second encompassed the winter of 1917–1918. The former may be defined as autonomist and the latter as separatist. Paradoxically, the task of building an independent state developed not on the old *samostiinyky,* but rather on the self-professed federalists. Neither the followers of Mikhnovskyi, who, after the outbreak of the Revolution, organized the Party of Socialist-Independentists, nor the émigré Union for the Liberation of the Ukraine had any major impact on the country's political development in 1917. The leadership of the Ukrainian Revolution rested in the hands of three parties, all of whom had a definitely federalistic outlook: the Marxist Social Democrats, the peasant-

---

Interior that "the Ukrainian movement—whose basic idea is the creation of an autonomous Ukraine under the scepter of the Habsburg dynasty—has been assuming ever greater expansion in recent times." The text of Baggamut's report has been published in *Ukrainskyi istorychnyi zhurnal,* No. 1 (Kiev, 1969), pp. 114–116. The Club of Russian Nationalists in Kiev sent, on January 13, 1914, a telegram to the Chairman of the Council of Ministers in St. Petersburg, which contained the following denunciation: "The plans of the *mazepintsy* consist in tearing away from Russia the whole of Little Russia, as far as the Volga River and the Caucasus, with a view toward incorporating it as an autonomous entity into Austria-Hungary." The telegram is reproduced in Oleksander Lototskyi, *Storinky mynuloho,* Vol. III, pp. 255–256. (The term *mazepintsy,* "the followers of Mazepa,"—the Cossack Hetman who in alliance with Charles XII of Sweden revolted against Peter I in 1708—was a Russian word of abuse for Ukrainian patriots. It implied that Ukrainians were traitors in the service of foreign powers.) Similar accusations appeared frequently in reactionary Russian newspapers such as *Novoe vremia, Moskovskie vedomosti, Kievlianin,* and others. Samples are to be found in S. N. Shchegolev, *Ukrainskoe dvizhenie kak sovremennyi ètap iuzhnorusskogo separatizma* (Kiev, 1912), pp. 476 ff.

oriented Socialist-Revolutionaries, and the party of the liberal intelligentsia, which assumed the name of Socialist-Federalists. They found themselves at the helm because at the time they in fact represented the Ukrainian political elite. Their purpose was to build an autonomous Ukraine as a component of an all-Russian federation, but within a few months the logic of events carried them beyond their original goal.

Students of the history of the Ukrainian Revolution must never lose sight of one crucial fact: the process of the crystallization of a modern nation was markedly retarded in the Ukraine. In this respect, there was a great difference between the Ukrainians and other Eastern European peoples. In the case of the Finns, the Poles, and the Czechs, national formation preceded the attainment of political independence. The Ukrainians, on the other hand, had the problem of statehood thrust upon them at a time when they were just beginning to emerge from the conditions of an amorphous ethnic mass. Memoirists and historians of the period rightly stress the structural deficiencies that hampered the Ukrainian cause in 1917: an inadequate mass national consciousness, the insufficient numerical strength and lack of experience of the leading cadres, and the predominance of alien ethnic elements in the country's cities.

Despite these obstacles, the Ukrainian movement demonstrated amazing strength soon after the fall of the tsarist regime. Volodymyr Vynnychenko, a prominent member of the Rada and head of the first Ukrainian autonomous government (General Secretariat), noted in his reminiscences: "In those days we were truly like gods; we were creating a whole new world out of nothing."[39] One may speak of the year 1917 as the Ukrainian *annus mirabilis*. Of decisive importance was the national awakening of the Ukrainian masses.

Furthermore, the Central Rada achieved some remarkable political success. The inclusion of representatives of the local Russian, Polish, and Jewish minorities transformed the Rada from an organ of the Ukrainian national movement into an authoritative legislative body, a territorial parliament. The Russian Provisional Government—the heir of the tsarist government which only yesterday had denied the very existence of a Ukrainian nation—was obliged to recognize the autonomy of the Ukraine in principle, although it tried to curtail both the size of the autonomous territory

---

[39] V. Vynnychenko, *Vidrodzhennia natsii,* Vol. I (Kiev-Vienna: Vyd. Dzvin, 1920), p. 258.

and the extent of the autonomous administration's competence. Since the suppression of the Hetmanate and the Zaporozhian *Sich* in the late eighteenth century, this was the first major political concession that Russia had ever made in favor of the Ukraine.[40]

It should be noted that even while adhering to a federalist program, the Rada initiated certain policies which claimed for the Ukraine, at least by implication, the rights of a sovereign state. An example of this was the drive for concentrating Ukrainian soldiers serving in the Russian army into special national units, the so-called "Ukrainianization of the bayonet."[41] The Rada also demanded the admission of a special Ukrainian delegation to the future peace conference. Finally, it was decided to convoke a separate Ukrainian Constituent Assembly, which was to meet independently of the All-Russian Constituent Assembly. However, the leaders of the Rada loyally supported Russia's war effort and avoided all contacts with those Ukrainian groups across the frontline—either Galician or émigré—that cooperated with Russia's enemies. Thus, as late as the summer of 1917, the Rada was still fully committed to the federalist concept.

The Third Universal—the proclamation of a Ukrainian People's Republic within the framework of a federated Russian Republic—was the climax of the entire preceding policy of the Rada, the fulfillment of the sincere aspirations of its leaders. But the historical process has a logic of its own which transcends the plans and the wishes of the actors. By the fall of 1917, the entire political constella-

---

[40] The Provisional Government recognized Ukrainian autonomy in principle by its Declaration of July 16, 1917. (For the text of the document, see Doroshenko, Vol. I, p. 114–115). By its "Instruction" of August 17, however, the Provisional Government limited the autonomous territory to five provinces (Kiev, Volhynia, Podillia, Poltava, and Chernihiv), excluding from it the industrial areas of the southern and eastern Ukraine. The number of departments of the General Secretariat (the autonomous Ukrainian government) was to be reduced from fourteen (as proposed by the Rada) to nine; not only military affairs, railways and communications, but even judicial matters and food supplies were to be removed from the competence of the Ukrainian administration. *Ibid.*, pp. 124 ff.

[41] Volodymyr Kedrovskyi, "Ukrainizatsiia v rosiiskii armii," *Ukrainskyi istoryk*, IV, 3–4 (New York-Munich, 1967), pp. 61–77; A. H. Tkachuk, "Krakh sprob Tsentralnoi Rady vykorystaty ukrainizovani viiskovi formuvannia v 1917 r.," *Ukrainskyi istorychnyi zhurnal*, No. 8 (Kiev, 1967), pp. 75–84.

tion had changed so radically that the Third Universal was already an anachronism at the time of its adoption. The swift current of events had eroded the foundations of the federalist concept. Two new factors entered the political scene: the disintegration of the Russian army and the Bolshevik seizure of power in Petrograd and Moscow.

It could not have been expected that the Ukraine, with its own meager resources or even with the aid of the Entente, might have been capable of carrying on the war against the Central Powers.[42] But as long as the war continued, there existed the acute danger that the Germans and Austro-Hungarians might move into the Ukraine, treating it merely as an occupied Russian territory. Even more threatening to the security of the country was the presence, in the Right-Bank Ukraine, of demoralized Russian troops, among whom Bolshevik agitators wielded much influence. While these remnants of the old imperial army did not offer any effective protection against Germany, they spread violence and anarchy in the country. Thus, it had become imperative for the Ukraine to terminate the war as quickly as possible by negotiating a separate peace with Germany and her allies. The circumstances were propitious because Germany, locked in deathly combat with her Western adversaries, also wished to end the war in the East. Moreover, Germany and Austria-Hungary needed Ukrainian foodstuffs and raw materials. This gave the Ukraine a certain bargaining strength, in spite of the disparity in military power. The circumstances demanded that the Ukraine embark on an independent foreign policy, which in turn necessitated breaking the constitutional links that still bound the country to Russia.

Separation had also become inevitable because of the nature of the new regime in Russia proper, which had come to power as a

---

[42] Relations between the Entente powers and the Ukrainian People's Republic in November-December 1917 have been extensively discussed by Oleh S. Pidhainy, *The Formation of the Ukrainian Republic* (Toronto and New York: New Review Books, 1966), pp. 283–400. However, it would seem that the author gives excessive importance to these tentative contacts. As a matter of fact, neither side was able to deliver the goods desired by the other party: the Ukraine was not in a position to shoulder the burden of a continued war against the Central Powers, while France and Great Britain could not offer effective protection against either the Germans or the Bolsheviks. Thus, objective conditions were adverse to cooperation between the Ukraine and the Allies at that time.

result of the October *coup d'état*. The crux of the matter was not that Lenin was more of a Russian chauvinist than his predecessor Kerensky. Quite to the contrary, among the Russian leaders of that time Lenin was the most broadminded on the nationalities issue and the most realistic in his appreciation of the Ukraine as a power factor. But, from the onset, Lenin's regime was marked by dictatorial and terroristic traits. To use latter-day terminology, this was an incipient totalitarian regime. The Central Rada, on the other hand, was an outgrowth of the libertarian and humanistic traditions of the pre-Revolutionary Ukrainian national movement. With all its shortcomings, the Rada strove to give to the Ukraine a democratic socialism of the European type. It was quite impossible to unite Russia and the Ukraine under a common federative roof; they were two countries whose respective internal developments were incompatible. Against those "blessings" which Bolshevism was bringing from the north, the Ukraine was obliged to protect herself by erecting the barrier of a state frontier.

In stressing the essentially democratic character of the Ukrainian People's Republic of 1917–1918, it is not intended to make this body politic appear in a more favorable light than it actually merits. The long subjugation under the rule of tsarist autocracy had lowered the Ukrainian community's level of civic culture. In this respect, the Galician Ukrainians, who had passed through the school of Austrian constitutionalism and parliamentarianism, were more fortunate than their compatriots under Russian imperial rule. The inadequate political and legal training of the Rada's leaders was reflected in the drafting of the Universals. These major state papers, which possessed the significance of fundamental laws, were wordy and overloaded with secondary matters, while the formulation of the salient points often lacked precision.

Another weakness of the Rada was its inclination toward utopianism in dealing with social and economic problems. Conditions in the Ukraine were such that a revolution necessarily had to be both national and social. Thus, the hegemony of left-wing elements in Ukrainian politics in 1917 is not difficult to understand. Ukrainian socialist parties were essentially democratic, and this differentiated them from the Russian Bolsheviks. They bore, however, the hallmarks of the Populist tradition, a nineteenth-century movement that profoundly affected the outlook of the radical intelligentsia both in Russia proper and in the Ukraine. The parties that controlled the Rada displayed a naive worship of "the people"—the peasantry. Moreover, the desire not to be outbid by Bolshevik demagoguery strengthened the tendency toward utopian schemes. This found a striking expression in the land law adopted by the Rada on January 18, 1918, whose main feature was the abolition of private ownership of the land.[43] It is true that the slogan of "socialization of land" enjoyed considerable popularity among the masses of the poorer peasants and agricultural workers, but this did not mean that the peasants really desired a collectivist organization of agriculture. In fact, this was quite unimaginable to them. A contemporary observer, well acquainted with conditions in the Ukrainian countryside, noted: "All peasants understand socialization simply as taking over the land from the landowners without compensation."[44] The Russian repartitional village commune (*obshchina*) was alien to the highly individualistic Ukrainian peasantry. A wiser Rada might have effected the necessary agrarian reform without overturning the principle of private land ownership, an ill-considered measure that caused a profound disturbance in the life of the countryside.

Mykola Kovalevskyi (1892–1957), a leading Ukrainian Socialist-Revolutionary and minister of supplies in the Rada government, records in his memoirs the conversations that he had with the German envoy to the Ukraine, Baron Adolf Mumm von Schwarzenstein, and the financial councilor at the German legation, Carl Melchior. The exchanges took place in the spring of 1918, after the Rada had returned to Kiev with German military support:

> During our conversations, Baron von Mumm and he [Melchior] tried to convince me about the impossibility of having agricultural production organized without the right of private ownership of land. What worried them most was that the breaking-up of the great estates would lower the productivity of Ukrainian agriculture. In addition, they tried to convince me that such an agrarian reform would ruin the finances of the state. Therefore, they thought, it would be preferable to demand from the peasants the payment of a so-called indemnity. The Frankfurt banker [Melchior] argued that by this measure the state would profit both politically and financially. According to him, the political advantage was to consist in the following: if the peasants

---

[43] See Illia Vytanovych, "Agrarna polityka ukrainskykh uriadiv, 1917–1920," *Ukrainskyi istoryk*, IV, 3–4 (New York-Munich, 1967), pp. 5–60.

[44] Ievhen Chykalenko, *Uryvok z moikh spomyniv za 1917 r.* (Prague, 1932), p. 22.

were to pay an indemnity, the influential class of great and middle landowners would not become alienated from the Ukrainian state. At the least, the hostility of that class, which still possessed some strength in the Ukraine, would be neutralized. As to the financial profit, the indemnity payments of the peasants—who, according to Melchior, had much cash hoarded—would flow into the state treasury, while the landowners would be reimbursed in long-term bonds. Thus, the state would make a huge profit on this transaction, and, most important, the country's finances would be put on a firm foundation. This stressing of a double profit was most characteristic of the German mind. I was somewhat shocked by this cynicism of the German negotiators, but I felt obliged to report the gist of each conversation to my government.[45]

As revealed in his memoirs, Kovalevskyi was generally a man of excellent political judgment. It seems surprising, then, that the advice which he received from Mumm and Melchior struck him as "cynical." To someone less influenced by Populist myths, this advice might have sounded rather like the voice of common sense. The Rada certainly committed a blunder by alienating the moderate and proprietary segments of the community. But for this, the rightist *coup d'état* of General Pavlo Skoropadskyi (1873–1945) on April 29, 1918, could probably have been avoided.[46]

In criticizing the doctrinaire character of the Rada's social and economic legislation, we should not overlook its constructive achievements in other fields. The record was particularly brilliant in deal-

---

[45] Mykola Kovalevskyi, *Pry dzherelakh borotby* (Innsbruck: Published by Maria Kovalevska, 1960), p. 471–472.

[46] One could argue that the radical nature of the Central Rada's agrarian legislation was a necessary result of the plight of the Ukrainian peasantry, whose interests it was bound to defend. This view, however, is refuted by the following observation. Agrarian conditions in Galicia were more unsatisfactory and the poverty of the peasants was greater than in the Dnieper Ukraine. Nevertheless, the law on agrarian reform adopted on April 14, 1919, by the National Council (parliament) of the Western Region of the Ukrainian People's Republic (eastern Galicia) preserved the principle of private land ownership by the small landholders; the question of indemnity for the great landowners, whose estates were to be expropriated, was to be settled by a separate future enactment. (Vytanovych, pp. 52–56). The contrasting Galician example proves that the Rada's policy of socialization of land was not simply a response to objective economic conditions; it was also determined by ideological preconceptions.

ing with the problem of the national minorities. A concerted effort was made to dispel the apprehensions of the minorities against Ukrainian statehood and to win their collaboration. The crowning achievement of this policy was the Law on National-Personal Autonomy of January 22, 1918, which guaranteed to the national minorities in the Ukrainian People's Republic full self-government in educational and cultural matters.[47] This law did honor to the humane and democratic disposition as well as to the statesmanship of the Rada's leaders.

Bismarck once said: "A statesman cannot create anything himself. He must wait and listen until he hears the steps of God sounding through events, then leap up and grasp the hem of His garment."[48] Translated from the language of poetical metaphor, this means that a statesman must have a feeling for the right moment, for the unique and unrepeatable opportunity; he must know how to adjust to this opportunity and how to take advantage of it. In the Ukrainian past such a great "opportunist" was the leader of the mid-seventeenth-century Cossack revolution, Bohdan Khmelnytskyi, whom contemporary Western observers compared with Oliver Cromwell.[49] But the men who stood at the helm of the Rada were not of the stuff of a Bismarck, a Cromwell, or a Khmelnytskyi. They made the transition from federalism to independence not from free volition, but under compelling circumstances. For them it was a hard and painful decision—in a sense a denial of their own past, a rejection of an old and beloved ideal. The inevitable step was

---

[47] For the text of the Law on National-Personal Autonomy, see Iakiv Zozulia (ed.), *Velyka Ukrainska Revoliutsiia: Kalendar istorychnykh podii za liutyi 1917 roku—berezen 1918 roku* (New York: Ukrainian Academy of Arts and Sciences, 1967), pp. 85–86. Two specialized monographs on this subject are: Henryk Jabłoński, *Polska autonomia narodowa na Ukrainie 1917–1918,* Publications of the Historical Institute of Warsaw University, III (Warsaw, 1948); Solomon I. Goldelman, *Jewish National Autonomy in Ukraine, 1917–1920* (Chicago: Ukrainian Research and Information Institute, 1968).

[48] A. J. P. Taylor, *Bismarck: The Man and the Statesman* (New York: Alfred A. Knopf, 1961), p. 115.

[49] Pierre Chevalier in his *Histoire de la guerre des Cosaques contre la Pologne* (Paris, 1663), calls Khmelnytskyi a "second Cromwell, who has appeared in Rus, and who is no less ambitious, brave, and clever, than the one in England." Quoted from the Ukrainian translation: Pier Shevalie, *Istoriia viiny kozakiv proty Polshchi,* trans. by Iu. I Nazarenko (Kiev: Vyd. Akademii Nauk URSR, 1960), p. 51.

finally taken, but not until much precious time had been lost. The Rada's leaders confused the public by their hesitant policy, which consequently weakened the country's cohesion in the face of the impending Soviet Russian invasion.

Some Ukrainian publicists in the interwar period, particularly those of the "integral nationalist" persuasion, blamed the Central Rada for not having proclaimed the independence of the Ukraine at an earlier stage of the Revolution.[50] These strictures now appear as rather naive. During the first months after the fall of tsarism the Ukrainian people were not yet ready for independence, either organizationally or psychologically. Moreover, the Provisional Government in Petrograd still possessed forces sufficient to suppress such an attempt. By autumn 1917 the situation had radically changed. The Bolshevik *coup d'état* precipitated the disintegration of the Empire. The old Russian army had succumbed to anarchy, while the new Red Army was still in an embryonic stage.

Let us for a brief moment give free rein to our imagination. What would have happened if the complete separation of the Ukrainian People's Republic from Russia had been proclaimed at the time of the Third Universal in November 1917, and if the peace treaty between the Ukraine and the Central Powers had been signed before the end of the year? It would have been easy for the Ukraine to receive from the Germans the needed technical assistance and the release of the Ukrainian military formations organized in Germany from among war prisoners. Also, Austria-Hungary would probably have been willing to lend to the Kiev government the legion of the Ukrainian *Sich* Riflemen (*Ukrainski Sichovi Striltsi*), a volunteer unit of Galician Ukrainians within the Austrian army.[51] In addition to the troops that the Rada already had at its disposal, these forces would have sufficed to uphold internal order in the country, to crush local Bolshevik uprisings, and to repulse the Soviet Russian invasion at the frontier. The Ukraine would have avoided the first Bolshevik occupation and the attending chaos, destruction, and terror. The Rada would not have been forced out of Kiev, nor would it have needed to ask for German armed intervention. As we

---

[50] This view has been recently restated by Petro Mirchuk, *Tragichna peremoha* (Toronto: Liga vyzvolennia Ukrainy, 1954), pp. 51 ff.

[51] On the history of this formation, see Stepan Ripetskyi, *Ukrainske Sichove Striletstvo: vyzvolna ideia i zbroinyi chyn* (New York: Chervona kalyna, 1956).

know, this intervention soon changed into an occupation, which did great harm to the Ukraine, morally and politically even more than materially.

Enough of these imaginative speculations. We are, however, entitled to stress the point that in the struggle between the Ukrainian People's Republic and Soviet Russia, the Ukrainian side, although finally defeated, also scored successes. In the field of military operations there was the disarming and the expulsion of the undisciplined and Bolshevik-controlled remnants of the old Russian army, concentrated in the Right-Bank Ukraine, and the suppression of the Bolshevik revolt in Kiev, the so-called Arsenal uprising of January 1918.[52] Among the political successes of the Rada, the following were of outstanding importance: the brilliant victory of the Ukrainian national parties in the elections to the Russian Constituent Assembly;[53] the complete triumph of the supporters of the Rada over the Bolsheviks at the First Congress of Soviets of the Ukraine, despite the fact that the Congress had convened on Bolshevik initiative;[54] and the firmness and astuteness displayed by the young Ukrainian diplomats during the Brest-Litovsk peace negotiations.[55]

---

[52] A detailed description of the Arsenal Uprising is to be found in *Peremoha Velykoi Zhovtnevoi sotsialistychnoi revoliutsii na Ukraini* (Kiev: Naukova dumka, 1967), Vol. II, pp. 49–58.

[53] "In Ukraine, the Bolsheviks obtained only ten percent of all the votes [in the election to the Russian Constituent Assembly], while in the central regions of Russia they received about forty percent." Jurij Borys, *The Russian Communist Party and the Sovietization of Ukraine* (Stockholm, 1960), p. 159. The Ukrainian parties collected 4.3 million votes, or fifty-three percent of all votes cast in the Ukrainian provinces. In addition, the Ukrainian Socialist-Revolutionaries obtained 1.2 million votes in joint lists with the Russian Socialist-Revolutionaries.

[54] On the All-Ukrainian Congress of Soviets, December 17–19, 1917, see Khrystiuk, Vol. II, pp. 69–74.

[55] Perhaps the greatest Ukrainian diplomatic success during the Brest-Litovsk negotiations was the secret protocol between the Ukrainian People's Republic and Austria-Hungary, signed on February 9, 1918, simultaneously with the main peace treaty. Austria-Hungary undertook the obligation to form a new "crown land" out of eastern Galicia (thus dividing the province of Galicia on ethnic lines) and Bukovina. The Ukrainian delegates were able to win this important concession by taking advantage of the difficult food situation in Vienna. The minutes of the Brest-Litovsk negotiations have been recently reprinted in Hornykiewicz,

The main accomplishment of the Rada was its determination not to bow to Bolshevik threats and violence, but rather to accept the challenge of the Petrograd *Sovnarkom* and resist the Soviet Russian invasion. The attitude of the Rada toward the Bolsheviks is documented by the text of the Fourth Universal:

> In an attempt to bring the Free Ukrainian Republic under its rule, the Petrograd Government of People's Commissars has declared war against the Ukraine and is sending its armies of Red Guards and Bolsheviks to our lands; they rob our peasants of their bread and without any remuneration export it to Russia. They do not even spare the grain set aside for seed; they kill innocent people and spread anarchy, thievery and apathy everywhere. . . . As for the Bolsheviks and other aggressors who destroy and ruin our country, we direct the government of the Ukrainian People's Republic to undertake a firm and determined struggle against them, and we call upon all citizens of our Republic—even at the risk of their lives—to defend the welfare and liberty [of our people]. Our Ukrainian People's state must be cleared of the intruders sent from Petrograd who trample the rights of the Ukrainian Republic.[56]

Similar ideas were expressed even more forcefully in a speech delivered on February 1, 1918, by Mykola Liubynskyi (1891–193?), the youthful member of the Ukrainian delegation at the Brest-Litovsk peace conference:

> The loud declarations of the Bolsheviks about the complete freedom of the peoples of Russia are nothing but a coarse demagogic device. The government of the Bolsheviks, which has chased away the Constituent Assembly and which is upheld by the bayonets of the mercenary Red Guards, will never decide to implement in Russia the just principles of self-determination, because it knows quite well that not only the several Republics—the Ukraine, the Don Region, Caucasia, and others—will not recognize it as their legitimate authority, but that even the Russian people themselves would gladly refuse them that right. The Bolsheviks, with their congenital demagoguery, have proclaimed the principle of self-determination both in Russia and here at the peace conference, exclusively because of fear of national revolution [in the borderlands of the former Russian Empire]. They rely on the mercenary gangs of the Red Guards to

---

Vol. II, pp. 49–222. The memoirs of the participants of the conference are collected in Ivan Kedryn (ed.), *Beresteiskyi myr* (Lviv: Chervona kalyna, 1928).

[56] See appendix below.

prevent the implementation of this principle in practice. They use evil and intolerable means: they close down newspapers, disperse political meetings, arrest and shoot civic leaders, and they engage in false and tendentious insinuations by which they attempt to undermine the authority of the governments of the young republics. They accuse noted socialists and veteran revolutionaries of being bourgeois and counterrevolutionary. . . . In this they follow the ancient French proverb: "Slander and calumniate, some of it will always stick."[57]

An American historian recently commented on the contrast between the Rada spokesmen and the Russian democratic leaders: "Nothing in the feeble and tearful accusations of the Martovs and Chernovs had come up to this standard of violence."[58] The universal historical significance of the struggle between the Ukrainian People's Republic and Soviet Russia lies in that it was not only a conflict between nations, but also a clash of two social and political systems —a contest between democracy and totalitarian dictatorship. This statement holds true in spite of all the obvious shortcomings of the Central Rada and in spite of the fact that the totalitarian nature of the Soviet regime was not yet fully developed.

From the point of view of the historical evolution of Ukrainian political thought, the importance of the events in the fall and winter of 1917 lay in the tremendous shift from federalism to a program of state independence. The federalist concept had already been undermined by the insincere and ambiguous policy of the Provisional Government toward the Ukraine. Now Bolshevik aggression delivered the death blow to this traditional Ukrainian ideology. Hrushevskyi called this great upheaval in Ukrainian political thought "purification by fire," and in several programmatic articles written in February and March 1918, he concluded:

The bombardment, occupation and destruction of Kiev were a summit and a culmination; this was the focal point in which were concentrated the immense and incalculable results of the Bolshevik invasion. . . . All our losses, painful and irreplaceable as they may be, we shall count as a part of the price for the restoration of our national statehood. . . . All our customary notions and formulas, all ideas handed down from the past, all plans formulated in other circumstances—all this must be set aside now; or, to be more precise,

---

[57] Hornykiewicz, Vol. II, p. 203.

[58] Adam B. Ulam, *The Bolsheviks: The Intellectual, Personal and Political History of the Triumph of Communism in Russia* (New York: Collier Paperback, 1965), p. 400.

it must be thoroughly scrutinized and reevaluated from the point of view of compatibility with the new task which history has placed before us. . . . What I consider outdated and dead, "a thing destroyed by fire in my study,"[59] is our orientation toward Moscow, toward Russia. For a long time this orientation was imposed on us by means of a forcible, insistent indoctrination until finally, as it often happens, a large part of the Ukrainian community had accepted it.[60]

Hrushevskyi's impassioned words illustrate the great change that had occurred in Ukrainian political thinking in the wake of the experiences of 1917.

An independent Ukrainian People's Republic, proclaimed by the Fourth Universal, did not survive. But the idea of *samostiinist*—confirmed by an armed struggle that lasted until 1921 and by the incessant efforts and sacrifices of the following decades—had become a common possession of Ukrainian patriots of all political persuasions, not only the democrats who claimed to be the rightful heirs of the Central Rada tradition but also the partisans of the monarchist-conservative and the "integral nationalist" camps.[61] The above statement applies in principle also to Ukrainian Communists. The brilliant publicist and member of the first Soviet Ukrainian government, Vasyl Shakhrai (d. 1919), wrote during the Civil War: "The tendency of the Ukrainian movement is national independence."[62] Shakhrai wanted the Ukraine to achieve the status of an

---

[59] Hrushevskyi's house, including his library and papers, burned down during the bombardment of Kiev by Bolshevik troops in January 1918. It was rumored at the time that Bolshevik artillery deliberately aimed at the building owned and inhabited by the Rada's president. The building was located on Pankivska Street, in an elevated part of the city. See Kovalevskyi, p. 444.

[60] Hrushevskyi, pp. 52–57.

[61] These political trends could, obviously, find overt expression only outside the USSR: among the Ukrainian populations of Poland, Rumania, and Czechoslovakia during the interwar period; among the exile communities in the countries of Western Europe; and among the Ukrainian immigrants in the United States and Canada. There is, however, some evidence that these non-Communist ideologies had a potential following also in the Soviet Ukraine—certainly during the 1920's and probably even later.

[62] Serhii Mazlakh and Vasyl Shakhrai, *Do khvyli: Shcho diietsia na Ukraini i z Ukrainoiu* (New York: Prolog, 1967), p. 82. The original edition of this pamphlet appeared in Saratov, 1919.

equal partner within an alliance of independent socialist states. In the course of the Revolution, the left-wing factions of the Ukrainian Social Democrats and Socialist-Revolutionaries adopted the Soviet platform and merged with the Bolsheviks, while retaining their nationalist loyalties.[63] A "national Communist" ferment was strong in the Ukrainian SSR in the 1920's, and, although it was subjected to severe repression during the Stalin era, recent evidence indicates that this tendency still thrives today.[64]

The men of the generation that made the great step from a program of federalism to that of national independence embraced the new ideal with the zeal of neophytes. They repudiated their pre-1917, federalist past, now rejecting it as a symbol of national immaturity and shameful weakness. This anti-federalist reaction of the interwar period is understandable from a psychological point of view, but it implied the partial loss to Ukrainian society of a valuable intellectual heritage. Pre-Revolutionary Ukrainian political thinkers and publicists had formulated a number of fruitful ideas, some of which became obsolete under the changed circumstances of a new reality, while others retained their validity. The strength of the old federalist concept was its breadth of vision. It placed the Ukrainian problem within a wide international context, organically connecting the goal of national liberation with the cause of political liberty and social progress for Eastern Europe as a whole. In contrast, an exclusive and almost obsessive concentration on the attainment of *samostiinist* increased the militancy of the

---

[63] On the subject of "nationalist deviations" within the Communist Party of the Ukraine, see Jurij Lawrynenko, *Ukrainian Communism and Soviet Russian Policy Toward the Ukraine: An Annotated Bibliography, 1917–1953* (New York: Research Program on the USSR, 1953). On the Ukrainian Left Socialist-Revolutionaries: Iwan Majstrenko, *Borotbism: A Chapter in the History of Ukrainian Communism* (New York: Research Program on the USSR, 1954). On the Ukrainian Independent Social Democrats: V. A. Chyrko, "Krakh ideologii ta polityky natsionalistychnoi partii ukapistiv," *Ukrainskyi istorychnyi zhurnal*, No. 12 (Kiev, 1968), pp. 24–35.

[64] The two most important documentary works available in English, which reflect the ideas of the contemporary intellectual opposition in the Ukrainian SSR, are the treatise of Ivan Dziuba (see note 23), and the *Chornovil Papers*, ed. by Viacheslav Chornovil (New York-Toronto-London: McGraw-Hill, 1968). See also George Luckyj, "Turmoil in the Ukraine," *Problems of Communism*, XVII, 4 (1968), pp. 14–20.

national movement, but it narrowed its intellectual insights and blunted its moral sensibility. As early as the 1890's, the democratic thinker Drahomanov was worried by the first symptoms of a xeno-phobic Ukrainian nationalism and raised his voice in warning against the dangers of chauvinism and national exclusiveness.[65]

Two parallel trends are noticeable in contemporary international relations; on the one hand, the continued drive for the emancipa-tion of formerly submerged peoples and a movement toward the formation of new nation states; on the other, a tendency toward an ever closer political, economic, and cultural interdependence of states and peoples and the emergence of new forms of international cooperation. Viewed from this angle, the two currents of Ukrainian political thought, federalism and separatism, may no longer appear mutually exclusive; rather, they are complementary. Still, their synthesis lies in the future.

In conclusion, it seems fitting to quote a passage from the work of the eminent historian of the Ukrainian Revolution, Vasyl Ku-chabskyi (1895–1945), who as a young officer played an active role in the struggle for Kiev in January 1918:

> The national self-consciousness and the elemental striving for free-dom of a people—who in their area of compact settlement between the Carpathians and the Don number some thirty million—will not disappear from this world again. This self-consciousness and this striving have been awakened by a tireless educational effort, and they have been tempered by the blood spilled in a hundred battles. The

---

[65] Drahomanov's polemics against the excesses of Ukrainian nationalism are contained in his last two works, which may be considered as his political testament, *Chudatski dumky pro ukrainsku natsionalnu spravu* (1892) and *Lysty na Naddnipriansku Ukrainu* (1894). In these writings Drahomanov stressed the necessity of basing national aspirations on uni-versal scientific and ethical values: "I acknowledge the right of all groups of men, including nationalities, to self-government, and I believe that such self-government brings inestimable advantages to men. But we may not seek the guiding ideas for our cultural, political and social activities in national sentiments and interests. To do this would lose us in a jungle of subjective viewpoints and historical traditions. Governing and con-trolling ideas are to be found in scientific thoughts and in international, universal human interests. In brief, I do not reject nationalities, but na-tionalism, particularly nationalism which opposes humanity and cosmo-politanism." *Lysty na Naddnipriansku Ukrainu* (2nd ed.; [Vienna?]: Partiia Ukrainskykh Sotsiialistiv-Revoliutsioneriv, 1915), p. 38.

great ills, by which this people is now afflicted, can still handicap it politically for decades. But when there will arise from this nation's great sufferings a new stratum of leaders—equipped with boldness, and intellectually equal to the country's very difficult international situation—then the Ukraine shall become, so it seems, *the* problem of future Eastern Europe.[66]

These words were written in 1929, but we can endorse them today, more than half a century after the Fourth Universal proclaimed the sovereignty of the Ukrainian nation and the independence of the Ukrainian People's Republic.

---

[66] W. Kutschabsky, *Die Westukraine im Kampfe mit Polen und dem Bolschewismus in den Jahren 1918–1923* (Berlin: Junker und Dunnhaupt Vlg., 1934), p. 2.

CHAPTER NINE

The Church and the Ukrainian Revolution: The Central Rada Period

Bohdan R. Bociurkiw

THE SUDDEN COLLAPSE of the tsarist regime in March 1917[1] threw the Orthodox Church in the Ukraine into a state of anxiety, confusion, and ferment. Although there had been little sympathy in ecclesiastical circles for state domination over the Church, and although the Rasputin scandal had weakened confidence in the last tsar, the Revolution could not immediately destroy the long-entrenched belief in the interdependence of Orthodoxy and autocracy shared by the episcopate and a considerable portion of the clergy. Not yet capable of standing on its own feet, the Church had to continue to depend upon state power, but now this power had passed into the hands of political parties which had long attacked the reactionary orientation of the Church and were favoring reforms entailing the surrender of many, if not all, of its past privileges. Uncertain of its future amid the rapid disintegration of the old order, the Church was inclined to fix its hopes on the forthcoming *Sobor*. Yet, though all elements in the Church felt the need for revision of both its relation to the state and its internal organization, differences over the nature and urgency of ecclesiastical reforms deeply divided the clergy.

While dutifully following the Petrograd Holy Synod in pledging their loyalty to the Provisional Government, the bishops of the Ukrainian dioceses displayed little enthusiasm for the Revolution.

---

[1] All dates in the text are given according to the New Style (Gregorian calendar). Dates of periodicals listed in the footnotes are, as a rule, according to the Old Style (Julian calendar), until March 1918.

Compromised by their close collaboration with the extreme rightist and chauvinist groups, several leading Church figures in the Ukraine soon found themselves under attack from both the revolutionary authorities and the now increasingly vocal progressive elements among the clergy and laymen. In April, Archbishop Vasilii of Chernihiv, disowned by his own clergy, was arrested by the local authorities as "dangerous to public order" and taken to Petrograd to await trial.[2] In Kharkiv, a committee representing the gubernia's public organizations forced Archbishop Antonii Khrapovitskii to leave his diocese "in view of his harmful activity."[3] Both Archbishop Evlogii Georgievskii of Volhynia and Archbishop Agapit Vyshnevskyi of Katerynoslav came under the attack of the revolutionary authorities, who made unsuccessful attempts to have the bishops removed from their sees.[4]

While the rank and file clergy in the Ukraine appeared more favorably disposed toward the new order than were their superiors, they, too, came to suffer from the widespread suspicion of the Church's continued counterrevolutionary orientation. According to a contemporary account, "hundreds of priests, deacons and psalmists were expelled from their posts and had to wander from place to place. . . . Everywhere, laymen began to intervene in ecclesiastical affairs, [they] seized church keys from pastors, as well as money and property, and even took upon themselves to appoint pastors."[5] In the Volhynia diocese alone, some sixty parish priests were expelled by verdicts of the village assemblies during a two-week period in April.[6] A similar situation prevailed in the Kiev gubernia, causing the Kievan clergy committee to issue a special appeal to the peasantry calling for moderation.[7] In Kharkiv, the diocesan congress beseeched the gubernia authorities to prevent "self-willed outbursts"

---

[2] *Posledniia novosti,* March 3, 1917. In May 1917, Vasilii was replaced by Bishop Pakhomii (Kedrov).

[3] *Russkiia vedomosti,* April 16, 1917. Antonii's removal was also demanded by the Ukrainian gubernia congress, which branded him an "enemy of the Ukrainian Church." Earlier that spring, Khrapovitskii refused to permit the reading of the Gospel in Ukrainian during the Easter services, arguing that "no great nations pray in the language spoken in the market place" (*Utro Rossii,* April 21, 1917).

[4] *Rech,* April 7, 1917; *Odesskiia novosti,* August 24, 1917.

[5] *Trybuna,* January 2, 1919.

[6] *Russkiia vedomosti,* April 26, 1917.

[7] *Novoe vremia,* April 8, 1917.

against the clergy, since "in many localities, priests are being removed from parishes without trial and investigation; they are being deprived of their vocation, arrested and locked in jails."[8]

With the hitherto dominant conservative elements in the Church temporarily silenced and disorganized, the initiative passed into the hands of the progressive clergy and laymen. Though numerically weak and largely restricted to the diocesan centers and theological schools, they were now able to draw support from V. N. Lvov, the liberal Ober-Procurator of the Holy Synod, and from sympathetic public authorities in order to challenge the power of the conservative episcopate and the consistories. Within the first weeks of the Revolution, "commissariats for ecclesiastical affairs" were formed by gubernia executive committees to supervise, on behalf of the revolutionary authorities, the administration of the dioceses. At the same time, executive committees of clergy and laymen were elected in each diocesan center by meetings of the local priests and Church intelligentsia. Led by progressive elements, these committees were to provide the rank and file clergy and laymen with an autonomous voice in dealing with the civil authorities and the hierarchy. Their most immediate task was the convocation of the diocesan congresses of clergy and laymen to discuss the future of the Church under the new order.

Despite some opposition from the episcopate,[9] diocesan congresses were held in the spring and summer of 1917 in all Ukrainian gubernias. The congresses voiced general consensus in favor of an early convocation of an All-Russian Church Sobor to undertake ecclesiastical reforms, but they split over the nature of the future reforms into conservative and liberal camps, on the one hand, and into Russian and Ukrainian factions, on the other. Greatly strengthened by the large lay participation, the liberals prevailed at most of these gatherings[10]—which adopted resolutions requesting the introduction of a conciliar principle of Church administration, including the election of bishops by the diocesan clergy and laymen —and then proceeded to elect diocesan councils to replace the un-

---

[8] *Russkiia vedomosti*, May 18, 1917.

[9] See, for example, *Rech*, May 5, 16, and 18, 1917.

[10] Conservative influence was more marked at the Odessa and Kharkiv congresses, both of which voiced demands for the continuation of the privileged legal status of the Russian Church. See *Russkiia vedomosti*, April 25 and May 21, 1917.

popular consistories. Several congresses voted in favor of the election of parish priests by their flock,[11] and at least one gathering (in Volhynia) called for the separation of church and state and the secularization of the parish schools.[12]

The principal issue dividing the diocesan congresses along national lines was the demand for Ukrainianization of the Church advanced by the nationally conscious Ukrainian clergy and laymen. While otherwise identifying themselves with the progressive camp, they viewed the "nationalization" of the Church as a necessary consequence of its democratization and a corollary of the Ukraine's anticipated evolution into an autonomous entity within a federated Russian state. As long as their aspirations did not involve complete ecclesiastical and political separation from Russia, the advocates of Ukrainianization were able to draw on support from many Russian Church liberals. On the other hand, the conservative elements, especially the episcopate, viewed any attempts at Ukrainianization as potentially subversive to the unity of both the Church and the Empire—an attitude that contributed much to the subsequent radicalization of the Ukrainian church movement.

The opponents of Ukrainianization proved to be strongest at the diocesan congresses in Chernihiv[13] and Kharkiv.[14] The first Odessa and Katerynoslav congresses evidently failed to take a stand on this issue; but when they reconvened in the summer, both adopted resolutions favoring a degree of Ukrainianization in church services and in the parish schools.[15] The clergy and laymen of the Volhynia diocese, having voted in favor of Ukrainian autonomy at their first congress in April, subsequently extended their support to the cause of an autonomous Ukrainian metropolitanate and the Ukrainianization of the Church schools.[16] By far the greatest measure of success was achieved by the Ukrainian group at the diocesan congresses in

---

[11] For example, the congresses in the Kiev, Poltava, Volhynia, Odessa, and Kharkiv dioceses. See *Russkiia vedomosti*, April 18, 23, and 25, 1917.

[12] *Rech,* April 25, 1917.

[13] D. Doroshenko, *Istoriia Ukrainy 1917–1923 rr.*, Vol. I (Uzhhorod: Svoboda, 1930), pp. 406–407; *Tserkovno-obshchestvennyi vestnik,* December 20, 1917.

[14] *Rech,* June 9, 1917.

[15] *Odesskiia novosti,* June 28, 1917; *Rech,* July 13, 1917.

[16] *Russkiia vedomosti,* April 23, 1917; *Vistnyk Soiuza Vyzvolennia Ukrainy,* October 7, 1917, p. 653.

the Kiev, Poltava and Podillia gubernias—the traditional strong-holds of the national movement.

The April congress of the Kievan diocese was dominated by a Ukrainian-liberal majority which, against strong objections from the Russian conservatives, renamed the gathering the "first *Ukrainian* Diocesan Congress" and resolved that "in the autonomous Ukraine, the Church should be independent from the [Petrograd] Synod." Chaired by Archpriest Vasyl Lypkivskyi, the gathering voted to support the Ukrainianization of church services, ecclesiastical administration, and the parish schools, and it called for the convocation of an All-Ukrainiia congress of clergy and laymen.[17] To replace the Kievan consistory, the Congress elected a pro-Ukrainian diocesan council headed by Archpriest Kapralov.

The most elaborate program for Ukrainianizing the Orthodox Church was adopted at the May congress of clergy and laymen from the Poltava diocese. Its principal provisions read:

1) In a free, territorially autonomous Ukraine, there must be a free, autocephalous Church, independent from the state in its internal order.

2) The Orthodox Church shall be the first among equal religious organizations in the Ukraine and shall, together with them, receive financial assistance from the state.

3) The Autocephalous Ukrainian Church shall have a conciliar constitution which should permeate the entire organization of the Church.

4) Church services in the Ukrainian Church shall be celebrated in Ukrainian . . .[18]

---

[17] *Russkiia vedomosti*, April 18, 1917; Iu. Samoilovich, *Tserkov ukrainskogo sotsial-fashizma* (Moscow, 1932), p. 28; I. Vlasovskyi, *Narys istorii Ukrainskoi Pravoslavnoi Tserkvy*, Vol. IV, Pt. 1 (New York: Ukrainska Pravoslavna Tserkva v Z.D.A., 1961), p. 13. According to Metropolitan Vasyl Lypkivskyi (*Istoriia Ukrainskoi Pravoslavnoi Tserkvy, Part 7: Vidrodzhennia ukrainskoi tserkvy* [Winnipeg, 1961], p. 7), the Kievan congress elected a special commission to convene an All-Ukrainian Sobor of clergy and laymen, headed by Bishop Dymytrii (Verbytskyi) of Uman, one of the vicars of the Kievan metropolitan. See V. V. Zenkovskii, "Vospominaniia (1900–1920); Piat mesiatsev v vlasti (moe uchastie v ukrainskoi zhizni)," Pt. 1 (1952) (Unpublished manuscript; Archive of Russian and East European History and Culture, Columbia University), p. 12.

[18] *Pro ukrainizatsiiu tserkvy: doklad prochytanyi na poltavskomu eparkhiialnomu zizdi dukhovenstva i myrian, 3–8 travnia 1917 roku* (3rd ed.; Lubny, 1917), p. 8.

The Poltava gathering proposed a series of concrete measures to be immediately introduced in all Ukrainian dioceses: the reading of Gospels and sermons in the Ukrainian language; the publication of Ukrainian translations of church books; an immediate end to the established practice of filling episcopal sees in the Ukraine with Russians; and the complete Ukrainianization of parochial and theological schools. The meeting called upon the clergy to support the cause of national-territorial autonomy. It also decided to establish contacts with other dioceses in order to consider in greater detail the Ukrainianization question and the convocation of a Ukrainian Church Sobor as a preliminary step toward an All-Russian Sobor.[19]

A similar line was taken by the Podillia diocesan congress, at which a strong Ukrainian group was led by the army chaplain, Oleksander Marychiv. The meeting adopted a resolution which "expressed hope that with the autonomy of the Ukraine, the autocephaly of the Ukrainian Orthodox Church will also be realized."[20]

An opportunity for united action presented itself to the Ukrainian Church movement when the All-Russian Congress of Clergy and Laymen met in Moscow in June. Led by I. Morachevskyi, sixty-six Ukrainian delegates from ten dioceses addressed a joint appeal to the Congress calling upon it to support the cause of Ukrainian autonomy before the Provisional Government (which had just turned down the autonomist demands of the Rada) and to endorse before the Holy Synod the request for the convocation of a Ukrainian Church Sobor, which should decide the future of the Church in the Ukraine. While declining to intervene in the current political controversy between Kiev and Petrograd, the Moscow congress gave its overwhelming support to the proposition that "should the Ukraine become an independent state, the Ukrainian Church, too, should be autocephalous; should there be an autonomous Ukraine, the Church should also be autonomous." The gathering approved, in principle, the use of national languages in the Church and offered its support to the proposed Sobor of the Ukrainian dioceses.[21]

Evidently encouraged by the response from the Moscow congress, the Kievan diocesan council proceeded on June 30 to elect a

---

[19] *Ibid.*, pp. 8–10.

[20] Doroshenko, Vol. I, p. 407; Samoilovich, p. 28.

[21] Samoilovich, pp. 32–33; *Odesskii listok,* June 23, 1917; *Odesskiia novosti,* June 23, 1917; *Dokladnaia zapiska Sv. Sinoda Ukrainskoi Pravoslavnoi Tserkvi . . . ob istorii i kanonicheskikh osnovaniiakh avtokefalii Ukrainskoi Pravoslavnoi Tserkvi* (Kharkiv, 1926), p. 1.

commission for the convocation of a Ukrainian Sobor.[22] The commission, however, encountered stiff opposition from the local episcopate, and, in July, the Petrograd Synod flatly rejected all Ukrainian demands:

> The Synod refuses to consider the question of establishing a separate Ukrainian Church; it is not intended to raise this question at the All-Russian Local Sobor since there was never an autocephalous church in the Ukraine and the Kievan Metropolitan has been subordinated to the Patriarch of Constantinople, and, since the end of the seventeenth century, to the Moscow Patriarch and, by succession, to the Synod.[23]

Having failed to secure the blessing of the Russian episcopate, the Kievan commission decided to present the ecclesiastical authorities with a *fait accompli* and published, on July 22, an appeal to "the clergy and laymen" announcing the convocation of a Ukrainian Church Congress to be held in Kiev between August 12 and 18.[24] At the last moment, however, the new Ober-Procurator of the Holy Synod, A. V. Kartashev, prohibited the Congress on the grounds that it would interfere with the election of delegates to the All-Russian Sobor, scheduled to meet in Moscow on August 28.[25] Any remaining hopes of securing a strong Ukrainian representation at the Moscow Sobor were dispelled when the two-stage elections in the Ukrainian dioceses produced a solid pro-Russian majority.[26] Though faring somewhat better, the liberals, too, failed to dominate the elections. In both cases, it seems, the mode of representation and the indirect method of elections worked against the liberal and Ukrainian elements, for they drew their strength primarily from among the urban clergy and the lay intelligentsia. But a far more important cause of their failure was a marked shift to the right in the attitudes of the rank and file clergy.

Several factors combined to bring about a gradual reassertion of traditional conservative attitudes among the clergy. Probably the most important in this respect was the disenchantment of the rural parish priests with the effects of the revolution on their relations

---

[22] Samoilovich, pp. 32–33.

[23] *Rech,* July 13, 1917.

[24] *Bezvirnyk,* No. 1 (1931), p. 45.

[25] *Russkiia vedomosti,* August 2, 1917.

[26] Samoilovich, p. 33.

with parishioners and their social and economic status. The numerous expulsions of pastors by their flocks, the laymen's attempts to control the administrative and economic affairs of the parish, the peasantry's designs on ecclesiastical and monastic lands, all contributed to a decline in the rural clergy's sense of security and prestige. Accustomed to relying on the civil authorities for protection and support, the clergy found the local representatives of the new order largely indifferent and, occasionally, hostile to their predicament. The clergy's anxiety increased as the Provisional Government proceeded to remove disabilities imposed by tsarist law on other religious denominations and to place parish schools under the Ministry of Education—a tendency that the priests feared would eventually culminate in a complete separation of the Church from the state and school. The growing distrust of the Provisional Government's motives and of its capacity to cope with increasing anarchy in the country and at the front made the clergy more and more inclined to close their ranks around the conservative episcopate and to submerge their differences in a common front against the "wreckers of the church."[27]

These developments greatly strengthened the hand of the episcopate in dealing with its liberal and Ukrainian opponents and, at the same time, galvanized into action the dispersed reactionary elements whose influence now rapidly increased in the urban parish councils. The latter—products of the early progressive upsurge in the Church—soon became, together with the local "unions of pastors," weapons in the hands of the episcopate and the reactionaries against "anti-canonic" activities of the "commissariats for ecclesiastical affairs" and diocesan councils.[28] These organs of "revolutionary democracy" within the Church lost the powerful support of the Ober-Procurator of the Holy Synod when, in July, the liberal V. N. Lvov was replaced by A. V. Kartashev, who was more inclined to accede to the wishes of the episcopate. Symbolic of the changed mood in the Church was the reelection, in August, of the banished Antonii Khrapovitskii—an archenemy of progressive and Ukrainian tendencies—as Archbishop of Kharkiv.

The emergent movement for the autonomy and Ukrainianization of the Church was given a hostile reception by nearly all bishops in

---

[27] See B. V. Titlinov, *Tserkov vo vremia revoliutsii* (Petrograd: Byloe, 1924), pp. 60–64.

[28] See P.V.L. [Lypkivskyi] in *Trybuna*, January 3, 1919.

the Ukraine.[29] The Russian ecclesiastical leadership initially attributed little significance to this development. By June, however, after the Ukrainian Rada challenged the Provisional Government on the issue of Ukrainian autonomy, it became a matter of primary concern. The subsequent compromise between Petrograd and Kiev and the official recognition of the Rada's General Secretariat as an autonomous government sharply divided Russian political circles; the Kadets joined the rightist groups in opposition to Petrograd's Ukrainian policy. The reality of Ukrainian autonomy suddenly gave substance to the demands for an ecclesiastical self-government and de-russification of the Church. The dual threat to the unity of the Russian Empire and the Russian Church not only strengthened the determination of Russian ecclesiastical authorities to oppose even minor concessions to the Ukrainian demands, but also served to split the liberal ranks within the Church on the Ukrainian issue. The belief in the Church's special mission to preserve "one indivisible Russia," long nurtured under the tsarist regime, once again reasserted itself among the Russian and Russian-oriented majority of the clergy in the Ukraine. This helps to explain the Synod's reaction to Ukrainian requests in June and the subsequent banning of the proposed Ukrainian Church Congress. It also explains the marked sharpening of the Russo-Ukrainian conflict within the Church.

The main battle was waged in Kiev, where a Ukrainian progressive coalition, backed by the Kievan "commissar for ecclesiastical affairs," E. Pospilovskyi, controlled both the local executive committee and the diocesan council of clergy and laymen. From the very beginning, it encountered determined resistance from Metropolitan Vladimir (Bogoiavlenskii), who refused to recognize the "arbitrary" and "anti-canonical" resolutions of the diocesan congress and to replace the consistory with the elected Diocesan Council. Appeals to the Synod and the intervention, in May, of the Ober-Procurator, Lvov, failed to impress the Metropolitan, who was supported by the upper stratum of the clergy and by local Russian nationalist circles.[30] The stalemate continued until Lvov's departure from the post of Ober-Procurator. In August, the Metropolitan

---

[29] The only bishops who displayed some sympathy for the movement in 1917 were Feofan (Bistrov) of Poltava and a Kievan vicar, Dymytrii (Verbytskyi) of Uman.

[30] See *Russkiia vedomosti,* May 27, 1917; and *Rech,* July 30, 1917.

counterattacked with a pastoral letter which, having condemned liberal tendencies in the Church, challenged the *bona fides* of the Ukrainian Church movement:

> It is dreadful for us to hear them speak of the separation of the South-Russian Church from the One Orthodox Russian Church. Have they, after such a long life in common, any reasonable grounds for these attempts? . . . None whatsoever! I testify, on the basis of my personal experience, that in all dioceses and metropolies in which the Lord honored me to serve, everywhere the teaching of Orthodoxy and morals has been preserved pure and unchanged, everywhere there is a unity in Church teaching, liturgy, and ceremonies. Who are the ones who strive for separation? Who benefits by it? Naturally it delights only internal and external enemies. The love of one's own motherland must not overshadow and overcome our love for all Russia and the One Orthodox Russian Church.[31]

The Metropolitan's message failed to answer the arguments of the Ukrainian movement, which were addressed not to the doctrinal but to the national and political orientation of the Orthodox Church in the Ukraine. Vladimir's phraseology and reasoning reflected well the attitudes of the dominant Russian strata in the Church. Divorced from the national and cultural aspirations of the Ukrainian people and frequently ignorant of its separate existence,[32] they failed to appreciate the potential strength and viability of the Ukrainian Church movement. Because of its novelty and impatience in the face of the canonic and hierarchical obstacles raised by its opponents, this movement appeared to the Russian episcopates as an artificial, politically inspired faction that was alien to the "South-Russian" believers and destined to pass away with the return of peace and order to "Holy Rus."

The failure to secure any of its major objectives and the increasing hostility of the ecclesiastical authorities caused some defections

---

[31] *Kievskiia eparkhiialnyia vedomosti*, No. 32–33 (1917), pp. 261–262.

[32] One of the participants in the Ukrainian church movement in Kiev, the priest P. Korsunovskyi, relates that, when accused by a Ukrainian delegation of being alien to Ukrainian aspirations, Metropolitan Vladimir "simply could not understand what they were talking about. Surprised, he inquired: 'What is a Ukraine? What is a Ukrainian people? Are not Little Russians the same as the Russian people?'" P. Korsunovskyi, "Tserkovnyi rukh na Ukraini v pershi roky revoliutsii," *Dnipro* (1925), cited in Vlasovskyi, Vol. IV, p. 19.

from the Ukrainian Church movement and contributed to its radicalization. Representative of the deepening frustration in its ranks was an article published in a September issue of the leading Ukrainian daily, Nova rada. The author, evidently an adherent of the movement, noted the victory of anti-democratic and imperialist tendencies at the Moscow Sobor and concluded that the only course left to the Ukrainian clergy was to break away from the Russian Church by revolutionary means.[33] Having exhausted ecclesiastical channels for bringing about the realization of its objectives, it is not surprising that the Ukrainian church movement now turned for support to Ukrainian organizations and authorities.

The relationship between the Ukrainian church movement and the dominant political and social forces shaping the course of the Ukrainian Revolution in 1917–1918 was one of considerable complexity and ambivalence. The few nationally conscious clergymen and laymen who launched the movement for the Ukrainianization of the Orthodox Church were guided by religious motives—a desire to end the Church's alienation from the life of the people, to make the Orthodox liturgy and teachings accessible to the masses, and to bring life into the atrophied body of the Church. But they also shared national, social, and political aspirations with the Ukrainian intelligentsia and the predominantly peasant following of the Revolution. In contrast to the passive and indifferent mass of their fellow priests and their openly hostile ecclesiastical superiors, these nationally conscious individuals welcomed the formation of the Rada in March 1917 and even sent their representatives to that body and to the Ukrainian National Congress in April.[34] They supported the Ukraine's claim to autonomy at diocesan congresses and at the All-Russian Congress of Clergy and Laymen in June. Later, they used their influence to assist in the work of the embryonic Ukrainian government.[35] Undoubtedly, the leaders of the Ukrainian Church movement, brought up as they were in the Orthodox tradition of close correspondence between the religious and political life of the people, viewed a national church as an important force in the process of nation-building and expected that the emergent Ukrainian government would throw its full weight behind the movement's attempts to de-russify the Church.

---

[33] S. Hai, "Polozhennia dukhovenstva," Nova rada, September 10, 1917.
[34] Doroshenko, Vol. I, p. 406.
[35] Russkiia vedomosti, June 23, 1917.

These expectations were not wholly fulfilled. The alienation of the established Church from Ukrainian cultural, social, and political aspirations and its use as an intrument of russification and reaction had left among the Ukrainian intelligentsia a legacy of bitterness and hostility to the official Church. This alienation, together with the strong socialist influence among the last two generations of the Ukrainian intelligentsia, combined to produce widespread anticlerical, if not atheistic, sentiment. The two parties dominating contemporary Ukrainian political life—the Socialist-Revolutionaries and the Social Democrats—considered religion as "a private matter" for both the Party and the state and favored, as soon as possible, the separation of the Church from the state and schools and the nationalization of the land owned by the Church and the monasteries.[36] While the SR's and SD's tended, with few exceptions, to minimize the importance of the ecclesiastical issue and preferred to leave the Ukrainian church movement to its own fate, smaller political groups, the liberals[37] and the nationalists,[38] ascribed somewhat greater importance to the Ukrainianization of the Church. As early as March, representatives of the Petrograd Ukrainian community, in which these groups carried considerable influence, approached Prime Minister Lvov with a request for a government instruction "that the clergy must not be persecuted for the use of the Ukrainian language in sermons" and asked for "the removal, as soon as possible, of the Orthodox church administration from Galicia" and for the "return to the Greek-Uniate Church of its rights."[39]

The most constructive attitude toward the question of ecclesiastical ukrainianization was adopted by the nationalists. Addressing a mass meeting in Kiev in April 1917, the leading nationalist

---

[36] For a discussion of the treatment of religion in the contemporary programs of the Ukrainian socialist parties, see I. Sukhopliuiev, *Stavlennia sotsiialistychnykh partii II Internatsionalu do relihii* (Kharkiv, 1932), pp. 284, 294–306. See also "Proiekt: Prohrama Ukrainskoi Partii Sotsiialistiv Revoliutsioneriv (UPSR)," *Boritesia-Poborete*, No. 6 (1922), p. 42.

[37] The old Ukrainian Progressivist Association (TUP) and the Ukrainian Socialist-Federalists.

[38] Primarily, the Ukrainian National Party and the Ukrainian Party of Socialists-Indepedentists, which the former party joined along with several small nationalist groups in December 1917.

[39] P. Khrystiuk, *Zamitky i materiialy do istorii ukrainskoi revoliutsii 1917–1920 rr.*, Vol. I (Vienna, 1921), p. 124.

ideologist, Mykola Mikhnovskyi, advocated autocephaly for the Ukrainian Orthodox Church under its own Patriarch.[40] At its December 1917 Congress, the Ukrainian Party of Socialist-Independentists passed a separate resolution, which declared:[41]

1) The Church in the Ukraine must be independent and Ukrainian, according to its historical traditions.

2) Divine services should be celebrated in the Ukrainian language.

3) Every nation must be inviolable in its religious affairs, as the freedom of confession and convictions is the foundation of true popular liberty.[42]

The importance of the nationalists' sympathetic attitude toward the aspirations of the Ukrainian Church movement derived not from their weight in the Rada (where they constituted a small minority), but from the considerable influence that they had developed in Ukrainian military circles. The Ukrainian church movement found some of its earliest proselytizers and leaders among military chaplains, some junior officers, and especially former seminarians who had been exposed to clandestine Ukrainian circles that were active in these institutions before the war. Another source of support came from Ukrainian peasant organizations, in particular from among the influential cooperative workers and the "Ukrainianized" soldiers who returned to their villages. Thus, by the end of April, the Kiev gubernia peasant congress instructed its delegates to the All-Russian Congress of Peasants' Deputies to demand also "that the word of God in the Ukraine's churches be read in the Ukrainian language."[43]

It was to Ukrainian soldiers, the "peasants in uniform," that the

---

[40] M. Kovalevskyi, *Pry dzherelakh borotby: spomyny, vrazhennia, refleksii* (Innsbruck, 1960), pp. 259–60. As early as 1900, Mikhnovskyi attacked, in his program of the Revolutionary Ukrainian Party, the use of the "language of our oppressors in the Orthodox Church" (M. Mikhnovskyi, *Samostiina Ukraina* [Munich: Ukrainskyi patriot, 1948], p. 19.

[41] *Ukrainska Partiia Samostiinykiv-Sotsiialistiv (U.N.P.)* (Vienna: Nakl. Ukrainskoi partii samostiinykiv-sotsiialistiv [U.N.P.], 1920), p. 80.

[42] An even greater similarity of views with the Ukrainian church movement appears in the later Socialist-Independentist program adopted in 1919, which provided for "an independent Ukrainian church," "an elected clergy," and a conciliar form of ecclesiastical government (see *ibid.*, pp. 79–80).

[43] Khrystiuk, Vol. I, p. 46.

frustrated Ukrainian Church movement turned for assistance in the fall of 1917. The occasion was the massive Third Ukrainian Military Congress, which met in Kiev during the first days of November. No doubt influenced by the news of the Bolshevik seizure of power in Petrograd and sharing the Congress's impatience with legal niceties as far as the Ukraine's right to self-determination was concerned, the Ukrainian military clergy prevailed upon the Congress to pass, on November 9, a special resolution endorsing the objectives of the national church movement:

> In a free democratic Ukrainian Republic there must be a free, auto-cephalous Orthodox Church, independent from the state in its internal order, with a conciliar constitution . . . , in the Ukraine the liturgy should be celebrated in the Ukrainian language.[44]

The Congress proceeded to appoint an "Organizational Committee for the Convocation of the All-Ukrainian Church Sobor," consisting of some thirty military chaplains and army representatives.[45]

If the movement still hesitated, doubting the prudence of revolutionary tactics, two subsequent events may have relieved such doubts. On November 12, the Moscow Sobor voted, against the opposition of its liberal minority, to re-establish the Patriarchate of Moscow, and on November 20 the Rada issued its Third Universal proclaiming a *de facto* independent Ukrainian People's Republic. The So-

---

[44] *Ibid.*, p. 194.

[45] *Bezvirnyk*, No. 1 (1931), p. 45. A somewhat different version was supplied by Ivan Shram ("Iak tvorylasia Ukrainska Avtokefalna Tserkva," *Na varti*, No. 5–6 (1925): "By the end of November, Ukrainian Orthodox activists [*revnyteli*] began to organize in the barracks of the Doroshenko Regiment. An initially small Action Circle decided to establish a "Ukrainian Church Committee" which would demand an immediate convocation of the All-Ukrainian Church Sobor. Archbishop Oleksii [Dorodnytsyn], known Ukrainian patriot, doctor of ecclesiastical history, who lived in retirement at the Lavra [Monastery], was invited to assume chairmanship of the Committee. After several days of meetings, a distinct tendency crystallized in the Committee—immediately to declare auto-cephalous status for the Ukrainian Church, to elect Archbishop Oleksii as the All-Ukrainian Metropolitan, and to convoke the Sobor only afterwards to sanction a *fait accompli* and to elaborate in detail the basic forms of church administration . . . Unfortunately, the deeds were different from the words" (p. 17).

bor's decision to restore a monarchical system of ecclesiastical government, which was interpreted in Ukrainian circles as a victory for the reactionary and imperialistic elements within the Church, and the Ukraine's new political status with its canonic implications, led the Ukrainian church movement to assume an organized form and to press for formal recognition and support from Ukrainian authorities.

Late in November, the leaders of the movement formed a "Brotherhood of Resurrection" (*Bratstvo Voskresennia*) in Kiev. The chairmanship was assumed by the deposed Archbishop of Vladimir, Oleksii Dorodnytsyn, whose conversion to the Ukrainian cause at last provided the national church movement with a leader of episcopal rank.[46] The founding meeting adopted resolutions calling for the autocephaly of the Ukrainian Church, the cessation of links with the Patriarch, and the speedy convocation of an All-Ukrainian Church Sobor.[47]. At the same time, Ukrainian church circles turned to the General Secretariat with a request for governmental intervention to end the opposition of the ecclesiastical authorities to Ukrainianization of the Church. An old supporter of the Ukrainian church movement, State Secretary Oleksander Lototskyi, brought up this matter at a November meeting of the government, pointing out "the necessity of bringing matters of ecclesiastical administration into the general sphere of the Ukrainian government's activities, and of establishing certain external controls over the administrative activities of the leading organs of the clergy to prevent them from misusing [their authority] in church matters." This, Lototskyi argued, "had to be done as long as the separation of the church from the state had not been formally implemented and as long as our alien episcopate was making use of the state apparatus and various governmental means."[48] However, Lototskyi's plea for a constructive church policy aroused a stormy debate with

---

[46] A Ukrainian by origin, Dorodnytsyn was dismissed by the Synod in March 1917 for his alleged links with Rasputin. For Dorodnytsyn's denial of this charge, see *Novoe vremia*, March 25, 1917. See also Dorodnytsyn's letter explaining his motives for joining the Ukrainian movement, and his response to attacks against him for "Ukrainophilism" in *Kievlianin*, December 6, 1917.

[47] *Russkiia vedomosti*, November 23, 1917; *Tserkovno-obshchestvennyi vestnik*, November 24, 1917, p. 3.

[48] O. Lototskyi, "Znevazhena sprava," *Tryzub*, III, 12 (March 20, 1927), p. 7.

the socialist majority, which defeated the proposal on the grounds that "our ideal is a system where religion has to become a private matter; therefore, the establishment of any administrative institution for this sphere would be a departure from this ideal."[49]

Noting the government's "utterly apathetic position" on the ecclesiastical question, the newspaper *Nova rada* sadly observed:

> Members of the *Mala Rada,* adhering to higher, inaccessible socialist ideals and party purism, have not dealt, unfortunately, with the clearly vital affairs of the Ukrainian Church, which should be of concern also to them as cultured people . . .[50]

Despite this setback, the Ukrainian church movement proceeded with its plans for ecclesiastical independence from Moscow. On December 6, the "Organizational Committee for the Convocation of the Ukrainian Church Sobor" held a joint meeting with the leaders of the *Bratstvo Voskresennia* and some members of the old Church Congress Committee elected by the Kievan diocesan council. It is hard to determine which factor was of greater importance in prompting this important meeting—the news of Metropolitan Tikhon's election as the "All-Russian Patriarch" or a telegram from Moscow recalling Archbishop Oleksii from Kiev, which organizers of the meeting inevitably interpreted as a Russian attempt to deprive the movement of its only patron within the episcopate. The gathering decided to merge the three organizations, with their largely overlapping membership, into a "Provisional All-Ukrainian Orthodox Church Council" (*Tserkovna Rada*), a body of some sixty members with Archbishop Oleksii Dorodnytsyn as honorary chairman. The actual leadership of the Council was assumed by the curate, Oleksander Marychiv, as chairman, with Colonel Tsvichynskyi and Deacon Durdukivskyi as vice-chairman and secretary, respectively.[51] Pointing to the "separation of the Ukrainian State

---

49 *Ibid.,* p. 8; Samoilovich, p. 36.

50 Cited in Doroshenko, Vol. I, p. 411.

51 Samoilovich, pp. 36–38; Friedrich Heier, *Die Orthodoxe Kirche in der Ukraine von 1917 bis 1945* (Köln-Braunsfeld, 1953), pp. 40–41; Vlasovskyi, Vol. IV, pp. 15–16. According to Vlasovskyi, the chairmanship of the Rada was first offered to Bishop Dymytrii of Uman, who declined this offer. Among members of this body were also the priests V. Lypkivskyi, N. Sharaievskyi, P. Tarnavskyi, A. Hrynevych, E. Kapralov, S. Fylypenko, P. Pashchevskyi, P. Korsunovskyi, N. Marynych, V. Khomenko, and S. Petikhyn; deacons Rafalskyi and Botvynenko; P. Maziukevych; and military representatives Andriienko, Holyk and Halamiiv.

from the Russian State" and to the election of the Patriarch, "who might extend his power also upon the Ukrainian Church," the *Tserkovna Rada* took a revolutionary step in proclaiming itself a provisional government of the Orthodox Church in the Ukraine until the convocation of an All-Ukrainian Sobor. Resolutions adopted at this constituent meeting provided for the inclusion in the *Tserkovna Rada* of representatives from the dioceses, episcopate, monasteries, theological institutions and certain lay organizations, but it was stipulated that "all representatives should be Ukrainian by origin and conviction," a restriction which, along with other provisions, was obviously designed to prevent Russian church elements from taking over the new institution. The meeting appointed commissars for individual dioceses and explicitly prohibited the honorary chairman, Dorodnytsyn, from complying with Moscow's order transferring him to a monastic post in Russia.[52]

At the same time, the *Tserkovna Rada* issued a call for an All-Ukrainian Church Sobor to meet in Kiev on January 10. In an intensely nationalistic proclamation, "To the Ukrainian People," which echoed the language of the Central Rada's Universals, the All-Ukrainian Church Council stated the motives and objectives of the forthcoming Sobor:

> Once, at the time of the Hetmanate, you were yet free, but having united with tsarist Moscow, you have lost your freedom, not only political but also ecclesiastical. Now, having rebuilt your People's Republic, you should have restored your once independent, autocephalous, holy Church. . . .
>
> But the Russians, having rid themselves of a temporal tsar, have created a new spiritual autocrat—the Patriarch of Moscow—in order to usher also our Ukrainian people into a new spiritual slavery. . . .
>
> In order not to fall into this spiritual captivity, you should immediately elect your All-Ukrainian Orthodox Sobor of clergy and laymen; at [this Sobor] you should restore the ancient independence of the Ukrainian Church, confirmed by the Treaty of Pereiaslav [1654], and illegally destroyed by Moscow. . . .
>
> Only the All-Ukrainian Church Sobor . . . has the right to decide the fate of your Church and to recognize or not to recognize the newly-elected Patriarch of Moscow; therefore, the latter should not be now mentioned [in liturgical prayers] in the churches of the Ukraine. . . .

---

[52] The resolution is cited in full in Heier, pp. 40–41.

The *Tserkovna Rada*'s message also set forth the mode of representation at the projected Sobor, which was calculated to prevent its domination by the Russians entrenched in the higher echelons of the Church. Not only were laymen favored in the distribution of Sobor seats, but the document restricted membership in the Sobor to "Ukrainians by birth and invariably sympathetic to the Ukrainian cause, which must be confirmed in the credentials issued to them by their electors."[53]

The revolutionary nature of the *Tserkovna Rada*'s action did not prevent it from resolving, at the same time, to send a delegation to the Moscow Sobor to deal with the questions pertaining to the Ukrainian Church and the convocation of the Sobor in Kiev. This suggests both the *Tserkovna Rada*'s reluctance to sever completely its canonic links with Moscow and its expectation that the radical measures adopted on December 6 would frighten the Russian church leadership into making concessions to Ukrainian demands.[54]

The pace of events now quickened. The local Russian church circles reacted vehemently to the *Tserkovna Rada*'s coup by staging a series of protests. On November 24, a meeting of the Kievan "Union of Parish Councils" condemned the "arbitrary and anti-canonic attempt to create an autocephalous Ukrainian Church" as eventually leading to "Union" and "submission to the Vatican and the Pope"; it requested the Patriarchate to "prevent" the convocation of the Ukrainian Sobor and to unfrock the *Tserkovna Rada* clergy unless they "renounce their designs." At the same time, the Kievan meeting dispatched a pledge of loyalty to Patriarch Tikhon, "the spokesman of the Russian Orthodox idea," under whose banner "the unity of the Russian people will be preserved."[55]

Meanwhile, forewarned on December 3 of the impending "threat to ecclesiastical peace and unity" in the Ukraine, the Moscow Sobor began to consider the crisis. Shortly thereafter, the caucus of Sobor delegates from the Ukraine met. While it appears that Metropolitan

---

[53] Cited in full in Doroshenko, Vol. I, pp. 408–409.

[54] According to Shram (pp. 17–18), differences developed within the "Ukrainian Church Committee" between supporters of a radical break with the Russian Church (initial founders of the Committee) and those who, out of consideration for the Orthodox canons, wanted to bring into this body all bishops of the Ukraine. The latter group included O. Marychiv and V. Lypkivskyi.

[55] *Tserkovno-obshchestvennyi vestnik,* December 1, 1917, p. 3.

Vladimir remained adamantly opposed to any compromise with the Ukrainians, the less extreme counsels prevailed in the caucus, whose conclusions were reported to the Sobor plenum on December 6 by Archbishop Evlogii of Volhynia. They recommended that a regional (*oblastnyi*) Church Sobor be held in Kiev as soon as possible under the chairmanship of Metropolitan Vladimir "to consider the new situation and the ordering of local ecclesiastical affairs in the new political circumstances." After some deliberation, it was decided to send a delegation to Kiev, which should "announce the Sobor's decision to convene a regional Ukrainian Sobor and establish relations with the Ukrainian Central Rada and church organizations for the sake of mutual reconciliation."[56] When the Sobor learned of the *Tserkovna Rada*'s resolutions, an angry debate erupted at the session; a number of speakers condemned any concessions to the *Tserkovna Rada,* some pleaded for caution, others favored compromise with the Ukrainians in view of the changing political situation. Finally, a new resolution was adopted, which pledged to send a strong "pacifying-enlightening" delegation to Kiev, headed by Metropolitan Platon, as the Patriarch's plenipotentiary. The delegation was "to establish relations with the Kievan clergy and to take measures assuring that a regional Ukrainian Sobor, against which the Local Sobor does not protest in principle, be convened on a canonical basis and not arbitrarily."[57]

The subsequent course of events is blurred by contradictory accounts. One version describes the arrival in Moscow on December 12 of a *Tserkovna Rada* delegation led by the priest O. Marychiv. He later reported that the delegation received a sympathetic hearing from Patriarch Tikhon, who authorized the *Tserkovna Rada* to convoke the All-Ukrainian Sobor and promised to send his official

---

[56] *Ibid.,* November 24, 1917, p. 3; *Russkiia vedomosti,* November 24, 1917. A Sobor member, Myrovych, argued in favour of autocephalous status for the Ukrainian Church "because after the Rada's Universal which had been favorably received by a significant portion of the clergy, there emerged in Southern Russia an independent Ukrainian republic connected only federally with the rest of Russia." Liberal Professor F. L. Mishchenko supported Evlogii's proposal.

[57] *Russkiia vedomosti,* November 25 and 28, 1917. The Sobor delegation included, in addition to Platon, S. A. Kotliarevskii (former Deputy Minister of Confessions), Prince G. N. Trubetskoi, the priest Ia. Botvynovskyi, and K. K. Myrovych (lecturer at the Kievan Theological Seminary).

blessings later with the Moscow Sobor's delegation.[58] However, when the latter delegation arrived in Kiev in December and entered into negotiations with the All-Ukrainian Church Council, the irreconcilability of their respective positions led to a complete deadlock, with Metropolitan Platon breaking off the talks after four days. The Ukrainian side accused Platon of demanding the *Tserkovna Rada*'s dissolution and of refusing to concede even autonomy to the Ukrainian Church.[59] It is likely that the extreme anti-Ukrainian position maintained by Metropolitan Vladimir and the local Russian clergy might have affected both Platon's and his delegation's attitudes.

The failure to reach agreement brought about renewed hostilities between the *Tserkovna Rada* and Russian ecclesiastical circles. On December 22, the *Tserkovna Rada*'s representatives visited Vladimir and requested that he and his vicar, Nikodim, should leave Kiev within three days. At the same time, the *Tserkovna Rada* attempted to take over the Kievan consistory and did succeed in temporarily Ukrainianizing the diocesan press organ.[60] Earlier, on December 21, the *Tserkovna Rada* published an order requesting all clergy in the Ukraine to offer liturgical prayers for "the God-loved and divinely-protected Ukrainian State, its supreme ecclesiastical authority—the All-Ukrainian Church Council—and the Ukrainian Army."[61] Two days later, the *Tserkovna Rada* issued an appeal to the Ukrainian population calling for their wholehearted support of the Ukrainian government in resisting the Soviet Russian invasion.[62]

---

[58] *Rech,* November 30, 1917; Vlasovskyi, Vol. IV, p. 17. According to Metropolitan Antonii Khrapovitskii, Tikhon declared to the Ukrainian delegates: "I shall never give my consent to any autocephaly of the Ukrainian Church, but autonomy, even the widest, is in your hands." Bishop Nikon [Raklitskii], *Zhizneopisanie Blazhenneishago Antoniia, Mitropolita Kievskago i Galitskago,* Vol. IV (New York: Izd. Severo-Amerikanskoi i Kanadskoi eparkhii. 1958), p. 234.

[59] Vlasovskyi, Vol. IV, p. 17.

[60] *Kievlianin,* December 11, 1917. On January 11, 1918, the same paper carried a rather improbable story that two *Tserkovna Rada* members subsequently paid a midnight visit to Metropolitan Vladimir offering him the post of a Ukrainian Patriarch and, when he refused, they allegedly demanded from him a contribution of 100,000 rubles for the needs of the Ukrainian Autocephalous Church. See also Heier, p. 43.

[61] *Odesskii listok,* December 10, 1917.

[62] Samoilovich, pp. 37–39.

In the meantime, the continuing efforts of the Ukrainian church movement to win the active support of the Ukrainian government began to bear fruit. In what amounted to an official recognition of the All-Ukrainian Church Council, its representative was seated in the Central Rada, and the latter's representative joined the Council. The government established the office of a Commissar for Religious Affairs (within the General Secretariat for Internal Affairs) and on December 27 declared that henceforth all communications with the Patriarch and the Church authorities in Russia must be carried exclusively through the Commissar.[63]

The shift in governmental attitude toward the Russo-Ukrainian conflict within the Church might have been the decisive factor in persuading the Russians to seek a compromise with the *Tserkovna Rada*. Of equal importance might have been the sudden arrival, on December 23, of a group of Moscow Sobor members, evidently led by Archbishop Evlogii, who, by-passing Platon and Vladimir, entered into negotiations with the *Tserkovna Rada*.[64] On December 24, Metropolitan Vladimir presided over a joint meeting of the Kievan union of clergy and representatives of parish councils which resolved "to ask the Central Rada why it had recognized the self-appointed All-Ukrainian Church Council"; at the same time, however, the meeting clearly indicated the readiness to reach a compromise on the issue concerning Ukrainianization of the Church:

> The higher church authorities—the Kievan Metropolitan, together with the clergy and representatives of the parish church organizations of Kiev—take this opportunity to declare openly to the Ukrainian Central Rada and all the leaders of the Ukraine's national revival, that they not only do not oppose the renovation of ecclesiastical life in accordance with the national peculiarities of the Ukraine, but also welcome such renovation and shall cooperate in every way in realizing this sacred cause.[65]

Two days later, the conference of the "Union of the Parish Councils" requested the higher church authorities to allow the convoca-

---

[63] *Ibid.*, p. 39.

[64] *Ibid.*, p. 41; Heier, p. 43; Metropolitan Evlogii, *Put moei zhizni* (Paris, 1947), p. 308. According to Heier, this group of Moscow Sobor members "approved and authorized the *Tserkovna Rada*, on behalf of the All-Russian Sobor, to function as an organ convening the All-Ukrainian Sobor."

[65] *Kievskii pravoslavnyi vestnik*, No. 2 (1918), p. 43; Samoilovich, p. 41.

tion of the Ukrainian Sobor "for the sake of pacification."[66] Meanwhile renewed negotiations with the *Tserkovna Rada* initiated by Evlogii soon produced a compromise formula, which declared that "the All-Ukrainian Church Council, headed by bishops of the Ukrainian dioceses, is the only legal organ for the convocation of the All-Ukrainian Church Sobor."[67] A new mode of representation and decision-making for the forthcoming Sobor, partly based on the practice of the Moscow Sobor, was agreed upon. Thus, the entire episcopate was to be included in the presidium of the Sobor and to provide its chairman. The bishops were to form a separate "chamber" of the Sobor with veto power. Each district (*povit*) and each gubernia center was to be represented by a clergyman, a deacon, a psalmist, and three laymen; every monastic and theological institution was entitled to one representative. At the same time, the entire *Tserkovna Rada* (some 60 members) was to be included among the Sobor members; in addition, one delegate was to be admitted from every Ukrainian military unit. Upon this compromise project the Patriarch and the All-Russian Sobor now duly bestowed their blessings.[68]

The agreement clearly bore the marks of a truce rather than a lasting reconciliation between the two ecclesiastical camps. Neither side believed in the sincerity of the other. The Ukrainians counted on both governmental backing and the weight of their lay and military representatives to assure a favorable outcome at the Sobor. Russian ecclesiastical circles were at least assured of the bishop's veto over favorable Sobor decisions. Meanwhile, the Soviet Russian invasion of the Ukraine and the shrinking control of the Central Rada over Ukrainian territory emboldened Metropolitan Vladimir and the more extreme Russian elements; they now attempted to revise the original terms of the compromise with the *Tserkovna Rada* and to force the postponement of the Sobor, probably in anticipation of the imminent fall of the Ukrainian regime.[69] At the same time, measures were taken to deprive the Ukrainians of their only supporter among the bishops; on December 31, the Patriarch again ordered Archbishop Dorodnytsyn to Moscow, and, when the

---

[66] *Ibid.*

[67] *Ibid.;* Lypkivskyi, *Istoriia ukrainskoi pravoslavnoi tserkvy,* p. 9.

[68] *Ibid.,* pp. 9–10; *Odesskii listok,* December 13, 1917.

[69] See the resolution adopted early in January by a meeting of the Union of Pastors and the executive of the Union of Parish Councils, cited in *Odesskii listok,* December 23, 1917.

latter did not comply, he was suspended by a decision of Metropolitan Platon and other bishops on the very day of the opening of the Sobor.[70]

The First All-Ukrainian Church Sobor, which opened in Kiev's ancient St. Sophia Catherdral on January 20, 1918, brought together 279 delegates, including bishops of nearly all the Ukrainian dioceses. The Soviet-Ukrainian war prevented the attendance of some delegates from the eastern gubernias of the Ukraine, and in at least two dioceses (Poltava and Kherson) local bishops failed to make arrangements for elections, thus depriving the Sobor of a quorum. In its national make-up, the Sober was predominantly Ukrainian, though, as far as the future of the Ukrainian Church was concerned, its membership was divided into centralist, autonomist, and autocephalist orientations.[71]

Elections of a presidium and commissions had taken up much of the Sobor's time. While the honorary chairmanship was assumed by Metropolitan Vladimir, the youngest of the participating bishops, Pimen (Pegov) of Balta, was made chairman after a bitterly contested election; two other bishops and members of the *Tserkovna Rada* made up the rest of the presidium.[72] Six commissions were formed, each headed by a bishop, to consider such questions as supreme church administration in the Ukraine, diocesan and parish administration, the Ukrainianization of the Church, and educational, economic, and personnel questions.[73]

Obviously, the Sobor's primary task was to determine the future relationship of the Ukrainian Church to the Moscow Patriarchate and to the Ukrainian State. The gathering had no doubt about the position of the Central Rada. In his passionate welcoming address, the government's representative, A. M. Karpinskyi, reminded the

---

[70] Vlasovskii, Vol. IV, p. 25.

[71] Heier, p. 44; *Rech,* January 30, 1918; Samoilovich, pp. 42–44.

[72] According to Vlasovskyi (Vol. IV, pp. 27–28), Pimen was elected chairman on the mistaken assumption that he was sympathetic to the Ukrainian church movement.

[73] Each commission was chaired by a bishop; Metropolitan Antonii of Kharkiv—supreme church administration; Archbishop Agapit of Katerynoslav—diocesan and parish administration; Archbishop Evlogii of Volhynia—Ukrainianization; Bishop Vasilii of Kaniv—education; Bishop Nikodim of Chyhyryn—economy; and Bishop Feodor of Pryluky—personnel questions. Heier, p. 44.

Sobor delegates that the Ukraine had been invaded by the Russians and warned that the General Secretariat "will not tolerate Muscovite ecclesiastical guardians in our state." In the name of the Ukrainian People's Republic, he demanded that the Sobor "grant autocephaly to the Ukrainian Church."[74]

The Sobor agreed to issue a call to defend the Ukrainian regime against the Bolsheviks,[75] but it procrastinated with regard to changing the ecclesiastic status quo. While some work had begun in the commissions,[76] no decisions were reached on any of the substantive questions by February 1, when the Bolshevik uprising in Kiev and the approach of the Soviet Russian troops persuaded the majority of the remaining Sobor delegates to adjourn until May 23. At the last stormy session, the Ukrainian delegates vainly demanded an immediate vote on the autocephaly of the Ukrainian Church against the determined opposition of the pro-Russian camp, which now appeared to be intent on gaining time in expectation of the demise of the Ukrainian Republic. In frustration, fifty-three Ukrainian delegates issued a joint declaration stating that "the Sobor did not reveal its Ukrainian character before the people and failed to answer questions demanding immediate decision." Before dispersing, the authors of the declaration decided to form a Brotherhood of SS. Cyril and Methodius to continue the work of the *Tserkovna Rada,* which had dissolved itself after the convocation of the Sobor.[77]

---

[74] D. Skrynchenko, "Vseukrainskii tserkovnyi sobor," *Kievskii pravoslavnyi vestnik,* No. 4 (1918), p. 90.

[75] Samoilovich, p. 44. The Sobor adjourned before the appeal could be published.

[76] Upon the invitation of the Sobor commission on Ukrainianization, Professor Ivan Ohiienko (after the Second World War, Metropolitan Ilarion of Winnipeg) delivered at one of the sessions a paper outlining the program for gradual Ukrainianization of the Church. It was to proceed through the following stages: 1) the adoption of Ukrainian pronunciation of Church-Slavonic liturgical texts; 2) the rendering of litanies in Ukrainian; 3) the celebration of the entire Mass in the Ukrainian language; 4) the Ukrainianization of other Church services and of the ecclesiastical administration (interview with Metropolitan Ilarion, August, 1958). Cf. Heier, pp. 44–45. According to Professor Ohiienko, he had helped to draft the program of the *Tserkovna Rada* and, in December 1917, the latter asked President Hrushevskyi to appoint Ohiienko as Minister of Confessions. See his "Moie zhyttia," *Nasha kultura,* I, 3 (1935), p. 452.

[77] *Nova rada,* March 14, 1918; Samoilovich, p. 44. The vote for the

Meanwhile, on January 22, 1918, the Central Rada proclaimed the full sovereignty of the Ukrainian National Republic and, on February 9, concluded a separate peace treaty with the Central Powers. On the same day, however, Kiev was finally captured by Soviet troops, and the Ukrainian government was forced to evacuate westward and to seek military assistance from Germany and Austria-Hungary. But the Bolshevik tide was soon reversed. By early March, German and Ukrainian forces recaptured the city, ending a reign of terror which claimed, among many other victims, Metropolitan Vladimir.[78]

Following the Central Rada's return to Kiev, the autocephalists, organized in the Brotherhood of SS. Cyril and Methodius, appealed to the government to reconvene the All-Ukrainian Sobor and to proclaim by state law the autocephaly of the Ukrainian Church. The government, however, did not proceed beyond the establishment of a Department of Confessions within the Ministry of Internal Affairs. The advantages of this belated change in the official attitude toward ecclesiastical affairs were largely nullified by the choice of an odious figure, the self-unfrocked former Krasnoiarsk Bishop, Nikon (Nikolai) Bezsonov, to head the new department.[79] The latter's orders to the Church, including the provision, on April 1, for the departmental clearance of all ecclesiastical communications with the Moscow Patriarchate, were ignored by the episcopate.[80] Sensing the political instability of the Central Rada, the Russian church leadership was intent on postponing any changes in the ecclesiastical status quo. The six bishops from the Ukraine who attended the Moscow Sobor met on April 2, 1918, and decided to postpone the second session of the All-Ukrainian Sobor until after diocesan con-

---

adjournment was 94 to 42. The meeting of the SS. Cyril and Methodius Brotherhood took place only on March 24, 1918, after the Central Rada's return to Kiev.

[78] A version accusing Ukrainian nationalists of instigating Metropolitan Vladimir's murder has been circulated widely by both Bolshevik and Russian émigré writers. But Metropolitan Antonii Khrapovitskii, who supervised the investigation of the murder, has denied this allegation. See Bishop Nikon, pp. 221–222.

[79] Samoilovich, p. 48. See also Evlogii, pp. 288–289. In April 1917, the Kievan council of public organizations favored Nikon as a replacement for Metropolitan Vladimir (*Russkiia vedomosti*, March 21, 1917).

[80] Samoilovich, p. 48.

gresses of clergy and laymen had been held in all eparchies of the Ukraine. Characteristically, the bishops requested these congresses not only to resolve the issues of autocephaly and Ukrainianization of the Church, but also to reconsider the representation system adopted for the All-Ukrainian Sobor through a compromise reached in December 1917 between the *Tserkovna Rada* and the episcopate.[81]

The continuing stalemate on the ecclesiastical front generated much bitterness among the supporters of Ukrainian autocephaly. Symptomatic of the growing desperation of the Ukrainian church movement was an article in *Nova rada,* which called for a radical break with the Russian Orthodox Church through the repudiation of the authority of the Russian bishops, the organization of a separate Ukrainian autocephalous church with its own episcopate, and the struggle for control of churches throughout the Ukraine:

> Nationally conscious and idealistic [*ideine*] clergy should be obliged to pledge in writing that they will recognize only the ecclesiastical authority approved by the state and not to subordinate themselves to any agents of the Moscow Patriarchate. In the beginning, even a protopresbyter could be placed at the head of these [Ukrainian] priests; later, [they should be headed by] a bishop, but one elected from among the white clergy.

This, the author felt, was the only way to liberate the Ukrainian Church "from the chains of the All-Russian religious oppression, which throughout the centuries has been exploiting for its insatiable interests the material and intellectual resources of our Fatherland."[82]

The Central Rada's days were, however, numbered. Impatient with its continued insistence on Ukrainian sovereignty and its socialist orientation, the Germans intervened in April 1918 and replaced the Rada with a quasi-monarchical regime headed by Hetman Pavlo Skoropadskyi. The necessities of political survival made the new regime much more cautious than its predecessor in the realization of Ukrainian national objectives and much readier to seek compro-

---

[81] *Kievskii eparkhialnyi vestnik,* No. 1, May 2/15, 1918, pp. 2–4. The bishops' resolution clearly suggested the exclusion from the All-Ukrainian Sobor of "persons not elected by the dioceses," which would have barred from the Sobor most members of the former *Tserkovna Rada* and representatives of the Ukrainian military units.

[82] P. Maziukevych in *Nova rada,* April 5, 1918.

mise with Russian interests in the Ukraine, interests which were reinforced at that time by a mass of politically vocal refugees from Soviet Russia.

These characteristics of the Hetman regime had a profound effect on the subsequent course of the Russo-Ukrainian struggle for the control of the Church. Encouraged by the political orientation of the new government and taking full advantage of its vacillating ecclesiastical policy, the conservative Russian elements within the Church were now able to consolidate their strength and to turn the balance of power in their favor, thus frustrating again the Ukrainian attempts to emancipate the Church from Russian control.

As a result, the Russo-Ukrainian conflict within the Orthodox Church passed beyond the point of reconciliation. The uncompromising centralist and conservative position of the episcopate and its open support of the anti-Ukrainian political forces compelled the Ukrainian church movement to seek the realization of its objectives through the belated intervention of the Directory, which replaced the Hetman regime by the end of 1918. But when the new Russian invasion prevented the implementation of the January 1919 decree proclaiming autocephalous status for the Orthodox Church in the Ukraine, the movement turned to revolutionary extra-canonic means, which eventually resulted in the emergence, under the Soviet regime, of the Ukrainian Autocephalous Orthodox Church.[83]

---

[83] On the subsequent devolopments, see Vlasovskyi, Vol. IV; Ivan Sukhopliuiev, *Ukrainski avtokefalisty* (Kharkiv, 1925); Samoilovich, chapters IV and V; John S. Reshetar, "Ukrainian Nationalism and the Orthodox Church," *The American Slavic and East European Review,* X, 1 (Seattle, Wash., 1951), pp. 38–49; and Bohdan R. Bociurkiw, "The Autocephalous Church Movement in Ukraine: The Formative Stage (1917–1921)," *The Ukrainian Quarterly,* XVI, 3 (New York, 1960), pp. 211–223.

CHAPTER TEN

The Great Ukrainian Jacquerie

Arthur E. Adams

It is the central thesis of this study that if the events of
1918–1920 in the Ukraine are to be accurately interpreted, they must
be viewed as parts of a vast and elemental social revolution in which
agrarian rebellion played a predominant role. According to this
thesis, urban social processes and the actions of intellectuals and
political parties, which have long occupied the center of the historical stage in our analysis of these years, must share the limelight with
the Ukrainian Jacquerie. More specifically, it is contended here
that the political parties active in the Ukraine had, as their chief
task, to engraft themselves somehow upon a torrential agrarian
social upheaval whose complex manifestations and principal characteristics were not then and are not even now fully comprehended.
Thus, whether consciously or not, the political parties clearly
struggled to lead and organize a cataclysmic social process which
they had little power to control; and, as a result, each of them
failed until the Jacquerie had exhausted itself. The purpose of this
essay is to examine the character of the agrarian upheaval, its influence on political events, and its relationships with the principal
political parties active during this period in the Ukraine.

As a beginning, we must attempt at least a rough definition of
the agrarian phenomenon that we wish to discuss. Subsequent pages
will add concrete detail to the bare outline presented at this point.
Briefly, the "agrarian upheaval" may be characterized as a peasant-
Cossack Jacquerie, a series of bloody rebellions, expressing in the
most violent terms the agrarian population's protest at the conditions of its life. This Jacquerie was of immense proportions. It was
led by no single group or class or party. Many of its local explosions
were legitimized and sustained by traditions and cultural values
with roots deep in the Ukrainian past, and its various manifestations

247

were complicated by the differing historical traditions, agrarian institutions, economic conditions, political experiences, and ethnic conflicts existing in the highly diversified regions of the Ukraine. Chronologically, the duration of the Jacquerie, through many months of swiftly evolving political and economic crises, of national awakening, and of military action against both domestic and foreign enemies, brought a complex series of intense pressures, first upon one local region, then upon another. The result was a social chaos so turbulent that it literally destroyed the best-laid plans of political parties and governments.[1]

In studying events in the Ukraine after 1917, scholars customarily focus attention on the actions of a number of political leaders and parties, the governments they established, the armies they raised, and the negotiations or battles they carried on with other parties, governments, and armies. It is obvious, of course, that Ukrainian and Russian political parties and governments, as well as the military expeditions of Western nations, were vital factors in the determination of events during these years of revolution, civil war, and intervention. Equally obvious are the significant influences of Ukrainian Rada and Directory politics, and of the theories, deeds,

---

[1] The distinguished political scientist Chalmers Johnson defines a Jacquerie rather narrowly as a "mass rebellion of peasants with strictly limited aims—the restoration of lost rights or the removal of specific grievances." He recognizes, of course, that people other than peasants may be involved. The Ukrainian Jacquerie was more complex. While it fulfills the requirements of Johnson's definition, it was also, in part, a continuation of the processes of disorganization and breakdown that followed the collapse of the old regime in 1917; from then until 1920, various substructures of the old social system were seeking to achieve a variety of "new orders." In addition, the Ukrainian Jacquerie embraced a series of anarchistic rebellions by groups that idealized the traditions and supposedly absolute personal freedoms of the distant past. Moreover, intervention by foreigners (including Russian Bolsheviks and Denikin's White armies) provoked a variety of more or less conscious nationalistic responses. Finally, civil war and the chaotic rise and fall of governments further complicated the course of the Jacquerie, compelling partisan bands and leaders to identify their aims variously at different times. See Chalmers Johnson, *Revolution and the Social System*, Hoover Institution Studies, No. 3 (Stanford, California, 1964), pp. 31 ff.; and also his later work, *Revolutionary Change* (Boston: Little, Brown and Co., 1966), pp. 136 ff.

and schisms of the Social Democrats, Socialist-Revolutionaries, Socialist-Federalists, Progressivists, *Borotbists*, Bundists, Anarchists, and others. It is necessary, therefore, to emphasize that it is not our purpose either to denigrate the influence of these political organizations or to detract from the reputations of their often courageous and intelligent leaders.

Nonetheless, the roles of the political parties have often been so overemphasized as to give the impression that *all* the important forces at work in the Ukraine were concentrated in party centers and in the governments they established. Such overemphasis implies, erroneously, that one may gain complete understanding of the events of 1918–1920 by focusing on the activities of the political parties. Emphasis on a single influential factor to the exclusion of all others frequently weakens the analysis of complex historical processes, for, all too often, major historical events are determined variously—by the character of the actors, by economic, social, political, and cultural influences, or by a sometimes indecipherable procession of accidents or confluence of social forces. The period of the Ukraine's long agony, ending at last with the Bolsheviks' victory in 1920, is a fascinating and tragic example of man's tangled history. To be understood, it must be examined from many sides. Therefore, the very significant role of the rural population in Ukrainian history, which has too often been thrust into the wings of the historical stage, will be brought into focus here.

Any effort to identify the motives of the peasant rebellions of 1918–1920 must begin with a consideration of the most powerful and glorious of all Ukrainian traditions—that of the Zaporozhian Cossacks. No matter what the Zaporozhians may have been in the sixteenth and seventeenth centuries, whether the founders of a great Ukrainian state or treacherous, irresponsible marauders, their struggles against Polish kings and Russian tsars in the seventeenth and eighteenth centuries left a dramatic and noble legacy for the Ukraine's agrarian folk. From the Zaporozhians came a genuine egalitarianism, an anarchistic love of personal freedom that expressed itself in a profound distrust of all authority, and a proud tradition that, when a true Cossack is oppressed, he will rebel and fight with a fine disregard for consequences. This tradition was diffused throughout the Ukraine by the dispersal of the Zaporozhians under Catherine the Great, and it was preserved by Cossack groups that settled in the Kuban and in Turkish and western Ukrainian territories.[2]

To the Cossack tradition must be added that of the *haidamaks*, the peasant brigands whose history goes back at least to the seventeenth century. When Polish nobles tried to enslave free peasants on the Dnieper's Right Bank, those peasants rose with scythes and hayforks and massacred their oppressors without mercy. These uprisings were so extensive and bloody that only the brutal intervention of the Empress Catherine's armies brought the peasants under control.[3]

Events of the past have little significance as motivating forces in later times unless they are somehow transferred to succeeding generations. That the Cossack traditions remained an integral part of the Ukraine's culture at the beginning of the twentieth century is unquestioned. They came into the present century in several ways. The first was through the early development of Ukrainian patriotic and nationalist literature. Scarcely had Catherine succeeded in breaking up the Zaporozhian regiments and scattering them throughout the Ukraine than Ukrainian poets, publicists, and historical scholars began to write of the past with a romantic fervor that gathered force through the years of the nineteenth century. This writing both preserved and glorified Cossack traditions, making the ideals of the past the basis of Ukrainian political objectives in the twentieth century.[4] Also, while students, professors, and Ukrainian publicists eulogized the Ukraine's past, the people themselves preserved the old traditions with a special devotion: although the Zaporozhian Host was dispersed, Cossack settlements (*stanytsi*) preserved the old military distinctions and organizational frame-

---

[2] Mykhailo Hrushevskyi, *A History of Ukraine* (New Haven, Conn.: Yale University Press, 1941), pp. 156–161, 178–179, 452–460; W. E. D. Allen, *The Ukraine: A History* (Cambridge: Cambridge University Press, 1941), pp. 229–232, 259–261; N. D. Polons'ka-Vasylenko, *The Settlement of the Southern Ukraine (1750–1775)* (New York: The Ukrainian Academy of Arts and Sciences in the U.S., 1955), pp. 319–331.

[3] Hrushevskyi, pp. 436–445; *Ukraine, A Concise Encyclopaedia*, Vol. I (Toronto: University of Toronto Press, 1963), pp. 660–661; *Entsiklopedicheskii slovar*, Vol. VII (St. Petersburg: Tipo-litografiia I. A. Efrona, 1894), pp. 871–873.

[4] *Ukraine*, Vol. I, pp. 561–569, 960–966, 1007–1017, 1019–1030; Hrushevskyi, pp. 477–482, 484–485, 501–511; Allen, pp. 242–247, 254–255.

work; Cossack political ideas, pride in daring horsemanship and headstrong courage, and the distinctive love of freedom remained. Similarly, service in the Cossack regiments of the tsar's armies helped to keep the traditions vigorous.[5]

As for the *haidamaks,* we too often assume that violent peasant uprisings were over and done with in the eighteenth century. In fact, peasant uprisings continued up to the twentieth century, so that widespread peasant violence both preceded and accompanied the 1905 Revolution.[6] In the Ukraine, peasant rebellions had never ceased.

Before the First World War, peasant land hunger, overpopulation, and an unstable economy created new reasons for dissatisfaction and drove hundreds of thousands into emigration.[7] Through the war itself, particularly during the revolutionary year 1917, the old traditions found their counterparts in the loudly trumpeted slogans of revolutionary parties suddenly made bold by the tsar's abdication. Soldiers deserting from the western and southwestern fronts brought back to their villages the pent-up frustrations of defeat along with the exciting idea that reforms made by the people themselves could open up better ways of life. Meanwhile, the Ukrainian Rada proclaimed the ideals of national autonomy and social democracy and began to move toward political separation from the Russian state. The Bolsheviks at Petrograd and Moscow took power in early November and decreed that peasants everywhere should seize and redistribute the lands and farm implements of the nobility, the

---

[5] *Entsiklopedicheskii slovar,* Vol. XIII, pp. 883–886; *Ukraine,* Vol. I, 362–364.

[6] I. I. Ignatovich, *Krestianskoe dvizhenie v Rossii v pervoi chetverti XIX veka* (Moscow: Izd. sotsialno-ekonomicheskoi literatury, 1963), Chapters VI, VII, and VIII; N. N. Firsov, "Krestianskie volnenia do XIX veka," in A. K. Dzhivelegov *et al.* (eds.), *Velikaia reforma,* Vol. II (Moscow: Tipografiia T-va I. D. Systina, 1911), pp. 48–49, 53, 55, 58–62; Geroid T. Robinson, *Rural Russia Under the Old Regime* (New York: The Macmillan Co., 1932, 1967), pp. 138–139, 152–155; see the documentary series, *Krestianskoe dvizhenie v Rossii v XIX-nachale XX veka* (Moscow: Izd. 'Nauka,' 1960–65) and also the series under the same title covering the years from 1900 through 1917.

[7] Konstantyn Kononenko, *Ukraine and Russia: A History of the Economic Relations between Ukraine and Russia (1654–1917)* (Milwaukee, Wisc.: Marquette University Press, 1958), pp. 86–88.

church, and the bourgeois farmer.[8] All these influences added tinder to the flames of peasant rebellion that were to sweep the Ukraine.

By early 1918, the demoralizing processes of Russia's political revolution and military collapse and the breakdown of the Rada's authority definitely marked the end of the old order in the Ukraine. The defenders of the *ancien régime*, its police, its harsh laws, and heavy punishments were paralyzed. Legitimate central authority ceased to exist. Ukrainian Cossacks and peasants, their appetites whetted by disorder and the disappearance of external restraints, recalled with more than usual enthusiasm their traditional faith in freedom and violence. It was as if the old Zaporozhian and *haidamak* Ukraine was beginning to realize that it had the power to shake off the puny reins of the Rada and Bolshevik governments, and it began to think more earnestly than before of restoring old equalities and remembered freedoms.

Into the vacuum of power, where some 33 million people lived (approximately 75 percent of them engaged in agriculture), the Germans moved their occupation troops in February and March of 1918.[9] By April, Hetman Pavlo Skoropadskyi pushed aside the Rada government to establish his mockery of a Cossack government, supported by German bayonets.[10] The Ukrainian agrarian folk— shocked into excited hope by revolution and the end of the imperial regime, by the land they had seized from wealthy proprietors and by the angry gangs of soldiers who had come home bearing stolen weapons—abruptly found themselves subjects of both the Germans and the Hetmanate government, whose chief missions were to force the countryside to give up its food and livestock to the foreign occupiers and to restore the former land relationships.[11]

---

[8] Allen, p. 279; John S. Reshetar, Jr., *The Ukrainian Revolution, 1917–1920: A Study in Nationalism* (Princeton, N.J.: Princeton University Press, 1952), pp. 47–50, 60–63, 89; Alexander Baykov, *The Development of the Soviet Economic System* (New York: The Macmillan Co., 1948), pp. 16–18.

[9] *Ukraine,* Vol. I, pp. 169, 174.

[10] V. Miakotin, "Iz nedalekogo proshlogo," in S. A. Alekseev (ed.), *Revoliutsiia na Ukraine po memuaram belykh* (Moscow: Gosudarstvennoe izd., 1930), p. 222.

[11] Iwan Majstrenko, *Borotbism: A Chapter in the History of Ukrainian Communism* (New York: Research Program on the USSR, 1954), pp. 62–63; I. Kapulovskii, "Organizatsiia vosstaniia protiv getmana," *Letopis revoliutsii,* No. 4 (Kharkiv, 1923), pp. 95–102; Ia. Shelygin, "Partizanskaia

With German patrols and Skoropadskyi's collection units scouring the country for provisions, the peasant-Cossack village population began to express its fury in the only way open to it.

The swift burgeoning of rebellion from April through June 1918 is well documented. Numerous pitched battles between peasant rebels and German troops have often been described and need not be detailed here; yet it is useful to point out that within the space of a few weeks some 19,000 Germans lost their lives in the effort to suppress the *haidamaks,* and for a time whole regions were cut off from Hetmanate and German authority.[12] Spattering across the Ukraine, these uprisings provoked others, and rebellious acts grew steadily in numbers and seriousness from May through June. At this point, crushing German retaliations reduced the peasant action for a few weeks, but soon the uprisings increased. This was a hydra-headed monster that could be neither isolated nor suppressed.[13]

A pertinent question to be asked concerning these first months of the Jacquerie is what role the political parties played in fomenting, creating, or directing the fighting. The answer that must be given is that while many parties and local leaders were involved, and while political ideas of many sorts saturated the Ukrainian atmosphere, no single party or leader can legitimately claim to have led the movement. And no one group was ever to control it.

Evidence concerning the influence of political parties is fairly conclusive. While the Ukrainian Socialist Revolutionary Party— SR's (organized first in April, 1917)—was active during these months, its innumerable factional schisms, lack of bold and vigorous leadership, and ineffective organization prevented it from playing an effective role. The *Borotbists,* a radical, peasant-oriented faction

---

borba s getmanshchinoi i avstro-germanskoi okkupatsii," *ibid.,* No. 6 [33] (1928), p. 64; M. Gorkii, I. Mintz, and R. Eideman (eds.), *Krakh germanskoi okkupatsii na Ukraine (po dokumentam okkupantov)* (Moscow: Gosudarstvennoe izd., 1936), pp. 28–29, 168–170.

[12] Reshetar, p. 174; *Krakh germanskoi,* p. 167; A. S. Bubnov, S. S. Kamenev, M. N. Tukhachevskii, and R. P. Eideman (eds.), *Grazhdanskaia voina, 1918–1921,* Vol. I (Moscow-Leningrad: Izd. Voennyi Vestnik, 1928–30), pp. 35–46.

[13] *Krakh germanskoi,* pp. 170–171; V. Primakov, "Borba za sovetskuiu vlast na Ukraine," in *Piat let Krasnoi Armii: sbornik statei, 1918–1923* (Moscow, 1923), pp. 184–187.

of the SR's, was similarly too poorly organized and led to exert great influence. Nor did the important Ukrainian Social Democratic Labor Party direct the movement, for its main strength lay in the cities, and it had few agents among the peasants.[14] Even the Bolsheviks, who since the event have argued that their influence was predominant, and that indeed they masterminded the rebellions, were in fact working in the dark. The universal uprising which their "Ukrainian" headquarters ordered for August 7, 1918, misfired and provoked retaliations that cost the lives of many Ukrainian partisan fighters who were not even aware that the order had been given. This fiasco so clearly demonstrated the weakness of Bolshevik organization and communications in the Ukraine that the careers of the men who had initiated it went into temporary eclipse.[15]

It must be concluded that angry villagers, sick of German agrarian policies and Skoropadskyi's military rule and stirred up by a wide variety of political ideas and local leaders, rose more or less spontaneously. This is not to imply that political leadership was lacking or that political ideas were not present. The point to be emphasized is that the rebels made use of whatever weapon, idea, or political organization fell to hand. They followed with almost equal enthusiasm any local leader or political group that promised to lead them against the enemy—the foreign despoiler and his collaborators.[16] Thus, although each partisan band may have had its ideology, expressed in more or less conscious form, the peasants as a whole fought for objectives more elemental and deeply felt than those embedded in party programs. To generalize these peasant objectives, one might say that they fought for their land, for an end to military oppression, for the food that Skoropadskyi's troops tore from the mouths of their families, and for freedom to run their own affairs. As violence bred a taste for more violence, some of the *haidamak* gangs turned to plunder and rape and anti-Semitic pogroms. They fought to kill Germans, to raid, and to burn and carouse through a

---

[14] Majstrenko, pp. 37–42, 64–69.

[15] M. Ravich-Cherkasskii, *Istoriia Kommunisticheskoi partii (b-ov) Ukrainy* (Kharkiv: Gosudarstvennoe izd. Ukrainy, 1923), pp. 83–88.

[16] I. Mazepa, *Ukraina v ohni i buri revoliutsii, 1917–1921*, Vol. I (2nd ed.; n.p.: Vyd. 'Prometei', 1950–51), pp. 55–56; Majstrenko, pp. 89–92; M. A. Rubach, "K istorii grazhdanskoi voiny na Ukraine (perekhod Grigoreva k sovetskoi vlasti)," *Letopis revoliutsii*, No. 3 [8] (Kharkiv, 1924), p. 177.

countryside where the hated foreign order and authority were fast disappearing.

At its height the Jacquerie seemed to follow an evolutionary process that had its own innate laws and unseen ends. With the irresistible force of a tidal wave, it swept aside or crushed whatever stood in its way. These characteristics and their impact upon political developments are well illustrated by the swiftly changing relationships between the peasants and the Directory, which rose in late November 1918 to drive out Skoropadskyi.

Again the basic facts are well know. A Ukrainian National Union was formed by the nationalist parties in July and August to work for the establishment of an independent, democratic national state. On November 14, following the collapse of Germany, this Union, under the leadership of Volodymyr Vynnychenko, proclaimed a Directory of five nationalist leaders to be the legitimate political authority in the Ukraine. In its proclamation the Directory pledged itself to establish an independent Ukrainian National Republic (UNR). Simultaneously, Symon Petliura, a member of the Directory and its chief military figure, issued an appeal to the nation for arms and men, and in the space of a few days thousands upon thousands of peasants, Cossacks, and townsfolk flocked to the Directory's blue and yellow banners.[17]

By mid-December, when Skoropadskyi abdicated and fled from Kiev disguised in a German uniform, the army of the Directory already embraced nearly 100,000 men, while new recruits continued to pour in, both from the cities and from the outlying areas.[18] Cossack chiefs (*otamans*) at all levels, village elders, school teachers, sergeants, self-made captains, colonels, and citizens of every rank—all rushed to support the nationalist independence movement. Thus, for a brief moment in history, it appeared that the active majority of the Ukrainian peasant-Cossack population was pro-Directory, pro-UNR, and pro-Petliura—nationalist, democratic, and irredentist. The UNR's army appeared sufficiently strong to prevent Russia's Bolsheviks from making a successful invasion from the north, as well as to fight off the Russian (Monarchist) troops of the White General, Anton Denikin, who threatened the Ukraine from the

---

[17] Reshetar, pp. 199–201.

[18] Volodymyr Vynnychenko, *Vidrodzhennia natsii*, Vol. III (Kiev-Vienna: Vyd. Dzvin, 1920), pp. 244–245.

southeast. At this moment of triumph the Ukrainian nationalist leaders were fully persuaded both that they were in command and that the Ukrainian people wanted a national republic governed by Ukrainians.

In reality, however, the peasants and Cossacks who poured into Petliura's formations had little or no comprehension of the Directory's political and social programs.[19] They knew only that they were sick of the Germans and of Skoropadskyi's police. They rose to seize the lands Skoropadskyi had forced them to return to the big landowners, to rid themselves of armed food collectors, to attack and plunder withdrawing German units, to rob stores in the cities —in sum, to profit in any way possible from the chaos.

With certain exceptions, the men who led the Directory's armies also failed to understand the real aims of the government they served. Thus the reactionary colonel, Petro Bolbochan, who acted as Petliura's chief commander on the Left Bank of the Dnieper, suppressed local urban workers' and peasants' assemblies, employed Russian officers in his units, and left Skoropadskyi's officials in place in the villages. In mid-January 1919, after losing Kharkiv to Bolshevik troops, Bolbochan moved to the province of Poltava, where he showed himself ruthlessly hostile to the peasants' social revolution.[20] In peasant eyes, his rule was only a continuation of the Hetmanate, now doubly infuriating because so much had been expected.

Other Directory commanders were reactionary Russian Officers, Cossack partisan adventurers, or local ruffians who hated Jews or saw in the Ukraine's chaos a splendid opportunity for sacking undefended villages and cities. Such men as *Otaman* Hryhoriiv, who led partisan bands in the central areas around Katerynoslav and Aleksandriia, Struk of Chernihiv province, Anhel and Ihnatiiev-Mysevra in Poltava province, and a host of lesser leaders were only nominally controlled by the Chief *Otaman* Petliura.[21] All did very

---

[19] Reshetar, pp. 200–201, 218–219; Vynnychenko, Vol. III, pp. 124–127.

[20] *Ibid.*, pp. 146–147, 181, 184–186.

[21] Other *otamans* and partisan leaders who played significant roles during the Jacquerie were: Shepel, in Podillia province; Zelenyi, in Kiev and Poltava provinces; Shuba, in the Lubny district; Kotsur, a village school teacher; Sokolovskyi, in the Radomyshl region west of Kiev; Bozhko, in the territory between Bar and Mohyliv-Podilskyi, who proclaimed the restoration of the Zaporozhian Cossack state; Tiutiunnyk, Iatsenko, Klymenko, Popov, Holub, Mordylev, Volynets, Sokil, Diachenko, and, of

much as they wished, and, if any of them listened to a restraining voice, it was to that of the men who followed him, for any self-styled *otaman* who set himself at the head of a peasant or Cossack band had to be sensitive to its moods. Each of these leaders (with his band) represented but a single wave in the great sea of rebellion, though each regarded himself as independent, sovereign, and free. At a later date, Volodymyr Vynnychenko understandably evaluated this *"otamanshchyna"* with bitter words: "There was neither punishment, nor justice, nor trials, nor control over these criminals and enemies of the revolution and the national movement. The whole system of military authority was constructed and consciously based, by the chief and by the lesser *otamany*, on the principle that there would be no control."[22]

Almost from the very day that the peasants and Cossacks rose to swell the ranks of Petliura's armies, they sensed that the Directory (so far as they were able to perceive its intentions) was not the agency that would lead them to freedom. Seeing only local military representatives like the brutal Bolbochan, those who had rushed to join the Directory armies began to have second thoughts.[23]

Nor were the vacillations of the Directory government calculated to persuade the masses that the new utopia was about to be established on earth. The Marxian socialists of the Ukrainian Social Democratic Labor Party hesitated too long before implementing their goal—the establishment of a socialist workers' dictatorship in the Ukraine, the establishment of a *non-Bolshevik* people's government.[24] While they hesitated, new reasons for moderating their

---

course, the powerful Makhno, who was joined in the southeastern steppe by many less well-known men. Reshetar, pp. 251–252; Majstrenko, pp. 91–92, 235–236; William Henry Chamberlin, *The Russian Revolution, 1917–1921*, Vol. II (New York and London: The Macmillan Co., 1935), pp. 223–225; Elias Heifetz, *Slaughter of the Jews in the Ukraine in 1919* (New York, 1921), pp. 65–66, 312, 338–347; B. V. Kozelskyi, *Shliakh zradnytstva i avantur (Petliurivske povstanstvo)* (Kharkiv: Derzhavne vyd. Ukrainy, 1927), pp. 19–22, 28–29; P. Arshinov, *Istoriia makhnovskogo dvizheniia (1918–1921 gg.)* (Berlin: Izd. 'Gruppy russkikh anarkhistov v Germanii,' 1923), pp. 214–215.

[22] Vynnychenko, Vol. III, p. 188.

[23] Pavlo Khrystiuk, *Zamitky i materialy do istorii ukrainskoi revoliutsii, 1917–1920 rr.*, Vol. IV (Vienna, 1921–22), pp. 27, 41, 77–78; Majstrenko, pp. 93–94; Reshetar, p. 257.

[24] Vynnychenko, Vol. III, pp. 131–138; Khrystiuk, Vol. IV, pp. 5.9.

radical social programs multiplied on every side. To advocate a Soviet government smacked of Great Russian Bolshevism, something no Ukrainian nationalist cared to associate himself with, since in January 1919 the Directory was at war with invading Bolshevik forces.

Similarly, the economic and social realities of the Ukrainian situation posed perplexing problems. For example, out of a population that, as noted earlier, probably approached 33 million, only some 300,000 could be classified as industrial workers,[25] and the majority of these were concentrated in a few highly industrialized areas in the eastern and southern regions of the Ukraine. Could a proletarian dictatorship be founded in such a society? In the minds of the most clearheaded Social Democrats, the new socialist order needed to establish economic and social equality for all workers— urban, agrarian, and intellectual; but strong democratic and conservative forces within the Directory raised stern objections to these ideas.[26] Individual party leaders, discussing these and similar issues, were brought to the realization that their utopian plans for the Ukraine were simply infeasible.[27] Meanwhile, both the parties and the administrative agencies of the Directory established only the most desultory contacts with the agrarian masses.[28]

In January, with Bolshevik troops advancing from the northeast and with French troops at Sevastopol and Odessa supporting Denikin's agents, it was impossible to argue that the Directory's first task was daring social reform. There was no time for the development of reform programs or the establishment of efficient provincial and local administrative offices; there was no reason for disseminating in newspapers, manifestoes, and handbills information about programs that were not yet decided upon and that might never be implemented. There was time only for fighting, and this was work for Petliura. In varying degrees it became clear to all nationalist leaders that if the Directory was to keep itself alive, the radical as-

---

[25] Jurij Borys, *The Russian Communist Party and the Sovietization of Ukraine* (Stockholm, 1960), pp. 57–59, 61; *Ukraine,* pp. 169, 174.

[26] Khrystiuk, Vol. IV, pp. 50–55; Mazepa, *Ukraina,* Vol. I, pp. 78–81; Arnold Margolin, *Ukraina i politika Antanty* (Berlin: Izd. S. Efron, 1921), pp. 98–103.

[27] Mazepa, Vol. I, p. 95; Khrystiuk, Vol. IV, pp. 54–55.

[28] M. G. Rafes, *Dva goda revoliutsii na Ukraine: èvoliutsiia i raskol "Bunda"* (Moscow: Gosudarstvennoe izd., 1920), pp. 144–148, 152.

pirations of the rampaging masses had to be ignored; the people had to be thrust away from direct participation in local government and prevented from exercising any kind of paralyzing parliamentary control while crucial defense efforts were underway.[29] The Directory's tragedy, in sum, was that it could not fight without the people and that it was forced to seek victory on the battlefield before it could devise and implement reforms that might have won it lasting popular support. Given this dilemma, the nationalists' great experiment was doomed.

What is especially pertinent to the present analysis is the fact that, despite the Directory's first successes and the apparent enthusiasm of the Ukrainian masses, its political parties and leaders failed to establish control over what was essentially but one phase of the Jacquerie. And, because of its inability to formulate and implement programs that would meet the demands of the agrarian population, the Directory lost peasant-Cossack support. The army that had burgeoned so rapidly in November and December 1918 began in January to melt away with equal rapidity until, by February 1919, Petliura's command had shrunk to about 21,000.[30] To put this within the framework of the thesis being argued here: the movement of the agrarian social revolution coincided for a few weeks with the fall of Skoropadskyi and the rise of the Directory. But, as the Directory faltered in its implementation of new programs, turning cautious and conservative in order to preserve its very life, the forces of the Jacquerie swept past it to embrace another, more radical political group, which seemed to promise a program that *would* suit peasant tastes. Specifically, even before the year 1918 had run its course, many of the Directory's peasant-Cossack supporters were already going over to the Bolsheviks.

What had been true for the Directory in the first weeks of its existence was also to be true for the Bolsheviks from late December 1918 until early March 1919. The small Military Revolutionary Committee that arrived at Kursk on November 20 to organize a "Red Army" for what came to be known as the Bolsheviks' "Second Campaign" in the Ukraine started its work under conditions that seemed to promise inevitable victory. Although it is generally as-

---

[29] Vynnychenko, Vol. III, pp. 184–185; Mazepa, Vol. I, pp. 74–76, 81, 94–95.

[30] Reshetar, p. 257.

sumed that a Russian Red Army came to conquer the Ukraine and defeat the Directory's forces in early 1919, nothing could be further from the truth. The Bolshevik military commander, Vladimir Antonov-Ovseenko, received little help from Moscow. Supported by a military revolutionary committee, whose other members were Georgii Piatakov, Volodymyr Zatonskyi, and briefly, Stalin, and aided by the small Communist Party of the Ukraine (CP(b)U), Antonov-Ovseenko was to build his army out of the people of the Ukraine.[31]

The masses of armed peasantry that had supported the Directory in mid-December flowed into the Bolshevik camp in January and February. While this movement is sometimes referred to as a reversal of direction, it would seem more accurate to describe it as only a continuation of the peasants' movement toward radical solutions for their social and economic problems. Essentially, the agrarian masses shook off a political organization that could not satisfy their needs, and for a few months many thousands of peasants joined whatever new political group promised the most radical reforms.[32]

It is important to remember that, while the Ukrainian peasants and Cossacks may have recognized in Bolshevik slogans the same radical-egalitarian utopianism that had long been the core of the Ukrainian folk's traditional culture, the hordes of peasants and partisans that joined Antonov-Ovseenko's Red Army formations were not and did not become members of the Communist Party. Nor do they appear to have been swayed to Bolshevism by the decidedly weak and inadequate propaganda and organizational efforts of the Bolsheviks in the first months of 1919.[33] To repeat: as with the Ukrainian nationalists, the Bolsheviks appeared to be moving in the same direction that the Jacquerie moved. For a few months in early 1919 there was an illusion that the two forces had joined for a common cause, and on the Bolshevik side there were fierce efforts to force the Jacquerie to serve the ends of the Communist Party. But the alliance was unnatural and temporary.

---

[31] Arthur E. Adams, *Bolsheviks in the Ukraine: The Second Campaign, 1918–1919* (New Haven, Conn.: Yale University Press, 1963), pp. 25, 36–40, 50–53, 66–70.

[32] Reshetar, pp. 258–259.

[33] A. G. Shlikhter, "Borba za khleb na Ukraine v 1919 godu," *Litopys revoliutsii*, No. 2 [29] (Kharkiv, 1928), pp. 102–105, 109–118, 128; Kh. Rakovskii, "Ilich i Ukraina," *Letopis revoliutsii*, No. 2 [11] (Kharkiv, 1925), pp. 9–10.

When the new Provisional Soviet government of the Ukraine sent its first units against Kharkiv in early January, Bolshevism was still something of an unknown quantity to the Ukrainian peasants and Cossacks of the Left Bank and the southern steppes. Consequently, there was a considerable store of passive good will for Bolshevism among the peasants. Although there had been shocking instances of Bolshevik brutality in the Ukraine in early 1918—as, for example, during the bloody occupation of Kiev carried out in February by the Red commander, Mikhail Muravev—there were also several reasons why it was possible for the peasant to be sympathetic to the Bolsheviks.[34] Many had met Bolsheviks under circumstances that placed them in an ideal light. Ukrainian soldiers on the western and southwestern fronts in 1917 had known Bolshevik agitators to be courageous advocates of a Soviet government, and Lenin himself had enunciated the slogan, "Peace, Land, and Bread." Others had seen Red troops retiring eastward under German pressure in March and April of 1918, a fact that seemed to make the Bolsheviks defenders of the Ukrainian land against the foreign conquerors.

Thus, as the Red Army of the Ukraine moved westward from Kharkiv in early 1919, few Ukrainian peasants on the Left Bank were aware that the Bolshevik utopian ideals of pre-November 1917 and early 1918 had been superseded by Lenin's obsessive determination to consolidate his power at all costs. Few could understand that the very possession of power had brought into prominence the Bolshevik leader's exclusivist and elitist principles; few realized that despite its exciting slogans, the Bolshevik party had no immediate interest in the needs and desires of the Ukrainian populace. The thousands of peasants who joined the Bolshevik Army of the Ukraine did so because they believed they were joining to fight for the common cause—that is, for themselves. They adhered to ideals that they understood to be the ideals of the Bolsheviks, but they abhorred the party, ironically emphasizing this point by calling themselves "non-party Bolsheviks."[35]

By early February 1919, the characteristics of the peasant cause were clearly recognizable. Three main features appear to have had

---

[34] Vladimir A. Antonov-Ovseenko, *Zapiski o grazhdanskoi voine,* Vol. I (Moscow-Leningrad: Gosudarstvennoe voennoe izd., 1924–33), pp. 143–155; Chamberlin, Vol. I, pp. 375–377.

[35] Adams, p. 165.

more or less universal significance. Of these, the first was disillusionment with the Directory government, disillusionment that was particularly strong on the Left Bank, where it had turned to active hatred under the suppressive actions of Bolbochan and his reactionary officers. As it became evident that the Directory in action meant censorship, military suppression, and rule by a conservative middle class, the aroused peasantry turned against the Directory with a ferocity similar to that which it had shown the Germans and Skoropadskyi. At that moment the Bolsheviks appeared on the scene, promising to help drive out the Directory, to establish an agrarian utopia, to uphold the peasant's right to govern himself. "If our own peasantry had not risen against us," Vynnychenko declared later, "the Russian Soviet government would have been powerless against us."[36]

The second characteristic of the peasant cause in 1919 was its primitive, egalitarian economic and political ideals. Among the peasants there was general agreement that the lands of the wealthy should be seized and divided in some just fashion among working farmers. This idea found its counterpart in Bolshevik promises.[37] Similarly, before there had been any extensive direct experience with the Bolsheviks, unsuspecting peasants and Cossacks could interpret the Bolsheviks' championing of soviets as a sincere effort to abolish all alien forms of government and to return political authority to the people themselves.

A third important feature of the peasant cause, less universal perhaps than the first two, but influential in the long run, was the presence of strong currents of *haidamak*-Cossack anarchism. There was a general readiness to march and fight for a variety of reasons other than political ideals and land reforms. Such motives ranged from a lust for plunder and killing to a thirst for glory. Surely, neither the Bolsheviks nor other parties consciously sought to enflame these currents; yet it is quite evident that the deepest strains of social anarchism—the desire to steal from the rich, to drink one's fill of vodka, to savor the wild pleasures of rape and murder—were strong among many partisan bands and influential in the determination of their conduct. As some of the Directory's *otamans* became

---

[36] Vynnychenko, Vol. III, p. 204.

[37] M. Kubanin, *Makhnovshchina: krestianskoe dvizhenie v stepnoi Ukraine v gody grazhdanskoi voiny* (Leningrad: Izd. 'Priboi,' 1927), pp. 55–56.

more and more violent, turning even to pogroms,[38] others rushed to join with the Bolshevik units as a way to legitimize their own will to violence. Thus, for a time, the Bolsheviks (as Petliura had done before them) accepted alliances with violent and ungovernable men whom they abominated, acting on the assumption that the ideal ends they worked for justified the use of any means.

Such support rendered the Bolshevik advance irresistible. In January, town after town on the Left Bank fell into their hands. Kiev, the Directory's capital, fell in the first days of February. At almost the same moment, in the central steppe regions, the powerful leader *Otaman* Hryhoriiv, Cossack and adventurer extraordinary, who called himself by Petliura's authority "*Otaman* of Zaporozhe," deserted the Directory and went over to the Bolsheviks. This act marked yet another decisive loss for the Directory, which retained only the fighting units of the Galician *Sich* Riflemen (*Sichovi Striltsi*) and some smaller partisan units.[39]

Hryhoriiv was a typical representative of the Jacquerie in the sense that he was motivated by deep and contradictory passions and ideas—hatred of authority, arrogance, willful independence—as well as intense and insatiable thirsts for vodka, power, and military glory. Added to these incompatible personal characteristics was a peculiar relationship with the *Borotbist* Party (Left SR's), which apparently influenced his thinking only when he wished it to do so. Like so many other partisan chiefs, Hryhoriiv led a rabble of peasants and Cossacks in which the middle and upper levels of the peasantry predominated, but which also contained a fair share of political agitators, adventuresome ruffians, and out-and-out criminals.[40]

Like the much more famous anarchist leader Nestor Makhno, whose band operated in the southeast, Hryhoriiv became for a few

---

[38] The kind of men involved is indicated in a list of more than thirty localities where pogroms took place during February and March 1919. A. I. Gukovskii, *Frantsuzskaia interventsiia na Iuge Rossii, 1918–1919 g.* (Moscow-Leningrad: Gosudarstvennoe izd., 1928), p. 81; see also Adams, pp. 152–155; Chamberlin, Vol. II, pp. 225–226.

[39] Rubach, pp. 178–183; Antonov-Ovseenko, Vol. III, pp. 166–167.

[40] Arshinov, pp. 108, 112–115; Rubach, p. 178; Antonov-Ovseenko, Vol. III, p. 223 and Vol. IV, pp. 68–69; Iu. Tiutiunnyk, "V borbe protiv okkupantov," in A. G. Shlikhter, *Chernaia kniga: Sbornik statei i materialov ob interventsii Antanty na Ukraine v 1918–1919 gg.*, Vol. II (Ekaterinoslav: Gosudarstvennoe izd. Ukrainy, 1925), pp. 211–216.

weeks one of the Bolsheviks' most powerful and successful military leaders.[41] It was Hryhoriiv, with his motley partisan "brigade" nominally under the command of Antonov-Ovseenko, who drove the French and Greek interventionist forces from Kherson, Mykolaiv, and finally, Odessa. It is a fascinating commentary on the role of the Jacquerie that one of the greatest "Red" fighters in the Ukraine during March and early April was no Bolshevik at all, but a twentieth century *haidamak*-Cossack who incessantly boasted of his total independence and of his indissoluble ties with the Zaporozhians.[42]

Like the Directory, the Bolsheviks failed to win leadership over the diverse elements of the Jacquerie. Both political groups rose to power in the Ukraine on a wave of aroused peasants; both were then deserted because of the failure to satisfy peasant expectations, and both subsequently had to defend themselves against the very people they presumed to lead. In the case of the Bolsheviks, the revulsion began almost as soon as they appeared in the Ukraine, and to a very great extent Bolshevik programs and policies were to blame. Thus, while they came preaching committee or soviet government, the system that they established was at variance with popular concepts of self-government. Instead of permitting the formation by villagers of their own elected soviets, to be composed of whatever group held local leadership, the Communists *decreed* the formation of pro-Bolshevik soviets or *appointed revkomy* (local Communist action groups), thus making it clear from the start that local "soviets" would be controlled by the Communist government of the Ukraine and manned exclusively by Bolsheviks. No other groups or parties were to be allowed to participate unless they explicitly accepted Bolshevik precepts.

In addition, the Bolsheviks decreed the establishment of *bidniak* (poor peasant) committees in the villages. These committees, composed only of "pro-Bolshevik members" and representing the "proletariat of the villages," were to be given political predominance. Thus, the Bolsheviks disenfranchised the middle and wealthy peasants and declared them class enemies of the Soviet

---

[41] Chamberlin, Vol. II, pp. 232–239; Arshinov, pp. 48–59, 215–220; Paul Avrich, *The Russian Anarchists* (Princeton, N.J.: Princeton University Press, 1967), pp. 209–217.

[42] Gukovskii, pp. 205–206; Adams, pp. 150, 187–214.

regime. Such policies left the non-Bolshevik and influential middle and wealthy peasants no alternative but resistance, and resist they did, with characteristic stubbornness.[43]

The Bolsheviks also decreed their own failure by supporting unpopular agrarian policies. Wedded to contradictory policies of propaganda and practice, they came to the Ukraine appealing to the peasants to seize and divide up the property of former landed proprietors, churches, monasteries, and rich peasants. But in practice the Bolsheviks were convinced that the land must be socialized, a term which, for them, meant the abolition of private farming (which had in the Ukraine far deeper roots than in the northern areas of Russia) and the establishment of communes—that is, one or another type of collective farm organization in which all members would work together and share the profits from land held in common.[44]

In the Ukraine, where the *mir* (commune) had not developed the deep roots typical of it in Russia proper, and where the private farm was virtually a natural right of the peasant farmer and the Cossack, the decree ordering that the land be organized into communal farms was regarded as nothing short of a declaration of war against all free farmers.[45] Other agrarian policies exacerbated this response. There were, for example, great estates in the Ukraine, some of them involved in livestock breeding, others producing such industrial crops as sugar beets and grain for alcohol. Breaking these estates into many small farms meant not only the destruction of their productivity but also the dispersal of their real property—livestock, farm implements, and refinery machinery. For good economic reasons, therefore, the new government withdrew these farms from the expropriation process, reserving possession to itself; and thus, in the peasants' eyes, it reneged on the promise that all land would be divided. Worse, to encourage the creation of communal farms, the Bolsheviks needed land that could be given to poor peasant

---

[43] *Sobranie uzakonenii i rasporiazhenii raboche-krestianskogo pravitelstva Ukrainy* (1st ed.; Kiev, 1919), No. 1, Art. 3, pp. 6–8; No. 3, Art. 29, pp. 29–31; No. 4, Art. 47, p. 48; B. M. Babi, *Mistsevi orhany derzhavnoi vlady Ukrainskoi RSR v 1917–1920 rr.* (Kiev, 1956), pp. 143–148; Shlikhter, pp. 116–117.

[44] N. N. Popov, *Ocherk istorii Kommunisticheskoi partii (bolshevikov) Ukrainy* (2nd ed.; Simferopol: Izd. 'Proletarii,' 1929), p. 197; *Sobranie uzakonenii*, No. 4, Art. 47: "Declaration of January 26," p. 47.

[45] Kubanin, pp. 55–59.

communes; moreover, they needed farm implements and livestock for such communes. To make such provisions, the Soviet government of the Ukraine decreed that approximately half of all land and all farm inventories would be retained by the state. Middle and rich peasants, who were hungry for more land themselves, saw this as further evidence of Bolshevik dishonesty.[46]

Still other Bolshevik policies increased peasant hostility. A huge and well-organized effort was mounted to collect provisions in the Ukraine for shipment to other fronts of the civil war and to the cities of Russia. Forcible confiscations were undertaken by armed *Cheka* units, Russian food collection detachments, and military provisioning units of the Red Army of the Ukrainian front.[47] Such actions, combined with exclusivist party politics and policies offensive to Ukrainian national feelings, mobilized the peasants to armed resistance.

In the month of April, Khristiian Rakovskii recounts that there were ninety-three separate armed uprisings against the Soviet Government of the Ukraine.[48] The memoirs of the Red Army commander Vladimir Antonov-Ovseenko reveal the desperation of his military situation, which forced him to deploy angry partisan forces not only against external enemies but also against other partisan forces that were raising the standard of rebellion. In mid-April, for example, Hryhoriiv defied Antonov's orders and withdrew his troops, now dubbed a "Red division," from Odessa to the "rest camps" around their home villages of Oleksandriia and Verbliuzhka.[49] Further to the west, other partisan groups, led by Zelenyi,

---

[46] *Sobranie uzakonenii* (1st ed.), No. 6, Art. 77, pp. 80–81; No. 9, Art. 111, pp. 123–124; (2nd ed.), Art. 271, pp. 369–370, 377–379. See also Popov, *Ocherk istorii*, pp. 196–99; Kubanin, *Makhnovshchina*, pp. 53–55.

[47] Popov, pp. 197–199; Shlikhter, pp. 113, 117–118, 123–124; Khrystiuk, Vol. IV, pp. 175–176; *Sobranie uzakonenii* (1st ed.), No. 1, Art. 7, p. 10; No. 2, Art. 13, p. 19; Kolomiets, "Vospominaniia o revoliutsionnoi borbe v Elizavetgrade v 1917–19 gg.," *Letopis revoliutsii*, No. 1 (Kharkiv, 1922), pp. 200–201; see also Heifetz, pp. 8–9, 58–62, 64–65, 68–69. Heifetz, as chairman of the All-Ukrainian Relief Committee for victims of the pogroms, made investigations in the field in early 1919. He blames the anti-Jewish sentiment, at least in part, upon the Communist use of Jews as Soviet government officials.

[48] Shlikhter, p. 106.

[49] Antonov-Ovseenko, Vol. IV, pp. 78, 80–81.

actively prepared for rebellion against the Bolsheviks.[50] In the southeast, where partisans stolidly held a part of the Bolshevik line against Denikin, Makhno openly declared the right of his people to govern themselves, making it clear that he would choose his own time for dealing with the Bolshevik dictatorship.[51]

Hryhoriiv's decision to rebel openly in early May was well timed. His uprising was accompanied by sympathy rebellions among other bands of lesser strength and by the successful attacks of Denikin against Makhno's sector of the Bolsheviks' southern front.[52] The Bolsheviks were badly shaken by the Hryhoriiv revolt and were compelled to take desperate measures, setting in motion the series of events that led to the collapse of the Soviet government of the Ukraine in August.[53]

As a footnote to Hryhoriiv's uprising, it is interesting to note that in some rather startling ways the leaders of various partisan bands were themselves victims of the radical peasants whom they tried to lead. By trampling over all obstacles to gain their most deeply desired objectives, the peasants victimized not only the Directory's leaders and the Bolsheviks, but also the native leaders who so often appear to have been part and parcel of the Jacquerie. In the case of Hryhoriiv, for example, there is good reason to believe that he was the leader of his rebellion only in a limited sense. His "followers," undisciplined and angry at the agrarian policies of the Bolsheviks, indicated both by word and deed (pogroms, murders of Bolshevik *Chekists,* attacks upon towns, and grumbling about Bolshevik policies) that if he did not lead an uprising, they would move without him.[54] The peasants, not Hryhoriiv, dictated. There is evidence to support the hypothesis that when Trotsky handed

---

[50] Khrystiuk, Vol. IV, pp. 131–133; Antonov-Ovseenko, Vol. IV, pp. 160–161, 171–172; Ravich-Cherkasskii, p. 122; N. I. Podvoiskii, *Na Ukraine: stati N. I. Podvoiskogo* (Kiev, 1919), p. 19.

[51] Arshinov, pp. 97–103, 109–110, 173.

[52] Antonov-Ovseenko, Vol. IV, pp. 222, 252–254, 304; "Grigorevskaia avantiura (mai, 1919 goda)," *Letopis revoliutsii,* No. 3 (Kharkiv, 1923), pp. 152–154; *Grazhdanskaia voina,* Vol. I, p. 91; *Chervonoe kazachestvo: sbornik materialov po istorii chervonogo kazachestva* (Kharkiv: Izd. "Put prosveshcheniia," n.d.), pp. 52–53; Kubanin, pp. 77–78.

[53] "Grigorevskaia . . . ," p. 153; Antonov-Ovseenko, Vol. IV, p. 304; Adams, pp. 358–373.

[54] Antonov-Ovseenko, Vol. IV, p. 80.

down an order to do so, in early June, Makhno submissively gave up the command of his brigade, because he had lost influence over the men he presumably commanded.[55]

The Jacquerie continued under Denikin and into 1920, when the Bolsheviks returned in force.[56] Space does not permit detailed examination of the later stages of this history, but the meaning of the events of the last phase must at least be summarized. That the Bolsheviks ultimately managed to consolidate their political authority in the early months of 1920 can be explained in part by the lessons they had learned from an earlier attempt, the chief lesson being that the Jacquerie could not be controlled or redirected by half measures. To suppress it demanded a highly centralized army, a ruthlessly efficient political organization, and policies designed to disarm and please the peasants. These the Bolsheviks possessed when they returned. While winning on the battlefields, they made public concessions to private farming, to the middle peasants, and to national pride.[57]

But there is another significant explanation for the Bolsheviks' ultimate victory. The Jacquerie, at least in its most influential and torrential phases, had burned itself out. With the exception of Makhno, its greatest leaders were dead or driven out of the Ukraine; thousands of brave men had died in the fighting—in the ranks of Ukrainian nationalist and Bolshevik and White Russian armies, and in independent partisan units. Ravaged by typhus, hunger, and cold, exhausted by years of campaigning, and anxious to return to the land and make it produce, the peasants and Cossacks simply went home. In 1920, the Jacquerie collapsed, and

---

[55] Kubanin, pp. 77–78.

[56] Kozelskyi, *Shliakh zradnytstva i avantur;* D. Kin, "Povstancheskoe dvizhenie protiv denikinshchiny na Ukraine," *Letopis revoliutsii,* No. 3–4 [18–19] (Kharkiv, 1926), pp. 70–74 ff.

[57] V. I. Lenin, *Sochineniia,* Vol. XXIV (3rd ed.; Moscow: Marx-Engels-Lenin Institute, 1928–37), pp. 169–171, 552–554, 655–660, 811–813n.; *Vsesoiuznaia kommunisticheskaia partiia(b) v rezoliutsiiakh ee sezdov i konferentsii* (1898–1926 gg.) (3rd ed.; Moscow-Leningrad, 1927), pp. 252–253; M. A. Rubach *et al.* (eds.), *Radianske budivnytstvo na Ukraini v roky hromadianskoi viiny, 1919–1920: zbirnyk dokumentiv i materialiv* (Kiev: Vyd. Akademii Nauk Ukrainskoi RSR, 1957), pp. 23–24, 26–30, 39–40, 47, 49, 55–56; S. Barannyk, Kh. Mishkis, and H. Slovodskii, *Istoriia KP(b)U v materialakh i dokumentakh (khrestomatiia 1917–1920 rr.)* (2nd ed.; Kiev: Partvydav TsK KP(b)U, 1934), pp. 497–501.

the Bolsheviks proceeded with the establishment of their "new order."

Although this was the end of the great rebellion, the ideals and traditions that had guided it did not disappear. Bolshevik troops were kept busy in the years immediately following 1920, hunting down and destroying groups of "bandits" that would not or could not give up. The conduct of the Ukrainian peasantry during the period of the New Economic Policy and through the era of collectivization provides good evidence that the rural folk were not readily giving up their basic ideals. And events during the Second World War—the quick dissolution of collective farms in some areas and the existence of some independent partisan groups—suggest that the forces that drove the rural masses of the Ukraine to rebellion between 1918 and 1920 were still alive.[58]

Several significant conclusions are suggested by the evidence examined above. Most important is the obvious need for further detailed examination of the role that the social convulsion, here called a Jacquerie, played in Ukrainian events. It is quite evident that we are not at present able to define clearly and positively the aims and objectives of the peasant masses; nor can we accurately portray the levels of comprehension of political and social ideals that existed in the villages. The difficulty is that, while some partisan movements have been examined in considerable detail, it is extremely difficult to form completely reliable general statements concerning the common aims and drives of the steppe farmer, the Galician peasant, and the peasants of Poltava gubernia. So great indeed have been the variations of historical experience among the peasant-Cossack population of the several regions of the Ukraine that the very use of such terms as "peasants" and "Cossacks" might well be questioned, on the grounds that they have no well-defined meaning applicable to all separate groups. So too, such questions as the direct influence of historical traditions on the peasant population, and the degree to which party propaganda and general news penetrated to the village in 1918 and 1919, need much more thorough and objective investigation than they have received in the past.

---

[58] Chamberlin, Vol. II, p. 239; Kubanin, p. 161; John A. Armstrong, *Ukrainian Nationalism, 1939–1945* (2nd ed.; New York: Columbia University Press, 1963), pp. 98–100, 144, 150, 154, 165, 249–254.

Finally, the evidence considered here indicates that parties, political leaders, and governments, overconcerned with their own roles in these years, have largely failed to record their own weakness before the onrush of the Jacquerie. It cannot be said that during 1918–1920 any one party or group of parties determined events. All contributed to the vast panorama; but, fundamentally, the Jacquerie followed its own bloody course, until its human elements could fight no longer. To the question: "Who best represented the Ukrainian peasants and Cossacks?" the answer must be: "The peasants and Cossacks themselves." No party was quick enough or bold enough, no party possessed an organization that could win and hold intellectual authority or establish lasting control over these champions of agrarian social revolution. Instead, the peasants and Cossacks rose in anger, fought with a stubborn and unreasoning violence that overwhelmed every political group, and at last collapsed from sheer exhaustion.

CHAPTER ELEVEN

Nestor Makhno and the Ukrainian Revolution

Frank Sysyn

CONTROVERSY HAS SURROUNDED the person of Nestor Makhno from his first appearance as an insurgent commander in the summer of 1918. Was he an ideological anarchist struggling for a new order or a cutthroat profiting from the turmoil of the Civil War? Was he favorably disposed to the Jewish population or a pogromist? These and other issues have been disputed from the turbulent years of the Civil War to our own day.[1] Lack of concrete information has served only to increase interest in the legendary *Batko* (Father) Makhno, and it is not surprising that he figures prominently in many literary works, the most recent being Oles Honchar's *Sobor* (Cathedral).[2] Interest in Makhno also has been revived by the New

---

[1] The range of opinion has been extreme. For example: "In the Ukrainian liberation struggle, Makhno's role was so negative and destructive that he deserves only to be ignored." F. Meleshko, "Nestor Makhno ta ioho anarkhiia," *Novyi shliakh* (Winnipeg), December 18, 1959, p. 3; "*Batko* N. Makhno was a capable leader of the Zaporozhian faction of our National Liberation Movement and led an unceasing struggle against the enemies of our people, without surrendering under any circumstances, without betraying his people and without sparing his own strength or life." Vasyl Dubrovskyi, "Batko Nestor Makhno—ukrainskyi natsionalnyi heroi," *Chornomorskyi zbirnyk,* Vol. VI (Hertzfeld, 1945), p. 5. For disputes on other issues, see the newspapers *Delo truda* (Paris) and *Volna* (New York). The ardor with which polemics on Makhno have continued may be seen in the recent exchanges in *Novoe russkoe slovo* (New York), January 23, February 2, March 2, March 15, 1969.

[2] Aleksei Nikolaev, *Zhizn Nestora Makhno* (Riga: Izdevnieciba 'Obshche dostupnaia biblioteka,' n.d.); Aleksei Nikolaev, *Batko Makhno* (Riga: Izdevnieciba 'Laikmets,' n.d.); Aleksei Nikolaev, *Pervyi sredi ravnykh*

271

Left, especially by Daniel and Gabriel Cohn-Bendit, who see in Makhno a model for the young revolutionary for whom Communism is irrelevant.[3]

For all the interest that Makhno has evoked, remarkably little scholarly work has been devoted to him or to the movement he led. The problems of separating truth from legend and of gathering the extremely dispersed source material have presented considerable obstacles. Furthermore, very little documentation concerning Makhno (newspapers, proclamations, personal papers) has survived or is available in the West.[4] Because of the controversy surrounding Makhno and the lack of scholarly studies about him, it has been difficult to evaluate his relationship to the Ukrainian Revolution. This study will focus on the most crucial issue—Makhno's perception of the Ukrainian question.

There is no definitive biography of Makhno and no thorough evaluation of his movement. A general outline of his life, however,

---

(Detroit: Izd. Profsoiuza, 1947); Vasyl Chaplenko, *Ukraintsi* (New York: All-Slavic Publishing, Inc., 1960); Oles Honchar, *Sobor* (Kiev: Radianskyi pysmennyk, 1968); Klym Polishchuk, *Huliaipilskyi 'Batko'*, 2 vols. (Kolomyia: Vyd. Oka, 1925–26); Iurii Ianovskyi, *Vershnyky*, in *Tvory*, Vol. II (Kiev: Derzhlitvydav, 1958), pp. 169–257.

[3] Daniel and Gabriel Cohn-Bendit, *Obsolete Communism, the Left-Wing Alternative* (New York: McGraw-Hill, 1968), pp. 220–234.

[4] The New York Public Library has one proclamation and three issues of *Put k svobode* (Huliai-Pole), Nos. 1–3; two other issues are in European libraries. L. J. van Rossum, "Proclamations of the Makhno Movement, 1920," *International Review of Social History*, XIII, Pt. 1 (Amsterdam, 1968), p. 249. Van Rossum's publication of eleven proclamations from the archive of the Italian anarchist Ugo Fedeli adds greatly to the fund of documents. A proclamation of the *Makhnivtsi* against anti-Semitism was published in *Volna* (New York), No. 58, October, 1924, pp. 39–42. Other proclamations are quoted in Petr Arshinov, *Istoriia makhnovskogo dvizheniia (1918–1921 gg.)* (Berlin: Izd. 'Gruppy russkikh anarkhistov v Germanii,' 1923). Selections from the protocol of the second meeting of the Huliai-Pole District Conference (February 12, 1919) are published in Petr Struve, "Ideologiia Makhnovshchiny," *Russkaia mysl*, No. 1–2 (Sofia, 1921), pp. 226–232. Three copies of the Kharkiv Makhno group's newspaper *Golos makhnovsta* are in the Soviet Union; they are cited in S. Semanov, "Makhnovshchina i ee krakh," *Voprosy istorii*, No. 9 (Moscow, 1966), p. 57. The Ukrainian-language newspapers *Shliakh do voli* (Huliai-Pole) and *Anarkhist povstanets* (Poltava) are unavailable.

has been established.[5] He was born in 1889 into a poor peasant family in Huliai-Pole, a rural center in the southern Ukraine not far from Zaporizhzhia. During the 1905 Revolution, Makhno joined an anarchist group in his native town. This terrorist group of anarchist-communists was tried for the assassination of a police official in 1908, and Makhno was sentenced to life imprisonment in Moscow's Butyrki prison.[6] There he received further instruction in anarchism from Petr Arshinov, a Russian worker from Kateryno-slav (Dnipropetrovsk). The February Revolution of 1917 freed Makhno from prison, and he returned immediately to Huliai-Pole, where he revitalized the anarchist group and became active in the revolutionary events of village life. The German and Austro-Hungarian occupation of the Ukraine in the spring of 1918 forced Makhno and his anarchist comrades to flee to Bolshevik Russia. From March to July 1918, he wandered through revolutionary Russia and met with Lenin and the famous anarchist, Prince Peter Kropotkin. In July, Makhno returned to Huliai-Pole and launched a guerrilla war against Hetman Skoropadskyi's government and the forces of the Central Powers. Peasant discontent in the Ukraine provided a favorable environment for the growth of Makhno's anarchist-influenced insurgent movement, and the overthrow of the Hetman's government left him in a position of considerable power in Katerynoslav gubernia and the surrounding areas.

Makhno proved to be a brilliant military leader for his peasant army. After December 1918, he sided with the Bolsheviks, whose invading Red Army was struggling with the Directory for the control of Kiev. In February 1919, Makhno negotiated an alliance with

---

[5] The outline given here includes the barest essentials to provide the reader with necessary background. A general sketch is found in David Footman, *Civil War in Russia* (London: Faber, 1961), pp. 245–303. See also Max Nomad, "The Warrior: Nestor Makhno, the Bandit Who Saved Moscow," in *Apostles of Revolution* (Boston: Little, Brown, and Company, 1939), pp. 302–342, and Victor Peters, *Nestor Makhno: The Life of an Anarchist* (Winnipeg: Echo Books, 1970).

[6] The most authoritative study of the 1906–1909 activities of Makhno and the Huliai-Pole group of anarchists is by G. Novopolin, "Makhno i guliai-polskaia gruppa anarkhistov (po ofitsialnym dannym)," *Katorga i ssylka*, No. 34 [5] (Moscow, 1927), pp. 70–77. Novopolin's work is based largely on the Odessa prosecutor's indictment of December 14, 1909, which charged fourteen people.

the Bolsheviks, who in turn called for the subordination of his
"Insurgent Revolutionary Army of the Ukraine" to the Red Army
Command. This alliance was soon strained because the Bolsheviks
attempted to assume command of Makhno's forces as well as the
territory that he controlled. Further dissension with the Bolsheviks
in the spring resulted from the agreement for mutual cooperation
between Makhno and the major anarchist group in the Ukraine, the
Nabat, led by Vsevolod Eikhenbaum (Volin). The *Nabat* group
saw in the *Makhnivshchyna* (Makhno movement) an opportunity
to put theoretical anarchism into practice, and it greatly strengthened anarchist influence on the *Makhnivshchyna* by providing the
necessary ideological cadres.[7] The threat of a common enemy,
Otaman Matvii Hryhoriiv, improved relations between the Bolsheviks and the *Makhnivtsi* (supporters of Makhno), which by the
spring of 1919 had deteriorated to the point of open hostility.
Hryhoriiv presented a far greater threat to Bolshevik rule than
Makhno did.[8] Makhno refused to join Hryhoriiv's revolt, and
during a meeting on July 27 assassinated him.

The mounting Denikin offensive in August and September 1919
swept both the Bolsheviks and Makhno from Left-Bank Ukraine.
Makhno retreated as far west as Uman, where he came into contact
with the Ukrainian *Sich* Riflemen (*Sichovi Striltsi*) and Petliura's
forces. Makhno and these Ukrainian formations, faced with the
threat from Denikin, agreed to tactical military cooperation on
September 21, 1919. However, four days later, Makhno moved alone
against Denikin and broke through the White Army's encirclement.
In lightning raids throughout Left-Bank Ukraine, he wrought con-

---

[7] The most thorough scholarly study of anarchist tendencies in the
Makhno movement is by Romuald Wojna, "Nestor Machno: anarchizm
czynu," *Z Pola Walki,* No. 2 [50] (Warsaw, 1970), pp. 45–76. See also
"Anarkhizm i makhnovshchina," *Anarkhicheskii vestnik,* No. 2 (Berlin,
1923), pp. 27–37. Attacks by anarchist enemies of Makhno such as Mark
Mrachnyi and Aaron Baron can be approached through a study of
Makhno's answers, published in the Paris anarchist paper *Delo truda* during the mid-1920's. An enlightening, but unfinished, discussion of the
relationship of anarchism to the *Makhnivshchyna* (chiefly a history of the
Nabat group) is the study of D. Ierde, "Politychna prohrama anarkhoma-
khnivshchyny," *Litopys revoliutsii,* IX, 1–2 (Kharkiv, 1930), pp. 41–50.

[8] Considerable attention is given to Hryhoriiv's revolt in Arthur Adams,
Bolsheviks in the Ukraine: The Second Campaign, 1918–1919 (New Haven,
Conn.: Yale University Press, 1963).

siderable damage on Denikin's rear forces and was thus instrumental in halting the White general's advance on Moscow.[9] With the defeat of Denikin, the *Makhnivtsi* reached the height of their power. By the fall of 1919, they occupied the large cities of Oleksandrivsk (Zaporizhzhia) and Katerynoslav and were able for a short period to concentrate on ideological work and the reorganization of their territory.

Early in 1920, the Bolsheviks reestablished their control of the Ukraine and initiated hostilities against the *Makhnivtsi*. Only Wrangel's autumn offensive caused a brief change in the situation. The Bolsheviks formed a new alliance with Makhno. This agreement was the final factor precipitating a break by most of the *Nabat* group with Makhno. Following the surprisingly easy defeat of Wrangel, the Bolsheviks renewed hostilities, and by November the *Makhnivtsi* were hard pressed by the Red Army. In August 1921, the remnants of the Makhno forces fled across the Rumanian border.

After detention in Rumania and a trial in Poland for "fomenting rebellion," Makhno went to Paris.[10] He remained active in anarchist circles, but he was troubled by the poverty and tribulations of exile, and the accusations by certain Russian anarchists that he was an anti-Semite. Despite these problems, before his death in 1934, he wrote numerous articles for the Paris journal, *Delo truda,* and he completed three volumes of his memoirs—a narrative of the *Makhnivshchyna* to December 1918.[11]

This brief outline suggests Makhno's importance in the history of

---

[9] Makhno's role in the struggle against Denikin is the basis of Nomad's epithet: "The Warrior: Nestor Makhno, the Bandit Who Saved Moscow," in *Apostles,* p. 302.

[10] For contemporary accounts of this very confusing period in Makhno's life, see Kazimir-Valerian Tesliar, "Pravda o muzhike-anarkhiste Makhno i anarkho-makhnovshchine," *Volna* (New York), No. 34–35, October–November, 1922, pp. 21–25; Gr. Anar. Molodezhi Varshavy, "Sud nad N. Makhno," *Volna,* No. 45, September, 1923, pp. 45–46.

[11] Nestor Makhno, *Russkaia revoliutsiia na Ukraine* (Paris: Federatsiia anarkho-kommunisticheskich grupp Severnoi Ameriki i Kanady, 1929), *Pod udarami kontr-revoliutsii* (Paris: Izdanie Komiteta N. Makhno, 1936), *Ukrainskaia revoliutsiia* (Paris: Izdanie Komiteta N. Makhno, 1937). These three volumes are hereafter referred to as Makhno I, II, III. The last two were issued posthumously under the editorship of Makhno's major anarchist colleague, Volin (Vsevolod M. Eikhenbaum).

revolutionary events in the Ukraine. Yet, if little has been done to research the life and thought of Makhno and the history of the movement that he led, almost nothing has been done to discuss his relation to the Ukrainian national reawakening. The standard histories of the *Makhnivshchyna* by Petr Arshinov and Vsevolod Eikhenbaum (Volin) included only a few perfunctory remarks about Makhno's attitude toward the Ukrainian question.[12] The matter is given a little more attention by the Soviet historian M. Kubanin, whose work is interesting chiefly for its assertion that Makhno converted to Ukrainian nationalism in 1920–1921.[13] The only work that deals specifically with any aspect of the problem is Lubomyr Wynar's short article, "The Relationships between Nestor Makhno and the Army of the Ukrainian National Republic, 1918–1920";

---

[12] Arshinov, *Istoriia makhnovskogo dvizheniia;* Voline [Vsevolod Eikhenbaum], *La révolution inconnue (1917–21)* (Paris: Les Amis de Voline, 1947), translated into English as *The Unknown Revolution (Kronstadt 1921, Ukraine 1918–21)* (London: Freedom Press, 1955).

[13] M. Kubanin, *Makhnovshchina* (Leningrad: Priboi, 1927). Early Bolshevik accounts vary in scholarly level. Many are mere propaganda tracts against an all-too-popular foe. Those which the contemporary Soviet historian Semanov describes as written "in the hot aftermath of the events" are Ia. Iakovlev, *Russkii anarkhizm v velikoi russkoi revoliutsii* (St. Petersburg: Izd. Kommunisticheskogo internatsionala, 1921), M. Ravich-Cherkasskii, *Makhno i Makhnovshchina* (Katerynoslav, 1920), R. Eideman, *Ochagi atamanshchiny i banditizma* (Kharkiv, 1921), D. Lebed, *Itogi i uroki let makhnovshchiny* (Kharkiv, 1921). Semanov's "Makhnovshchina i ee krakh" is one of two Soviet studies in recent years and is the only substantial discussion of the *Makhnivshchyna* which makes no use of Makhno's memoirs. Semanov's only comment is in note 81, p. 52, which mentions the first two volumes of memoirs and ascribes their editorship to Volin. This would lead one to believe that Makhno's writings were unavailable to Semanov, since he reveals no knowledge of the third volume and since, in fact, Volin did not edit Volume I, as is explained in detail in the introduction to Volume II. He and Makhno were having personal difficulties at the time. The other Soviet work is P. Kh. Bilyi, "Rozhrom Makhnovshchyny," *Ukrainskyi istorychnyi zhurnal*, XIV, 5 (Kiev, 1971), pp. 10–21, which is devoted to a narrative of the last phase of the *Makhnivshchyna*. It is especially valuable for information on early Bolshevik literature dealing with Makhno. Of considerable value is the account of the former *Makhnivets* anarchist I. Teper [Gordeev], *Makhno: Ot "edinogo" anarkhizma k stopam rumynskogo korolia* (Kiev: Molodoi rabochii, 1924).

it does not, however, treat in any detail Makhno's thinking on the Ukrainian question.[14]

Makhno and the *Makhnivshchyna* have often been viewed as being totally divorced from the Ukrainian national revival. This may partially be due to our own preconceptions of the 1917–1921 period. The relationship of a given historical figure to the Ukrainian question has been evaluated largely by his support of or opposition to a Ukrainian national state. In focusing attention on Ukrainian political movements, we have often overlooked a post-1917 "revolution" of even greater importance. This "revolution" was the acceptance of the idea of an entity with fairly well-defined borders called the "Ukraine," and the self-identification of the masses living in this area as "Ukrainians." This was a revolution in perception, and it brought about a general recognition that Ukrainians were a separate nation. Even the Russians or Poles, who had hitherto viewed Ukrainians as merely a part of their own nations, came to accept this new view. Although the degree to which the Ukrainian masses were nationally conscious before 1917 is debatable, and although many Russians and "Little Russians" (Ukrainians who believed that they were the Little Russian branch of an "All-Russian" nation) questioned the existence of a Ukrainian nation, by the 1920's the concepts "Ukraine" and "Ukrainians"

---

[14] Liubomyr Vynar, "Zviazky Nestora Makhna z Armiieiu U.N.R. (1918–1920)," *Rozbudova derzhavy*, No. 3 (Montreal, 1953), pp. 15–18. Wynar has also contributed another article that contains useful information on the relationship between the Makhno movement and the Ukrainian national movement: "Prychynky do rannoi diialnosty Nestora Makhna v Ukraini (1917–18)," *Rozbudova derzhavy*, No. 2 (Montreal, 1953), pp. 14–20.

The article by Dubrovskyi, "Batko Nestor Makhno," is an important work that contains a positive evaluation of Makhno's role in Ukrainian history. It is strictly a narrative, however, and does not analyze Makhno's thought on the Ukrainian question. The most useful commentary by a member of a Ukrainian political faction is Isaak Mazepa, *Ukraina v ohni i buri revoliutsii*, 3 vols. (Munich: Prometei, 1950–51). A nearly contemporary account of the *Makhnivshchyna*, and at the same time a particularly interesting Ukrainian political commentary on the movement, is A. S., "Makhnivshchyna," *Kalendar 'Hromada' dlia robitnoho naroda v misti i seli na rik 1926* (Lviv, 1925), pp. 105–109. The best work in English is *Nestor Makhno*, by Victor Peters, especially for its eyewitness accounts gathered on the *Makhnivshchyna*.

were almost universally accepted and had become analogous, for instance, to "Armenia" and "Armenians." The dynamics of the awakening of Ukrainian consciousness can be understood only by studying the countless individual experiences that composed it.

Makhno is an interesting subject for a number of reasons. First of all, whatever his own national self-identification, his ideological commitment to anarchism meant that he could never accept the philosophy of groups seeking to set up a state (including a national state). Secondly, he was a peasant with little formal education who was catapulted to a position of power as a leader of the peasant masses. Hence, a study of Makhno may help our understanding of the peasantry's relationship to the national awakening. Finally, Makhno allowed himself to be Russified in his youth, at least linguistically, and spent a good part of his life in Russian revolutionary circles.[15] Thus, at an early stage in his career he allied himself with the dominant Russian culture and group. Obviously, all these factors greatly affected Makhno's attitude on the Ukrainian question.

Little is known of Makhno's early life or of the Huliai-Pole environment. The town was overwhelmingly Ukrainian in population, but also included a substantial number of Jews and a small number of Russians, most of whom held government positions.[16] However, Huliai-Pole was located near the Russified centers of Katerynoslav and Oleksandrivsk, a factor of considerable importance for Makhno's future development. It is clear that the increase of political activism aimed at the Ukrainian countryside did not bypass Huliai-Pole. The first event of significance in Makhno's career was his politicization—conversion to an anarcho-communist group that had been established in Huliai-Pole by anarchists from Katerynoslav. In this way, Makhno and a number of other Ukrainian youth were brought into contact with the urban anarchist movement. Makhno's adherence to anarchism was to be of central importance throughout the rest of his life, and in order to understand his actions, as well as the major influences upon him, the relationship between anarchist theory and nationalism must be discussed.

---

[15] For Makhno's discussion of his Russification, see Makhno II, pp. 153–154.

[16] For a description of Huliai Pole, see Natalia Sukhogorskaia, "Vospominanie o makhnovshchine," *Kandalnyi zvon,* No. 6 (Odessa, 1927), pp. 37–38.

In anarchist theory, the solution of national problems is achieved with the overthrow of the state. In a stateless society, the bourgeoisie is no longer able to oppress the workers by playing on their nationalism. Also, the abolition of the state ends national oppression and allows the free development of all nations.[17] Classical anarchism does not recognize national questions.

Though most Russian anarchists in the pre-revolutionary period dismissed the question of nationalism as irrelevant, a minority thought that greater attention should be devoted to this issue. In 1910, Maksim Raevskii wrote in *Burevestnik* that "it is even possible to say that the national factor in the life of mankind is studied less in our literature than are all other important questions of social and political life."[18] Raevskii and the dean of Russian anarchists, Peter

---

[17] The general trend of anarchist thinking is outlined by P. Kropotkin, "Natsionalnyi vopros," *Listki "Khleb i Volia"* (London), No. 16, June 7, 1907, pp. 2–4.

[18] Raevskii viewed this lack of attention as the inevitable result of anarchism's development in uni-national states—above all in Western Europe. He maintained that anarchists in the multi-national Russian Empire must devote more attention to nationalism, citing two articles by Kropotkin as one of the few anarchist attempts to study and explain the growth of nationalism among the non-Russians of the Empire and above all among the working class. M. Raevskii, "Natsionalnyi vopros s tochki zreniia kommunisticheskogo anarkhizma," *Burevestnik* (Paris), No. 19, February 19, 1910, p. 13.

Kropotkin attributed the lack of anarchist discussion on the nationality question to the influence of French anarchist theorists, who looked on nationalism as a prop of the state and of reaction. He maintained that, although this view was correct for the French and other dominant nationalities, it did not apply to oppressed ones. He generalized from the history of the nineteenth century that no social revolution is possible while a nation is struggling for its liberation. Thus, it would follow from his argument that the success of the struggle for national freedom was a necessary precondition of the struggle for social revolution. Indeed, he believed that if each nation developed its own language and culture it would contribute to the progress of anarchism. Kropotkin, pp. 2–4.

Raevskii commented on the considerable criticism leveled against Kropotkin in anarchist circles because of his favorable attitude toward nationalist movements. He also called on anarchists to formulate tactics for dealing with nationalism among the workers of the oppressed nationalities of Russia. However, Raevskii challenged Kropotkin's assertion that nations struggling for national freedom could not enter the path of

Kropotkin, attempted to bring about a change in Russian anarchist attitudes toward the liberation struggles of the Poles, Georgians, Jews, and other minority groups. However, the prevailing tendency in the pre-1917 period was either lack of attention to the national factor, or, when it was alluded to, a simple denunciation of nationalism as a bourgeois manifestation. For those anarchists interested in the nationality issue, the limited literature on the subject gave little guidance.[19]

Anarchists were very active in the Ukraine after the 1905 Revolution. Their activity, however, was centered in the Russified cities of Katerynoslav, Kharkiv, Odessa, and Kiev. Given the ethnic configuration and cultural-linguistic characteristics of these centers, it was possible for the anarchist movement in the Ukraine to be culturally "Russian" and thus to avoid the national problem. It is impossible to estimate the number of Ukrainians in the anarchist movement. However, the lack of special Ukrainian anarchist groups or of periodicals in Ukrainian suggests that the number of Ukrainian-speaking or nationally conscious anarchists was not large.[20] The lack of evidence of Ukrainian activity in the anarchist movement is in marked contrast to the considerable material on the participation of Ukrainian Jews in the movement.[21] Even Raevskii, an anarchist interested in the nationality problem and a native of the Ukrainian city of Nizhyn, made no mention of Ukrainians in his discussion of the nationality problem in the Russian Empire.[22] A measure of the anarchists' lack of perception of a Ukrainian problem is revealed by the local reports, or "chronicles," in the pre-

---

social revolution. He cited the Jews, Poles, and Georgians as examples that the struggle for national freedom is an integral part of the struggle for social freedom. Thus, Raevskii saw the reawakening of oppressed nationalities and their struggle for freedom as a positive phenomenon in which anarchists should play a role.

[19] Interest was centered on Jewish nationalism, a very atypical form, given the Jewish minority status and the Zionist movement. Kropotkin's articles on the nationality problem were prompted by the inquiries of Marc Jahrblum, a Zionist anarchist. M. Raevskii (L. Fishelev) was Jewish.

[20] The formation of a specifically Ukrainian group of anarchists was announced in 1914. Its goal was to issue propaganda in the Ukrainian language. *Nabat* (Geneva), No. 1, July, 1914. There is no indication that this group undertook any activity.

[21] Paul Avrich, *The Russian Anarchists* (Princeton, N.J.: Princeton University Press, 1967), pp. 43–49.

[22] *Ibid.*, pp. 62–63.

1917 anarchist press. A study of these "chronicles" shows evidence of anarchist activity in twenty-five Ukrainian cities and villages.[23] In only six cases (all from northern Ukraine and not including a single major city) is there evidence of consciousness of the existence of a Ukrainian nation.[24] Thus, the pre-1917 anarchist movement in the Ukraine had neither contact with nor great awareness of the Ukrainian national movement. Linguistically and culturally, it was predominantly a Russian movement of the Ukrainian cities.

Makhno's anarchist leanings placed him in the world of Russian

---

[23] Katerynoslav (Dnipropetrovsk); Odessa and Balta (Odessa *oblast*); Cherkasy, Smila, Shpola, Zvenyhorodka, Uman, and Zolotonosha (Cherkasy *oblast*); Elizavethrad (Kirovhrad *oblast*); Vinnytsia and Pohrebyshche (Vinnytsia *oblast*); Melitopol, Oleksandrivsk (Zaporizhzhia) and Huliai-Pole (Zaporizhzhia *oblast*); Romny (Sumy *oblast*); Nizhyn (Chernihiv *oblast*); Zhytomyr and Berdychiv (Zhytomyr *oblast*); Lutsk (Volyn *oblast*); Novopavlivka (Voroshylovhrad *oblast*).

Newspapers consulted: *Listki "Khleb i Volia"* (*London*), No. 1, October 30, 1906, through No. 17, June 20, 1907; *Nabat* (Geneva), No. 1, July, 1914; Nos. 2–3, May–June, 1915; No. 4, April, 1916; *Anarkhist* (Geneva), No. 1, October, 1907; No. 5, March, 1910; *Burevestnik* (Paris), No. 1, July 20, 1906, through No. 19, February, 1910; *Buntar* (Geneva), No. 1, December, 1906; No. 1, May 15, 1908; *Khleb i volia* (London), No. 1, August, 1903, through No. 25, November, 1905; *Khleb i volia* (Paris), No. 1, February, 1909; No. 2, July, 1909; *Almanakh,* No. 1 (Paris, 1909).

[24] A report from Shpola mentioned the necessity for anarchist newspapers and leaflets in Ukrainian in order to work among the peasants and workers. A report from Chyhyryn informed of conversions to anarchism from the Revolutionary Ukrainian Party, while another from Romny (northern Poltava gubernia) told of the conversion of that city from a center of the Ukrainian "Spilka" to anarchism. *Anarkhist* (Geneva), No. 1, October 10, 1907, p. 33 and No. 2, April, 1908, p. 29.

One informant from Nizhyn wrote of distributing leaflets in the "Little Russian language." *Khleb i volia* (London), No. 11, September, 1904, p. 4. Another article outlined the beginnings of the anarchist movement in the Ukraine, including developments in Nizhyn; it also contained information on Ukrainian parties and stressed the paucity of anarchist literature (only in Russian) as opposed to Social Democratic literature (in three languages: Russian, Ukrainian and Yiddish). L. Pridesnianskii, "Pervye shagi anarkhizma na Ukraine," *Almanakh,* No. 1 (Paris, 1909), pp. 117–125.

Finally, a report from Chernihiv gubernia discussed the work of the Ukrainian Social Democrats. It mentioned the lack of influence of the Russian Social Democrats, referred to the activity of the *Bund* and commented on the large number of Jews among the "progressive" proletariat. *Khleb i volia* (London), Nov. 13–14, October–November, 1904, p. 8.

revolutionaries, a world that, though not Russian nationalist, was Russian in outlook and that viewed any "localist" or nationalist movement as a hindrance to the social revolution. Makhno's entrance into this "Russian" environment was reinforced by his confinement in Moscow's Butyrki prison, where he came under Arshinov's tutelage.[25] It was probably his long confinement there that linguistically Russified him.[26]

The Makhno who returned to Huliai-Pole in March of 1917 was not interested in a search for national identity but in social revolution and cooperation with anarchist forces. "Ukrainianism," a concept that he may well have first encountered at that time, was to him a bourgeois political movement of the village intelligentsia and merely another ideology to be combatted. The distinction between political activity on behalf of a Ukrainian state and the assertion of one's linguistic-national identity as a Ukrainian was still very vague. This was especially true in Katerynoslav gubernia, where Ukrainian political and cultural life were particularly underdeveloped.[27] To increase their strength, the Ukrainian political factions in the area cooperated in joint activities. The more rightist groups devoted their efforts to cultural work. The weakness of the Ukrainian political movement caused others, including Makhno and the anarchists, to consider "Ukrainians" as merely an amorphous political faction.

The young anarchist's entrance into the political life of the

---

[25] Arshinov joined the anarchist movement in 1906. From 1911 until 1917 he served with Makhno in Butyrki. Contacts between them were renewed in 1918 during Makhno's trip to Moscow. In April 1919, Arshinov joined Makhno and remained with him until the beginning of 1921 as a member of the Cultural Enlightenment Section and editor of *Put k svobode*. Volin, "Predislovie," in Arshinov, pp. 12–14.

[26] Mykola Irchan asserts that he was told this by Makhno. M. Irchan, *Makhno i Makhnivtsi* (Kaminets: Vyd. "Striltsia," 1919), p. 19. Makhno later admitted that by July 1918 he was no longer in command of his "native language." Makhno II, pp. 153–154.

[27] Mazepa discusses this weakness and illustrates it by pointing to these facts: (1) the first city election in Katerynoslav, in which Ukrainian parties won 9 out of 113 seats, was considered a victory; (2) throughout Katerynoslav gubernia, soviets and *dumas* were almost never controlled by Ukrainian political groups; (3) in the whole gubernia Ukrainians were able to publish only one weekly newspaper, and this was the result of a collective effort by all parties. Mazepa, Vol. I, pp. 25–26.

Huliai-Pole of 1917 meant a struggle with Ukrainian forces. Makhno and his group of anarcho-communists soon attained dominance in the Huliai-Pole Soviet and successfully opposed the activity of the major Ukrainian party, the Ukrainian Socialist-Revolutionaries. Makhno carried on a bitter struggle against the "Ukrainians," or, as he called them, the "socialist chauvinists," and contacts with urban anarchists only strengthened the Huliai-Pole group's antipathy. Marusia Nikoforova and other Oleksandrivsk anarchists visited the town and counseled the use of terror against Ukrainian parties.[28] Local anarchists responded by assassinating the major "Ukrainian" leader in the village, Semiuta-Riabko.[29] Makhno's deep antagonism to the Ukrainian movement was one of the factors leading to his cooperation, in January 1918, with Bolshevik forces in Oleksandrivsk against the forces of the Rada.[30] He viewed the Rada's invitation to the Central Powers to enter the Ukraine as the final betrayal of the revolution.[31]

Even before Makhno launched the guerrilla movement that was to become the *Makhnivshchyna,* and before the *Nabat* group of anarchists had any influence on him, the outline of his policies had emerged. This anarcho-communist peasant, who no longer had command of his native language, was suspicious of "Ukrainianism" (*ukrainstvo*) in general and was vehemently opposed to Ukrainian political formations. His anarchist persuasions made the culturally Russian anarchists of the Ukrainian cities his cohorts, and he felt comfortable working within this non-Ukrainian milieu. Finally, like so many other anarchists, he saw the Bolshevik movement as revolutionary and was willing to cooperate with it against what he viewed as the forces of reaction.[32]

---

28 B. Belash, "Makhnovshchina (otryvki iz vospominanii B. Belasha)," *Litopys revoliutsii*, VII, 3 (Kharkiv, 1928), p. 194. Makhno makes mention of a visit by M. Nikoforova on August 29, 1917. Makhno I, p. 62. In discussing the events of January 1918 and cooperation with the Bolshevik forces, Makhno mentions Nikoforova's role as a delegate to the Revolutionary Committee. Makhno II, p. 116.

29 Makhno I, pp. 189–191.

30 *Ibid.,* pp. 107–127.

31 *Ibid.,* p. 181.

32 See Avrich, pp. 122–203, for a general discussion of the Bolshevik-anarchist relationship. It must be remembered that, while the Bolshevik "purge" of anarchists ended cooperation between the two, the Bolshevik regime continued to hold a fascination for anarchists, since they often

Soon after Makhno returned to Huliai-Pole from Moscow, in July 1918, he launched the guerrilla movement that was to be the basis of his power. Peasant resentment against the conservative regime of the Hetman as well as the German and Austro-Hungarian occupation was widespread. In the northern and western areas of the Ukraine this discontent was utilized by the Ukrainian political forces of the Directory. At the same time, Makhno became a major leader of the anti-Hetmanate rebellions in the steppe areas of Katerynoslav and Taurida gubernias.[33] But already, from the first

---

continued to view it as "revolutionary." While Makhno was, of course, aware of the "purges," his subsequent alliances with the Bolsheviks must be placed in the context of the temporary weakness of Bolshevism in the Ukraine and the great strength of the "reactionary" forces represented by Denikin.

[33] The importance of the anti-Hetman movement in fomenting Ukrainian national consciousness and serving as a vehicle for the Directory's bid for power is asserted by Mazepa: "Discounting its eventual failure . . . the anti-Hetman rebellion played a historic role in the Ukrainian liberation struggle. It awoke Ukrainian consciousness in the people." Mazepa, Vol. I, p. 59. While this assessment is essentially true in the north and west, the anti-Hetman movement did not have a similar effect in the east and south. Petr Arshinov, who throughout his work shows the usual anarchist lack of concern for the nationality issue, asserts that: "The rebellion did not everywhere retain its revolutionary popular essence, its faithfulness to the interests of its class. At the same time that the rebellion in southern Ukraine took up the black banner of anarchism and went down the path of anarchy and self-rule for laborers, in the western and northwestern parts of the Ukraine, after the overthrow of the Hetman, the rebellion fell under the influence of elements of democratic nationalism, foreign and hostile to it (Petliurists) . . . In this manner, the uprising of the peasants of Kiev, Volhynia, Podillia, and a part of Poltava gubernias, although it had common roots with the other uprisings, in its later development did not find within itself its true historic tasks or its own organized force. It fell under the control of the enemies of labor and thus became a blind instrument of reaction in their hands." Arshinov, p. 48. Thus, Arshinov sees peasant rebelliousness as a tremendous force that could be harnessed and shaped by the politically conscious.

Others have attempted to explain on socio-economic grounds the difference between the area of the *Makhnivshchyna* and the territory controlled by the nationalists. "From one side the closeness of major working centers, and from the other the German and Greek colonies surrounding the Ukrainian peasantry, erased that with which the Ukrainian intelligentsia later tried to inoculate the *Makhnivshchyna*." Teper, p. 48.

contacts between the Directory forces of *Otaman* Havrylo Horobets and the *Makhnivtsi*, it was evident that Makhno was bitterly opposed to groups attempting to establish a Ukrainian state. Any hope that he could be won over to the Ukrainian national cause was destroyed by Chubenko and Myrhorodskyi, Makhno's emissaries to Horobets. One of the Directory officials present at this meeting described it in the following manner:

> They [the Makhno delegates] spoke Russian and under the slogans of battle with the "counterrevolution," "bourgeoisie," etc., did not want to hear of anything else. To the proposition of the Ukrainian Command that they enter into a common struggle for the resurrection of the Ukrainian state, they announced that they considered the Directory a counterrevolutionary force and that for them, revolutionaries, there was no common path with the Ukrainian nationalist bourgeoisie. In general their phraseology did not differ at all from that of the Bolsheviks.[34]

There was almost no common ground between Makhno, who stressed the needs of the revolution, and the Ukrainian forces, who emphasized Ukrainian cultural and national aspirations.

Throughout the complex political events of 1919–1920, Makhno's policy toward the Ukrainian problem was consistent. After the *Nabat* group of anarchists joined Makhno, several publications propounding ardent internationalism were founded. Ukrainian nationalism, as well as nationalism of any sort, was condemned in the movement's major organ, the Russian-language newspaper

---

M. Kubanin has discussed this difference as the result of the national compactness of the village in the nationalist region, which gave a nationalist hue to the hatred of the city, the greater percentage of trade carried on by Jews, and the high percentage of Polish landlords. Kubanin, pp. 29–30. Certainly more careful socio-economic analysis is necessary. Yet the role of the leader must not be underestimated. Thus, it would be interesting to see to what degree the regions held by Hryhoriiv and Makhno differed, and how much the direction of the movements they led was dependent on their leadership.

[34] Mazepa, Vol. I, p. 63. Makhno's reaction to proponents of Vynnychenko after the Directory's assumption of power was similar. In his memoirs he claims to have duelled verbally with the Ukrainian forces: "Where, I ask you, friend, in the revolutionary Ukrainian villages and cities, will you find among the workers such fools as to believe in the 'socialism' of the Petliurist-Vynnychenkist Ukrainian government or 'Ukrainian Directory' as it styles itself?" Makhno III, p. 154.

Put k svobode.[35] When *Otaman* Hryhoriiv rose in revolt against the Bolsheviks under the banner of Ukrainian nationalism and called for Makhno's assistance, the *Makhnivtsi* issued a condemnation:

> What does Hryhoriiv say? From the first words of his "Universal" he says that the people who crucified Christ rule the Ukraine, that they have come from rapacious Moscow. Brothers, is it possible that you do not hear in these words the dark call to the Jewish pogrom? Is it possible you do not feel the aim of *Otaman* Hryhoriiv to tear asunder the living brotherly link of revolutionary Ukraine from revolutionary Russia?[36]

Not only was the movement as a whole opposed to Ukrainian nationalism, but those both favorable and hostile to Makhno testify to his lack of nationalist feeling.[37] The degree of Makhno's hostility to Ukrainian nationalists is illustrated by Fotii Meleshko's account of his meeting with Makhno in 1919. Meleshko recalls that Makhno asked him whether he was afraid, since the anarchist leader was rumored to murder all "nationally conscious" Ukrainians.[38]

---

[35] For example, the issue of May 17, 1919, carried slogans such as: "Is it possible you do not know that all workers are equal, that the revolution does not know national enmity?" Arshinov, p. 204, quotes an October 1919 statement of the Makhno forces that independence for the Ukraine exists only in terms of the "self-determination of the laborers."

[36] *Put k svobode* (Huliai-Pole), No. 1, May 17, 1919, p. 3; and Arshinov, p. 112. The above newspaper issue also includes an article, "Grigoriev—Novyi Petliura," warning that Hryhoriiv wished to assist the bourgeoisie to enter the Ukraine with "fire and sword."

[37] Even Teper, who charged Makhno with having embraced Ukrainian nationalism just before his flight into Rumania in 1921, writes that: "Makhno himself was as far from nationalism as from the anti-Semitism, which so many people ascribe to him." Teper, p. 50. And, in discussing Ukrainian attempts to take control of the *Makhnivshchyna,* he says: "It would be comic to maintain that Makhno and the basic cadre of the *Makhnivshchyna* originating in Zaporizhzhia might sympathize with these national reformers." *Teper,* p. 49. Dubrovskyi, who casts Makhno as a Ukrainian national hero, nevertheless admits his inattention to the national problem, pp. 21–22. See also Arshinov, pp. 203–213; Semanov, p. 40; Kubanin, pp. 163–165.

[38] Meleshko, December 25, 1959, p. 3. The degree to which "Ukrainian" was a political and sociocultural term, not a national designation, is shown in a note from Halyna Kuzmenko that Meleshko cites: "My hus-

Makhno consistently refused military cooperation with Ukrainian nationalist forces. Only once did he come to an agreement with Ukrainian military groups. First contact was made with the "foreign" Galician *Sich* Riflemen near Uman at the height of the Denikin offensive in late September 1919.[39] Although an accord was reached and the Petliura forces accepted a group of Makhno's wounded, the agreement was in effect only four days.[40] The Makhno camp issued a pamphlet denouncing Petliura and later charged that he planned to betray them to the Whites.[41] Subsequently,

---

band wishes to see you. I pledge nothing will happen to you. Nestor treats Ukrainians well!"

[39] For accounts of this agreement, see Arshinov, pp. 137–138; Dubrovskyi, p. 12; Mazepa, Vol. II, pp. 112–113. The Galician *Sich* Riflemen were the major proponents of an alliance with Makhno. For their answer to Ukrainian critics of such an alliance, see Irchan, pp. 27–32.

[40] Dubrovskyi, p. 12, cites 3,000 as the number of wounded.

[41] Arshinov, p. 137. This evaluation of the Petliura forces' policy is also put forth by Kubanin, p. 109, who sees it as an attempt to buy off the Denikin forces; and by V. Rudnev, *Makhnovshchina* (Kharkiv: Bibl. "Oktiabria," 1928), p. 49. Mazepa, Vol. II, p. 113, contests this accusation, claiming that the declared war between the Directory and Denikin made it impossible. Meleshko, February 19, 1960, p. 3, sees the Petliura forces' inaction as a lost opportunity.

Wynar maintains that Makhno betrayed Petliura by abandoning the Ukrainian National Republic's forces, and he dismisses as spurious any allegations that Petliura planned to sacrifice Makhno to Denikin. "Zviazky," pp. 16–17. That the Petliura forces were far from satisfied with Makhno as an ally is evident from several proposals in an intelligence report of the Petliura counter-intelligence, dated October 4, 1919: ". . . 3) Makhno himself and his unit do not recognize any authority and are against it by its nature. They are incapable of being subject to the government and command of the Ukrainian National Republic even if they wished to; 4) As a major armed group of bandits, the *Makhnivtsi* are a constant and major threat to our front and rear, and therefore: 5) When military circumstances permit, it would be best to squeeze the units of Makhno into Denikin's rear where they would be a constant, solid threat for Denikin. For the liquidation of Makhno's banditry with his system of mobility, it would be necessary for the Denikinites to use three times as many forces as Makhno commands." "Makhno ta ioho viisko," *Litopys chervonoi kalyny* (Lviv, 1935), pp. 16–17.

Although this report does not indicate a plot to sell out Makhno to Denikin, it illustrates the potential danger of the Makhno alliance for

Makhno was charged with having planned to deal with Petliura as he had with Hryhoriiv.[42]

It would be a mistake, however, to label the *Makhnivtsi* as "anti-Ukrainian." Although they opposed the political goals of most "svidomi ukraintsi" (nationally conscious Ukrainians), they accepted the existence of a Ukrainian nation and used the terms "Ukraine" and "Ukrainians."[43] Opposing Denikin's restrictions on the use of

the Ukrainian People's Republic (UNR). Also, Makhno's flight to Denikin's rear forces, far from being an unexpected betrayal of the UNR forces, may have taken place through their influence (the discrepancy in dating may be a lag in recording the document). A final reason for Makhno to have distrusted the Petliura forces is that his emissary to them was both a Ukrainian nationalist and the leader of a plot against him (cf. footnote 50).

[42] This is undoubtedly one of the most perplexing aspects of the *Makhnivshchyna*. The first major allegation appears to be that of the former *Makhnivets,* Teper: "Whether this plan became known to Petliura even at present is unclear; in any case, the latter, a few hours before the appointed meeting-time, left Uman and in this way escaped the fate of Hryhoriiv." Teper, p. 51.

Another source of evidence for such a plot is F. Meleshko, a Directory proponent who spent some time among the *Makhnivtsi* in the summer of 1919. Meleshko, February 19, 1960. It is unlikely that knowledge of such a plot existed in the Petliura camp. It is known, however, that a group of dissatisfied Galician *Sich* Riflemen conspired to assassinate Petliura and that this group was later in contact with Makhno. Letter to the author by Zenon Jaworskyj, January 15, 1971. See also K. V. Gerasimenko, "Makhno," in *Denikin-Iudenich-Vrangel: Revoliutsiia i grazhdanskaia voina v opisaniiakh belogvardeitsev,* Vol. V (Moscow-Leningrad: Gosudarstvennoe izd., 1927), pp. 236–238.

[43] The movement even seems to have contained a strain of attachment to the Ukraine and the Ukrainian nation. A poem by "Staryi Makeich" in *Put k svobode* (Huliai-Pole), No. 1, May 17, 1919, p. 3, contains a tinge of Ukrainian feeling. In an appeal for revolutionary action, it concludes:

> And the brave ones went out,
>   Bidding adieu to their families,
> To chase the oppressors from
>   native Ukraine.

Thus, segments of the movements, while not nationalist, saw the *Makhnivshchyna* as their revolution in their native land. The role of the "newcomers" (*prishlie*) is illustrated by a poem in *Put k svobode* (Huliai-Pole)

the Ukrainian language in schools, the Cultural Enlightenment Section of the *Makhnivshchyna* issued the following order in October 1919, on the pages of *Put k svobode*.

> In the interest of the spiritual development of the people, the language of school instruction ought to be one to which the local population (teachers, students and parents) naturally inclines. The local population, not the authorities and not the army, ought to decide this question freely and independently.[44]

The need to communicate with the peasant masses led to the foundation of a Ukrainian-language newspaper, *Shliakh do voli*.[45] Specifically Ukrainian themes, such as historical subjects and literary allusions, were mentioned frequently in *Makhnivtsi* publications during the later phases of the movement's existence.[46]

The increase of Ukrainian-language materials in the *Makhnivshchyna* was a result of the work of a small group of Ukrainian intellectuals. The most important of these was Makhno's wife, Halyna Kuzmenko, a former teacher of Ukrainian language and history in the Hulaia-Pole Gymnasium.[47] Halyna used her influence to

---

No. 3, June 4, 1919, entitled, "To Ukraine . . . from the North," by Chashcharin, and asking that the Ukraine accept them in a brotherly manner.

[44] Arshinov, p. 204. Denikin protested the assertion that his movement was directed against the minorities by claiming that only the publicly supported schools were required to instruct in the "state" language. A. Denikin, *Ocherki russkoi smuty*, Vol. I (Berlin: J. Povolozky & Cie, 1926), pp. 142–144.

[45] Both Volin and Arshinov estimate that the *Makhnivshchyna* was overwhelmingly Ukrainian, with six to eight percent of its participants Russian, and substantial numbers of Greeks, Jews, and Caucasians. Arshinov, p. 203; Volin, *The Unknown Revolution*, p. 221.

[46] This is based on the observations of Iwan Majstrenko, *Borotbism: A Chapter in the History of Ukrainian Communism* (New York: Research Program on the USSR, 1954), p. 104, who had *Shliakh do voli* at his disposal. V. Holubnychy maintains that, while the *Makhnivtsi* literature was primarily in Russian at the beginning, it was later for the most part in Ukrainian. He also mentions the existence of a *Makhnivtsi* Ukrainian paper in Poltava (*Anarkhist-Povstanets*). V. Holubnychy, "Makhno i Makhnivshchyna," *Entsyklopediia Ukrainoznavstva: Slovnykova chastyna*, Vol. IV (Paris, Munich: Vyd. "Molode Zhyttia," 1962), pp. 1493–1494.

[47] Halyna, the daughter of a police official, was from Pishchanyi Brid,

Ukrainianize the cultural milieu of the *Makhnivshchyna*.[48] In the summer of 1919, a group of Ukrainian intelligentsia gathered around her in an attempt to convert the Makhno movement to the Ukrainian nationalist cause.[49] The available information is incomplete, but a plan may have been afoot to overthrow Makhno himself, and discovery of this probably was the factor precipitating his anti-Petliura pamphlet. One former supporter maintained that, after Makhno discovered these plans, he easily dislodged the Ukrainian nationalists from the movement.[50] Yet, the fact that

---

Elizavethrad (Kirovhrad) county, Kherson gubernia. She studied at the Women's Seminary in Dobrovelychkivka (Elizavethrad county) and in the fall of 1918 accepted a position in the newly opened Ukrainian State Gymnasium in Huliai-Pole. Her reasons for becoming one of a long string of Makhno's wives are reputed to have been her fears of the Denikin forces. The couple are reported to have married in her native village church during the summer of 1919. Meleshko, December 18, 1959, and December 21, 1959. Halyna later denied that there had been any religious rites. See her "Vidpovid na stattiu 'Pomer Makhno' v 'Novii Pori' vid 9-ho serpnia 1934 roku, hor. Detroita, Mych.," *Probuzhdenie* (Detroit), No. 50–51, September–October, 1934, p. 17. Another source maintains that the church wedding was necessary to please Halyna's parents, who were Old Believer peasants, and attributes her hatred of Denikin's Whites to their murder of her parents. Sukhogorskaia, p. 55. There is a rumor that she and Makhno were not on good terms in the emigration, but it is known that Halyna attended her husband's funeral in 1934 with their daughter. Meleshko, February 26, 1960, p. 3.

Teper, p. 44, describes Halyna as a person "who until 1922 remained of a rather strong chauvinist viewpoint." On the other hand, Nikolaev, in his novel on Makhno, *Pervyi sredi ravnykh,* based largely on the author's acquaintance with Halyna in Paris, writes with apparent total oblivion of the existence of a Ukrainian question. One may suppose that by the 1920's and 1930's Halyna toned down any Ukrainian nationalist sympathies.

[48] Sukhogorskaia (pp. 48, 53–54), a Russian teacher in Huliai-Pole, describes Halyna as the self-proclaimed patroness of education and the intelligentsia, as well as an organizer of cultural events.

[49] Halyna's role in the *Makhnivshchyna* was of considerable importance. She was her husband's constant companion even in battle and appears to have served as head of the movement's Punitive Commission. Dubrovskyi, p. 15.

[50] Teper, p. 51, is the major source. He charges that a group of Ukrainian intelligentsia became active in the *Makhnivshchyna* and were ac-

he allowed Ukrainian nationalists to work in his camp at all illustrates the need for Ukrainian cultural workers. The purported plot to convert the movement into an instrument of Ukrainian

---

cepted by the *Batko* because of his need for cultural workers; that this group began to feel stronger, especially because it attracted Makhno's wife to its side; and that they sought to take over the *Makhnivshchyna* when it was in close proximity to the Petliura forces at Uman. He maintains that they were easily defeated by the anti-nationalist Secretariat of the Makhno movement. Teper further asserts that Makhno's plan to kill Petliura originated from his reaction to this plot. While these charges can be properly evaluated only after closer study of the material on both sides, they would appear to be correct.

M. Irchan, who served as a press-attaché for the Galician *Sich* Riflemen and who visited the Makhno camp in mid-September 1919, reported: "There are two parties, the nationalists, that is the Ukrainian, and the apoliticals, that is, those indifferent to the national question. The first group is constantly growing. The Army has a relatively large percentage of educated people—doctors, teachers (male and female), and people well-known even from pre-war Ukrainian literature." Irchan, pp. 17–18.

The growth of Ukrainian cultural forces is also indicated in the memoirs of F. Meleshko, who relates that after being cut off from the Directory's forces he received a note from Halyna inviting him and some of his cohorts to the Makhno camp. Makhno proposed that they embark on cultural work with the implicit understanding that they would serve as negotiators with the Petliura forces if the need should arise. Meleshko, V. Nadaikasa. L. Voitsyk, T. Berezhniak, and T. Moldovanenko accepted, but they bolted from the Makhno forces within a month. Meleshko reports that Volin and Arshinov were absent from the camp and that one of the twelve members of the Revolutionary-Military Soviet was an ardent Ukrainian. Meleshko, however, gives no indication that his stay with the *Makhnivtsi* was occasioned by anything more than chance, or that there was a Ukrainian plot against Makhno. Meleshko, December 18, 1959, and February 29, 1960.

The most important indication that an attempt was made to overthrow Makhno and utilize his forces in cooperation with the Ukrainian National Directory is offered by an informant of Dubrovskyi, R. Kupchynskyi. He states that Makhno's emissary, Shpota, who "spoke often with us on Ukrainian themes" and who "disliked Makhno's anarchism," conspired with F. Shchus, one of the Makhno's major "generals," against the *Batko*, but that Makhno discovered the plot. He relates that Makhno's wife did not want to see the end of the agreement with the Ukrainian People's Republic and "would have been happy if Makhno's whole army had gone over to Petliura." Dubrovskyi, p. 12.

nationalism failed, but the need for cultural workers continued.[51] Halyna, whom Makhno does not seem to have suspected of plotting against him, did not cease in her attempts to Ukrainianize the movement. The activity of Ukrainian intellectuals, however, was merely a minor current in the *Makhnivshchyna*.

In fact, anarchists, many of them Russian and Jewish, provided the basic cadre of the movement in 1918–1919. The slogans of the movement were internationalist, and Ukrainian nationalism was opposed, though the latter was considered only a peripheral problem. Nonetheless, some Soviet historians have claimed that both the movement and Makhno turned to nationalism during the 1920–1921 period. M. Kubanin asserted that many of the ideological anarchists departed from the Makhno camp and that, under the influence of Halyna and a "chauvinistic" group, the peasant leader's pronouncements became more and more nationalistic. He also charged that Makhno cooperated with Petliura units in "mutual non-aggression pacts and joint action against Soviet power," and that Makhno's final transformation into a Ukrainian nationalist came just before his flight to Rumania, when he drew up a universal calling for the liberation of "Mother Ukraine"—*Nenka Ukraina*.[52] In 1928, Makhno wrote a rebuttal to Kubanin in which he totally dismissed the charges. He also asserted that Kubanin distorted anarchism's espousal of local autonomy so as to create trumped-up charges of nationalism. Unfortunately, he did not provide any substantial information on the period, and his assertion that Halyna did not even wish to win him over to nationalism does not coincide with what is known about her.[53]

There is considerable cause to doubt Kubanin's charge of Makhno's conversion to nationalism. The nationalist papers and pronouncements he refers to are never cited or quoted in his

---

[51] Both Arshinov and Volin are silent as to the question of Ukrainian influence in the Makhno camp. Arshinov's discussion of cultural and educational activities makes no mention of even using the Ukrainian language. Arshinov, pp. 175–179.

[52] Kubanin, pp. 165–166.

[53] Nestor Makhno, *Makhnovshchina i ee vcherashnie soiuzniki-bolsheviki* (*Otvet na knigu M. Kubanina*) (Paris: Izd. 'Biblioteki Makhnovtsev,' 1928), pp. 26–27. For an example of the Makhno movement's anticentralism (used in this case against the Bolsheviks), see Roshchin, "Dukha ne ugashaite," *Put k svobode* (Huliai-Pole), No. 2, May 24, 1919, pp. 1–2.

work.[54] Moreover, a Bolshevik proclamation issued sometime after November 1920—that is, after the Wrangel defeat—asserted that, unlike Petliura, Makhno was not a nationalist and did not appeal to nationalist sympathies.[55] Kubanin's statement that the number of anarchists with Makhno decreased considerably between 1919 and 1920 is, of course, correct. The increasing dissatisfaction of *Nabat* with Makhno led to a final break in November 1920, but this was not over the national question.[56] The alleged "truce, non-aggression pact, and joint action against the Soviets" with the Petliura bands is contradicted by Kubanin's own citation of his major informant on the period: "There was no official link with the Petliura detachments, excluding certain chance meetings, since the *Petliurivtsi* feared us as an opposing camp and avoided contacts."[57] It is true, but hardly significant, that on occasion there was cooperation between elements of the two groups, because both were so hard pressed by the Bolsheviks. Of more importance is Makhno's own admission that during 1920 former Petliura units joined his camp and introduced a nationalist element into his forces.[58] However, he claimed to have resisted this influence. The projected universal that Kubanin

---

[54] It is, of course, possible that what Majstrenko sees as an increase in Ukrainian themes, Kubanin views as nationalism.

[55] "Makhnovshchina, petliurovshchina, banditizm, antisemitizm i borba s nimi," *Volna* (New York), No. 58, October, 1924, pp. 37–39.

[56] As early as February 1920, the *Nabat* had expressed concern over Makhno's methods of leadership. In April, a new concordat was reached when Baron and Sukhovolskii were sent as emissaries to Makhno. After Makhno's new alliance with the Bolsheviks, only Volin, Arshinov, Berman, and Goldman remained faithful to the *Makhnivshchyna*. Aaron Baron and Mark Mrachnyi became especially virulent enemies of Makhno. Ierde, pp. 52–54.

[57] Kubanin, p. 111. Vynar, "Zviazky," p. 17–18, also asserts that cooperation between UNR and Makhno forces was of a local and minor character. Elsewhere, he maintains that Makhno's antagonism to Ukrainian forces had diminished considerably in this period. "Prychynky," pp. 17–18.

[58] Nestor Makhno, "Makhnovshchina i antisemitizm," *Delo truda* (Paris), No. 30–31, November–December, 1927, p. 16. It appears that in April 1920 a group of Ukrainian Socialist-Revolutionaries joined the *Makhnivtsi,* and one of their number became a member of the Revolutionary-Military Soviet. R. Ivanenko, "Pro shcho ne vilno zabuvaty (Makhnivshchyna)," *Ukrainskyi holos* (Winnipeg), August 29, 1962.

charged Makhno as planning to issue is discussed by a former Makhno supporter, Teper, in the following manner:

> Shortly before the flight to Rumania, Makhno decided to put into the archives all prior declarations and to take upon himself the composition of a new declaration in a completely different vein. Basically he proposed in it a project for the national liberation of the Ukraine. . . . But a part of the commanding staff protested strongly against this declaration, and he was forced not to push it any further.[59]

Far from seeing this declaration as the culmination of a process, Teper views it as a desperate, last-minute effort to secure Ukrainian nationalist support. Thus, he contradicts Kubanin's allegation of a steady process that culminated in this proposed manifesto. The problem of Makhno's conversion can be resolved only on the basis of new evidence.

Whether or not Makhno considered issuing a call for the liberation of the Ukraine as a last-ditch effort, the charge that he went over to the nationalist camp in 1920–1921 seems improbable.[60] What is possible is that the virulence of his opposition to Ukrainian nationalism decreased in the face of what he saw as even greater enemies. Also, the triumphs of Russian forces in the Ukraine (Bolshevik or White) and the increasing self-identification of the masses as Ukrainian may have led him to think in Ukrainian terms. It is significant that in the anarchist émigré press, in which Makhno was so often held responsible for the Jewish pogroms, no mention was made of any Ukrainian nationalism.[61]

The problem of Makhno's relationship to the Ukrainian question appears to be simple. A Russified Ukrainian peasant led a movement ideologically opposed to Ukrainian nationalist forces and staffed by a culturally Russian anarchist elite. From what is known of his life in emigration in Paris, his contacts were with Russian anarchists, not with nationally conscious Ukrainians.[62] He con-

---

[59] Teper, p. 114.

[60] Another indication that Makhno had not espoused Ukrainian nationalism in 1920 is that, when Wrangel called on him, in the summer of 1920, to join the struggle against the Bolsheviks, he did so in the name of Russian nationalism. Arshinov, p. 168.

[61] See Makhno's answer in *Makhnovshchina i ee vcherashnie,* as well as "Makhnovshchina i antisemitizm."

[62] Meleshko, December 18, 1959, asserted that Makhno "was not able

tributed to Russian anarchist publications and journals, and it would appear that his relations with his major Ukrainian contact, his wife Halyna, were strained.[63]

All the evidence is consistent, with one exception—Makhno's own history of the movement in his memoirs. Composed in the late 1920's and early 1930's, his writings reveal a man very much aware of his own Ukrainian identity and the appeal of Ukrainian nationalism to the masses. He even displays a considerable degree of Ukrainian patriotism.[64]

The memoirs contain numerous texts of speeches, purportedly made by Makhno, explaining the bankruptcy of Ukrainian nationalism. Long passages assert the correctness of Makhno's and other anarchists' programs for the liberation of the Ukraine and Ukrainians.[65] He describes the events of 1918–1919 as a process in which the "Russian Revolution in the Ukraine" became the "Ukrainian Revolution." One of the speeches quoted in the memoirs from the Revolutionary period includes a passage predicting that "Even should the Revolution in the Ukraine appear to be a continuation of the Russian Revolution, it will in its character and anti-state feeling be a Ukrainian Revolution."[66] Makhno also included passages extolling the special qualities of the Ukrainian soul. He thus describes his feelings while addressing a meeting in Huliai-Pole:

---

to gather around himself and his idea even ten Ukrainians in the emigration" (presumably he means nationally conscious Ukrainians) and that at his funeral there was only one Ukrainian, his wife.

[63] Mrs. Ida Mett, an acquaintance of Makhno from 1926 to 1929, confirms that relations were strained between Nestor and Halyna Makhno in that period. Letter of January 7, 1971, to author.

[64] The only work that has noticed the tone of Ukrainian patriotism in Makhno's memoirs is that by Max Nomad. He commented that: "Makhno was particularly bitter when writing about the Ukraine, his homeland, whose liberator he had hoped to become . . . Unwittingly he gave vent to the nationalistic longings of his countrymen." Nomad, p. 340. In fact, Makhno's commentaries are not as "unwitting" as Nomad presumed.

[65] See, for example, Makhno I, pp. 98, 104–105, 109–114, 157, 185; II, pp. 7, 72, 84; III, pp. 17, 155–156, 172–173.

[66] Makhno III, p. 59. Makhno's theory of a Ukrainian Revolution developing out of a Russian Revolution is illustrated in the titles of his memoirs. The first volume is entitled, "The Russian Revolution in Ukraine," while the third is "The Ukrainian Revolution."

I began to lose my equanimity and almost cried for joy at the breadth of development of the Ukrainian workers' and peasants' souls. Before me arose the peasants' will to freedom and independence, which only in the width and depth of the Ukrainian soul could so quickly and strongly manifest itself.[67]

In the memoirs, Makhno's interest focuses not only on the Ukrainian revolutionary soul, but also on Ukrainian culture. Although he wrote in Russian, Makhno prefaced the first volume with a note:

One thing alone must bother me in publishing this outline, and that is that it does not come out in the Ukraine and in the Ukrainian language. The Ukrainian nation is advancing culturally step by step toward a full definition of its own individual essence and this [the memoirs, F.S.] could be important. That I cannot publish my writings in the language of my people is not my fault but that of the conditions in which I find myself.[68]

The degree of Makhno's Ukrainianism even led Volin, the anarchist who edited the last two posthumous volumes, to attempt to tone down what he saw as ideological failings. Volin's commentary appended to the second volume asserted that "along with a fanatical faith in the peasantry (namely, in the *Ukrainian* peasantry) there existed in him [Makhno] a guarded, untrusting, suspicious relation to everything non-peasant (and *non-Ukrainian*)."[69]

---

[67] Makhno I, p. 185.

[68] Makhno I, p. 6.

[69] Makhno II, p. 159. Volin's discussion is devoted to two major attacks by Makhno on other anarchist movements. The first is Makhno's attack on urban anarchists for their ineffectiveness and their failure to give assistance to rural anarchists. Volin asserts that the urban anarchists were tremendously understaffed even for the needs of the cities. The second is Makhno's attack on the anarchists of Russia and their ineffectiveness compared to those of the Ukraine. Volin explains this in terms of the very different conditions existing in the Ukraine and Russia during the 1917–1921 period. He stresses the speed with which Bolsheviks assumed control in Russia and the degree to which the peasant disturbances against the Hetmanate created a favorable climate for anarchists in the Ukraine. Makhno's attacks were largely prompted by his resentment of what he saw as the halfhearted and tardy support of anarchists from the cities and from Russia for his movement. Of course, in the Ukraine, where the concepts "Ukrainian" and "peasant" were almost coterminous, Makhno's prorural disposition implied a pro-Ukrainian stance. That Makhno's

There are numerous factors that may have led Makhno toward interest in the national question and national consciousness. The manifest rebirth of the Ukrainian nation, the influence of his wife, the growing acceptance of the Ukraine as an entity in the 1917–1921 period, the bitterness of the struggle against the Russian Bolsheviks and the Russian Whites, all may have been contributing factors. However, the fact that he threw in his lot with the Russian anarchists of Paris illustrated that in emigration he was far from being a nationalist or anti-Russian.

The real explanation of Makhno's Ukrainianism lies in an article he published in 1926 in the anarchist newspaper, *Delo truda,* entitled "A Few Words on the National Question in the Ukraine."[70] Makhno emphasized the great changes that the Ukrainian masses had undergone during the years of Soviet rule. He maintained that the Bolsheviks and their Moscow-based power had betrayed the Ukrainian laborer and had thus given him a great distrust of the *prishlie* (the outsiders, newcomers, or foreigners). Makhno asserted that, although during the Revolution the Ukrainian laborers had not sympathized with or followed those who put forth the ideas of Ukrainian "self-determination," they later came to view this concept favorably. Accordingly, Makhno advised his anarchist brethren:

> The working masses sympathize with the idea of self-determination. At times they even affirm it in their life style. Thus, for example, they uphold their language and their culture, which in pre-revolutionary times were in the position of step-children. They keep up their life style, their customs, accommodating them to the achievements of their new life. The gentlemen state-builders have nothing against using . . . all these natural manifestations of Ukrainian reality, against which the Bolsheviks would be powerless to struggle, even if they wished . . . for their goal of the creation of an independent Ukrainian state.[71]

He saw the Soviet Ukrainianization policy of the 1920's as an attempt by the Bolsheviks to reverse their original error and to harness Ukrainian nationalism in their service. Thus, Makhno

---

memoirs go beyond this is testified to by Volin's emphasis on Makhno's "fanatic belief" in a "Ukrainian" peasantry. For examples of Makhno's disparagement of the Russian Revolution in comparison to the Ukrainian, see Makhno II, pp. 39, 142, 150.

[70] Nestor Makhno, "Neskolko slov o natsionalnom voprose na Ukraine," *Delo truda* (Paris), No. 19, December, 1926, pp. 4–7.

[71] *Ibid.,* p. 5.

asserted that even the anarchists' bitter enemy, the Bolsheviks, had to come to terms with a renascent Ukraine.

Makhno also warned anarchists that they must adjust to the new situation in the Ukraine in order to convince the laborers that not only foreign government but all governments were the source of oppression. Drawing upon the lessons of the past, he recalled that during the period of his activity:

> There was no time to scrutinize, and there was never any examination of all the "aliens" in our ranks. Faith in the Revolution took precedence over any discussion of who those "aliens" might be, and whether they were not our enemies.[72]

Makhno stressed that "much has changed in the psychology of the Ukrainian laborer," and because of the great attraction that Ukrainian self-determination had for the masses, he suggested that the anarchists' major task was to explain that an independent Ukrainian government would be as oppressive as alien rule. In order to fulfill this task, he warned anarchists that they must take into account the following:

> The Ukraine speaks Ukrainian, and because of this nationalism at times it does not listen to strangers who do not speak Ukrainian. One ought to consider this practically. If until this time anarchists have exerted a weak ideological influence on the Ukrainian village, it is because they cluster in the cities and do not take into consideration the national language of the Ukrainian village.[73]

In order to rectify this failing, he called for the formation of a Ukrainian anarchist organization to prepare to work under these conditions.

Makhno thus proposed Ukrainianization of the anarchist movement. The importance of this stand is obvious in view of the hostility and the lack of attention given by anarchism to the problems of nationality. Not even in the 1917–1921 period did the very active anarchist movements in the Ukraine begin to "Ukrainianize." The *Nabat* group chose the Ukraine as its field of action not because it had strong local roots, but simply because it saw greater potential for real revolution there.[74] Anarchist newspapers, mani-

---

[72] *Ibid.*, p. 5.

[73] *Ibid.*, p. 7.

[74] When the *Nabat* group met in Kursk in November 1918, it proclaimed that it would concentrate its work in the Ukraine, because there

festoes, and pamphlets were predominantly in the Russian language and at times reflected pre-Revolutionary Russian views toward the existence of a Ukrainian nation.[75] When Bolshevik victory forced most anarchists to leave the Ukraine, they emigrated essentially as *Russian* anarchists. Thus, the emigré anarchist movement of the 1920's was no better equipped to operate in a Ukrainian environment than was the anarchist movement of 1905. But now, as Makhno pointed out, the Ukraine was a definite entity and nationalism was a vital issue.

Those Russian anarchists who noticed the change in the Ukrainian mentality were hardly prepared to understand or analyze it.[76]

---

was a chance for a new "October" that might not fall under Bolshevik control. Ierde, p. 50.

[75] The resolutions of the conference of *Nabat* in Elisavethrad show no evidence that the group was taking into account the non-Russian composition of the area. *Rezoliutsii pervogo sezda Konfederatsii anarkhistskikh organizatsii Ukrainy "Nabat"* (Buenos Aires, 1923). As late as July 21, 1919, a conference of Kievan anarchists made a proclamation to the "Russian peasant and worker." "Vozzvanie kievskikh anarkhistov," *Nabat*, No. 25, July 21, 1919, pp. 1–2. A study of the issues of *Odesskii Nabat, Nabat* and *Kharkovskii Nabat* during the 1919–1920 period shows almost no awareness of the Ukrainian revival. Though the *Kharkovskii Nabat* carried frequent notices of the formation of a specifically Latvian language group of anarchists, no analogous Ukrainian group appears to have existed. A Ukrainian language journal was planned for village consumption, though it appears never to have been published. P. Rudenko, *Na Ukraine (povstanchestvo i anarkhicheskoe dvizhenie)* (Argentina: Izd. Rabochei gruppy v Resp. Argentine, 1922), p. 25.

[76] Emma Goldman and Alexander Berkman, American anarchists who remained Makhno supporters even after the Russian anarchist movement turned against him, sensed this change and mentioned it in the accounts of their travels in Soviet Russia and Ukraine in 1920. "In Soviet institutions, as among the people at large, an intensely nationalistic, even chauvinistic spirit is felt. To the natives, the Ukraine is the only true and real Russia; its culture, language, and customs are superior to those of the North. They dislike the 'Russian' and resent the domination of Moscow. The imported officials, unfamiliar with the conditions and psychology of the country, often even ignorant of its language, apply Moscow views to the population with the result of alienating even the more friendly disposed elements." Alexander Berkman, *The Bolshevik Myth* (London: Hutchinson and Co., 1925), p. 163. See also Emma Goldman, *My Disillusionment with Russia* (Garden City, N.Y.: Doubleday, Page and Co., 1923), pp. 211–241.

Their concern for the world or, at least, the all-Russian revolutionary movement evoked little interest in the Ukrainian question. Even Volin and Arshinov, who begin their works with almost romantic descriptions of the Ukrainian people, in practice recount the history of the *Makhnivshchyna* as a Russian movement.[77] Makhno, no matter how Russified he was, had strong attachment to his native Ukrainian countryside, and consequently took notice of the changes.

Even though the continuance of Bolshevik rule meant that anarchism was never put to the test in the Ukraine, Makhno's fear that the movement was too "Russian" for the new situation seems correct. His appeal seems to have had no effect, and there is certainly no indication that he formed a group of Ukrainian anarchists.[78] There is some evidence of Ukrainian anarchist activity in the Americas, but it was not the result of Makhno's activities. A few anarchist publications in the United States showed a distinct

---

[77] Volin begins his discourse on the *Makhnivshchyna* in terms that might well have served as an introduction for a nationalist publication: "Relatively cultivated and refined, individualistic and capable of taking the initiative without flinching, jealous of his independence, warlike by tradition, ready to defend himself and accustomed for centuries to feel free and his own master, the Ukrainian was in general never subjugated to that total slavery—not only of the body but also of the spirit—which characterized the population of the rest of Russia." Volin, *The Unknown*, p. 76. Arshinov, p. 41, in discussing the reasons why events in the Ukraine and Russia had taken such different courses, wrote that "A second still more important side in the life of the Ukrainian peasantry and workers (the local, not the alien—the *prishlie*) were the traditions of free life retained from bygone times." Despite these introductions, both authors actually proceed to describe the *Makhnivshchyna* as part of the Russian revolution and Russian anarchism. Arshinov states that: "The *Makhnivshchyna* is a revolutionary movement of the masses, prepared for by the historical conditions of life of the poorest strata of the Russian peasantry." Arshinov, p. 214. See also pp. 24, 33.

[78] One indication of this failure was Makhno's promise that he would republish his memoirs in Ukrainian as soon as a translator could be found, thus indicating the scarcity of culturally Ukrainian anarchists. The memoirs were never published in Ukrainian. Nestor Makhno, "K russko-ukrainskoi rabochei kolonii v Sev. Amerike i Kanade," *Delo truda* (Paris) No. 29, October, 1927, p. 20. The only translation of Makhno's writings into Ukrainian was his "Zapysky," a short commentary on the movement, in *Volia Ukrainy* (Newark, N.J.), No. 2, 1923, pp. 2–3.

Ukrainian consciousness[79] and engaged in the formidable task of trying to win over the largely Galician Ukrainian workers from the nationalist camp.[80]

Makhno's memoirs must be understood in terms of his new perception of the Ukrainian problem. The long passages recounting ideological sparring with Ukrainian nationalists were an attempt to convince the "Ukrainian laborers" that the nationalist philosophy was still bankrupt. The apology for the Russian text of the memoirs is understandable in view of his recognition that to influence the Ukraine the Ukrainian language was indispensable.[81] Perhaps to make his own former indifference to Ukrainian language and culture more palatable, he recounted the following incident. Returning from Russia to the Hetman-ruled Ukraine, he was rebuffed by a railwayman whom he had addressed in Russian, and he was forced to speak in Ukrainian.

> I was struck by this demand, but it couldn't be helped, and I, not having proper command of my native language, Ukrainian, was forced

---

[79] See *Vilna hromada* (New York, 1922) and *Volia Ukrainy* (Newark, N.J., 1923). While these groups were not founded by Makhno, they had great respect for the *Batko*. On October 20, 1923, Arshinov wrote to *Volia Ukrainy* requesting financial support for the defense of Makhno, who was being tried in Poland for supposedly fomenting disturbances among Ukrainians in Eastern Galicia. *Volia Ukrainy* (Newark), No. 2, 1923. For an example of their adulation of Makhno, see "Buv chas borotby i na nashom grunti," *Volia Ukrainy* (Newark), No. 2, 1923.

[80] Just how formidable this task was is obvious from reading the article by A. S. "Makhnivshchyna," pp. 105–109. "It appears that, under anarchism, there will be communes of nations: Polish, Ukrainian, Muscovite, that create one great union (association) of nations. But are we Ukrainians sure that the Muscovite commune will give up Ukrainian wheat from the rich fields of the Dnieper-Ukraine, or the Polish commune, Galician oil? No, we are not sure. Imperialism (the tendency to exploit other nations) has been formed in Poles and Muscovites for centuries, this spirit of rule is passed at birth from father to son." (p. 108).

[81] Makhno's recognition that knowledge of the Ukrainian language was necessary for any future anarchist work in the Ukraine is confirmed by Mrs. Ida Mett. She writes in a letter of January 7, 1971: "Je me souviens qu'un jour il m'a dit que s'il retourne en Ukraine un jour, il faudrait sans doute apprendre la langue ukrainienne tout simplement comme nécessité." Mrs. Mett's commentary lends support to the possibility that perception of new realities, and not an active self-identification as a Ukrainian, was the cause of Makhno's Ukrainianism in his memoirs.

to disfigure it . . . I put a question to myself—in whose name is this demanded of me . . . such a butchering of a language when I don't know it. I understood that this demand did not originate with the Ukrainian working people.

I was convinced that for such Ukrainians [the Hetman supporters] only their Ukrainian language is necessary, and not the full freedom of the Ukraine and of its working people.[82]

Makhno was thus interested in presenting himself and the anarchists as the only true purveyors of freedom for the Ukraine. The nationalists were not the only group he took to task on the Ukrainian issue. He was also intent on exposing what he saw as the hypocrisy of Bolshevik Ukrainianization policy. This is evident from his own account of the famous encounter with Lenin. Makhno claimed to have said to Lenin: "Anarcho-communists in the Ukraine (or, since you Communist-Bolsheviks attempt to shun the word Ukraine and call her 'the South of Russia')—anarcho-communists in this 'South of Russia' . . ." Later, when Lenin informed Makhno of the border between Ukraine and Russia (post-Brest-Litovsk) Makhno gibed: ". . . and you still consider the Ukraine 'the South of Russia'?" Lenin answered ". . . to consider is one thing, comrade, to see in life another."[83] Makhno uses this technique of emphasizing his own acceptance of the Ukraine, as opposed to the Russian chauvinist attitude of his enemies, in recounting conversations with Iakov Sverdlov. Sverdlov: "So you, comrade, are from the South of Russia." Makhno: "Yes, I'm from the Ukraine."[84] In view of Makhno's contention that the Bolsheviks had embarked on the Ukrainianization policy of the late 1920's as an attempt to conteract their initial mistakes, the memoirs should be seen as an effort to make the public aware of what he saw as the hypocrisy of Bolshevik attitudes toward the Ukraine.

Not only ideological enemies came in for attack on the Ukrainian issue; Makhno also settled scores with his anarchist enemy, Alexander Shapiro. Shapiro charged Makhno with anti-Semitism in numerous articles in the émigré anarchist press.[85] Thus, Makhno's

---

[82] Makhno II, pp. 153–154.

[83] Makhno II, pp. 134–135.

[84] Makhno II, pp. 121.

[85] For a discussion of Shapiro's attacks on Makhno for anti-Semitism, see "Dlia chego sushchestvuet anarkhicheskaia pressa," *Probuzhdenie* (Detroit), No. 14, November, 1930, p. 62.

description of a conversation about the Ukraine to which he adds the comment " (according to Shapiro, the South of Russia)," is in fact a counterattack charging his anarchist enemy with anti-Ukrainian Great Russian chauvinism.[86]

The vehemence with which Makhno criticized his enemies for anti-Ukrainianism merely emphasizes the development of his own Ukrainian national consciousness. The direction of Makhno's thinking is in fact a testimony to the triumph of the Ukrainian national revival in the years after the Revolution. For large segments of the Ukrainian population, the 1917 period and the revolt against the Hetman were crucial for the formation of a Ukrainian national consciousness. For Makhno, however, the crucial stage appears to have been the final imposition of Soviet rule. All the evidence supports the assertion that Makhno and the *Makhnivsti* carried on their struggle in an area where the Ukrainian issue was not of major importance. However, even in this area the influence of the Ukrainian revival was felt. In order to communicate on a large scale with the Ukrainian peasantry, the Makhno movement required Ukrainian-speaking cultural workers. Above all, the presence of a nationally conscious Ukrainian, Makhno's wife, introduced a limited Ukrainianization. The emergence of a nationally conscious Ukrainian nation in the 1920's, which prompted the Communist Party to introduce Ukrainianization, was the final decisive influence on Makhno's thinking. While he never became a nationalist, he did to a degree become a Ukrainian anarchist.

The evolution of Makhno's thought on the nationality issue was particularly complex because of his involvement in the "Russian" anarchist movement. The dilemma of the Ukrainian radical in the pre-Revolutionary period was to integrate Ukrainian national aspirations, which often seemed provincial and minor to the revolutionary youth, with the more important "All-Russian" or universal problems. The sons and daughters of the Ukrainian intelligentsia faced this problem early in their development. But, Makhno, who emerged from the nationally amorphous mass of peasantry, initially paid little attention to the implications of the Ukrainian revival in the Russian Empire. This was especially true

---

[86] Makhno II, p. 100. He also uses this tactic in describing a conversation with the anarchist Lev Chernyi. He reports that they discussed the anarchist movement in the Ukraine, "which he never recognized and called the 'South of Russia'." Makhno II, p. 96.

because the anarchists, the group with which he identified, were antagonistic to nationalism and isolated from those segments of the population most influenced by the rise in national consciousness. Like many of his contemporaries during the Revolution, Makhno viewed "Ukrainian" as more a political than a national designation. By the 1920's, however, "Ukrainians" had emerged as a full-fledged nation, and one that could contain all shades of political thought—from legitimate monarchist to communist. "Ukrainianism" was no longer identified with agrarian populists. Consequently, the Ukrainian nation could even contain an anarchist element. Just as there were French, Spanish, and Russian anarchists, who were by no means nationalists, there could also be Ukrainian anarchists. Makhno's thinking and writings reflected this emergence of a modern Ukrainian nation.

CHAPTER TWELVE

The Germans and the Union for the Liberation of the Ukraine, 1914–1917

Oleh S. Fedyshyn

AMONG THE FOREIGN powers that were active in Eastern Europe during the First World War and in Russia during the Civil War, none can rival Imperial Germany and the decisive role it played in influencing the destinies of this area. This was especially true of the years 1917–1918, the period during which Germany attained an overwhelming political, military, and diplomatic superiority in this part of the world. Few areas of the east came to be as deeply affected by the German factor as was the Ukraine. Since the conclusion of a separate peace treaty between the Ukraine and the Central Powers, which took place at Brest-Litovsk on February 9, 1918, and the subsequent occupation of the Ukraine by the German and Austrian forces have been treated in depth elsewhere,[1] this essay shall deal primarily with the period from the outbreak of the First World War to the disintegration of Russia, the development that more than anything else made the German advance in the east possible.

The accusation that the German *Drang nach Osten* and the Ukrainian national movement were in some kind of alliance, or even that Ukrainian separation was simply an Austro-German intrigue, came to be voiced with increasing frequency in Russian circles in the period following the Crimean War of 1854–1856. Such claims had no basis in fact and must be dismissed as the fore-

---

[1] Oleh S. Fedyshyn, *Germany's Drive to the East and the Ukrainian Revolution in World War I* (New Brunswick, N.J.: Rutgers University Press, 1970).

runners of similar inventions fabricated in the period immediately preceding and during the First World War. Nevertheless, the Ukrainian Rada's most reluctant and by no means predetermined decision to conclude a separate peace with the Central Powers gave further credence to accusations of Ukrainian Germanophilism. The Rada's opponents used this as evidence for the alleged weakness and artificiality of the Ukrainian national movement. It is seldom noted that this fateful and unpopular decision was made after weeks of desperate and completely futile attempts by the Rada to secure Allied assistance. Also, this step was taken in the face of imminent defeat at the hands of the Red Guards, which would have resulted in the incorporation of the Ukraine into Soviet Russia. While saving the Rada from complete collapse, the German intrusion into Ukrainian affairs further increased the antagonism between the Ukrainians and the Russians, deepened the split among Ukrainian social classes and political groups, and strengthened Allied suspicion and resentment toward the Ukrainians. This last factor was to have a crucial effect on the course of the Ukrainian Revolution, in particular after the withdrawal of the Central Powers' forces in late 1918.

Among the latter, only Austria-Hungary had a long-standing direct interest in the Ukrainian problem. This was due largely to the fact that the Ukrainians, then known in the Dual Monarchy as Ruthenians, constituted a majority in eastern Galicia, northern Bukovina, and Carpatho-Ruthenia. Because of Polish, Rumanian, and Hungarian pressures on the Ukrainian elements in these areas, some groups developed a pro-Russian orientation. It is not surprising, therefore, that in the course of the nineteenth century these areas came to be viewed by Russian Pan-Slavists as irredentist territories, and with the outbreak of the First World War they became the object of Russia's official war aims. Because of the considerably freer political conditions in the Habsburg Empire, eastern Galicia became the "Piedmont" of the Ukrainian national movement, and Vienna was soon regarded as the center of anti-Russian activities abroad as well as the real power behind various Ukrainian groups and organizations that aimed at establishing national autonomy or even complete independence for this, the second largest Slavic people. At the time, there were about thirty million Ukrainians in the Russian Empire and some five to six million in Austria-Hungary.

Generally speaking, Vienna studiously refrained from exploiting these anti-Russian forces[2] and was as a rule more sympathetic to Polish than to Ukrainian political aspirations in Galicia. It must be noted that in the Russian Ukraine, where the Ukrainian national awakening had its origin, no Ukrainian publications whatsoever were permitted; Ukrainian educational, cultural, and academic institutions, not to mention political organizations, were completely suppressed. On the other hand, in Lviv, the cultural center for Ukrainians in eastern Galicia, the renowned historian and later leading revolutionary, Mykhailo Hrushevskyi, was permitted by the Austrian authorities to offer courses in Ukrainian history. Furthermore, Galicia was where virtually all Ukrainian publications were produced (many of which were smuggled into Russia), where Ukrainians were able to establish an academy of arts and sciences, the Shevchenko Scientific Society, and where scores of Ukrainian scholars and political leaders from Russia were permitted to carry on their activities without any hindrance from the Austrian authorities.

The Austrians were thus well informed about the Ukrainian question and showed some sympathy for the movement, but because of the strong opposition of the Poles and Magyars—the two most influential national groups in the Habsburg Monarchy who had a claim to the Ukrainian-populated provinces of eastern Galicia and Carpatho-Ruthenia, respectively—Vienna proved both unable and unwilling to exploit the Ukrainian factor in its military and political offensive after the outbreak of the First World War.[3]

In the pre-war period the Germans had even less interest in or sympathy for the Ukrainian national movement. True, as early as the reign of Catherine the Great (the second half of the eighteenth century), thousands of German settlers, who later came to be known as the colonists, emigrated to Russia, and some of them settled down on the fertile plains of the Ukraine. It was also around this time that Johann Gottfried von Herder, the well-known German philosopher and ethnographer, who was impressed with the wealth of Ukrainian folklore, prophesied: "The Slavs had been the stepchildren of history, but this would change in the course of time, and the

---

[2] Helga Grebing, "Österreich-Ungarn und die 'Ukrainische Aktion'," *Jahrbücher für Geschichte Osteuropas*, VIII (Breslau, 1959), p. 272.

[3] Fedyshyn, chapters I–III.

Ukraine might become one day a new Hellas."[4] Moreover, in 1791, toward the end of Catherine's rule in Russia, the Ukrainian autonomists sent one of their leaders, Vasyl Kapnist, to Prussia on a secret mission.[5] But these were isolated instances of German interest, and it was not until the second half of the nineteenth century that a number of German writers began to show a more serious interest in the Ukrainian national movement with definite political implications, some of them going so far as to advocate the breakup of the Russian Empire and the formation of a separate Ukrainian state.[6] The pro-German orientation on the part of some political exiles from the Russian Ukraine, who were especially active in eastern Galicia, was not developed until shortly before the outbreak of the First World War.

Incidentally, neither Chancellor Bismarck nor his successors ever showed much interest in a plan aimed at dismembering Russia. He not only refused to consider such bold schemes but even went along with the tsarist russification policy in the Baltic provinces, which had strong and well-organized German communities.[7]

German settlers in the Ukraine, numbering about 600,000, and Germany's investments in Russia, totaling 441.5 million rubles and constituting 19.7 percent of the country's foreign capital, had no influence on the Ukrainian national movement in the period before the First World War.[8] Nor is there any evidence, despite Soviet as-

[4] Cited in Walter Laqueur, *Russia and Germany* (London: Weidenfeld & Nicolson, 1965), p. 19.

[5] Ivan L. Rudnytsky, "The Intellectual Origins of Modern Ukraine," *The Annals of the Ukrainian Academy of Arts and Sciences in the U.S.A.*, VI (New York, 1958), pp. 1381–1405. This article, incidentally, is one of the best short studies on the subject.

[6] Good examples of such writings are the memoranda of Kurt von Schlötzer, who served as the Second Secretary of the Prussian Embassy in St. Petersburg in the 1860's, published under the title "Politische Berichte aus Petersburg," *Preussische Jahrbücher*, CCXIX (Berlin, 1930), pp. 1–27, and Eduard von Hartmann's "Russland und Europa," *Gegenwart*, Nos. 1–3 (Berlin, 1888).

[7] Otto Fürst von Bismarck, *Gedanken und Erinnerungen*, Vol. I (New York-Stuttgart: Cotta Vlg., 1898), pp. 104–107; Gustav A. Rein, *Die Revolution in der Politik Bismarcks* (Göttingen-Berlin-Frankfurt: Musterschmidt Vlg., 1957), chapter V; Martin Göhring, *Bismarcks Erben, 1890–1945* (Wiesbaden: F. Steiner Vlg., 1959), chapter I.

[8] For further details and the sources on which these data are based, see Fedyshyn, chapter I.

sertions, that these factors had anything to do with the development of the Reich's policies in this part of the world. Soviet historians are still committed to the thesis that from the mid-nineteenth century Germany worked actively for the dismemberment of Russia and the creation of an independent Ukraine.[9]

Unlike Austria-Hungary, which because of its large Ukrainian population had a direct interest in the national movement, Germany had on the eve of the First World War no vital stake in the further development of this question. It is not surprising, therefore, that at this point only Germany's eastern experts possessed some familiarity with the still weak Ukrainian national movement. Germany's official circles and general public became aware of the problem only after the opening of hostilities.

At the beginning of the war, German *Ostpolitik* contained no definite plans for the Ukraine. Most of the articles, pamphlets, and monographs about Russia's nationality problem that were published during the war viewed the Ukraine as a pivotal area in the east as well as the region where Russia was vulnerable. Such views were not so much a reflection of the Reich's official war aims as they were a testimony to the aggressiveness and anti-Russian feeling among the country's eastern experts and political commentators, many of whom were Baltic Germans. This literature did help to familiarize the general public in Germany, Austria, and other European countries with the eastern problem; moreover, the works of well-known and respected writers like Dr. Paul Rohrbach and Professor Theodor Schiemann also served as a source of encouragement to the Ukrainians orienting themselves toward the Central Powers. But these writings had virtually no influence on the Reich's official policy makers. True, Schiemann was on friendly terms with the Kaiser, who often sought his advice; the latter, however, did not have as much say in the formulation and implementation of the Reich's policies as his position and public pronouncements would lead one to believe. Rohrbach's role in the development of German *Ostpolitik* during the war period was even more limited.[10]

---

[9] One of the best-known proponents of the thesis, which has never been substantiated by any reliable sources, is A. S. Erusalimskii, *Vneshniaia politika i diplomatika germanskogo imperializma v kontse XIX veka* (Moscow: Izd. Akademii Nauk SSSR, 1951).

[10] Klaus Meyer, *Schiemann als politischer Publizist* (Frankfurt-am-Main: Welt und Geschichtsbild, 1956); Paul Rohrbach, *Um des Teufels Hand-*

In spite of all this agitation and the seemingly uncontrolled anti-Russian hysteria in wartime Germany, the Russian school, led by Otto Hoetzsch, a well-known professor of Russian history and a Reichstag deputy, continued to enjoy a surprising amount of covert sympathy and support among the military and civilian bureaucracy. While the group organized around Professor Hoetzsch published less and was often overwhelmed by opponents from the *Osteuropa*, *Mitteleuropa* and Pan-German schools, they nonetheless did exert more influence on official circles than one would expect. Of course, Hoetzsch's Russian school suffered a complete defeat with the conclusion of the Ukrainian and Russian treaties of Brest-Litovsk in February and March of 1918, but even during this brief eclipse his orientation continued to enjoy the support of such influential Reichstag leaders as Stresemann and Rathenau, as well as of numerous high-ranking governmental bureaucrats and military officers both in Berlin and in the east. Despite the continued German presence in the Ukraine and other eastern territories, the Russian political orientation in Germany regained an even higher degree of influence in the summer of 1918 than in 1915–1916—a time when Russo-German reconciliation was viewed as a viable possibility, and when Berlin, instead of talking about a free Ukraine, supported Vienna's plan for the establishment of a Polish state oriented toward the Central Powers. Continuing this earlier tradition, the Germans sought to establish better working relations with the Bolsheviks in Petrograd, and they also made overtures to the Russian Right in the Ukraine, the Don, and other areas of the south.

Considering the traditional and deeply rooted pro-Russian orientation of the Reich's official circles and Austria's long-standing concern with the Ukrainian question, it is not at all surprising that with the outbreak of the First World War it was Vienna rather than Berlin that sought to exploit the Ukrainian movement. With this in mind, the Austro-Hungarian authorities permitted the organization of the Union for the Liberation of the Ukraine—*Soiuz Vyzvolennia Ukrainy*. It was established in Lviv (officially Lemberg, the capital of Galicia) on August 4, 1914, by a small group of Ukrainian political émigrés from Russia with the support of Galician Ukrainian leaders. This constituted a drastic departure from Vienna's

---

schrift (Hamburg: Hans Dulk, 1953). For additional sources on these two German writers see also Fedyshyn, chapter II.

traditional policy of cooperating with Russia against various revolutionary and subversive elements and organizations.[11]

  The founders of the Union were self-styled non-partisan political exiles from the Russian Ukraine—Oleksander Skoropys-Ioltukhovskyi, Mariian Melenevskyi (Basok), Andrii Zhuk, Volodymyr Doroshenko, Dmytro Dontsov, and Mykola Zalizniak.[12] Dontsov and Zalizinak left the organization several weeks after it was founded, but the latter continued to cooperate with the Austrians independently and served as liaison during the Brest-Litovsk negotiations.[13] While political leaders from both Russia and Galicia limited themselves at the outbreak of the war to modest autonomist demands, the Union openly committed itself to the restoration of an independent and socialist Ukrainian state.[14] Initially, the Union was oriented toward Vienna rather than Berlin. This was quite natural, since the organization came into existence on Austrian soil and expected that the Habsburg armies would soon move victoriously into the Ukraine. The Union's programs were financed jointly by Vienna and Berlin, although neither Austria-Hungary nor Germany would commit itself publicly or privately to a plan calling for the restoration of an independent Ukraine. In spite of grandiose schemes, ranging from a manifesto to the Ukrainian people—to be issued in the name of the two Kaisers—to a planned commando raid by a volunteer Ukrainian force in the Kuban, the Union's programs during the first several months of the war were limited largely to propaganda and publication activities on the territory of the Cen-

---

[11] Grebing, p. 272; Volfdieter Bihl, "Osterreich-Ungarn und der 'Bund zur Befreiung der Ukraina'," in *Osterreich und Europa: Festgabe für Hugo Hantsch zum 70. Geburtstag* (Graz-Vienna-Köln: Verlag Styria, 1965), pp. 505–518; and an earlier account by one of the principal leaders of the Union for the Liberation of the Ukraine, Oleksander Skoropys-Ioltukhovskyi, "Moi 'zlochyny'," *Khliborobska Ukraina*, Vol. II (1920–1921), pp. 201–205.

[12] *Ibid.;* and the Austrian Foreign Office documents pertaining to the Ukraine: Theophil Hornykiewicz (ed.), *Ereignisse in der Ukraine, 1914–1922* (Horn, Austria: Verlag F. Berger for the W. K. Lypynsky East European Research Institute, Philadelphia, 1966), Vols. I and II.

[13] Hornykiewicz, Vol. I; and Ivan Kedryn-Rudnytskyi (ed.), *Beresteiskyi myr* (L'viv-Kiev: Chervona kalyna, 1928).

[14] This line was presented in virtually all of the Union's publications. Its official organs were *Die ukrainischen Nachrichten* and *Vistnyk Soiuza Vyzvolennia Ukrainy*.

tral Powers and other neutral countries, including the United States.[15]

Financial assistance furnished to the Union for the Liberation of the Ukraine was not very impressive. The amount received from Vienna during the first five months of the Union's existence was a mere 227,944 crowns;[16] and this was the period of closest cooperation between the Union and Vienna, a time when Austria hoped to accomplish specific military and political objectives in the east with Ukrainian assistance. A considerable portion of the money was spent on the purchase of office furniture and equipment, development of a library and research facilities, and other basic necessities for the launching of the Union project. The activities of the Union were supported cautiously by Vienna as a strictly wartime measure designed to weaken or even, it was hoped, to bring about the collapse of the Russian war effort. To sponsor openly a movement aiming at the dismemberment of Russia would have been too risky, for such action could have endangered the system on which the Habsburg Monarchy itself was founded.[17] Still, in the initial months of the war, Vienna was quite serious about its Ukrainian undertaking and such high-ranking Austrian officials as Count Alexander Hoyos, Permanent Secretary of the Foreign Office, were associated with it.

As for the Germans, they too began to explore the possibility of exploiting national movements among Poles, Ukrainians, Jews, and other ethnic groups in Russia for the benefit of their military effort. However, the Kaiser rather than the German Foreign Office took the initiative in this matter. On his suggestion, Count Bogdan Franz Servatius von Hutten-Czapski, a Prussian nobleman and a Polish patriot, was appointed to the Supreme Headquarters as its "eastern expert," but, as it turned out, this individual was more interested in the restoration of "historical Poland" (including Lithuania, Belorussia, and large portions of the Ukraine) than in pro-

---

[15] For a full discussion of the Union's activities during the early months of the war, see Fedyshyn, chapter II.

[16] Skoropys-Ioltukhovskyi, "Moi 'zlochyny' "; also O. Skoropys-Ioltukhovskyi and A. Zhuk to Consul E. Urbas, "Report on the Union's Finances," Vienna, December 16, 1914, Hornykiewicz, Vol. I, pp. 170–171.

[17] See, for example, the correspondence of Count Ottokar Czernin von und zu Chudenitz (Vienna) to Prince Chlodwig von Hohenlohe (Berlin), August 27, 1914, cited in Hans J. Beyer, *Die Mittelmächte und die Ukraine* (Munich: Isar Vlg., 1956), pp. 3–4.

voking revolution among the oppressed peoples of Russia. Consequently, these early efforts proved quite insignificant.[18]

It was not until the spring of 1915, following the transfer of its headquarters from Vienna to Berlin, that Germany began to show greater interest in the activities of the Union for the Liberation of the Ukraine. This move was paved by Hutten-Czapski's resignation in September 1914, but it was above all the result of Vienna's disillusionment with the Ukrainian movement and its decision, taken as early as December 1914, to abandon the plan of revolutionizing the Ukraine.

The Union's break with Vienna did not mean the termination of its activities on Austro-Hungarian soil, since Vienna's financial assistance did continue, albeit in the considerably reduced form of 16,000 crowns per month.[19] Nor did Berlin's takeover result in any real change in the Reich's official stand *vis-à-vis* the Ukrainian movement. To be sure, Union leaders were privately given the assurance of continued German support for their efforts. This was done, for example, by the Under-Secretary of State, Arthur Zimmermann, at a special meeting on November 3, 1915, with the Head of the Central Bureau of the Union in Berlin, Oleksander Skoropys-Ioltukhovskyi.[20] The Union's activities, in the meantime, were financed and supervised by a special "non-governmental agency"—the Intermediary Agency of Frankfurt on the Oder—headed by Friedrich von Schwerin, a high-ranking Prussian official and one of the Reich's most active annexationist advocates.[21] Officially, Berlin (and this was Bethmann Hollweg's deliberate policy) remained non-committal, retaining a completely free hand in the east, especially with respect to the Ukraine. Following the transfer of its main office to Berlin, the Union continued its propaganda activities on the eastern front by printing and distributing leaflets and other similar materials. These efforts, however, were never given much emphasis and their effectiveness was without doubt very limited.

---

[18] Bogdan F. S. von Hutten-Czapski, *Sechzig Jahre Politik und Gesellschaft*, 2 vols. (Berlin: E. S. Mittler, 1936).

[19] Hornykiewicz, Vol. I.

[20] Document No. A 31872-15, November 3, 1915, *German Foreign Office Archives* (National Archives Collection, Washington, D.C.), microfilm No. 21.

[21] Skoropys-Ioltukhovskyi, "Moi 'zlochyny' "; Fritz Fischer, *Griff nach der Weltmacht* (Düsseldorff: Droste Vlg., 1961), pp. 126, 187, 199, 346, 438.

Even less significant and successful were German attempts to enlist the Union's collaboration for special projects behind the front lines. The organization's leaders did not conceal their distaste for such activities. Consequently, the Union had virtually no contact with the Russian Ukraine. A reliable Union source mentions only one individual who made two trips from the Ukraine to Germany in the course of the war.[22] German secret files on this matter are very scarce. A careful search by this writer produced only a reference to German assistance in helping the Union to send several Ukrainian propagandists across the front line in 1916, and a plan (probably never carried out) to send propaganda and sabotage missions made up of Ukrainian volunteers behind the front lines in January 1917.[23]

The Union's successful information and publication activities abroad were of much greater significance. While concentrating primarily on the territory of the Central Powers, where such propaganda activities could be conducted more or less without restrictions, the Union maintained two very successful information centers in Switzerland throughout the war, as well as smaller offices or missions at different times in Rumania, Sweden, Norway, Italy, Great Britain, and the United States.[24] The Union also carried out cultural and educational work in Ukrainian areas occupied by German and Austrian troops during the 1915–1916 campaigns: western Volhynia, Pidliashshia (Podlasie), and especially Kholm (Chełm), which had a mixed Ukrainian and Polish population. Kholm was viewed as a historically Ukrainian territory and as a testing ground for the determination of German and Austrian aims toward the Ukraine as a whole. Berlin's attitude toward Ukrainians in these occupied areas was generally sympathetic. Vienna's position was considerably more complex. The Austrians encouraged cultural programs in Volhynia—where Ukrainian leaders were being confronted by local Russophiles—but at the same time maintained an unmistakably pro-Polish posi-

---

[22] Skoropys-Ioltukhovskyi, p. 218. He was Ievhen Helytsynskyi, a member of a Ukrainian socialist underground organization in Kiev.

[23] Skoropys-Ioltukhovskyi, "Moi 'zlochyny'," and an unnumbered memorandum of the German War Ministry, marked "very secret," dated Berlin, January 5, 1917, signed by General Emil Friedrich. *German Foreign Office Archives,* microfilm No. 109.

[24] For German and Austrian writings on the Ukraine during the First World War, see Dmytro Doroshenko, *Die Ukraine und das Reich* (Leipzig: Verlag S. Hirzel, 1942), chapters V and VI.

tion in Pidliashshia and Kholm.[25] Like the Ukrainians, the Poles also viewed developments in the Kholm area as an index of Berlin's and Vienna's future intentions, and the Austrians were careful not to do anything there that would offend them. The Kholm area, incidentally, remained a bone of contention between Ukrainians and Poles not only until the collapse of the Central Powers in late 1918 but for decades thereafter.

Among the Union's various activities, none was more important than its work among Ukrainian prisoners of war. This was the organization's favorite project and the field in which it achieved the greatest success. Already in the first months of the war, Union representatives were allowed to visit various prisoner of war camps in Austria-Hungary and Germany in order to determine the number of interned Ukrainians; they used this opportunity to improve the prisoners' lot. The number of prisoners, according to a Ukrainian source, was approximately 500,000, but many of them did not possess a sufficiently high degree of national consciousness to be interested in the Union and its programs. An official German source put the number of prisoners at 300,000 as of August 1918.[26] Given the vagueness of the term "Ukrainian," and the fact that in the spring of 1918 two divisions were formed out of these Ukrainian prisoners and dispatched to the east, the two sources are not too far apart. Whatever their exact number, it was the second largest national group among prisoners captured by the Central Powers in the east, and the Union rightly viewed the work among them as its most important task.

It was not until the spring of 1915 that the Austrian authorities, following the Union's request, permitted the organization of two special camps for Ukrainian prisoners. The number in these two camps eventually reached 30,000. Later that year, three similar camps, with approximately 50,000 inmates, were established in Germany. This happened only after the Union succeeded in removing

[25] Dmytro Doroshenko, *Istoriia Ukrainy*, Vol. I (Uzhhorod: Svoboda, 1930), pp. 34, 39; and Beyer, pp. 14–15. One of the most reliable works on the Reich's policy in Poland during this period is Werner Conze's *Polnische Nation und deutsche Politik im Ersten Weltkrieg* (Köln-Graz: Böhlau Verlag, 1958).

[26] Zenon Stefaniv, *Ukrainski zbroini syly v 1917–1921 rr.* (Kolomyia: Vyd. 'Nasha Slava,' 1935), p. 49; German War Ministry to Foreign Office, Communication No. 697/18, Berlin, August 22, 1918, *German Foreign Office Archives*, microfilm No. 53.

a number of obstacles, the most important of them being opposition from the German Foreign Office.[27] (It is interesting to note that the Poles and Finns were separated from their Russian comrades virtually at the outbreak of the war, and soon thereafter the Germans permitted the organization of special camps for Russia's Georgians and Mohammedans.) The decision of Ukrainian and other non-Russian prisoners of war to join special "national" camps was a fateful one and could some day result in the most far-reaching consequences for them and their families. In the event of Russia's victory or a Russo-German separate peace, their return home would have been completely out of the question.

Initially, very few Ukrainians who were transferred to these camps were nationally conscious to the point of supporting the Union's separatist position. Nonetheless, they could be considered potential supporters of the Ukrainian national movement, and the Union leaders were confident that, given time, they could be won over, an expectation that proved fully justified. After all, no one was forced to move to these special camps, and those Ukrainian prisoners who disapproved of the Union's aims and programs simply remained in the general camps for Russian prisoners of war on the territory of the Central Powers.[28]

The period from the spring of 1915 through March 1917 was a rather difficult one for the Union for the Liberation of the Ukraine. By the end of 1914, Vienna had already lost interest in the Ukrainian movement, and the transfer of the Union's headquarters to Berlin did not really result in any dramatic improvement of its position nor did it affect in any significant way its programs. The painstaking and quiet educational work with Ukrainian prisoners of war and the continuation of propaganda activity among the Central Powers and neutral states were the Union's principal tasks during this rather uneventful and difficult period. The exciting days of festive appeals and proclamations and of bold schemes and great expectations—so characteristic of the first months of the war—gave way to prosaic drudgery and hopeless wartime routine. The future of Poland, as a part of the *Mitteleuropa* plan, occupied Berlin's and

---

[27] Skoropys-Ioltukhovskyi, pp. 115–117.

[28] The best source on the Union's educational work among the Ukrainian prisoners of war is Omelian Terletskyi, *Istoriia ukrainskoi hromady v Rashtati* (Kiev-Leipzig: Ukrainska nakladnia, 1919). He was personally involved in this program as a teacher.

Vienna's attention during 1915 and 1916 rather than revolutionizing the Ukraine.

Thus, on the eve of Russia's collapse in March 1917, neither Berlin nor Vienna had committed itself to the Ukrainian national movement. Both retained a completely free hand in the east and would certainly have abandoned the Union and the idea of independent Ukrainian statehood to conclude a separate peace treaty with any Russian government willing to come to terms.

The Russian Revolution was without doubt the most important event to occur during the First World War. Obviously, nothing affected the general situation in the east as profoundly as did the collapse of the Russian Empire. The Germans and the Austrians generally hailed it as a welcome and positive development that would bring the war to an end, at least on the eastern front, but few people thought that this would automatically bring about the revitalization of the earlier rather bold and far-reaching plans and programs, most of which had never been fully developed and seriously thought through. German official spokesmen, while hoping to see an early end to Russia's war effort, were certainly not prepared to speak in terms of permanently dismembering the Russian Empire. Even General Ludendorff found it advisable to observe rather cautiously that "the outbreak of the Russian Revolution was a factor upon which no general could dare to count with certainty."[29]

The developments in the Ukraine did little to encourage Berlin to resume its earlier attempts to revolutionize the non-Russian areas of the former tsarist empire. The establishment of the Ukrainian Rada in March 1917 was far from being a revolutionary step, nor did it reflect the separatist position of the Union for the Liberation of the Ukraine and other Ukrainian nationalist groups abroad. One of the first measures taken by this autonomous regional administrative body was to proclaim allegiance to the Provisional Government in Petrograd, which was firmly and openly committed to continue the war on the side of the Allies until a victorious end. Incidentally, the Ukrainians only asked at this point for "cultural autonomy for the Ukrainian people and its democratic intelligentsia."[30]

---

[29] Erich Ludendorff, *Ludendorff's Own Story*, Vol. II (New York & London: Harper, 1919), p. 14.

[30] Cited in S. M. Dimanshtein (ed.), *Revolutsiia i natsionalnyi vopros*, Vol. III (Moscow: Ogiz, 1930), p. 32. For a more complete discussion of the rise of the Rada, see John S. Reshetar, *The Ukrainian Revolution, 1917–*

Nor could the Germans find much encouragement in the fact that the Rada was headed by Professor Mykhailo Hrushevskyi, the noted Ukrainian historian who in the pre-war period held a chair in Ukrainian history in Lviv. Of course, he could not have retained this position without the approval of the Austrian authorities, but he did not feel that he owed any political debts to Vienna. Hrushevskyi went to Lviv to teach Ukrainian history simply because he could not have done this anywhere else. In order to dramatize his political independence and to refute once and for all the accusation that he was an Austrophile, Professor Hrushevskyi returned to Kiev at the outbreak of the war, only to be arrested immediately and deported by the Russian authorities as a dangerous political opponent of the regime. Before his deportation, he did have an opportunity to criticize publicly the Vienna-sponsored Union for the Liberation of the Ukraine. It is equally significant that, following his return from exile, Hrushevskyi again criticized the Union in May and September 1917 in his official capacity as head of the Rada. Hrushevskyi's negative attitude toward possible collaboration with the Central Powers, and the fact that the latter had no support within the Rada and no direct ties with any Ukrainian leaders, contributed further to Berlin's pessimistic view regarding the prospect of German-Ukrainian cooperation in the foreseeable future.[31]

Thus it is not surprising that Berlin and Vienna were slow in exploiting the enthusiasm with which the Union and the Ukrainian prisoners of war, already organized into national camps, greeted the collapse of the tsarist empire. The Germans permitted the formation of a Finnish volunteer battalion as early as 1915, and the Georgian Legion was organized in the course of 1916.[32] But it was not until late April 1917 that the Germans, following an earlier request by the Union, agreed to establish a special military training camp for the Ukrainian prisoner of war officers at Hannover-Münden. Two months later, in June 1917, Vienna reluctantly followed

---

1920 (Princeton, N.J.: Princeton University Press, 1952), chapter II. A more comprehensive but less critical work is Oleh S. Pidhainyi, *The Formation of the Ukrainian Republic* (Toronto-New York: The New Review Books, 1966), chapters I–IV.

[31] Doroshenko, *Istoriia Ukrainy*, Vol. II, pp. 11, 36; and Beyer, p. 27.

[32] Walther Hubatsch, *Germany and the Central Powers in the World War, 1914–1918* (Lawrence, Kansas: University of Kansas Publications, 1963), p. 106; and Fischer, p. 154.

the German example by establishing a similar Ukrainian officer training camp at Josephstadt, Austria.[33] The uncertain and ambivalent position of Berlin and Vienna on the delicate question of converting Ukrainian prisoners of war into military units is further dramatized by the fact that it was not until almost one year later, in the spring of 1918, that these troops were finally permitted to be returned to the Ukraine—only to be disarmed and disbanded by the Germans as a hostile and unreliable military force.[34]

There is no evidence whatsoever that the Germans had any part in the process of the "Ukrainianization" of Russia's southwestern front—i.e., the organization of separate Ukrainian formations in the months following the collapse of tsarist Russia. German military commanders and intelligence officers in the east studied these developments closely, but they did not seem to ascribe much importance to them.[35] On the whole, the Germans preferred to remain neutral in this process of differentiation and disintegration within the former Russian Empire, confining themselves to such innocuous measures as the publication of Ukrainian literature. In fact, Berlin made the publication of Ukrainian materials one of its most important projects during the period from March 1917 to the conclusion of the Ukrainian treaty in February 1918. A Galician-Jewish businessman, Jakob Orenstein, was given a contract to publish these materials. The project was launched with the publication of 50,000 copies of selected poems by the Ukraine's foremost poet and national prophet, Taras Shevchenko. As much as 250,000 marks was allotted, and this explained the increase in the Reich's financial assistance to the Union's work at this point.[36]

Still, the total amount of money provided by Berlin and Vienna to the Union in the course of 1917 was not that impressive—several hundred thousand marks from the Reich and sixty to seventy thousand crowns from the Dual Monarchy. In the meantime, millions were given to Parvus (Alexander Helphand) alone to provide Rus-

---

[33] Doroshenko, *Istoriia Ukrainy,* Vol. I, p. 35.

[34] *Ibid.,* Vol. I, pp. 38–39, 382, and Vol. II, pp. 33, 167. See also Mumm (German Ambassador in Kiev) to Foreign Office (Berlin), Telegram No. 296, April 13, 1918; *German Foreign Office Archives,* microfilm No. 36.

[35] *German Foreign Office Archives,* microfilm Nos. 2116–2128.

[36] The Chancellors Michaelis and Hertling, as well as several high-ranking German diplomats, were directly involved in this publication project. For further details, see Fedyshyn, chapter III.

sian socialists, both in Russia and abroad, with the necessary funds to carry on their work. The German secret files reveal that the Russian Bolsheviks were the principal beneficiaries of the Reich's financial assistance. The total amount allocated for subversive activities in Russia during the First World War range from Eduard Bernstein's estimate of fifty million marks to the figure of thirty million suggested by Zeman and Scharlau, on the basis of new evidence.[37] As for the Union, its usual monthly allowance, spent mainly on educational work among some 80,000 Ukrainian prisoners of war, was about 25,000 marks. The total spent by the Union during the three-year period from 1915 through 1917 was 743,295 marks.[38]

The Germans also supported Ukrainian information centers in neutral countries; these sums, however, were never very large. The Information Bureau in Lausanne, for example, which was one of the most active German-sponsored Ukrainian propaganda centers abroad, had a monthly allowance of 5,000 Swiss francs.[39] It may be interesting to add that throughout 1918 the Germans continued to support the Union's work among the Ukrainian prisoners of war. The Union's monthly allowance during this period was reduced to 12,000 marks.[40] The two Ukrainian governments during the German occupation of the country in 1918—the Rada and the Hetmanate—had nothing to do with these matters, and, as far as can be ascertained, they neither approved nor disapproved. With regard to the Habsburg Monarchy, one Austrian scholar states that "sev-

---

[37] Secretary of State Richard von Kuhlmann to his Liaison Officer at the Supreme Army Command, Baron Kurt von Lersner, Telegram No. 1610, AS 3640, Berlin, September 29, 1917, cited in Z. A. B. Zeman (ed.), *Germany and the Revolution in Russia, 1915–1918* (London: Oxford University Press, 1958), p. 70; Kuhlmann to Lersner (To be communicated to the Emperor), Telegram No. 1925, Berlin, December 3, 1917, cited in George Katkov, "German Foreign Office Documents on Financial Support to the Bolsheviks in 1917," *International Affairs,* XXXII (London, 1956), p. 189; Z. A. B. Zeman and W. B. Scharlau, *The Merchant of Revolution: The Life of Alexander Israel Helphand (Parvus), 1867–1924* (London: Oxford University Press, 1965), p. 231.

[38] Skoropys-Ioltukhovskyi, p. 233.

[39] German Embassy (Bern) to the Imperial Chancellor (Berlin), Communication No. 3706, Secret, November 30, 1917, *German Foreign Office Archives,* microfilm No. 110.

[40] War Ministry to Foreign Office, Communication No. 697/18, Berlin, August 22, 1918, *ibid.,* microfilm No. 53.

eral large sums" were given to the Union during this period—38,000 crowns in October and 12,000 in December 1917! The organization received another 30,000 crowns from Vienna in April 1918, and then was furnished a monthly allowance of 3,000 crowns for the remainder of the year.[41]

A careful reading of German Foreign Office documents failed to produce any evidence of direct financial assistance by Germany to the Ukrainian Rada or to any other political group active in that country prior to the conclusion of the Treaty of Brest-Litovsk in February 1918. Nor did the Union for the Liberation of the Ukraine have much success in facilitating a political rapproachment between Kiev and Berlin in the period following the March Revolution in Russia, despite the Reich's increased financial support of the Union's activities, which could be construed as Germany's encouragement of the Ukrainian national movement. The Rada continued to be wary of German plans for the east and did not abandon the hope of solving the Ukrainian problem within the framework of an all-Russian federation. Similarly, the relations between the Union and the Ukrainian Rada remained cool. As early as April 15, 1917, the Union publicly proclaimed its "official mandate exhausted" and promised to limit its future activities to work among the Ukrainian prisoners of war and the defense of Ukrainian interests in the territories occupied by the German and Austrian forces (i.e., Volhynia and Kholm). But this did little to improve relations between the Rada in Kiev and the small group of Ukrainian exiles in Berlin who were oriented toward the Central Powers and who at one time considered themselves to be the nucleus of a future Ukrainian government.[42] The latter felt compelled to state repeatedly that it had "neither official nor any other ties with the Union for the Liberation of the Ukraine in Germany."[43]

The lack of any cooperation or understanding between the Union and the Rada, and the latter's suspicion of German intentions, were not the sole reasons for the absence of relations between Berlin and Kiev before the Brest-Litovsk negotiations. The vagueness and un-

---

[41] Bihl, p. 515.

[42] Doroshenko, *Istoriia Ukrainy,* Vol. I, p. 36.

[43] See, for example, the statement published in *Nova rada* (Kiev), No. 118, August 22, 1917, cited in *German Foreign Office Archives,* microfilm No. 109.

certainty of German plans for the east were equally important factors. German Foreign Office archives show conclusively that it was not until the opening of peace talks at Brest with an independent Rada delegation in January 1918 that the Reich began in earnest to develop concrete plans for the Ukraine.[44]

In the light of the above evidence, it is not at all surprising that support of the Union for the Liberation of the Ukraine by Vienna and Berlin between 1914 and 1917 was quite cautious and half-hearted; this was also true following the collapse of tsarist Russia. The Union represented a small group of Ukrainian patriots who found themselves on the territory of the Central Powers at the outbreak of the war. Since these Ukrainian patriots were aware of Berlin's and Vienna's direct interest in the east, and since they followed the example of their Galician compatriots, the orientation of this group toward Austria and Germany can easily be understood. Only if Russia were defeated by the Central Powers could the non-Russian peoples of the tsarist empire have any hope for the fulfillment of their national aspirations. Obviously, the Ukrainians were not the only ones to stake their future on foreign powers; the subjugated peoples in other empires—the Czechs in Austria-Hungary or the Irish in the British Empire—also looked to other states for assistance.

The Union had practically no ties and no following in the Ukraine, and its influence over the Rada through 1917 was so limited that it can be dismissed altogether. Furthermore, the Union played no role whatsoever during the Brest-Litovsk negotiations, and after the German occupation of the Ukraine it had no influence on either Berlin or Kiev. The Ukrainian Revolution of 1917 was without question an independent and truly spontaneous development in which neither the Allies nor the Central Powers played any significant part. It was not until the conclusion of a separate peace treaty with the Rada, on February 9, 1918, and the occupation of the country in the spring of that year, that Germany, with the reluctant assistance of a dying Habsburg Monarchy, came to play a decisive role in the destinies of the Ukraine.

---

[44] This thesis is fully developed in Fedyshyn, especially chapters III and IV.

CHAPTER THIRTEEN

Allied Policy and French Intervention in the Ukraine, 1917–1920

George A. Brinkley

ALLIED INTERVENTION IN Russia was initially a result of the latter's "defection" from the First World War.[1] The problem of keeping Russia in the war had in fact prompted intervention even before the March Revolution, and it had steadily increased as the country passed through the period of gradual disintegration under the Provisional Government. What the Allies lacked in November 1917, when the Bolshevik coup converted a growing problem into a crisis, was a common policy toward the "Russian question." The Allied conference on war aims, which met in Paris on November 29, found the situation still too confused for simple decisions, but it was evident now that the Bolsheviks were seeking to withdraw from the war, and the Allies agreed that above all it was necessary to prevent a collapse of the eastern front.

Therefore, during the first week of December, Britain and France (with the support of the United States) initiated steps to seek out pro-Allied elements in Russia that would be willing and able to continue resistance against the Central Powers. They turned to the

---

[1] Among secondary sources in English, the following should be noted: John Bradley, *Allied Intervention in Russia, 1917–1920* (New York: Basic Books, 1968); J. M. Thompson, *Russia, Bolshevism, and the Versailles Peace* (Princeton, N.J.: Princeton University Press, 1966); J. S. Reshetar, *The Ukrainian Revolution, 1917–1920* (Princeton: Princeton University Press, 1952); and R. H. Ullman, *Anglo-Soviet Relations, 1917–1921,* 2 vols. (Princeton: Princeton University Press, 1961–68). The most recent Soviet collection, *Grazhdanskaia voina na Ukraine, 1918–1920,* 3 vols. (Kiev: Izd. 'Naukova dumka,' 1967), brings together many previously published documents on the intervention.

South,[2] where new armies were known to be forming and where both already had established interests and contacts. By early December 1917, Britain and France had decided to aid the Russian Volunteer Army that was being organized by General Alekseev and was soon to be led by General Kornilov in the Don area. Both also began considering plans for further action, the British particularly through Iran and Transcaucasia and the French through Rumania and the Ukraine, to build an alliance of forces in the South.

French interest in the Ukraine was in part related to past economic investment there, but in December 1917 it was much more directly a result of: (1) the fact that the large French mission in Rumania under General Berthelot had entered close relations with the Russian commander on that front, General Shcherbachev, who was assisting the Ukrainian Rada in the reorganization of Ukrainian troops in the area; (2) the existence of a military mission in Kiev under General Tabouis, which had good contacts with Ukrainian leaders; and (3) the presence in the Ukraine of an impressive armed force in the Czechoslovak Legion which had, on November 28, formed an association with the Rada and for which preparations were already being made in December to give it the status of an Allied force under French command. When the French government established a special commission for Russian affairs on December 7, the Czech leader, Eduard Beneš, was included, while the head of the Czech national movement, T. G. Masaryk, went to Russia to look into the Legion's situation and bring it under his direction.

These preliminary steps were further coordinated in consultations between the two Allies on December 22—appropriately, the day the Bolsheviks opened peace negotiations with the Central Powers at Brest-Litovsk. Through British initiative, an agreement was signed on December 23 that divided the South into two zones of responsibility. Accordingly, the British were to develop forces in a zone "southeast of the Black Sea," including the Caucasus region and Transcaucasia, while France was to bear responsibility for the area "north of the Black Sea," including the Crimea, the Ukraine, and Bessarabia. Both would simultaneously approach the Volunteer Army and the Cossacks in the South, and in case they were open to

---

[2] See Bradley, pp. 10–18. The term "South" or "South Russia" is used here as it was commonly used by the Allies, with both geographical and political implications.

persuasion, the Bolsheviks in the north.[3] On the next day the Allied Supreme Council announced that everyone willing to continue the war would get Allied support.

Considering the general disintegration that followed the Bolshevik coup, especially after the abrupt dismissal of the Constituent Assembly in January, any effort to restore a front against the Central Powers would necessarily encounter widely differing political circumstances along that front. For the Allies, however, political considerations were at this point decidedly secondary to the overriding military objective. The one real criterion for Allied aid was simply that the recipient be able to offer resistance to German and Turkish penetration. The first Allied agreement on intervention was, therefore, not calculated to favor any one ideology or solution to the "nationalities problem." Contacts were established during December with the indicated elements, and all were offered help to continue the war.

The greatest activity could be observed in the Ukraine. On December 23, the Allied Supreme Council approved the designation of the Czechoslovak Legion as an Allied army and agreed to finance its operations. On December 29, General Tabouis was given new credentials as "Commissioner of the French Republic to the Government of the Ukrainian Republic." He and his British counterpart, Bagge, immediately promised a major program of "financial and technical aid."[4] These appointments were not regarded as recognition of Ukrainian independence (which, in the sense of separation from Russia, was not declared by the Rada until January), but there was no doubt that a serious commitment was being undertaken. The Ukraine was, indeed, being treated with special urgency because it was considered essential to Allied operations in Rumania and to the main-

---

[3] *Documents on British Foreign Policy, 1919–1939,* First Series (London: H. M. Stationery Office, 1947–63), Vol. III, pp. 369–370 (hereafter: *British Documents*); and *Papers Relating to the Foreign Relations of the United States, 1918, Russia* (3 vols; Washington, D.C.: U.S. Government Printing Office, 1931–32), Vol. I, pp. 330–331 (hereafter: *Foreign Relations, 1918, Russia*).

[4] E. Evain, *La problème de l'indépendence de l'Ukraine et la France* (Paris: F. Alcan, 1931), pp. 100–108; A. D. Margolin, *Ukraina i politika antanty* (Berlin: S. Efron, 1921), pp. 365–368. See also Foreign Minister Shulhyn's account: A. Choulguine, *L'Ukraine, la Russie et les puissances de l'entente* (Berne: Imp. Réunies S.A. Lausanne, 1918), pp. 31–41.

tenance of a blockade against the Central Powers.[5] By early January 1918, the French mission in Kiev had assumed major responsibility for organizing military forces in the Ukraine and had established a common recruiting office and supply commission for Ukrainian, Polish, Czechoslovak, and Rumanian troops in the area.

In the winter of 1917–1918, however, this scheme existed largely in the minds of a few men; implementing it proved to be extremely difficult. The failure to achieve significant results can be attributed chiefly to: (1) the initial success of the Bolsheviks in driving into the Ukraine and capturing Kiev in February; (2) the inability of the Allies to provide real help from outside at this point; (3) the rejection by the Czechoslovak Legion (on Masaryk's decision) of French requests to join in the struggle for the Ukraine; and (4) the decision, made by the Ukrainian government in desperate circumstances in January, to sign a separate peace with the Germans. After it became clear during talks in January that the Allies could not offer sufficient aid, the Ukraine then dispatched a delegation to Brest-Litovsk, where on February 9 it signed a peace with the Central Powers and invited German aid. Foreign Minister Shulhyn, who had been in closest contact with the Allies, chose to dissociate himself from this action and resigned his post.

On February 7, just as Bolshevik forces were taking Kiev, Masaryk signed an agreement with them to preserve strict neutrality on the part of the Czechoslovak Legion. Declaring the Legion under Allied authority, he began hurried negotiations with both the Bolsheviks and the Allies looking toward the evacuation of the Legion before the Germans entered the area. He was assured of Allied support for this action on February 18, and two days later he ordered the Legion to leave the Ukraine and move eastward to the Transiberian railway and thence to Vladivostok. The German aid sought by the Rada soon turned into an occupation which, while it stopped the Bolshevik invasion, also paved the way for the overthrow of the Rada by the conservative faction led by Skoropadskyi. The latter, establishing himself as Hetman, adopted a policy of cooperation with the German command and received its support.

From the point of view of the Allies, the period beginning in February 1918 and continuing until the Armistice in November was

---

[5] *Foreign Relations, 1918, Russia,* Vol. I, p. 331, and Vol. II, pp. 656–663.

a period of almost complete failure in the South. At the same time, however, the Allies were becoming more deeply involved elsewhere in Russia. The center of attention shifted chiefly to Siberia as the focus for the proposed reconstruction of the eastern front; of its two flanks, only the one in the north could be developed substantially, although a brief effort in August was made in the South at Baku. While this is not the place to discuss developments in other areas, such as Siberia, it is important to recall the cumulative impact of the events of this period, including the Brest-Litovsk peace in March, the German occupation of (or establishment of strong influence in) virtually all the borderland states from Finland to Georgia, the May revolt of the Czechoslovak Legion against the Bolsheviks after a clash with Austro-Hungarian soldiers released by Moscow, the Socialist Revolutionary uprisings in July, which were provoked especially by the growing cooperation between Moscow and Berlin, and the new agreements entered into by the Soviet government and Germany in August.

These events convinced the Allies that military intervention in Russia was not only "urgently necessary in order to save Russia" from German domination, but that it was also "essential in order to win the war" against the Central Powers and avoid consequences that could "only be described as disastrous to the Allied cause."[6] The most immediate result was the Allied military intervention in Siberia and the north, but these developments also produced far-reaching effects on Allied thinking about future actions in the South. Before taking up the events in the South after November, it would be useful to note more particularly some of the assumptions and conclusions that shaped Allied (and especially French) policy. After mid-1918, not only were the Bolsheviks branded as allies of the Germans, but many of the anti-Bolshevik elements, including some of the non-Russian nationalities, had also come to be regarded as unreliable because of their willingness to turn to the Germans for help. Equally important is the fact that during this period the Allies became committed to a course of aiding a loyal and (they hoped) united force of Russian political and military elements forged into an alliance in Siberia, an area notably lacking any serious nationality problem. Thus, when the Ufa Directorate was established in Siberia in September, both Britain and

---

[6] Allied Supreme War Council statement, July 2, 1918, *ibid.*, Vol. II, pp. 241–246.

France soon identified it as the kind of government desired, because it united the Socialist-Revolutionaries (who had widespread popularity) and the "Whites" (the "stable" conservatives who had armed forces). Both notably stood for the restoration of Russia and had a record of opposing any dealing with the Germans.

The attitude of the French in particular was influenced by the position that any given element took *vis-à-vis* the Germans in the February–November 1918 period. Quite predictably, French spokesmen, from Premier Clemenceau and Foreign Minister Pichon down to low-ranking representatives, indicated a distrust and dislike of any who had collaborated with the Germans. Former Russian Foreign Minister Miliukov, for example, was bitterly denounced by Clemenceau for having proposed that the Volunteer Army cooperate with the Germans, while the Don Ataman, General Krasnov, was refused aid because he had accepted supplies from German forces in the Ukraine. With respect to the latter, it may be noted that, while good relations existed with certain Ukrainian leaders, such as former Foreign Minister Shulhyn, in November 1918 Pichon made specific reference to collaboration between an independent Ukraine and the Germans, implying that separatism should be opposed because it had been a vehicle of German penetration.[7]

It has been said by many that the surrender of the Central Powers in November 1918 eliminated the reason for the intervention, and in a sense it certainly did. In Allied (especially French) thinking, however, there was no abrupt end to the broader outlook as to the purposes of the intervention; this outlook had been acquired in the course of events and through commitments entered during the summer and fall of 1918. As far as the French were concerned, continuation of the intervention was necessary precisely in order to fulfill its original purpose—to oppose the Germans.[8] After November, this required the removal not only of German troops but also of German influence and the elimination of the consequences of German occupation. This meant defeating the Bolsheviks and restoring Russian unity under pro-Allied leadership. Since the major armed force in the South now was the Volunteer Army, an element that had re-

---

[7] V. A. Maklakov Archives (of the Russian Embassy in Paris) (ms., The Hoover Institution), Series B, Packet I, Dossier 6 (hereafter as: B, I, 6).

[8] See Foreign Minister Pichon's statement, *Annales de la chambre des députés, Débats parlementaires* (Paris: Assemblée Nationale), Tome III (1918), pp. 3334–3335, session of December 29, 1918 (hereafter: *Débats parlementaires*).

mained consistently anti-German and had sought the reunification of Russia, this task was made quite complex by virtue of the fact that the population in the South was predominantly non-Russian—indeed, often anti-Russian—and the area had become a jigsaw puzzle of independent governments.

Thus, the French could not ignore the nationalities, particularly the Ukrainians, and indeed they had no desire to do so; but they also could not, without violating the logic of their own policy, fail to support the Volunteers and their goal of Russian unity. Consequently, the same desire for a strong coalition that stimulated Allied interest in the Ufa Directorate also prompted an inclination to favor unity between Russian armed forces and non-Russian national movements in the South. Not only was unity necessary for victory, but for both historical and future reasons the French were motivated by a desire to have a strong, great power ally in Russia. Individual secessionist states such as the Ukraine, even in combination with other states formed out of the old empire, could not provide such an ally, especially if there was any possibility that they might be an instrument of German policy.

For all these reasons, the slogan of national self-determination could be viewed favorably only so long as it did not go beyond the demand for cultural and political autonomy, such as had been the case during the period of the Provisional Government and more generally up until January 1918. Foreign Minister Pichon did not regard Ukrainian nationalism as something with "deep roots in the population" and saw no basis for separation of the Ukraine from Russia.[9] The French were also never very impressed with the Volunteer Army, but, as Pichon put it to the French ambassador in London, "the dismemberment of our ally cannot be the end sought by our policy, and consequently we must not encourage that dismemberment.... [Since] none of the parts [of Russia] can assure by itself its own existence and development ... our policy [in South Russia] must be based on the one force which exists there, the Volunteer Army, mediocre though it may be."[10] The French came to favor democratic federation as the best way to take national minority rights into account and restore unity, but the actual resolution of

[9] Pichon to Berne, November 7, 1918, Maklakov Archives, B, I, 6.

[10] Pichon to Cambon, March 3, 1919, Maklakov Archives, B, II, 11. On the role of the Volunteer army, see G. A. Brinkley, *The Volunteer Army and Allied Intervention in South Russia, 1917–1921* (Notre Dame: University of Notre Dame Press, 1966).

such a problem was regarded as something to be left to a Constituent Assembly; it was not a task for the French themselves to undertake. The French role was seen rather as that of aiding in a common struggle against the Bolsheviks, after which the Russians and the non-Russians could work out their own solutions.

There is much, of course, that could be disputed. It could be argued, for example, as one version of the policy of *cordon sanitaire* later suggested, that the most practical opposition to the Bolsheviks would be that based on a dismemberment of Russia and the erection of a "fence" of new states from the Baltic to the Black Sea. Allied policy was in fact to some extent always torn between the two alternatives, and in 1920 it did show a drift toward the second, the borderland *cordon*. But until then the dismemberment of Russia was definitely resisted, for it was felt that such a policy could well impede the attempt to destroy Bolshevism in its home base while offering in the smaller states what at the time appeared to be a somewhat dubious basis for a barrier to either Bolshevik or German influence. An Eastern European *cordon* between Russia and Germany might indeed become the necessary goal, but only if the continued existence of a Bolshevik Russia were assumed. If there was a choice (and the French believed there was) between eradicating the major threat on the one hand and simply containing it on the other, priority would be given to the former.

Even if the principles in French policy were evident, they did not automatically provide an adequate guide to practice. On the contrary, the belief that the Bolsheviks could be defeated by a united effort evidently tended at first to produce an assumption that unity would naturally follow. When Allied activity was resumed in the South in November 1918, there was no apparent effort to adjust policy to the needs of intervention in a civil war as opposed to intervention for continuing an international war. Clemenceau launched the second phase of French intervention in the Ukraine with new directives in October, knowing that the war with Germany would soon be over, but neither he nor Pichon indicated any change in policy or approach that would take that fact into account. Indeed, in view of the situation in the South, it is striking that both Britain and France entered the new intervention simply assuming or hoping, rather than planning, for an alliance of all anti-Bolshevik forces.

The continuity in Allied policy was affirmed by the renewal of the December 1917 zone agreement in November 1918. Allied troops were directed to move into South Russia in accordance with the division of responsibility that delegated the Ukraine and Crimea to France and Transcaucasia to Britain. The aim of this military intervention, as French Foreign Minister Pichon expressed it, was "to come to the aid of associations and groups in Russia devoted to the Entente and to permit elements faithful to our alliance and respectful of our contracts . . . to organize themselves effectively and fight against ruin and anarchy, the consequences of which can extend to ourselves." Nothing in this policy, he added, "constitutes any interference in the internal affairs of Russia."[11]

Thus, when Clemenceau issued instructions for the preparation of the French intervention, he merely ordered General Berthelot, commanding French forces in Rumania, to establish contacts with groups loyal to the Allies. He indicated to General Franchet d'Espérey, Allied commander in the East, that the purpose of the intervention was to eliminate German presence and influence, then to isolate and ultimately destroy Bolshevism. While Franchet d'Espérey complained that extension of French operations into the Ukraine was ill-advised because of the inadequacy and low morale of French troops, Clemenceau was strongly supported both by Berthelot and by the former chief of French military missions in Russia, General Niessel. The French Premier issued orders on November 2 and 3, which designated Berthelot to command operations in Rumania, the Ukraine, and the Crimea, and which called for the initiation of naval operations to move troops by sea to Odessa.[12]

The first real efforts to prepare the intervention politically were made not in Paris but in Iaşi and Bucharest, where Allied representatives, apparently with only vague instructions though a very strong sense of urgency, assumed responsibility for taking action.[13] It was they who initiated new relations with the Ukraine and decided to seek cooperation with Skoropadskyi. Following their advice

---

[11] *Débats parlementaires,* III (1918), p. 3334.

[12] Clemenceau's instructions are in *Les Armées françaises dans la Grande Guerre* (Paris: Ministère de la Guerre, État-Major de l'Armée, 1934), Tome VIII, Vol. III, Annexes, Vol. 3, pp. 120–125. Franchet d'Espérey's views are quoted in Jean Xydias, *L'Intervention française en Russie, 1918–1919; souvenirs d'un témoin* (Paris: Éditions de France, 1927), p. 115; and in Paul J. L. Azan, *Franchet d'Espérey* (Paris: Flammarion, 1949), pp. 240–241. General Niessel's report is in the Maklakov Archives, B, I, 12.

[13] *Foreign Relations, 1918, Russia,* Vol. II, pp. 644, 678, 699–706, 709.

that a complete break with the preceding (German) period was essential for the Ukraine, Hetman Skoropadskyi approved the establishment of a new Ukrainian government under S. N. Gerbel, and that government issued a statement, on November 14, hailing the Allies as friends and calling for the restoration of unity on the basis of an "All-Russian" federation. There remained the need to put this apparent Ukrainian cooperation into the context of a larger "All-Russian" agreement.

Relations with the Volunteers (now commanded by General A. I. Denikin) were established by General Berthelot on November 15, the very day of his return to Bucharest. There, in conference with General Shcherbachev, his acquaintance of earlier days, Berthelot laid out his conception of the Allied (French) plan: an Allied (mostly French and Greek) force of some twelve divisions would soon enter the Ukraine through Odessa and thence move into a large area stretching from the Don on the east to Kiev on the north and Bessarabia (already occupied by Rumanian troops by agreement with Shcherbachev) in the west. This occupation force would maintain order while the Germans were evacuated and while anti-Bolshevik forces were being organized for the campaign that would ultimately defeat the Bolsheviks. General Shcherbachev, who got the impression that the main purpose of the intervention was to aid the Volunteers to restore an "All Russian" state, conveyed this plan to General Denikin and received the latter's full approval.[14]

Further political groundwork for the intervention was prepared in a conference that opened in Iaşi on November 16.[15] This aspect of the preparations was handled by the French "consul," Emile Henno, who had previously been director of intelligence in the Tabouis mission in Kiev and now, in Iaşi, had assumed the role of representing the Allied missions in Rumania in the matter of contacts with various elements in the Ukraine and elsewhere in the South. On Henno's initiative, some thirty persons, representing a relatively broad range of organizations and views from socialist to

---

[14] E. G. Val [von Wahl], *K istorii belago dvizheniia: deiatelnost Generaladiutanta Shcherbacheva* (Tallin: Izd. avtora, 1935), pp. 34–37. See also the Volunteer Army's *Ocherk vzaimootnoshenii vooruzhennykh sil Iuga Rossii i predstavitelei frantsuzskago komandovaniia*—referred to as the "Orange Book" (Ekaterinodar, 1919), pp. 233 ff. (full text in Denikin Archives, Columbia University); cited here as published in *Arkhiv russkoi revoliutsii,* Vol. XVI (Berlin: Gessen, 1925).

[15] Journal of Meetings and other materials in P. N. Wrangel Archives (ms., The Hoover Institution), Military Archives, File 143.

monarchist, were invited to Iaşi to advise the Allies on intervention policy. Although there was no Ukrainian delegation as such, the Ukrainian government cooperated with the arrangements (many of the delegates came from Kiev and Odessa), and two persons (V. I. Hurko and N. N. Shebeko) indirectly represented the Hetman's views.

The conference, meeting from November 16 to 23, was largely concerned with producing an appeal to the Allies and a proposal on what political authority should be supported by the intervention. The former, hastily formulated because of the rush of events in the Ukraine, urged all possible speed in the introduction of Allied troops and called on the Allies to require the Germans to maintain order until they were officially authorized to leave. The conference thus went on record, perhaps rather more strongly than many of its participants desired, for maintenance of the status quo in the Ukraine until orderly change could be achieved. The delegates were unable to reach any agreement on the form that political authority should take once changes could be introduced, but they did express a generally held opinion on the necessity of a single Russian military commander for all operations in the South, the majority favoring Denikin.

On the surface it may have appeared that a basis for unity had been established in Iaşi. However, the conferees there, mostly conservative Russians, came out in favor of retaining Skoropadskyi mainly because the alternative to him, the Directory led by Vynnychenko and Petliura, was ostensibly separatist, socialist, and suspected of being pro-Bolshevik. While the conference called for reconciliation with the Ukraine, it also demanded suppression of "chauvinistic Ukrainians." Henno, who engineered the Iaşi conference, was determined to stop the "anarchy," which he blamed particularly on Vynnychenko and Petliura. When he then set out for Kiev, only to find his trip cut short in Odessa by Petliura's troops, his proclamation of Allied policy contained a strong warning against any interference with "the re-establishment of order and the reorganization of Russia begun by patriotic Russians and powerfully supported by the Allies." The Allies, he declared, were coming to support "the regeneration of Russia as a power," and anyone who attacked existing authorities or created disturbances would be held "personally responsible" and would be "severely punished."[16]

---

[16] *Foreign Relations, 1918, Russia,* Vol. II, p. 701.

As it turned out, neither the Germans nor the Volunteers were willing to make any effort to keep Skoropadskyi's new government from falling. The Germans, indeed, turned their backs on Skoropadskyi and cooperated in the Directory's takeover of Kiev, while the Volunteers, who regarded both Skoropadskyi and the Directory leaders as pro-German traitors, spent the little time available quarreling over military command in the Ukraine rather than taking any action. When French forces finally reached Odessa on December 17, they were confronted by a new declaration of Ukrainian independence by the Directory and found Petliura's troops in control. All Henno had behind him in the part of Odessa left unoccupied by Petliura was a small detachment of Volunteers and a Polish brigade. He asked them to "clear the city" for the landing of the French troops; hence, the 1,800-man detachment of the 156th French Colonial Division from Salonika went ashore in the midst of an open battle with Ukrainian forces. The French officer in charge, General Borius, having instructions simply to support local "patriots," approved Henno's suggestion to recognize the Volunteer commander, General Grishin-Almazov, as military governor of the city.[17]

The actions, promises, and threats of both Berthelot and Henno were to some extent a distortion of French policy by over-zealous individual spokesmen; but, even so, the fault seems to have derived largely from the failure of the French government to anticipate such developments. Foreign Minister Pichon had indeed been informed prior to the Iaşi conference of the new contacts with the Ukrainian government and of the reversal of policy it was willing to make. In this regard, he was probably also influenced by a note from former Foreign Minister Shulhyn, on November 6, stating that the Hetman's government had dealt with the Germans only out of necessity and now sincerely sought a restoration of relations with the Allies. Shulhyn was at this time serving as Ukrainian minister in Sophia and from there had maintained contact with Allied representatives. Moreover, Pichon had also received favorable comment on the reorganization of the Ukrainian government from the leader of the Russian Political Conference in Paris, Ambassador

---

[17] P. Khrystiuk, *Zamitky i materiialy do istorii ukrainskoi revoliutsii, 1917–1920,* Vol. IV (Vienna: Ukrainskyi sotsiologichnyi institut, 1922), pp. 6, 15 ff.; A. G. Shlikhter (ed.), *Chernaia kniga: sbornik statei i materialov ob interventsii antanty na Ukraine v 1918–1919 gg.* (Kharkov: Gosizdatelstvo Ukrainy, 1925), pp. 93, 111 ff.; Xydias, p. 160 ff.

Maklakov, and he agreed with the latter's assessment that it provided a real basis for cooperation.[18]

In view of these assurances, Pichon had evidently assumed that things were going well and required no further action on his part. As noted before, he seems to have accepted the identification of the Directory as pro-Bolshevik and separatist and had ruled out relations with it for this reason. He had probably also been led to believe (because of the apparent success with Skoropadskyi and reports of accord between the new Ukrainian government and the Volunteers) that the Directory's bid for power would not be successful and need not be taken seriously. In any case, when Paris realized that its previous plans and assumptions had gone awry, it immediately reassessed the situation and took steps to bring French actions more in line with the new conditions in the Ukraine. In fact, by the time the intended commander of the Odessa headquarters, General d'Anselme, arrived with his staff in January 1919, a number of important decisions had been made that considerably altered the course of French policy as hitherto enunciated by Berthelot and Henno.

A trend against the intervention was indeed evident in the Allied countries already at the end of 1918. By January 1919, when the Peace Conference opened in Paris and discussed the Russian question, the demand for an end to intervention had become quite strong.[19] From the beginning of the conference, two of the Allied leaders, Lloyd George and Wilson, objected to any prolongation or enlargement of the intervention and agreed on the desirability of bringing the conflict to a close as soon as possible. In opposition to these views, Foreign Minister Pichon and Marshal Foch openly condemned any dealing with the Bolsheviks and spoke as advocates of intervention, the latter offering plans for an army recruited in the border states to join in the liberation of Russia. However, Clemenceau, while not in accord with Wilson and Lloyd George on these questions, was troubled by the enormous difficulties already en-

---

[18] The Shulhyn, Pichon, and Maklakov notes are in the Maklakov Archives, B, I, 6.

[19] *Papers Relating to the Foreign Relations of the United States: The Paris Peace Conference, 1919,* 13 vols. (Washington, D.C.: U.S. Government Printing Office, 1942–1947), Vol. III, pp. 471 ff., 581–584, 649 (hereafter: *Paris Peace Conference*).

countered in Russia and grudgingly accepted even the idea of calling a peace conference. It would, he reasoned, at least be one way to reduce criticism at home, and it might even provide "a unique opportunity... of indicting Bolshevism and its abuses before the whole world."[20]

The result, of course, was the famous "Prinkipo Proposal" approved by the Allied Council of Ten on January 22. Broadcast the next day to all factions in Russia, it called for an immediate cessation of hostilities and the convocation of a peace conference on February 15 on the Prinkipo (Princes) Islands in the Sea of Marmara.[21] However, as a partial result of French (Pichon) and even British (Churchill) reassurances to the anti-Bolshevik elements that rejection would not affect Allied support, the peace proposal failed. The Bolsheviks accepted, but with confusing conditions, and many of the non-Russian states rejected the invitation, in part because they interpreted it as contrary to their separation from Russia. The Ukrainian Bolsheviks, vying for power and recognition, accepted the proposal, but the government of the Directory, which made the withdrawal of Bolshevik troops a prerequisite to any negotiations, returned a negative reply.

With the failure of the Prinkipo Proposal, pro-interventionist factions in the Allied governments, particularly those headed by Foch and Churchill, attempted to fill the policy vacuum by new initiatives in Paris, but the leaders of all the Allied governments now were reluctant to be drawn further into the civil war. While they declined to become involved in new peace efforts, such as the Bullitt proposals, the Allies also refused to adopt suggestions for recruiting additional troops for use in the struggle and rejected a proposal to establish an Allied coordinating agency to direct the intervention. All agreed that existing commitments should continue to be honored, but Allied policy early in 1919 was decidedly opposed to the use of their own troops in battle and was in general opposed to the maintenance of forces in Russia for any prolonged period.

Clemenceau was clearly disheartened with the lack of a forceful Allied policy, but under the circumstances he was realistically prepared to scale down French policy accordingly. In fact, anticipating the opposition to the intervention expressed at the Allied

---

[20] *Ibid.*, Vol. IV, pp. 16–18.
[21] *Ibid.*, Vol. III, pp. 691–692.

conference, the French government had already decided that it would not be able, even with available reinforcements from Greek and Algerian troops, to mount the full-scale occupation described earlier by Berthelot. Explaining French policy to a very critical Assembly, both Clemenceau and Pichon indicated that only a small "defensive front" would be established around Odessa. It was made clear that there was no intention of allowing Allied troops to become involved in the fighting, but the French government did expect to use these troops to form a protective shield that would enable the "healthy elements" in the zone to organize and carry out their own struggle against the Bolsheviks.[22]

An important decision flowing out of this more limited view of the French role was that the intervention could be continued only if the necessary agreements could be reached with the Ukraine. French policy, as Franchet d'Espérey put it, was "neither to dismember Russia nor to impose on her this or that form of government," but to cooperate with "local governments" to permit the restoration of order.[23] D'Anselme's Chief of Staff, Colonel Freydenberg, who assumed responsibility for implementing French policy in Odessa in January, added that, while France preferred to see Russia reunited, the tasks ahead could be accomplished only by "making use of all anti-Bolshevik forces, including the Ukrainians."[24] Now, of course, that meant finding a way to work with those whom Henno had so vigorously denounced.

The French command in Odessa, cut off from the interior, faced not only a problem of too few troops, even after the arrival in January of two Greek divisions, but also an increasingly difficult economic and political situation. The Volunteer command in Odessa proposed to move into the surrounding area to recruit new troops and establish a more secure economic and military base, but this raised the very serious problem of more conflict with Ukrainian troops. Colonel Freydenberg, who categorically rejected any plan that might involve French troops in battle, and who had become increasingly dissatisfied with the performance of the Volunteer

---

[22] *Débats parlementaires,* Tome III (1918), pp. 3334–3335.

[23] Xydias, p. 202.

[24] A. I. Denikin, *Ocherki russkoi smuty,* Vol. V (Berlin-Paris, 1926), p. 34. Also interviews with Freydenberg quoted in the "Azbuka" reports in the Maklakov Archives, B, II, 3; and M. S. Margulies, *God interventsii,* Vol. I (Berlin: Z. J. Grzhebin, 1923), pp. 285, 289.

authority in Odessa, therefore brushed aside Russian objections and invited the Directory to send representatives for negotiations.[25]

On the question of the zone around Odessa, results were quickly achieved. In talks arranged through General Grekov, an agreement was reached to lift the blockade of the city and to permit French and Greek troops to occupy an area bordered by a line running from the Dniester at Tiraspol through Berezovka and Mykolaiv to the Dnieper at Kherson. Further talks, on economic and political questions, were then begun with an expanded Ukrainian delegation, including Dr. Osyp Nazaruk and Serhii Ostapenko. Now, however, far more difficult problems arose, in part because of the very nature of the French goal—that is, Russian-Ukrainian cooperation. Freydenberg had the unenviable task of trying to bridge the gap between a Ukraine which was not only an independent state already but one under leadership that had come to power renouncing the "All-Russian" approach and, on the other side, Russian elements, particularly the Volunteers, who were determined not to cooperate with "separatists" even if they were anti-Bolshevik. Given the situation, Freydenberg's "solution" was probably the only logical one.

According to Freydenberg's plan, Southwestern Russia (the French zone) should be divided into two parts, one Ukrainian and one Russian. Each of these would have its own political authority (preferably some sort of "directorate") and its own military forces. At the same time, a higher authority, with military and political functions, would be established to coordinate the efforts of the two units to maintain order and pursue the military struggle to victory. This higher authority would have the nature of a coalition, including representatives of both parts but also a third element, which would hold the balance of power and thus act as the real coordinator. This third element, of course, would be the French command. Freydenberg also considered the possibility of organizing special "mixed" brigades, which would operate under French officers and would form a kind of buffer force between the respective Ukrainian and Russian armies.[26]

This plan would of necessity involve a substantial reorganization of the political and military structure in the South, at least in terms

---

[25] On subsequent talks see Margolin, pp. 109 ff.; S. Ostapenko, "Direktoriia i frantsuzskaia interventsiia," in A. G. Shlikhter, *Chernaia kniga;* and numerous materials in the Maklakov Archives, B, II, 3.

[26] Denikin, Vol. V, p. 35.

of the elimination of the Volunteer authority in Odessa and the establishment of a supreme authority with headquarters in that city. It soon developed, further, that not only the Volunteer Army would be affected. Colonel Freydenberg insisted that the Ukrainian Directory be reorganized too, by the removal of its more radical leaders, so as to make it more suitable for the French plan. Vynnychenko (who was considered the most pro-Bolshevik) was evidently the prime target, but others were also suggested. Therefore, the formation on February 13 of a new government under Ostapenko went a long way toward satisfying Freydenberg's conditions for agreement, but the terms still had to be worked out.[27]

Petliura, who as commander of Ukrainian forces was an extremely important figure in these negotiations, resigned from the Social Democratic Party to assuage French concern, but he also demanded recognition of the Ukraine and the restriction of Ukrainian military operations to Ukrainian territory as his conditions for cooperation. Freydenberg's often expressed exasperation with Petliura might, indeed, have led to a breakdown of talks but for the arrival of a new and very effective negotiator for the Ukrainian side, Dr. Arnold Margolin. During February, Margolin was able to establish very good relations with the French command and to bolster his bargaining position by organizing a cooperative bloc with Belorussian and Cossack representatives in Odessa. Together with these he advocated a policy of "federation from below," a plan that provided for both the recognition of existing regional governments and their ultimate reunification in a voluntary federation.[28]

The terms of agreement that then emerged between the French command and the Ukraine represented a remarkable example of Ukrainian flexibility and of French military diplomacy in action. According to most accounts, agreement was reached not only on the establishment of a joint military command, but also on the political and economic questions involved, including acceptance of the idea of a future federation and the restoration of a major French economic role in the Ukraine (particularly in the form of railroad and industrial concessions). In return, France would support the Ukraine both economically and politically, with *de facto* recognition for the interim period before reunification, and the use of

---

[27] Margolin, pp. 123–124; V. Vynnychenko, *Vidrodzhennia natsii,* Vol. III (Kiev-Vienna, 1920), p. 255 ff.

[28] Margolin, p. 112 ff.

French good offices to bring about cooperation with Poland, Rumania, and other governments.[29]

Negotiation and implementation were, of course, two very different things; there was as yet neither any formal acceptance of the indicated terms by the French and Ukrainian governments nor any agreement with the Russian side, particularly with Denikin. Freydenberg approached the latter problem on two levels, negotiating simultaneously with diverse Russian organizations in Odessa and with the Volunteer military government, to some extent playing one off against the other. Several plans were proposed for the formation of a new government in Odessa for Southwestern Russia, each including a major role for Denikin as military commander. None, however, received the latter's approval, even though Freydenberg insisted that his purpose in seeking agreement with the Ukraine was solely that of "using their forces for the fight against the Bolsheviks" and for the restoration of a "united and strong Russia."[30]

The irreconcilable confrontation between Denikin's uncompromising adherence to the policy of "One Russia" (which excluded federation) and the Ukraine's insistence on at least temporary recognition as an autonomous republic made acceptance of the French plan impossible. General Berthelot, who made a last effort to sway the Volunteers before resigning his post in March, found it a hopeless task. Consequently, when the military situation became increasingly precarious in March (because of the collapse of the Directory and Bolshevik advances, including Grigorev's attack on Kherson and Mykolaiv), the French command decided to proceed without the Volunteers. Under the impact of a forced withdrawal of French and Greek troops from the outer perimeter, the French command declared a state of siege in Odessa, on March 14, and imposed a new regime on the city. When Volunteer authorities objected, orders

---

[29] Various "texts" of the agreements are in A. I. Gukovskii, *Frantsuzskaia interventsiia na iuge Rossii, 1918–1919* (Moscow: Gosudarstvennoe sotsialno-ekonomicheskoe izd., 1928), pp. 142–143, 146; A. G. Shliapnikov (ed.), *Les alliés contre la Russie avant, pendant et après la guerre mondiale: faits et documents* (Paris: Delpeuch, 1926), pp. 286–288; E. E. Iakushkin, *Frantsuzskaia interventsiia na iuge, 1918–1919* (Moscow: Gosizdat, 1929), pp. 31–32; and Shlikhter, pp. 134–135. General confirmation of the areas of agreement may be found in Khrystiuk, Vol. IV, p. 104; Margolin, pp. 109–124; Vynnychenko, Vol. III, p. 251 ff.

[30] See interview of February 24, 1918, in Maklakov Archives, B, II, 3.

were issued on March 22 expelling the Volunteer Governor-General, Grishin-Almazov, and Denikin's personal representative, General Sannikov.[31]

The French command, with General Franchet d'Espérey playing a direct role for the first time, made a vigorous effort to make up for lost time in the last hectic days of March. General A. V. Shvarts, an independent not favored by the Volunteers, was named commander (with Ukrainian General Prokopovych to be a deputy commander) and given a mandate to recruit both Russian and Ukrainian troops. A civil authority, to include a mixed Russian and Ukrainian cabinet, was established under D. F. Andro de Langeron, a conservative "French Ukrainian." Both the new military command and the "government" thus established, however, were clearly operating under the French command, a fact that discredited them from the outset. The result was an almost complete revolt against the French in Odessa. Denikin vehemently denounced French actions as a *coup d'état,* the workers began a Bolshevik-inspired uprising, and most of the Russian organizations, conservative and socialist, joined in a common protest, accusing the French of attempting to set up a "colonial regime."[32]

French efforts to restore confidence met with little success. In spite of an announced "resolute decision" to remain in Odessa and the arrival of more Allied troops on March 26, the French command in fact recognized the hopelessness of the situation and had already so advised Paris. The intervention, in Franchet d'Espérey's opinion, had become an "absurdity."[33] Accordingly, in discussions in the Allied Council of Four on March 17, 25, and 27, Marshal Foch called for abandoning the established policy and turning instead to the Eastern European countries, particularly Rumania and Poland.[34] On March 27, the decision was made in Paris (over British objections) to evacuate Odessa.[35] General d'Anselme received corresponding orders on April 2, and the next day he initiated a panicky

---

[31] The French command's orders are collected in the Maklakov Archives, B, II, 1.

[32] Volunteer "Orange Book," *Ocherk vzaimootnoshenii,* p. 247; Denikin, Vol. V, p. 47.

[33] Azan, p. 246.

[34] *Paris Peace Conference,* Vol. IV, pp. 379–383.

[35] See Pichon's public announcement of March 29, *Débats parlementaires,* Tome I (1919), p. 1448, and a note on British objections in Denikin, Vol. V, p. 69.

withdrawal of Allied troops, leaving many, including some Volunteers, behind to fend for themselves. What was left of Petliura's troops had already taken refuge in Podillia and Galicia, while those Volunteers, Poles, Ukrainians, and others who escaped from Odessa sought safety in Bessarabia.

The evacuation of French troops in the Crimea (Sevastopol) followed, from April 19 to April 30, under a truce with the Bolsheviks. As Franchet d'Espérey explained it to Denikin, the evacuation "resulted exclusively from the impossibility of supplying provisions for them [in Odessa and Sevastopol], in consequence of which disorder threatened to break out.... If there had been no fear of dooming the populations of these two cities to starvation, we would have remained in position."[36] Obviously, the problem was somewhat broader than that and included, in addition to the complications already noted, the fact that French soldiers and sailors were approaching a state of mutiny. Whatever the reasons for the withdrawal, it certainly marked the end of French military presence in the South and brought French relations with both Ukrainians and Russians to their lowest point.

Anglo-French talks in session at the time of the evacuation revealed a strikingly undaunted attitude on the part of the French. This was partly the result of their growing rivalry with the British. Cooperation between the Allies had never been much more than a theoretical proposition in the South, and French action in Odessa had produced considerable tension between them. The British had especially objected to what they alleged was a pro-Ukrainian and anti-Volunteer bias in French policy, but in their meeting on April 4 the French repudiated the idea of an agreement with the Ukraine and indicated a desire to restore harmony by rebuilding their relations with Denikin. As a supplement to the Allied zone agreement, they proposed a "protocol," which declared that France would not interfere with operations by the Volunteers in the French zone. It further promised the return to Denikin of Russian ships seized at the time of the evacuation and assured access for the Volunteers to supplies "located in the zone of French operations," a reference to previous French opposition to Russian use of stores in the Ukraine and also to Rumania's failure to turn over Russian material left in Bessarabia (while at the same time supplying arms to Petliura).[37]

---

[36] Denikin, Vol. V, p. 69.
[37] Text in Shliapnikov, pp. 290–291, and Denikin, Vol. V, pp. 67–68. On the Rumanian aspect see *British Documents*, Vol. III, pp. 585–586;

Coming after the evacuation of French troops, this declaration of policy was certainly less impressive than it might have been earlier. While the April protocol made it clear that the French did not intend to abandon their zone entirely, especially to the British, it was evident that the British had much greater influence (although not control) over Denikin. Instead, Denikin's reaction to the French overture (which he did not receive until June when he was also first informed of the Allied zone agreement) was a rejection on the grounds that it was not relevant to his operations. With assurances of full support from the British (thanks especially to Churchill) and, in his view, a record of little support of any kind from the French, he saw no need for further concern over his relations with the latter.

Thus, while the French were cautiously feeling their way toward a possible renewal of their influence in the South, the British and Volunteer attitudes were not very amenable. Although formally respecting the French zone, the British view (privately stated by Curzon in a letter of June 11 to Balfour) was that real cooperation with the French was no longer possible and that the Ukraine, as a part of Russia, "should properly fall within General Denikin's sphere of influence, and consequently under our control. . . ."[38] When, in July, Denikin requested British assistance to establish Volunteer bases and begin operations in the Crimea and the Ukraine, the British informed the French government of their decision (already made without consultation) to comply with the Volunteer request. The French consented, having little choice in the matter, but reminded the British that there were still very considerable French interests in the zone that would require appropriate protection.

Although the French were to play a rather secondary role in the surge of battle in the Ukraine during the second half of 1919, they were by no means out of the picture. French diplomacy became an increasingly important factor, especially during the autumn. At that time, the British commitment was, in spite of Churchill, subjected to reconsideration and subsequent reduction, while the possible role of Poland began to receive greater attention, in particular from the French. Thus the question of further French intervention during this period soon came to focus on the possibility of a Volunteer-Ukrainian-Polish alliance under French auspices.

In July 1919, Denikin's Volunteers began their major offensive

---

Denikin, Vol. V, p. 183; and materials in Wrangel Military Archives, File 8.

[38] *British Documents,* Vol. III, p. 366.

and were driving northward through the Ukraine; Polish troops, having invaded Galicia, were occupying the territory west of the Zbruch River; and newly combined Ukrainian forces—those of Petliura and those (now led by Grekov) of the West Ukrainian Republic, which had just been overrun by the Poles—were moving eastward toward Kiev, hoping once again to recover their capital. In spite of the inherent contradictions, the French supported all three operations, and through Margolin and Maklakov in Paris they urged the Volunteers, Ukrainians, and Poles to cooperate and to establish contacts.[39]

When the Volunteers and the Ukrainians almost simultaneously reached Kiev, a clash was avoided, in part because of these efforts and because the Galician commander (now General Tarnavskyi) decided to enter into talks with the Volunteer commander, General Bredov. Agreement was reached on August 31 between these two forces, and, with considerable prodding from the Allies, negotiations were begun for further cooperation. But, even as this progress was being recorded, Petliura chose to take another road. On September 1, he signed a truce with the Poles and thus began a fateful association with Piłsudski, the enemy of his Galician supporters. Although in October Petliura made one of his strongest appeals for French support, he did so now as a self-identified ally of Poland and as an enemy of the Volunteers (for whom, of course, the feeling was mutual).[40]

Polish-Volunteer talks, begun at Denikin's headquarters in September with a mission under General Karnicki, offered new hope of an alliance, and both Britain and France responded by appointing new high-level representatives to promote this goal. General Charles Mangin was assigned by Paris in November to go to South Russia and prepare the ground for Volunteer-Polish cooperation, while his British counterpart, Sir Halford Mackinder, went first to Warsaw to urge Piłsudski's immediate support. Clemenceau even reversed his government's previous ruling against further credit for aid to the Volunteers in October and issued orders to French repre-

---

[39] See correspondence between Maklakov and Pichon in Maklakov Archives, B, II, 4, and French note to the Ukrainian delegation in Paris in Margolin, pp. 145–146, 372–373.

[40] See S. V. Petliura, "Un appel du président Petliura à la démocratie française," addressed to M. Jean Pélissier, October 28, 1919 (in Ukrainian Delegation Propaganda, The Hoover Institution).

sentatives to do everything possible to bring Volunteers, Ukrainians, and Poles together in a common effort.[41]

However, these efforts were not successful. On the one hand, Poland's territorial ambitions and her fear of Great Russian power (identified with the Volunteers) and, on the other, Denikin's refusal to concede more than the "Curzon Line" before a restored Russian government could negotiate a final settlement created a deadlock in the Polish-Volunteer negotiations that not even French mediation could resolve. (French-supported efforts to bring Rumania into an alliance with the Volunteers encountered the very same difficulties.) When the Volunteers were at the peak of their success in November, Piłsudski decided, in part because of Karnicki's report on Volunteer attitudes,[42] that he did not want to support Denikin and, instead, entered a secret truce with the Bolsheviks.[43] When, in December, the Volunteers were in retreat, Piłsudski promised to mount a new offensive against the Bolsheviks, but not until the spring.

On December 5, Petliura and Piłsudski began negotiations that subsequently resulted in an alliance. The basis of this pact, formally concluded only the following April, was already provided by Petliura's willingness to concede Galicia to Poland and Piłsudski's decision not to join with the Volunteers, but after their defeat to restore an independent Ukraine. In spite of intense efforts by General Mangin to revive Polish-Volunteer talks in December and French appeals to Piłsudski to begin operations immediately, no results were forthcoming. A new agreement between Denikin and the Galician army in November[44] and Piłsudski's new association with Petliura in December had only further alienated the two major forces. By the beginning of 1920, the retreating Volunteers were little more than a disorganized band of soldiers seeking refuge where they could find it, especially in the Crimea.

---

[41] Maklakov Archives, B, II, 4.

[42] Karnicki to Piłsudski, November 15, 1919, cited in Bradley, p. 196.

[43] See Piotr S. Wandycz, "Secret Soviet-Polish Peace Talks in 1919," *Slavic Review*, XXIV, 3 (Seattle, Wash., 1965), pp. 425–449.

[44] Denikin recognized the Galician government and gave Galician troops autonomous status in the Volunteer army, an arrangement never accepted by the head of the West Ukrainian Republic, E. Petrushevych. In December the Galician delegation in Paris broke with the Directory and formed a separate Ukrainian National Committee, which denounced Petliura's policy. See Committee statements in Maklakov Archives, B, II, 3; see also Margolin, p. 188.

With the defeat of the force that they had always regarded as "the only one in South Russia worthy of support," the British decided to end their intervention and seek a settlement with the Bolsheviks. Similarly, Clemenceau concluded that the intervention had failed, and that the only viable policy was to erect a "barbed wire entanglement around Russia" based chiefly on "a strong Poland."[45] Although there was no inclination on the part of France to enter relations with Moscow, negotiations for exchange of prisoners and repatriation of Russian soldiers in France were entered into, and they resulted in an agreement with Litvinov, which was subsequently signed on April 20 in Copenhagen. According to a joint communiqué published later by the Bolsheviks, the French representative (Duchesne) even made a promise that France henceforth "will not intervene in the internal politics of Russia and will not support any aggressive measures against the Soviet Republics of Russia and the Ukraine."[46]

The year 1920 did not, as this might suggest, bring a quick end to war and intervention, for on April 26 Piłsudski and his new ally, Petliura, began the promised spring campaign in the Ukraine. Moreover, Millerand replaced Clemenceau, and the French responded with new plans for an active intervention to regenerate the Russian Civil War. General Weygand had already drawn up a new version of the Foch plan in January, and Millerand now made it the basis of a French policy, relying primarily on the Polish military action but also looking toward a renewal of Volunteer efforts.[47] When the Polish-Ukrainian offensive began in April, Denikin had just resigned, assuming that the Volunteers would soon be evacuated abroad. However, his successor, General Petr Wrangel, who had been one of his severest critics, soon began to reorganize the Volunteer remnant in the Crimea and prepare it for more than evacuation.

The British, now seeking Soviet cooperation to end hostilities, strongly opposed the new war and warned the Volunteers against becoming involved. But French urging overcame any hestitation Wrangel might have had. In the face of a virtual ultimatum from London, Wrangel notified Mangin on May 30 that he was "quite

---

[45] *Paris Peace Conference,* Vol. IX, p. 848; *British Documents,* Vol. II, pp. 744–745.

[46] *Dokumenty vneshnei politiki SSSR,* Vol. II (Moscow: Gospolitizdat, 1958), p. 462.

[47] Bradley, pp. 172–173.

disposed to cooperate with the Polish and Ukrainian forces."[48] With this in mind, he began an offensive on June 7, keeping his troops east of the Dnieper to facilitate cooperation. On the diplomatic side, Wrangel's chief representative, Petr Struve, renounced Denikin's "One Russia" policy and called for federation among the "existing new separate entities."[49] Wrangel himself entered into talks with Ukrainian representatives (from the Ukrainian National Committee) in the Crimea and sent his Chief-of-Staff, General Makhrov, to Warsaw to seek ties with Poland and to investigate the possibility of cooperation with Russian and Ukrainian forces there.[50]

Meanwhile, British-French relations were reaching a crisis. At the Spa conference held in early July,[51] Lloyd George vented his intense displeasure with Poles, Ukrainians, Volunteers, and French alike; at his insistence, an appeal was sent to the Soviet government on July 11, calling for a cessation of military operations and an agreement to negotiate. Millerand not only refused to associate France with such polices but privately began a campaign to frustrate British efforts. Indeed, thanks in part to the Bolshevik rejection of both appeals and warnings from the British, French policy appeared to be on its way to success, even in persuading the Rumanians to supply arms to Wrangel. Such success as there was, however, was rather short-lived, for the Bolsheviks were reversing the tide of battle even while the Spa conference was still in progress. Kiev had already been lost again in June, and, by the end of July, Warsaw was threatened. The Red Army crossed the Curzon line and brought in its trail a ready-made Communist regime for Poland, which would at last serve to export the Revolution to the west.

In a desperate effort to pull victory from defeat, Millerand dispatched Weygand to Warsaw and, after another conference with the British at Hythe on August 8 and 9, announced his decision to recognize Wrangel's government and provide all possible support to enable the Volunteers to resume the offensive, which had been halted late in June.[52] Wrangel not only sent his troops out again in

---

[48] Wrangel Archives, Diplomatic Correspondence, Case I, File 5.

[49] Struve to Millerand, June 20, 1920, *ibid.*

[50] On Makhrov's activities see P. S. Makhrov, "General Wrangel i B. Savinkov" (ms., Columbia University).

[51] *British Documents,* Vol. VIII, p. 502 ff.

[52] *Ibid.,* p. 725 ff. See also Millerand to Bazili, August 10, 1920, Wrangel Archives, Diplomatic Correspondence, Case I, File 5; and Millerand to Foch, August 16, 1920, Wrangel Military Archives, File 48.

August but, through Makhrov, entered into new arrangements with the Ukrainians and Poles. One Russian unit that had taken refuge in Poland, the Bredov Corps, had already been sent to rejoin the Volunteers, and by mid-October Makhrov had established a working agreement with Boris Savinkov, the important Russian Socialist Revolutionary leader who had Piłsudski's personal backing.

Savinkov had gone to Poland in January 1920, after serving the previous year as a key man in the Russian delegation in Paris. With the financial support of the Polish High Command, he had succeeded in reorganizing various Russian forces in Poland, which, in alliance with Poland, would continue the war and strive to establish a democratic federation in Russia.[53] Under special arrangements, worked out with some difficulty between Savinkov and Makhrov, a new "Third" Russian army was organized in Poland. It was to be under Savinkov's "Political Center," although it recognized Wrangel as military commander. Savinkov and Makhrov then also worked out an agreement with Petliura's forces, and in October the Third Russian army and the Ukrainian army began operations side by side with the full support of the Polish Chief-of-Staff, General Rozwadowski.

These developments, which under other circumstances might have been termed a most remarkable success in fulfilling the hopes for unity and the plans of the French for a joint offensive, were in October 1920 not considered a crowning achievement but a pathetic farce. They were indeed acts of desperation, for, as the tide of battle had been turned once again with new Polish victories in August and September, the pressures to make peace had been revived and this time not only by the British. By October, virtually everyone was ready for peace; the struggle had been too long, and the prospects for the greater victories once dreamed of were now too dim. Poland, therefore signed an armistice agreement with the Bolsheviks on

---

[53] See B. V. Savinkov, "Letter from the Representative of the Russian Political Committee in Poland to General Wrangel," October 15, 1920 (ms., The Hoover Institution); Savinkov Statement of Policy, January 1920, Maklakov Archives, B, II, 1; Agreement of August 27, 1920, between Savinkov and Russian forces in Poland, and Statement of the (Savinkov) Political Committee, October 2, 1920, in the P. N. Miliukov Personal Archives (ms., Columbia University); and Savinkov's testimony in *Ispoved Savinkova: protsess Borisa Savinkova* (Berlin: 'Russkoe Ekho,' 1924), p. 82. Further material may be found in the Jozef Pilsudski Institute of America.

October 12; this went into effect six days later, a date that automatically became a deadline for military operations.

The operation that put Russian and Ukrainian troops in the field together was thus in fact a mutual attempt to escape before the terms of the armistice came into effect, requiring the disarming and internment of such forces still in Poland. The effort was in vain; both Russians and Ukrainians were defeated and driven back into Poland, where they were then disarmed and eventually released as civilians. Wrangel, who on October 19 received Count de Martel, the newly appointed French "High Commissioner," was in turn forced to abandon the struggle within a few days.[54] Turning his ships over to France as security for assistance rendered, Wrangel led his army into permanent exile in November. The war and the intervention were finally over.

The intervention was an obvious failure. At the crucial moment it failed, in part because of Denikin's myopic refusal to cooperate with the French effort to reach agreement with the Ukraine. The only real possibility of cooperation lay in general acceptance of federation as the basis of unity, and, much to its credit, the Ukraine was willing, while the Volunteers were not. Denikin always argued that such matters had to be left to a Constituent Assembly, but in fact he rejected compromise with the Ukraine both because he feared its consequences and because he believed it unnecessary. Contrary to the impression he gave, his views were not all reactionary, but he completely lacked the practical statesmanship necessary for the leading role he insisted on playing. And one of his most serious mistakes was in believing that he could win the war alone.

However, the French intervention also failed because of the inability of any of the three Ukrainian governments—the Rada, the Hetmanate, and the Directory—to hold on to their own territory. That can be blamed partly on the Bolsheviks, partly on the Germans, and partly on Makhno and the very great role that anarchy and anarchism played in the Ukraine. But the fact remains that the instability of the Ukrainian governments and their failure to organize effective military forces not only upset French efforts but also made it easy for Denikin to refuse his coopera-

---

[54] P. N. Wrangel, *Always With Honor* (New York: Speller, 1957), pp. 297–298.

tion. One may speculate that the outcome might have been quite different in the spring and summer of 1919 if the Ukrainian government and army had been more of a match for the Bolsheviks and the anarchists. The possibility that the French might be able to influence Volunteer policy—and even keep them out of the Ukraine, since the original Volunteer plan was to follow the Volga route to Moscow—was eliminated by the collapse of the Directory and the French evacuation that followed.

The Volunteers and the Ukrainians were not alone at fault, for the Allies also failed. Certainly theirs was a difficult task, especially in view of the deep-seated antagonism between Russians and non-Russians. Furthermore, the Allied countries had an enormous amount of popular opposition to intervention; and, in this respect, Lloyd George and Wilson were more representative of the public mood and the limits that it placed on Allied policy. However, even in terms of the advocates of intervention, such as Pichon and Churchill, Britain and France were never really united on policy and action; being divided, they were much less effective in seeking unity among those whom they were aiding. Both sought the overthrow of the Bolsheviks and the restoration of Russia as a federated democratic republic, but they came unprepared to deal with the political complexity of such a goal, and in their improvisations they most often undermined their own efforts.

Perhaps it would have been better for Russia if the Allies had not intervened at all. Certainly the effort to keep Russia in the First World War contributed first to the fall of the Provisional Government and then to the disintegration that set the stage for later failures. On the other hand, prior to November 1918 it would have been asking too much to expect Allied policy makers not to do what at the time seemed to be imperative if they were going to win the war. Moreover, to assert that it was only the postwar intervention that was a mistake is to ignore the continuity in Allied policy. Neither Britain nor France could simply stop history at one point in time and get off. They continued to intervene after November 1918 largely because they had intervened before and because they could not make peace. Unless one takes a view of Allied interests completely different from those held by the leaders themselves (including Wilson and Lloyd George), it is difficult not to conclude that the Allies in fact did what they had to do—and no more.

Perhaps, as Churchill has suggested, circumstances in both Russia and the Allied countries conspired to produce an effort that was just enough to do the most harm and gain the least advantage.[55] But, if that was the case, then it should be added that in the final analysis they were all—Allies, Russians, Ukrainians, and others— not the creators so much as the victims of those circumstances which caused their failure.

---

[55] W. S. Churchill, *The Aftermath* (London: Thornton Butterworth, 1929), p. 273.

CHAPTER FOURTEEN

America and the Ukrainian National Cause, 1917–1920

Constantine Warvariv

WE ARE DEALING with a topic around which many accusations, misunderstandings, and half-truths have accumulated for over half a century on both sides of the Atlantic.[1] Many Ukrainians and friends of their cause are often mystified at the treatment that the Ukrainian people and political aspirations received in American official and non-official channels.[2] We also know that false preconceptions and misunderstandings on both sides cannot be dissolved in short order; this requires time, patience, the avoidance of harmful insinuations, and, above all, a scrupulous dedication to scholarship.

This essay will analyze American responses to the Ukrainian

---

[1] See M. Suprunenko, *Ukraina v period inozemnoi interventsii i hromadianskoi viiny, 1918–1920* (Kiev, 1951); R. H. Symonenko, *Imperialistychna polityka SShA shchodo Ukrainy v 1917–1918 rokakh,* (Kiev: AN URSR, 1957). See also A. V. Likholat, *Rozgrom natsionalisticheskoi kontrrevoliutsii na Ukraine, 1917–1922* (Moscow: Gospolitizdat, 1954); A. E. Kunina, *Proval amerikanskikh planov zavoevaniia mirovogo gosudarstva v 1917–1920 gg.* (2nd ed.; Moscow: Gospolitizdat, 1954).

[2] See Nicholas D. Chubaty, "America and the Russian Empire," *The Ukrainian Quarterly,* VII (New York, 1951); Clarence A. Manning, "Ukraine and American Diplomacy," *ibid.,* IV (1948); Roman Smal-Stocki, *The Captive Nations: Nationalism of the Non-Russian Nations in the Soviet Union* (New York: Bookman Associates, 1960), especially pp. 7–12. See also an admirable work, reflecting a wide breadth of objective historical knowledge and personal experience, written by a learned American lawyer and former member of the Ukrainian government, the late Arnold D. Margolin, *From a Political Diary: Russia, the Ukraine and America, 1905–1945* (New York: Columbia University Press, 1946).

attempt to establish national statehood in the aftermath of the First World War. It is based primarily on published and unpublished documentary materials located in the National Archives, the State Department, and the Library of Congress. Chronologically, this study will cover the period from March 1917, when Romanov rule ended and the Ukrainian people, along with other non-Russian nationalities, undertook to establish a free existence, to July 1920, when the Ukrainian People's Republic ceased to exist as a separate political entity and the whole country was in the hands of Soviet troops. Occasionally, it has been necessary to move beyond this time period in order to clarify some relationship or idea concerning American policy toward Russia.

For a better understanding of American foreign policy during and immediately following the First World War, it is necessary to review briefly the influence of the past. A tradition of friendship toward the Russian Empire was from the beginning an important aspect of American foreign policy. Nonetheless, it is one of the singular coincidences of history that, in the early years of American national existence, tsarist Russia was the last of the great powers to recognize the new revolutionary government of the United States, just as that country, a century and a half later, was to be the last great power to recognize the new government of the Soviet Union. Historically, there were almost no causes for friction between the two countries. They were geographically isolated and followed divergent paths in the arena of world politics.

The provisions of the Treaty of Commerce and Navigation, signed on December 8, 1832, long remained satisfactory to both countries, and commerce flourished uninterrupted. The determining factor that perpetuated cordiality between the two distant and radically different lands was common hostility toward Great Britain.

When the clash of rival imperialisms led to the Crimean War in 1854, Great Britain and France supported Turkey against its northern neighbor, but American sympathies inclined toward Russia. This war furnished another occasion for the conclusion of a formal agreement between the two countries, the "Convention as to the Rights of Neutrals at Sea," signed in Washington on July 24, 1854. By the 1860's a tradition of friendship had been established, and this was confirmed during the following decade.

During the American Civil War, Russian sympathies were on the side of the Union, while Great Britain and France sympathized with the Confederacy. Tsar Alexander II made his sentiments known at once and never wavered from them during the struggle.[3] In September 1863, when the future of the Union seemed dark and it was felt that the threats of European intervention in the American Civil War would soon materialize, Russian friendship was manifested in a dramatic manner that was to linger long in the American public mind. On September 11, a Russian squadron appeared in San Francisco and another at New York with alleged "sealed instructions" to assist the Union, should Great Britain and France take hostile action.[4] It is more probable, however, that the fleets may have come to find a safe winter haven in neutral ports and to escape being bottled up at home in the event of a recrudescence of the Anglo-Russian conflict; both the content and the very existence of the "sealed instructions" remain very doubtful. But in the United States the visits were hailed with grateful rejoicing as a clear indication that at least one European power was prepared to stand by the Union.

The Alaska purchase closely followed these events. From 1868 to 1914, no fewer than nine Russian-American treaties or conventions were concluded. It is obvious that all of these grew out of limited problems related to direct contacts between the two countries and did not include the larger stakes of diplomacy. When the First World War broke out in August 1914 between the Triple Entente and the Central Powers, the Tsar found the United States not only officially neutral but indifferent to the Russian cause. However, economically speaking, Russia became an important factor, placing an ever-increasing number of orders for war supplies with American manufacturers. For example, before 1914, United States exports to the Russian Empire amounted to about $35 million a year, but, during the fiscal year 1916–1917, the exports reached almost $560 million.[5]

But the American nation knew little of the forces that had produced the catastrophe. Nor did the war aims of the Tsar enlist its sympathy or support. The friendly sentiments toward the Entente that soon manifested themselves were directed toward France,

---

[3] James Morton Callahan, *Russo-American Relations during the American Civil War* (Morgantown, W.V.: Department of History and Political Science, West Virginia University, 1908), p. 2.

[4] *Ibid.*, pp. 10–11.

[5] See *Current History*, XXIII (Philadelphia, 1926), p. 624.

Great Britain, and Belgium rather than toward autocratic Russia. On March 15, 1917, when Nicholas II announced the abdication, and a "Provisional Government" headed by Prince Lvov was created, the news of this sudden and almost bloodless collapse of the autocracy was greeted in Washington with great satisfaction. David R. Francis, then the United States Ambassador to Russia, felt confident that the control of affairs was in safe hands. He informed the Department of State of the revolution in a telegram dated March 17, 1917,[6] and the following day he asked Washington to extend formal recognition to the new government:

> I request respectfully that you promptly give me authority to recognize Provisional Government as first recognition is desirable from every viewpoint. This revolution is the practical realization of that principle of government which we have championed and advocated, I mean government by the consent of the governed. Our recognition will have a stupendous moral effect especially if given first. Rodzyanko [President of the Duma] and Milyukov [minister for Foreign Affairs] both assure me that Provisional Government will vigorously prosecute the war; furthermore upon Russia's success against the Central Empires absolutely depend the salvation of the revolution and the perpetuity of the government it establishes. . . .[7]

Two days later, Secretary of State Robert Lansing authorized Francis to recognize the new government on behalf of the United States.[8] This prompt recognition was dictated as much by the imminent entry of the United States into the war as by considerations of the stability of the new government and its ability to fulfill its inernational obligations. Moreover, fighting side by side with the autocratic tsarist regime would have made it difficult, if not impossible, to accept the Wilsonian thesis that the war was being fought to "make the world safe for democracy." The advent of an apparently democratic regime in Russia removed a most embarrassing obstacle to the successful operation of the machinery of war propaganda. In his war message to Congress of April 2, 1917, President Wilson clearly defined this attitude toward the March Revolution:

---

[6] *Papers Relating to the Foreign Relations of the United States, 1918, Russia* (3 vols.; Washington, D.C.: Government Printing Office, 1931–32), Vol. I, pp. 3–9 (hereafter: *Foreign Relations, 1918, Russia*).

[7] *Ibid.*, p. 6.

[8] *Ibid.*, p. 12.

Does not every American feel that assurance has been added to our hope for the future peace of the world by the wonderful and heartening things that have been happening within the last few weeks in Russia? Russia was known by those who knew it best to have been always in fact democratic in heart, in all the vital habits of her thought, in all the intimate relations of her people that spoke their natural instinct, their habitual attitude toward life. The autocracy that crowned the summit of her political structure, long as it had stood and terrible as was the reality of its power, was not in fact Russian in origin, character or purpose; and now it has been shaken off and the great, generous Russian people have been added in all their naive majesty and might to the forces that are fighting for freedom in the world, for justice, and for peace. Here is a fit partner for a League of Honor.[9]

This spirit of optimism and confidence in the "regenerative soul of Russia" was common among many American political and intellectual leaders at the time. In part, it was an expression of their wish to keep the Russian army fighting on the eastern front, thus speeding up the day of the final victory over the "enemy of mankind"—Germany. It was in this spirit that the United States Treasury advanced to the Provisional Government the sum of nearly $188 million;[10] this may have delayed its fall, but it could not prevent Russia's disintegration. The Ukrainian people, like all the other nationalities of the Empire, acclaimed the fall of tsardom in the belief that the time had come for the beginning of a new and hopeful era. While the Provisional Government granted some concessions to the Finns (their Constitution was approved on March 6, 1917) and issued a vague proclamation to the Poles, it was stubbornly reluctant to say or do anything that would recognize Ukrainian national aspirations.

The Ukrainian question made its first appearance on the American political scene several months before the United States' entry into the First World War. On January 24, 1917, a resolution was introduced in the House of Representatives, and simultaneously in the Senate, requesting that the President designate and appoint a day on which funds could be raised for the relief of the Ukrain-

---

[9] *Ibid.*, p. 17. For the full text of the war message, see James Brown Scott (ed.), *President Wilson's Foreign Policy: Messages, Addresses, Papers,* (New York, 1918) pp. 282–283.

[10] United States Secretary of the Treasury, *Annual Report for 1920,* Exhibit 25, showing cash advances made in 1917, p. 330.

ians, "especially for those in war-stricken Galicia, Bukovina, and other Provinces of Austria."[11] This measure was the result of the initiative taken by the Very Reverend Father P. Poniatyshyn, Administrator of the Ruthenian Catholic Diocese in the United States. He successfully enlisted the interest and support of his state's congressional leaders, Representative James A. Hamill and Senator William Hughes, both of New Jersey, who introduced the resolutions in their respective Houses. The measure was favorably considered by the Senate Committee on Foreign Relations, was passed unanimously by both Houses, and was signed by the President of the United States on March 2, 1917. It became Public Law Resolution No. 52 and is published in the United States Statute at Large, Chapter 154, of 1917 (page 999).

Of particular interest are the remarks by Hamill and others that appear in the Appendix to the Congressional Record of the 64th Congress, 2nd Session. Their speeches contain more or less accurate information about the Ukraine and describe Ukrainians as "a typical example of a people who have been actually submerged; they are, in fact, a forgotten race, and yet these Ukrainians constitute a nation just as clearly and sharply defined as are the Poles, the Russians, or the Bulgarians."[12] It should also be pointed out that on the eve of the Paris Peace Conference, Hamill introduced another, more far-reaching resolution requesting the American Commission to present before the International Peace Conference a petition calling for "the right of all Ukrainian territories to freedom, independence, and self-determination."[13] This resolution was referred to the Committee on Foreign Affairs for further study, but it was never acted upon.

Another interesting Congressional document, which indicates that the Ukrainian Revolution as well as the national revolutions of other non-Russian peoples had left some imprint on American public opinion, is to be found in the Senate Bill of June 29, 1918, introduced by Senator King of Massachusetts. This bill authorized the organization of a so-called "Russian Legion," to be composed

---

[11] United States Congress, 64th Congress, 2nd Session, House Joint Resolution 350 (*House Report* No. 1422, Vol. I), and Senate Joint Resolution No. 201 (*Senate Report* No. 1013, Vol. I).

[12] *Ibid.*, 64th Congress, 2nd Session, Appendix, pp. 522–523.

[13] *Ibid.*, 65th Congress, 3rd Session, House Joint Resolution 369 of December 13, 1918 (House Document 1868).

of Russian residents (although non-citizens) in the United States. According to the proposal, the precondition for joining the Legion was that:

> [No] man shall be enlisted in it until he has furnished satisfactory evidence that he will faithfully and loyally serve the cause of the United States and the cause of a united and independent Russia and that he desires to fight the Imperial Government of Germany and Imperial Government of Austria and any other nations with which the United States and its allies are now at war. . . . The force so raised . . . may be transported to Russia to be used against the common enemy either with our own troops or with those of Russia or any nation associated with us in the present war. . . .[14]

When the discussion of this resolution began, many senators raised questions as to what was meant by "a united and independent Russia." Senators Lodge, Wadsworth, McCumber, and Brandegee strongly opposed that precondition. They questioned whether there is "a united Russia," since there were many other nationalities who did not desire to be part of such an entity.

As a result of this interesting debate, the bill was substantially amended. The name was changed from "Russian Legion" to "Slavic Legion," and it was to be an "organization of volunteers [composed of Yugo-Slavs, Czecho-Slovaks and Ruthenians (Ukrainians)] belonging to the oppressed races of the Austro-Hungarian or German Empires resident in the United States but not citizens thereof nor subject to the draft." All references to Russia were removed from the revised bill which, however, was never enacted.[15]

The turbulent events in the former Russian Empire, complicated by a series of national revolutions, evoked further comments in the American press.[16] On November 28, 1917, the *New York Times*

---

[14] *Ibid.*, 65th Congress, 2nd Session, pp. 8480–8482.

[15] *Ibid.*, p. 8514.

[16] Although the Ukraine and Ukrainians were comparatively little known in this country during the First World War, a score of editorials and articles that appeared in leading American periodicals of that day were unusually well informed, and in some respects more objective and sympathetic toward the Ukraine's quest for freedom then was the case during the Second World War. For a detailed survey, see Stephen Shumeyko, "American Interest in Ukraine during World War I (as revealed in American periodical comments)," *The Ukrainian Quarterly*, II, 1 (New York, 1945), pp. 66–79. See also: Leonid Ivan Strakhovsky, *American Opinion about Russia, 1917–1920* (Toronto: University of Toronto Press, 1961).

speculated on the future of Russia in an editorial entitled, "Will Russia Break Up?"

> Speculations on the fate of Russia have usually assumed as a basis the continued existence of the country we now know by that name, within its present geographical boundaries. It is quite possible, however, that that vast empire will disappear, resolving itself into its constituent elements. The declarations of independence by Finland, the Ukraine, and other factors in the empire—the latest such declaration, that of Caucasus, was reported only yesterday—may be symptoms. Russia is an enormous bundle of nations, which . . . have been tied together by the string of Tsardom. The string has been cut. The bundle may fall apart.

Following the Ukrainian Declaration of Independence on January 22, 1918, various comments appeared in American periodicals and newspapers. Some of these were brief editorials pointing out that, instead of the seemingly one mighty Russian nation composed of a single homogeneous Russian people, the country was actually composed of many subjugated races striving for freedom, or at least autonomy. Brief, unbiased accounts of the Ukrainian political scene also appeared. Finally, some articles—written by prominent American journalists and scholars—presented unusually well-informed and comprehensive discussions of the Ukrainian national movement extending from the formation of the Kievan Principality to modern times.[17]

Questions as to the ability of the Russian Empire to remain intact also began to arise in the diplomatic dispatches of American missions in various European capitals. In a telegram dated January 9, 1918, the American Ambassador to Russia, David R. Francis, reported to Secretary of State Lansing that he had visited the French Ambassador in Petrograd, who told him that "France desired to recognize the Ukraine but his government [first] had cabled ministers in England and Italy suggesting or requesting *concerted* action." The telegram also informed Lansing that the Ukrainian delegation was admitted to the peace conference (at Brest-Litovsk), a fact that he, Francis, thought was "very significant, and indicates that the Soviets are abandoning the policy of all-Russian subjection." The telegram ends with the following recommendation:

> [I am] beginning to think separate peace improbable, perhaps impossible, and am inclined to recommend simultaneous recognition of

---

[17] See, for example, *New York Times Current History Magazine* for March 1918.

Finland, Ukraine, Siberia, perhaps Don Cossacks Province and Soviet as *de facto* government of Petrograd, Moscow and vicinity . . .[18]

A similar opinion was transmitted to Washington on January 14, 1918, by the American chargé d'affaires in Denmark, Mr. Grant-Smith.

At present the Allies have apparently no definite connection with the *de facto* governments, are cut off from the Ukraine, Finland and other separatist movements while some Austro-Germans have entered into direct relations with each group and consequently are enabled to pursue their plans unhindered.

He then asks:

Should such a course be deemed advisable, is not the United States from tradition, recent entry on the scene, Latin American experience with *de facto* governments and especially in the light of the President's recent message, the best suited among Germany's opponents to undertake the task?[19]

In response to these and other messages, the Department of State instructed its diplomatic posts, which were still maintained in some cities of the former Russian Empire, to provide answers to a number of specific questions, particularly with regard to the political, military, and economic conditions in certain areas. Following are some excerpts from a reply to the Department's questionnaire concerning the Ukraine, which the American Consul-General in Moscow, Maddin Summers, transmitted to Washington on January 14, 1918.

The Ukrainians set up a rival organization at Kiev and gradually extend their influence. Their small numbers, not more than a hundred intellectuals in the beginning, it is stated, dictated a cautious policy until they should win adherence in the army and among the peasants. They now have a Rada or parliamentary assembly, a ministry or general secretariat, a voluntary army, control of the staff of the southwest and Rumanian fronts, now combined in one front. . . .

The avowed policy of the Ukraine is to take the lead in creating a federal republic in Russia. There is, however, a pro-Austrian party, with partisans, it is supposed, in the ministry. There is also an open and skillful Austrian propaganda. A motive for secession from Russia

---

[18] *Foreign Relations, 1918, Russia,* Vol. I, p. 336.
[19] *Ibid.,* p. 338.

would be the hope of attaching to their republic the Ukrainians of Galicia, Bukovina and Transylvania. . . .

The leading factors of the situation are the traditional cult of the Little Russian language and literature and national customs; the historical distrust of the Little Russians for Poles and Russians; the attempts of the [tsarist] autocracy to suppress the Little Russian nationality; the land question; and the Austrian propaganda. . . .

There are said to be about 35,000 regularly organized Ukrainian volunteers in Kiev. Russian, that is non-Ukrainian troops, are disarmed in passage, and Ukrainian troops are hindered as far as possible from reaching the Ukraine from other fronts, and of course are disarmed. Nevertheless, the concentration of Ukrainian soldiers from other fronts is going-on steadily and there is likewise a steady withdrawal of other elements from the Ukraine front, so called. . . .

The soldiers of Ukraine origin probably have more discipline and better fighting qualities than the average of the Russian armies taken as a whole. The Ukrainian volunteers cheerfully salute officers, conduct themselves in an orderly fashion and are ardent patriots, but have still to prove their military value.

The Maximalist [Soviet] Ukraine movement, launched at Kharkov, is gaining ground in the provinces of Kharkov and Ekaterinoslav. The Maximalists are also crowding the Ukrainians in the eastern half of Chernigov. Little is heard of the Ukrainians in Volhynia, but they have a stout party in Mogilev. Both sides are disposed to negotiate and to try to outwit one another. . . . Bessarabia, with strong Ukrainian and Rumanian elements, has an obscure autonomous movement.

The Black Sea coast districts are not definitely aligned with any party. The fleet is divided. . . .[20]

I have purposely dwelled at length on this report to illustrate that rather objective information was available to those who requested it.

Shortly before, American Consul-General Summers transmitted to the Secretary of State the text of a note of the Ukrainian government dated December 21, 1917, and addressed to all belligerent and neutral powers, which according to Summers, "deserves careful consideration in view of the growing importance of the Ukrainian front."[21] This ably composed note informed "the powers and peoples of the world of the attitude of the Ukrainian Republic toward the peace negotiations beginning at Brest-Litovsk" between the representatives of the Soviet Russian government and the

---

[20] *Ibid.,* pp. 345–347.
[21] *Ibid.,* p. 415.

Central Powers. It provided the *raison d'être* for the Ukraine's entrance into the negotiations and declared that:

> The Ukrainian Republic, having now upon its land the Ukraine front, and making its entry independently into the arena of international affairs in the person of its General Secretariat, which is bound to conserve the interests of the Ukrainian people, ought to take part on a parity with other powers in all peace negotiations, conferences and congresses. [point 7]

The note ended with a commentary on the future form of government:

> Peace in the name of the whole of Russia can be concluded only by a federal government [of the future federation], which requires the recognition of all the republics and politically organized territories of Russia; and, if such a government should not be formed in the early future, then the only authority capable of concluding peace is the representative body of all these republics and territories. [point 9][22]

There is good reason to assume that the American source of information about events in the Ukraine during late 1917 and early 1918 was Douglas Jenkins, formerly American Consul at Riga, who was sent on December 12, 1917, to Kiev "with instructions to consult Summers in Moscow, concerning establishing a consulate at Kiev."[23] In one of his telegrams to Secretary Lansing, Ambassador Francis reported that he had "cautioned Jenkins against recognizing any government, [but] gave him discretion as to opening a consulate [in Kiev]."[24] Washington's official position at that early date concerning the recognition of Ukrainian independence was cryptically stated in a message from Lansing to Francis dated January 15, 1918:

> French Embassy [in Washington] advises that General Tabouis, the French Commissioner at Kiev, is being instructed to recognize Ukraine as in fact an independent Government. This [i.e., American] Government not disposed as yet to recognize any independent governments until the will of Russian people has been more definitely expressed on this general subject. The public utterances of the President have defined clearly the sympathy of the United States for democracy and self-government.[25]

---

[22] *Ibid.*, pp. 415–417.
[23] *Ibid.*, Vol. II, p. 649.
[24] *Ibid.*, p. 650.
[25] *Ibid.*, p. 657.

On the basis of numerous diplomatic exchanges among the Allies concerning recognition of the Ukrainian People's Republic in the period before Brest-Litovsk, it is possible to assume that the position of the United States remained open or, at least, not finally determined. Evidence supporting this assertion is also provided by the dramatic, last-minute attempts between the Allies and the Ukrainian Republic to reach some accommodation and to forestall the negotiations at Brest-Litovsk. Since this was the first (and last) official negotiation between the representatives of the Ukrainian government and all the "Big Four" Powers, it is worth quoting in full the pertinent State Department documents:

The Ambassador in France (Sharp) to the Secretary of State. Telegram. Paris, January 22, 1918. Following joint telegram dated Jassy, January 18, received from the Ministers of the United States, Italy, England, and France:

Yesterday morning we received a visit from the delegates of the Ukraine, Messrs. Galip, Undersecretary of State for Foreign Affairs, and Galicinsky, the Director of Finance. From the rather vague statement made to us by Mr. Galicinsky, we gathered following:

(1) That on account of the state of public opinion the Ukraine does not consider itself bound to recognize the treaties concluded under the regime of the Tsar;

(2) That having no army she is unable to continue the war and that as regards the Brest-Litovsk conference, the desire for peace is so widespread among the Ukrainian population that the government of the Rada would be unable to withstand this current, especially if the Bolsheviks manage to conclude peace with the Austro-Germans;

(3) That the Ukrainian government is apparently engaged in recruiting troops of which the greater number will be by voluntary enlistment for maintaining order in the interior, as well as for fighting the Bolsheviks and incidentally for guaranteeing the independence of the country against foreigners;

(4) That the Ukraine has no intention of allowing any interference in its internal affairs on the part of other states of Russia; as for her part, she undertakes to respect scrupulously the independence of these states. (Nevertheless Mr. Galip added that his country does not exclude the possibility of a federal union between her and the other parts of Russia and that he had even tried to get into communication with the union of south Russia and with Bessarabia, but we ourselves have gathered the impression that the federalist tendency had rather weakened in Ukraine lately);

(5) That as a result of her internal conditions and of her relations

with the other states of Russia, as well as with foreign powers, the economic and financial situation of the Ukraine is particularly serious.

As a result of what preceded, Mr. Galip has formulated the following demands: (1) Recognition of the independence of Ukraine by the great powers of the Entente and nomination of the Allied diplomatic representatives at Kiev; (2) Financial support to the Ukrainian Government; and (3) Facilities on the part of the Entente for supporting the Ukraine with manufacturing products.

In the course of conversation, Mr. Galip admitted that the military situation would change completely if there were Allied forces in Russia, if the Allied powers were masters of communications with Vladivostok, and if agreements could be concluded with Turkey and Bulgaria, whose representatives at Brest-Litovsk had apparently made advances to the Ukrainian delegates and shown a certain resentment against Germany and Austria-Hungary. We informed the delegates that we would reserve our reply pending a discussion. Consequently, this morning we called upon them and stated: (1) That in the first place, the Allied powers must ask the Ukraine, even if it could not carry on the war financially, to give us at least an understanding that it would conclude no separate peace; (2) That the Ukrainian Government should at the same time undertake to enter into no degrading relations with our enemies; (3) That the authorities should organize with the assistance of the Allied military mission an armed force that would be sufficient to assure not only order in the interior but also to render the country independent of an attack from outside; (4) That the Ukrainian Government should enter into relations with other Russian autonomous states as well as with Rumania so as to present a solid front to the Central Empires who are the natural adversaries of the principles of nationalities as has again been confirmed by the Brest-Litovsk negotiations; (5) That the Ukrainian Government should undertake to facilitate the revictualing of Rumania and to take to this end the means for assuring the regular service of the railways in conjunction with the measures that the Bessarabian Government is now adopting for these purposes with the assistance of the Rumanian Government.

At the same time, we considered it our duty not to let pass unprotested Mr. Galip's statement regarding treaties concluded under the Tsar's regime. We remarked in this respect that the powers entered into war not for a cause which interested the Tsar and his government but at the request of Russia for the cause of a small Slavonic people which the Central Empires wished to crush; that the war provoked by the Germanic powers had therefore been carried on by the Allied powers to defend the principles of nationalities in accordance with sentiments manifested at all times by the Russian people. Consequently, the Allied powers had treated through the mediation of the Imperial Government with entire Russia and the fundamental principles of the treaties of allegiance ought to be accepted and recognized by all the states of Russia, especially the Ukraine.

We finally decided that the attitude of the great Allied powers towards the Ukraine from the point of view of recognizing her independence, her financial help, and military collaboration was dependent on the reply which we received on the above five points. The French Minister added that he was already authorized to acknowledge the independence of Ukraine and that he was ready to do so immediately on receipt of a satisfactory answer from the delegates. Mr. Galip having informed us that he had not the necessary powers to undertake the engagements we asked of him but that he would refer by telegram to the Rada, we decided to have another interview with the Ukrainian delegates as soon as the reply reached them.

The language of the Ukrainian delegates agrees with the information received from the Allied agents in Kiev showing that the Entente can at present expect no effective help from the Ukraine. All that we can ask of her is to gain time to allow the Allied powers to act for the improvement of the general situation on this front.... We again expressed the opinion that the only means of attaining this and consequently of deciding the attitude of the Ukraine in a manner conformable with the interests of our cause is to send to Russia international [force] under the conditions we have indicated. It is well to note that this impression is shared by the Rumanian Government which has also had interviews with the delegates of the Ukrainian Government.

Sharp[26]

On January 26, 1918, Ambassador Sharp sent Washington the following joint telegram from the Ministers of the United States, England, France, and Italy, dated Iaşi, January 23:

The head of the Ukrainian delegation has communicated to us the following information:

The Ukrainian delegates at Brest-Litovsk have received full powers to negotiate peace with the Central Empires. The latter are insisting especially on the resumption of economic relations. They ask to exchange their manufacturing products against provisions from Ukraine. The government at Kiev not disposing of an army, and being obliged to employ its feeble police forces against the Maximalists,

---

[26] *Ibid.,* pp. 660–663.

cannot resist the pressure of the Germanic powers. According to Mr. Galip, the Ukraine, even after conclusion of peace, will endeavor to safeguard its future, to maintain good relations with the Allied powers, to organize itself with their help and to limit to the inevitable minimum the amount of provisions sent to our enemies. Mr. Galip also states that the Ukraine will assist in the revictualing of Rumania and the evacuation of national Czech, Serbian, and Transylvanian armies. It is doubtful in the present state of anarchy and in presence of the German occupation, whether the Ukraine will have the means of conforming to the intentions if they are sincere. . . .

Sharp[27]

Nothing, however, came of this offer. The Ukrainian representatives resumed their negotiations at Brest-Litovsk and on February 9, 1919, signed the peace treaty with the Central Powers.

Meanwhile, on January 8, President Wilson delivered an address to Congress that included the famous Fourteen Points, the sixth of which called for:

The evacuation of all Russian Territory and such a settlement of all questions affecting Russia as will secure the best and freest cooperation of the other nations of the world in obtaining for her an unhampered and unembarrassed opportunity for the independent determination of her own political development and national policy and assure her of a sincere welcome into the society of free nations under institutions of her own choosing; and, more than a welcome, assistance also of every kind that she may need and may herself desire. The treatment accorded Russia by her sister nations in the months to come will be the acid test of their good will, of their comprehension of her needs as distinguished from their own interests, and of their intelligent and unselfish sympathy.[28]

Reference to "the independent determination of her own political development and national policy" was interpreted by some as supporting the territorial integrity of the Empire. There is also evidence that this position was *not* endorsed at all governmental levels. Colonel House, for example, was inclined to favor the breakup of the Russian colossus. After discussing the question with

---

[27] *Ibid.*, p. 664.

[28] Ray Stannard Baker and William E. Dodd (eds.), *Public Papers of Woodrow Wilson*, Vol. I (New York: Harper and Brothers, 1925), pp. 159–160.

President Wilson on September 19, 1918, House commented: "I am not in agreement with the President as to leaving Russia intact." House went on to explain that Russia "is too big and homogeneous for the safety of the world. I would like to see Siberia a separate republic, and European Russia divided into three parts."[29] There is further evidence indicating that Secretary Lansing also suggested that the Baltic provinces and the Ukraine become autonomous states within a Russian confederation, with Poland and possibly Finland becoming independent.[30]

As we have indicated before, there was undoubtedly some public support for the position of Lansing and House within the United States, particularly from areas with large concentrations of Eastern European immigrants. Senator Lodge of Massachusetts, claiming to represent "the real feeling of the people of the United States and certainly the Senate of the United States," suggested that the peace conference consider the formation of an independent Ukraine and of separate Baltic states under American and Allied protection.[31] The separation of non-Russian territories, with the possibility of their later confederation in a Great Russian-Siberian state, was also envisaged by the American journalists Frank Cobb and Walter Lippmann, who, at Colonel House's request, undertook in October 1918 to prepare a "commentary" on the Fourteen Points of President Wilson. The following are pertinent excerpts from their memorandum, which Colonel House sent to President Wilson for comments:

> The first question is whether Russian territory is synonymous with territory belonging to the former Russian Empire. This is clearly not so, because proposition 13 stipulates an independent Poland, a proposal which excludes the territorial reestablishment of the Empire. What is recognized as valid for the Poles will certainly have to be recognized for the Finns, the Lithuanians, the Letts, and perhaps also for the Ukrainians. Since the formulating of this condition these subject nationalities have emerged and there can be no doubt that

---

[29] Cited in John M. Thompson, *Russia, Bolshevism, and the Versailles Peace* (Princeton, N.J.: Princeton University Press, 1966), pp. 192–193.

[30] Robert Lansing, *The Peace Negotiations: A Personal Narrative* (Boston: Houghton Mifflin Co., 1921), pp. 192–193.

[31] In a memorandum to the veteran American diplomat Henry White, member of the American delegation to negotiate peace. See Allan Nevins, *Henry White: Thirty Years of American Diplomacy* (New York: Harper and Brothers, 1930), p. 354.

they will have to be granted an opportunity of free development . . .

This can mean nothing less than the [recognition] by the peace conference of a series of [*de facto*] governments representing Finns, Esths, Lithuanians, Ukrainians. This primary [act] of recognition should be conditional upon the calling of national assemblies for the creation of *de facto* governments, as soon as the peace conference has drawn frontiers for these new states. The frontiers should be drawn so far as possible on ethnic lines, but in [every] case the right of unhampered economic [transit] should be reserved. No dynastic ties with German [or] Austrian or Romanoff princes should be permitted, and every inducement should be [given] to encourage federal [relations] between these new states. Under proposition 3 the economic sections of the treaty of Brest-Litovsk are obliterated, but this proposition should not be construed as forbidding a customs union, a monetary union, a railroad union, etc., of these states on the same terms.

As for Great Russia and Siberia, the peace conference might well send a message asking for the creation of a government sufficiently [representative] to speak for these territories. It should be understood that economic rehabilitation is offered provided a government carrying sufficient credentials can appear at the peace conference.

The essence of the Russian problem then in the immediate future would seem to be: (1) the recognition of provisional governments; (2) assistance extended to and through these governments.

With respect to Point 10, which stated that "The peoples of Austria-Hungary, whose place among the nations we wish to see safeguarded and assured, should be accorded the freest opportunity of autonomous development," the Cobb-Lippmann memorandum commented:

This proposition no longer holds. Instead we have (today) the following elements:

. . . (2) *Galicia*. Western Galicia is clearly Polish. Eastern Galicia is in large measure Ukrainian (or Ruthenian) and does not of right belong to Poland.

There also are several hundred thousand Ukrainians along the north and northeastern borders of Hungary and in parts of Bukovina (which belonged to Austria).

As for an independent Polish state (Point 13), which should include the territories "inhabited by indisputably Polish populations," the memorandum suggested:

On the east, Poland should receive no territory in which Lithuanians or Ukrainians predominate. . . . The principle on which frontiers [of the Polish state] will be [delimited] is contained in the President's word "indisputably." This may imply the taking of an impartial census before frontiers are marked.[32]

President Wilson, however, responded in lukewarm fashion to the work of Cobb and Lippmann, noting that their analysis was a satisfactory interpretation of the principles involved, but that the detailed application of these principles should be reserved for the peace conference.

Another important source of semi-official information that sheds light on the American attitude toward the many thorny questions associated with the Russian question is the archive of the so-called Inquiry.[33] Organized at the behest of President Wilson in early September 1917, the Inquiry was composed largely of academicians —in particular, political and social scientists. Its purpose was to prepare the United States government's program for peace in advance of the termination of military hostilities. Throughout its existence, the Inquiry's staff, numbering about 150 scholars, produced and collected nearly 2,000 separate reports and documents on virtually every region of the globe, plus at least 1,200 maps. At the end of the war, certain members of the group accompanied President Wilson to Paris, where they served as advisers to the American delegation and, in some cases, as negotiators on international commissions.

Archibald Cary Coolidge, professor of Eastern European and Middle Eastern history at Harvard University, was placed in charge of the Eastern European Division, which included Russia and its European provinces. When Coolidge went overseas in April 1918, he was replaced by Robert H. Lord, assistant professor

---

[32] *Foreign Relations, 1918: Supplement I, The World War*, Vol. I, (Washington, D.C.: Government Printing Office, 1933), pp. 408–413.

[33] The American preparatory commission, known as the Inquiry, functioned under the direction of Colonel House for some fourteen months prior to the armistice. It provided the earliest precedent for use by the United States government of numerous scholars whose special talents were directed toward the shaping of American foreign policy. There is no complete single listing of the reports and documents prepared by the Inquiry. *An Inventory of Records of the American Commission to Negotiate Peace*, compiled by H. Stephen Helton and published by the National Archives ("Preliminary Inventories No. 89"), serves as a useful, though incomplete, guide to the Inquiry's production.

of modern European history at Harvard. Professor Coolidge, who had been mainly responsible for bringing together the staff of the Eastern European Division, seemed confident that he had recruited at least some of the best students for this work. He once said of Frank A. Golder, his top Russian adviser: "I have not thought of any man better than Golder for Russia. He is a very conscientious worker and has been in the country recently."[34] Golder authored at least two extensive studies dealing with the Ukrainian problem. His point of view is well illustrated in the conclusion to one of his reports, entitled "Ukraine" and dated February 15, 1918:

> The Ukraine has ceased to be a local question and has become a world problem. On its proper solution depend the future peace and welfare of the world. In the first place the Ukrainians in Russia and Austria (those in Hungary are very ignorant and nothing is heard of their desire for nationality) must be brought together so that such intrigues as have been going on during the last two decades may not be repeated. In the second place, the Central Powers must not be permitted to get the upper hand in Ukraine. This is a matter of the greatest importance which the Germans realize fully, but the Allies do not seem to. Control of Ukraine gives the Central Powers possession of the richest part of Europe; it gives them not only the route to Bagdad but also to India and China.
>
> Under Germany the Ukrainians have no future. With their high percentage of illiteracy they are quite incapable of managing their country, and that work they will hand over to the Germans as they have already the mineral resources, and the natives will never be anything more than capitalistic slaves. The hardships felt under Russia, the prohibition to write pamphlets in Ukrainian, will be nothing as compared with the humiliations they will have to endure under their German and Magyar masters. Russia driven beyond the Volga and from the Baltic will either relapse into barbarism or will make so little progress that it will not be able to play any great part in the world's movements.
>
> From the point of view of all concerned there seems to be but one honest solution to the Ukrainian question, and that is union with Russia. The causes that have estranged them are now removed. There is no good reason why they should not live in harmony in the future, and there are many reasons why they would. . . .
>
> For the sake of the peace of the world, for the sake of Russia and

---

[34] Coolidge to James T. Shotwell, November 3, 1917, Inquiry Archives, file No. 97, National Archives. Shotwell, professor of history at Columbia, joined the Inquiry in the capacity of director of research.

Ukraine, for the sake of the Central Powers themselves, Great Russia and Little Russia must be united into a strong and free nation.[35]

It is interesting to note that, despite earlier (1918) recommendations encouraging reunion "within a federalized or genuinely democratic Russia" of the border regions in the south and west, the Inquiry's leaders proved to be capable of changing their mind as the new situation required. Prior to the Paris Peace Conference, there was not a single Inquiry report that tried to come to grips with the possible menace of Bolshevism to European security. Bolshevism in Russia was viewed strictly as a temporary, abnormal condition. All of the Inquiry's original plans assumed the imminent establishment of a democratic constitutional government in Russia.

Nevertheless, in its "Outline of Tentative Recommendations" of January 21, 1919, the Inquiry displayed an awareness of the real situation, concluding that if the Bolshevik regime continued in power then "there seems to be no alternative to accepting the independence and tracing the frontiers of all the non-Russian nationalities under discussion."[36] The formation of an independent Ukrainian state was specifically recommended, "provided Ukrainian nationalism is strong enough to justify that decision." Assuming sufficient ardor and enthusiasm among the Ukrainian population and the rise of a separate nation-state, the Inquiry report further suggested the advisability of eastern Galicia's being annexed to an independent Ukraine. Should that not happen, the alternative would have the territory annexed to the new Polish state, providing there were sufficient guarantees for an eventual plebiscite to decide popular preference in the area.

The Crimea, too, would be included in the proposed Ukrainian state. Geographic and economic considerations were paramount. An independent Ukraine would otherwise be lodged between the Crimea and Russia proper, without any outlet to the sea.

The status of "provisional independence" was recommended for Georgia, with the alternative of annexation to the Ukrainian state within some form of federal organization. Thus, in accordance with the Inquiry's recommendations of January 21, 1919, in the absence of a reconstituted democratic and federative government in Russia, the Empire would be broken up into a number of independent

---

[35] Inquiry Archives, typewritten document No. 188, National Archives.
[36] An Outline of Tentative Recommendations of January 21, 1919, Inquiry Archives, National Archives.

national states, extending from the Arctic Ocean to the Black Sea. These new states would consist of the former western regions of the Russian Empire: Finland, Estonia, Latvia, Lithuania, Poland, the Ukraine, and Armenia.

According to a recent and pioneering American study of the policies and operations of the Inquiry, it is not clear whether the establishment of these new independent nations was recommended to create a buffer zone separating Russia from Central Europe, or whether the Inquiry was simply attempting to apply the doctrine of self-determination to the ethnic groups within the Russian orbit. "From the existing evidence," the study concludes, "the latter seems to provide a more potent motive than the former."[37]

The Inquiry's recommendations also favored independence for Czechoslovakia and Hungary. By January 1919 the Czechoslovak Republic was already a *fait accompli*. The recommended Czechoslovak and Hungarian frontiers were theoretically based on ethnic considerations, although economic factors influenced considerably the drawing of the lines. As for the sizeable group of Carpatho-Ukrainians, the report favored their separation from Hungary, under whom they had suffered frequently in the past. The union of Carpatho-Ruthenia with the Ukraine was opposed for fear it might eventually lead to union with Russia. "It is certainly undesirable that Russia should extend across the Carpathians down to the Hungarian plain." Hence, the best alternative—and the one supposedly favored by many Carpatho-Ukrainians—was for Carpatho-Ruthenia to unite with the new Czechoslovak state. With the exception of the Ukraine and the peoples of the Caucasus, the Inquiry's recommendations varied only slightly from the final settlement for Eastern Europe that was incorporated into the peace treaties.

The foregoing demonstrates that on the eve of the Peace Conference, which commenced in Paris in January 1919, the United States delegation had at its disposal a series of expert recommendations for the solution of important questions affecting the future of the peoples of Eastern Europe. However, in the case of the Ukraine the advice of American experts turned out to be of little influence in changing Wilson's mind, and therefore the American position remained committed to the preservation of the territorial

---

[37] Lawrence E. Gelfand, *The Inquiry: American Preparations for Peace, 1917–1919* (New Haven and London: Yale University Press 1963), p. 215.

integrity of what was referred to as "Russia." The official attitude of the United States was reiterated by the Department of State when it ordered the Liquidation Commission not to extend credit sales of surplus stocks—clothing, medical supplies, and motor equipment stored by the American Forces in France—to the Ukraine.[38] According to a telegraphic report from the United States Commission to Negotiate Peace to the Secretary of State, "The recognized Ukrainian Mission in Paris, which has purchased large quantity American Army supplies, represents Petliura Government."[39] In response to the State Departments query as to what was the "recognized Ukrainian Mission, Paris," Mr. Frank Polk, American plenipotentiary at the Peace Conference, cabled on October 17, 1919, the following reply:

> With regard to the "recognized Ukrainian mission" in Paris, there has been for a good many months a Ukrainian mission here which has flooded this delegation with propaganda. We are not aware that

---

[38] The Liquidation Commission was established by an act of Congress for the purpose of disposing vast quantities of surplus war stocks of the American Expeditionary Forces in Europe—clothing, foodstuffs, medical supplies, and instruments of industry and transportation that were held in French warehouses. Such classes of stocks seemed peculiarly suitable for relieving hunger and the urgent want of the peoples of Eastern Europe. It was believed that the sales of these articles to the liberated peoples of Eastern Europe would also serve an important function in stabilizing the governments and institutions that were beginning to take shape, and that they would help to check the advance of Bolshevism.

According to the final report of the Commission, "In some instances it was felt desirable to make sales to cooperative societies or organizations, rather than to the Governments. In each case, however, the Commission has, either directly or through such cooperative society, taken Government obligations in payment for the stocks. . . . On the whole, the prices were rather higher than could have been procured at wholesale from any other purchasers. They were believed, however, to be fair and just when considered in the light of the quality of the securities and other circumstances associated with the transactions." U.S. War Department, Liquidation Commission, *Final Report of the United States Liquidation Commission, War Department,* by Edwin B. Parker, Chairman (Washington, D.C.: Government Printing Office, 1920), pp. 29–30 (hereafter cited as Liquidation Commission, *Report).*

[39] *Papers Relating to the Foreign Relations of the United States, 1919, Russia* (Washington, D.C., Government Printing Office, 1937), p. 779 (hereafter: *Foreign Relations, 1919, Russia.)*

it has been recognized by any one and it is dealt with on the same footings as the numerous delegations of other [un]recognized groups. The acting President of the mission is Count Tyszkevytch and the Vice President is Dr. Paneyko. . . . Paneyko confirms reported purchase by Ukrainian mission of war stocks from American Army but states they have been unable to ship them out of France. Do not know who American army authorities consulted in connection with sale but it would seem to have been an extraordinary action for them to take without getting views of the Department.[40]

This information infuriated the State Department, and Secretary Lansing ordered a thorough investigation of the transaction between the Ukrainian Mission in Paris and American military authorities. From the reports supplied to Washington by the Commission to Negotiate Peace and by Judge Edwin Parker, Chairman of the Liquidation Commission, we learn the following interesting details:

(1) In his letter of March 24, 1919, to the Chairman of the Liquidation Commission, President Wilson gave the former a broad mandate with respect to disposing of enormous stocks of surplus materials "at the earliest possible moment." The letter concluded with this specific advice:

> The sympathetic interest which American people must have in the alleviation of misery amongst the liberated people should lead us to entertain the most sympathetic view as to prices and terms upon which this material is disposed of to them. I would be glad, therefore, if the Commission could accept as its guiding principle in these negotiations the fact that it is not only securing a rapid liquidation of materials that may otherwise prove practically unsalable, but also that it has an opportunity to perform a fine human service by approaching the matter in the most sympathetic mind. . . .[41]

(2) In April 1919 the Commission was approached by the representatives of the Ukrainian Republic for the purchase of supplies. Judge Parker wrote to the Secretary-General of the Commission to Negotiate Peace:

> We told them that we were not in a position to sell to Ukraine as it has not been recognized by the United States. After conference with Mr. Hoover's organization and others, however, a partnership was

---

[40] *Ibid.*, p. 779.
[41] *Ibid.*, p. 787.

formed consisting of Ivan Petrushevich, Voldemar Timoshenko and Simon-Jean Cerf, who made the proposal No. 97, referred to in your letter. This proposal was prepared in May but not acted upon by the Commission until on or about June 6th, having undergone careful investigation in the meantime. The proposal contemplated the purchase of supplies aggregating in value in excess of $11,500,000. While the proposal was accepted, deliveries thereunder were stopped by the Commission, and property of the value of approximately $8,000,000 delivered.[42]

While the sale was made to the "Ukrailian" [sic] partnership, that partnership in turn sold to the Republic of Ukrania [sic] and took in payment the notes of the Republic of Ukrania, which they passed on to this Commission. A copy of one of these notes you will find enclosed, signed originally by three representatives of the Republic of Ukrania at the Peace Conference, and subsequently reexecuted by Mr. Hyro Sydorenko, a certified copy of whose credentials are now in our files.

Incidentally, I beg to advise that a Committee of the Peace Conference who had visited Russia, Esthonia, Ukrania and neighboring Provinces, waited upon this Commission several times, and with great earnestness urged that in the interest of humanity, as well as for business and political reasons, the surplus stocks of the American Army should be sold to these peoples, including the Ukrainians. As before stated, however, a considerable portion of the proposed purchase was cancelled and deliveries never made.[43]

(3) On December 5, 1919, after two months of an intensive investigation, Mr. Polk submitted to the Department of State his report concerning "the circumstances and present situation as regards the sale by the Liquidation Board of supplies to a Ukrainian Cooperative Society representing the Petliura government."

At the present time the bulk of the material, comprising six and one half million dollars worth of articles of clothing, blankets, etc., $1,000,000 worth of medical supplies and $300,000 worth of motor material including 75 Cadillac automobiles, is understood to be still stored in warehouses in France near Bordeaux and Marseilles.

According to a statement of the Ukrainian representatives, 600,000 francs worth have been sold to persons and corporations in France in

---

[42] The total property actually sold to the Ukrainian People's Republic under this transaction amounted to $8,500,222.67, including $1,128,951.24 worth of medical supplies. Liquidation Commission, *Report*, p. 30.

[43] *Foreign Relations, 1919, Russia*, pp. 785–786.

order to obtain funds to defray the expenses of transportation, storage and handling of the supplies. I understand further at the present time there is in Marseilles a ship chartered to take a cargo of these supplies to Galatz.

From conference with the Liquidation Board I gather that the sale was originally made some months ago at a time when the forces of Petliura were cooperating against the Bolshevik and when the Board considered the Ukraine [to be in a position] similar to that of the Baltic states [to which] sales were [also] made. I may add confidentially that Judge Parker is frank to admit that in view of events subsequent to the sale, the apparent collapse of the Petliura movement and the anti-Polish and anti-Denikin trend it has taken, it is unfortunate that the sale was ever made but that now it is too late for the Liquidation Board to retract and their chief concern is, if possible, to cover themselves financially unless political considerations should influence the Department of State to take up the matter.

The Liquidation Commission is now considering whether to accept [at this time] further signatures of the Ukrainian [notes] by officers of a cooperative society which purports to have purchased the goods from the Ukrainian Government for sale and distribution to civilian populations.

I [see] a number of embarrassing possibilities in the present situation. Notwithstanding French regulations to the contrary, it is very probable that the Ukrainians can succeed in liquidating the marketable supplies in France and realize sums to be used to further their propaganda or to ship other supplies to [forces in] south Russia which we might not particularly desire to assist at the present time especially as we have done so little to assist Denikin. In this connection Kramar, former Czech Premier, who has just returned from Denikin's headquarters, expressed the greatest surprise and astonishment at this . . . [sale] to the Ukrainian forces and spoke of the discouraging effect it would have upon Denikin if he knew of it.

The matter is of the most extreme urgency and yet so delicate that I did not feel that I could intervene decisively without instructions. In view of the fact, however, that I learned that a shipload of these supplies was about to be sent from Marseilles to Galatz, I have addressed a confidential note to Clemenceau outlining the situation in case the French authorities might desire to take precautions against the dissipation of the stocks in France or their possible shipment to Ukrainian forces.

A (number) of possibilities present themselves: (1) that no political action should be taken, but the matter left to the Liquidation Board, which should be left free to take such precautions as might be possible to protect itself against financial loss; (2) that the State Department should intervene and request or cooperate with the French authorities in sequestering these supplies; (3) that efforts should be made to arrange for the possible supervision of the distribution of these supplies in Russia by American Red Cross officials.[44]

In response to this report, Secretary Lansing sent a telegram on December 23, 1919, to the American Ambassador in France, Mr. Hugh Wallace. It stated that the State Department "regrets sale of supplies to Ukrainians by Liquidation Commission and would welcome any action to annul its effects which would not embarrass American authorities. Department concurs as to undesirability of Ukrainians obtaining funds in France through sale of supplies. . . . Distribution consisting of medical supplies by Red Cross now under consideration and will be discussed with Polk." The Ambassador was asked if he could "devise method to prevent Ukrainian use of other supplies."[45]

On January 20, 1920, Ambassador Wallace transmitted to the State Department the following digest of a note he received from the President of the Ukrainian Mission in Paris, dated January 16, 1920:

Twelve million dollars worth of American Army stocks were ceded to the Government of the Ukrainian Republic by contract signed June, 1919, through Liquidation Commission. Treasury notes of Ukrainian Government were accepted in payment. Transfer effected November 11th. Exact sum owed by Ukrainian Government determined at $7,844,600.90. By letter dated January 16th (1920) Liquidation Commission declared contract annulled and demanded surrender of stocks in return for the Ukrainian notes received. No motive or reason given. Colonel Noble of Liqidation Commission in several interviews indicated that measure was based on assumption that *de facto* Ukrainian Government no longer existed and consequently could not fulfill its obligations. President Ukrainian peace delegation earnestly protests and declares that Ukrainian Government has never ceased to exist and is at this moment endeavoring [apparent omission] in close union with Polish and Roumanian Governments to liberate its country from foreign and enemy incursions. Petliura still President and Commander-in-Chief of national Ukrainian Army. Government transferred to Rovno and therefore its scope of activity from a territorial point of view vaster than [that at] time of signing of contract when Government was at Kamenetz-Podolsk. States Ukrainian Government con-

---

[44] *Ibid.*, pp. 787–788.
[45] *Ibid.*, p. 789.

tinues to consider itself responsible for obligations assumed and insists upon exact execution of contract.[46]

Informing the State Department that this was the first correspondence that the Embassy had had on this subject with the Ukrainian
Mission, Ambassador Wallace requested instructions as to what
reply, if any, should be made to the Ukrainian note.[47] The State
Department instruction, dated January 28, 1920, was brief:

> Although this Department has informed the representatives of the
> Liquidation Commission in the United States of its belief in the in-
> advisability of allowing the Ukraine Mission in Paris to obtain large
> stocks of salvage surplus army supplies, it is not thought best that
> the Department appear as an active participant in the negotiations.
> You will, therefore, tell the Ukrainian Mission informally, if you
> consider it advisable to correspond with it, that the matter rests en-
> tirely in the hands of the Liquidation Commission and the Depart-
> ment of State can take no action in the matter.[48]

This hands-off policy on the part of the State Department can be
better understood in the light of its telegram dated October 29, 1919,
concerning the United States' general policy in respect to the
Ukraine. Addressed to the Commission to Negotiate Peace in Paris,
the message stated that:

> On the basis of past investigations the Department is disposed to re-
> gard the Ukrainian separatist movement as largely the result of
> Austrian and German propaganda seeking the disruption of Russia.
> It is unable to perceive an adequate ethnical basis for erecting a
> separate state and is not convinced that there is a real popular de-
> mand for anything more than such greater measure of local autonomy
> as will naturally result from the establishment in Russia of a modern
> democratic government, whether federative or not. The Department
> feels, accordingly, that the policy of the United States, while leaving
> to future events the determination of the exact character of the rela-
> tions that exist between Great and Little Russia, should tend in the

---

[46] *Ibid.*, pp. 589–590.

[47] Brig. General Edgar Jadwin, United States observer in the Ukraine,
who met with Petliura in September 1919, reported to the Department
that Petliura protested to him the non-delivery of clothing and equipment bought from the Liquidation Commission. Petliura also "requested
that Ukrainians in America be permitted to join his army." For a digest
of General Jadwin's report, see *ibid.* pp. 781–783.

[48] *Ibid.*, p. 790.

meantime, rather to sustain the principle of essential Russian unity than to encourage separatism.[49]

Thus, President Wilson's view, and therefore the American position, that the territorial integrity of the former Russian empire should be safeguarded remained intact. It was restated as late as August 10, 1920, in a formal reply to an inquiry from Baron Camillo Romano Avezzana, Ambassador of Italy in Washington, as to the position of the United States regarding the Soviet-Polish situation. Mr. Bainbridge Colby, the new Secretary of State, reaffirmed the Wilsonian principle of non-dismemberment:

> The United States maintains unimpaired its faith in the Russian people, in their high character and their future. That they will overcome the existing anarchy, suffering and destruction we do not entertain the slightest doubt. The distressing character of Russia's transition has many historical parallels, and the United States is confident that restored, free and united Russia will again take a leading place in the world, joining with the other free nations in upholding peace and orderly justice.
>
> Until that time shall arrive, the United States feels that friendship and honor require that Russia's interests must be generously protected, and that, as far as possible, all decisions of vital importance to it, and especially those concerning its sovereignty over the territory of the former Russian Empire, be held in abeyance. . . . We are unwilling that while it is helpless in the grip of a non-representative government, whose only sanction is brutal force, Russia shall be weakened still further by a policy of dismemberment, conceived in other than Russian interests.[50]

This repeated restatement of the policy of "united Russia" made the position of the United States government a moral one. In his report to Washington, dated December 22, 1920, the American Ambassador in Geneva, Mr. Gary, stated that this position had a "decisive influence on the non-admission of states bordering Russia to the League of Nations."[51] Continuing this theme, at least one reputable student of American policy toward Russia during these years has concluded: "In favoring settlement of the frontier dis-

---

[49] *Ibid.*, pp. 783–784.

[50] *Papers Relating to the Foreign Relations of the United States, 1920,* Vol. III (Washington, D.C.: U.S. Government Printing Office, 1936), pp. 465–466.

[51] *Ibid.*, p. 480.

putes arising out of Russia's revolution and civil war . . . on a basis which would keep Russia a united nation, the American Government felt that it had in part repaid to the Russian state an old debt of friendship, even though Russia's new government was regarded as one with which amicable relations could not be maintained."[52]

As already indicated at the outset of this study, the first significant factor that influenced much of official American thinking concerning the aspirations to independence of the Ukrainians and other non-Russian minorities of the Empire was the past heritage of friendship toward Tsarist Russia. It is only fair to say, however, that this curious feeling of amity had nothing to do with or in any way indicated American approval of Russia's handling of its internal minorities, problems about which even educated American citizens knew very little. The second element of paramount importance was the personality of President Woodrow Wilson. Wilson personally handled United States policy toward Russia, which in turn influenced the actions of the Paris Peace Conference towards Russia's neighbors. Imbued with sincere idealism, but removed from political reality, particularly in Eastern Europe, Wilson faced the greatest challenge of his political career. Preconditioned by superficial views on Russia, he was unable to realize the tragic contradiction between, on the one hand, his firm view that an ordered and peaceful world must rest on the principle of allowing people everywhere the inalienable right to determine their own fate, and on the other, his almost stubborn commitment to the preservation of the territorial integrity of the former Russian Empire.

Like most Americans of his time, President Wilson equated the Russian peoples with all the different nationalities of the Empire. As a result, he was unprepared for the disintegration of the Russian Empire into separate national entities that followed the March Revolution of 1917. The Revolution appeared as a vindication of his belief in the capacity of the Russian people for self-determination, and he sincerely viewed the overthrow of the Tsar as another milestone in the orderly advance of humanity toward its democratic destiny.

However, in spite of almost doctrinaire adherence to the three negative premises on which he formulated United States policy

---

[52] Frederik L. Schuman, *American Policy Toward Russia Since 1917* (New York: International Publishers, 1928), p. 216.

toward Russia—namely, no recognition, no intervention, and no dismemberment—Woodrow Wilson was not at all sure of the righteousness of his position. He once confided to Colonel House: "I have been sweating blood over the questions what is right and feasible to do in Russia. It goes to pieces like quicksilver under my touch."[53] A similar admission is found in a letter from Wilson to Masaryk, in which he openly admitted: "I have felt no confidence in my personal judgment about the complicated situation in Russia and am reassured that you should approve what I have done."[54]

Lastly, and most importantly, in the light of the documentary material presented in the course of this study, there is *no* evidence whatsoever of any Ukrainophobia on the part of any American official, private citizen, or group, as is sometimes alleged by Ukrainians both in the United States and abroad. Moreover, the Ukraine was not the only secessionist (independence-minded) colony of the former Russian Empire whose strivings toward independence during the turbulent years of the Great East European Revolution did not evoke sufficient sympathy and support from the world's greatest democracy. It was not until 1922 that President Harding formally recognized the independence of the three Baltic states of Estonia, Latvia, and Lithuania. It might also be well to remember an important lesson that the last two world wars and their aftermath should have taught: America, like any other nation in the world—to paraphrase a famous British statesman—has neither permanent friends nor permanent enemies. The only thing that is *permanent* is national interest, as conceived, rightly or wrongly, by those who bear the burden of responsibility for the nation's destiny.

---

[53] Charles Seymour, *The Intimate Papers of Colonel House* (New York: Houghton Mifflin Co., 1928), p. 386.

[54] Ray Stannard Baker, *Woodrow Wilson: Life and Letters,* Vol. VIII (Garden City, N.Y.: Doubleday, Page and Co., 1939), p. 323.

Appendix

THE UKRAINIAN TEXTS that served as the basis for the translation were taken from *Velyka ukrainska revoliutsiia: kalendar istorychnykh podii za liutyi 1917 roku—berezen 1918 roku* (2nd ed. New York: Ukrainian Academy of Arts and Sciences in the United States, 1967). These are reliable texts. The translators have tried to adhere as closely as possible to the originals in both style and tone. Translated by M. Bohachevsky-Chomiak and R. L. Chomiak.

First Universal[1] of the Ukrainian Central Rada[2] to all Ukrainian People whether residing in the Ukraine or beyond its borders.

Ukrainian people! Nation of peasants, workers, toilers!

By your will you have placed us, *the Ukrainian Central Rada,* to guard the rights and freedoms of the Ukrainian land.

Your finest sons, those who represent villages, factories, military barracks, all Ukrainian communities and associations, have elected us, *the Ukrainian Central Rada,* and ordered us to stand firm and defend these rights and freedoms.

Your elected representatives, nation, have expressed their will thus:

Let the Ukraine be free! Without separating from all of Russia, without breaking with the Russian state, let the Ukrainian people have the right to manage its own life on its own soil. Let a National Ukrainian Assembly (*Soim*), elected by universal, equal, direct, and secret balloting, establish order and harmony in the Ukraine. Only our *Ukrainian Assembly* has the right to establish all laws which can provide that order among us here in the Ukraine.

---

[1] The Universals were not numbered, but in broadsides they have always been referred to as the First, Second, etc.

[2] The Ukrainian term *Rada,* meaning council, has been retained in this translation. All italicizing and capitalizing follows the original.

Those laws which would govern the entire Russian state should be promulgated in the All-Russian Parliament.

No one can know better than we what we need and which laws are best for us.

No one can know better than our peasants how to manage their own land, therefore, we desire that after all the lands throughout Russia held by the nobility, the state, the monasteries, and the tsar have been confiscated and have become the property of the people, and after a law concerning this has been enacted by the All-Russian Constituent Assembly, the right to administer the Ukrainian lands shall belong to us, to our Ukrainian Assembly (*Soim*).

Thus spoke the electors from the entire Ukrainian land.

Having so resolved, they elected us, *the Ukrainian Central Rada,* from among their midst and commanded us to be at the head of our people, to stand for its rights, and to create a new order in a free *autonomous Ukraine.*

And so, we, *the Ukrainian Central Rada,* have fulfilled the will of our people, we took upon ourselves the heavy burden of building a new life, and have now begun this great task.

We thought that the Central Russian Government would extend its hands to us in this task, that in agreement with it, we, *the Ukrainian Central Rada,* would be able to provide order for our land.

But the Provisional Russian Government rejected all our demands; it pushed aside the outstretched hand of the Ukrainian people. We have sent our delegates (envoys) to Petrograd so that they might present our demands to the Russian Provisional Government.

Our major demands were the following:

That the Russian government publicly, by a special act, declare that it does not oppose the national will of the Ukraine, the right of our people to *autonomy.*

That the Central Russian Government have accredited to it our *Commissar on Ukrainian affairs* for all matters concerning the Ukraine.

That local power in the Ukraine be united under one representative from the Central Russian Government, that is, by a *Commissar in the Ukraine* chosen by us.

That a definite *portion of the monies* which are collected for the

Central Treasury from our people be turned over to us, the representatives of this people for its own national-cultural needs.

The Central Russian Government *rejected* all of these demands.

It was not willing to say whether or not it recognizes the right of our people to autonomy and the right to manage its own life. It evaded an answer, and referred us to the future All-Russian Constituent Assembly.

The Russian Central Government did not wish to include our Commissar; *it did not want to join us in the establishment of a new order.* Likewise, *it did not wish to recognize a Commissar for all the Ukraine* with whom we might bring our land to order and accord.

It also refused to return the monies collected from our own land for the needs of our schools, education and organizations.

And now, Ukrainian people, we are forced to *create our own destiny.* We cannot permit our land to fall into lawlessness and decline. Since the Russian Provisional Government *cannot* provide order for us, since it does *not want* to join us in this great task, then we must take it upon ourselves. This is our duty to our land and to the peoples who live on our land.

That is why we, *the Ukrainian Central Rada,* issue this Universal to our entire nation and proclaim: from this day forth we shall build our life.

Therefore, let each member of our nation, each citizen of a village or city know that the time has come for a great undertaking.

Hereafter, each village, each *volost,* each city or *zemstvo* governing board which upholds the interests of the Ukrainian Nation should have *the closest of organizational ties with the Central Rada.*

In places where for some reason administrative authority remains in the hands of people hostile to the Ukrainian cause, we prescribe that our citizens carry out a broad, vigorous organizational effort and enlightenment of the people and then *elect an administration.*

In cities and those areas where the Ukrainian population is intermingled with other nationalities, we prescribe that our citizens immediately *come to agreement and understanding with the democratic elements of these nationalities,* and jointly begin preparations for a new orderly existence.

The Central Rada hopes that the non-Ukrainian peoples living on our territory will also care for order and peace in our land, and that in this difficult time of disorder in the entire state, they join us in a united and friendly fashion to work for the organization of an *autonomous Ukraine.*

And when we complete this preparatory organizational work, we will call together representatives from all nations of the Ukrainian Land and will establish laws for it. These laws, this entire order which we shall prepare, the All-Russian Constituent Assembly must ratify by its own law.

Ukrainian people! Before your elected leadership—*the Ukrainian Central Rada*—stands a great, high wall which it must topple in order to lead its people to the open road.

Strength is needed for this. Strong, courageous hands are needed. The people's hard work is needed. But above all, for the success of this work, great means (monies) are needed. Until this time, the Ukrainian nation had relinquished all its means to the All-Russian Treasury, and it has not, nor does it now receive that which is its due.

Consequently, we, *the Ukrainian Central Rada,* order all the organized citizenry of our villages and towns and all Ukrainian community executive boards and organizations to institute a special tax on the population for our native cause, effective the first day of the month of July, to be transmitted accurately, immediately and regularly to *the treasury of the Ukrainian Central Rada.*

Ukrainian people! Your fate lies in your own hands. In this difficult time of universal disorder and ruin, prove by your unity and your statesmanship that you, a nation of workers, a nation of tillers of the soil, can proudly and with dignity take your place beside any organized nation-state, as an equal among equals.

Enacted in Kiev in the year 1917, in the month of June, on the tenth.

The Ukrainian Central Rada

Second Universal of the Ukrainian Central Rada

Citizens of the Ukrainian Land

The representatives of the Provisional Government have informed us of the measures which the Provisional Government will use in governing the Ukraine until [the convocation of] the Constituent Assembly.

While standing guard over the freedom won by the revolutionary people, recognizing each nation's right to self-determination, and deferring the establishment of the final form of this [right] to the Constituent Assembly, the Provisional Government extends its hand to the representatives of the Ukrainian democracy—to the Central Rada—and calls upon it to create, in agreement with it, a new life in the Ukraine for the benefit of the entire revolutionary Russia.

We, the Central Rada, having always stood for the Ukraine's non-separation from Russia, in order that we and all her peoples might jointly strive toward the development and welfare of all Russia and toward the unity of her democratic forces, accept with satisfaction this call of the [Russian Provisional] Government to common action and declare the following to *all citizens of the Ukraine:*

The Ukrainian Central Rada, elected by the Ukrainian people through its revolutionary organizations, will soon be expanded on a just basis by representatives of the revolutionary organizations of the other peoples who live in the Ukraine: subsequently, it will become that single supreme body of revolutionary democracy in the Ukraine which will represent the interests of the entire population of our land.

From its own midst, the expanded Central Rada will select anew a separate body—the General Secretariat—which will be responsible to the Rada and which will be subject to confirmation by the Provisional Government as the repository of the highest regional authority of the Provisional Government in the Ukraine.

All rights and means [of governance] will merge in this body, so that, as the representative of Democracy in all the Ukraine and as, at the same time, the supreme governing body in the land, it might be empowered to fulfill the complex task of organization and to establish order throughout the land, in accord with the entire revolutionary Russia.

In harmony with other nationalities of the Ukraine, and acting as an organ of the Provisional Government in the sphere of state administration, the General Secretariat of the Central Rada will follow steadfastly the road of strengthening the new order created by the revolution.

Striving toward an autonomous order for the Ukraine, the Central Rada, in agreement with the national minorities of the Ukraine, will prepare drafts of legislation for the Ukraine's autonomous structure, which will then be submitted for confirmation to the Constituent Assembly.

Considering that the establishment of a territorial branch of the Provisional Government in the Ukraine assures, within a plausible framework, the desired closeness of the administration of the Land (Ukraine) to the needs of the local population prior to the Constituent Assembly and recognizing that the fate of all the peoples of Russia is firmly tied to the overall achievements of the revolution, we emphatically oppose any plans to establish autonomy arbitrarily in the Ukraine before [the convocation of] the All-Russian Constituent Assembly.

As for the formation of Ukrainian military units, the Central Rada will have its representatives attached to the offices of the Minister of War, the General Staff, and the Supreme Commander, who will take part in the formation of separate units composed exclusively of Ukrainians insofar as such formation will be deemed technically feasible by the Minister of War, and will not jeopardize the fighting capacity of the army.

In making this known to the citizens of the Ukraine, we firmly believe that the Ukrainian democracy, which transferred to us its will, together with the revolutionary democracy of all Russia and her revolutionary government, will exert all its strength to lead the entire state, and particularly the Ukraine, to the full triumph of the revolution.

Kiev, in the year 1917, 3 July

The Ukrainian Central Rada

Third Universal of the Ukrainian Central Rada

Ukrainian people and all peoples of the Ukraine!

A heavy and difficult hour has fallen upon the land of the Russian Republic. In the capitals to the north a bloody civil struggle is raging; the Central Government has collapsed, and anarchy, lawlessness and ruin are spreading throughout the state.

Our land is also in danger. Without a single, strong national authority, the Ukraine may also fall into the abyss of civil war, slaughter and ruin.

Ukrainian people! You, together with the other fraternal peoples of the Ukraine, have placed us to guard the rights acquired through your struggles, [empowered us] to create order and to build new life on our land; and, we, the Ukrainian Central Rada, by your will, and in the name of establishing order in our country in the name of saving all of Russia, do now proclaim:

From this day forth, the Ukraine becomes the Ukrainian People's Republic.[3]

Without separating ourselves from the Russian Republic and maintaining its unity, we shall stand firmly on our own soil, in order that our strength may aid all of Russia, so that the whole Russian Republic may become a federation of equal and free peoples.

Until [the convocation of] the Constituent Assembly of the Ukraine, all power to establish order in our country, to promulgate laws, and to govern belongs to us, the Ukrainian Central Rada, and to our government—the General Secretariat of the Ukraine.

With power and authority in our native land, we shall use this power and authority to stand guard over freedom and the revolution, not only in our land, but also throughout all of Russia.

Therefore, we proclaim:

To the territory of the Ukrainian People's Republic belong regions inhabited for the most part by Ukrainians: the provinces of Kiev, Podillia, Volhynia, Chernihiv, Poltava, Kharkiv, Katerynoslav Kherson, Taurus (excluding Crimea). The final demarcation of the borders of the Ukrainian People's Republic as well as the annexation of parts of the Kursk, Kholm, Voronezh provinces and the neighboring gubernias and areas where the majority of the population is Ukrainian, will be determined in agreement with the organized will of the peoples.

---

[3] The name of the Ukrainian state established by the Third Universal was *Ukrainska Narodna Respublika*—literally, the Ukrainian People's Republic; hence, this form is used in the present translation. For various reasons—one of them being the connotation of "people's republic" as a communist state—the name "Ukrainian National Republic" has been accepted in publications and in everyday use. There are also those who favor the name "Ukrainian Democratic Republic" because, on the one hand, the word "democratic" does mean "of the people," and, on the other, some diplomatic representatives of the Ukrainian People's Republic used the term "Ukrainian Democratic Republic" on documents that they issued in languages other than Ukrainian. Since the purpose of this translation is to render as closely as possible the spirit and the letter of the four Universals of the Ukrainian Central Rada, it was deemed necessary to use the proper rather than the fashionable term for the Ukrainian state.

We declare the following to all citizens of these lands:

Henceforth, on the territory of the Ukrainian People's Republic, the existing property rights on lands of the nobility and on agricultural lands of other non-toiling ownership, including deeded lands, [lands owned by] monasteries and ministries, and church lands, are abolished.

In asserting that these lands are the property of the entire working people, and that they be recognized as such without compensation [to former proprietors], the Ukrainian Central Rada entrusts the Secretary General for Land Affairs to prepare legislation immediately to regulate the manner in which land committees, elected by the people, should manage these lands until [the convocation of] the Constituent Assembly.

The labor of the workers in the Ukrainian People's Republic must be placed on an orderly basis immediately. Now, we proclaim: *from this day forth, an eight-hour workday is instituted in all enterprises on the territory of the Ukrainian People's Republic.*

The difficult and terrible time which all of Russia and, with her, our Ukraine is experiencing, demands a proper organization of production, steady distribution of consumer products and a better organization of labor. Therefore, we charge the General Secretariat for Labor, together with the representatives of the workers, with the immediate establishment of *state control over production in the Ukraine,* guarding the interests of both the Ukraine and all of Russia.

For the fourth year blood is being spilt on the battlefields; and the strength of the peoples of the world is destroyed in vain. In the name of the Ukrainian Republic and in expression of its will, we, the Ukrainian Central Rada, shall firmly insist that *peace be instituted quickly. To this end, we shall use resolute means to force through the Central Government, both allies and enemies to begin peace negotiations at once.*

Likewise, we shall see to it that the rights of the Ukrainian people in Russia and outside Russia are not infringed upon by the peace treaty [that is negotiated] at the Peace Conference. However, until the beginning of peace, each citizen of the Republic of the Ukraine, together with the citizens of all other nations of the Russian Republic, should stand fast at his post, both at the battlefield and at home.

Recently, the bright achievements of the revolution have been dimmed by the reinstatement of the death penalty. We proclaim:

Henceforth, on the territory of the Ukrainian Republic, the death penalty is abolished.

All prisoners, all those detained for political activity committed prior to this date, including those sentenced and those not yet sentenced or charged, are hereby granted full amnesty. A law will be promulgated to that effect immediately. The court in the Ukraine should be just [and] in conformity with the spirit of the people. With that goal in view, we direct the General Secretariat for Justice to take all measures necessary to bring order to the judicial system and to assure its compliance with the legal conceptions of the people.

We direct the General Secretariat for Internal Affairs [as follows]:

To use all means to strengthen and broaden the rights of the local bodies of self-government which serve as organs of the higher administrative authorities in the localities, and to *establish its closest ties and cooperation with the organs of revolutionary democracy* which should constitute the best basis for a free, democratic life.

Furthermore, the Ukrainian People's Republic shall secure all freedoms won by the All-Russian revolution: freedom of speech, press, worship, assembly, association, strikes, inviolability of person and residence, and the right and opportunity to use the native language in dealings with all administrative agencies.

The Ukrainian people, who have fought long years for their national freedom and have won it today, shall firmly defend the free national development of all nationalities residing in the Ukraine; therefore, we proclaim: *The Great-Russian, Jewish, Polish and other peoples in the Ukraine are granted national-personal autonomy* to guarantee their own self-government in all matters of their national life; and we charge our general Secretariat for National Affairs to present to us, within the shortest possible time, legislative drafts for [guaranteeing this] national-personal autonomy.

The matter of provisions is the root of the power of government in this difficult and responsible time. The Ukrainian People's Republic should strain all its powers to save not only itself, but also the front and those parts of the Russian Republic which need our aid.

Citizens! In the name of the Ukrainian People's Republic within a federated Russia, we, the Ukrainian Central Rada, call upon all, to struggle decisively against all anarchy and destruction and to work towards the great fraternal construction of new governmental forms which will grant the great and weakened Republic of Russia health, strength, and a new future. The determination of these forms shall be made at the Ukrainian and All-Russian Constituent Assemblies.

The date for the election of the Ukrainian Constituent Assembly shall be December 27, 1917; the day of its convocation shall be January 9, 1918.

A law regulating the convocation of this Ukrainian Constituent Assembly shall be promulgated immediately.

Kiev, November 7, the year 1917

The Ukrainian Central Rada

Fourth Universal of the Ukrainian Central Rada

People of the Ukraine!

By your efforts, your will, and your word, a Free Ukrainian People's Republic has been created on Ukrainian soil. The ancient dreams of your ancestors—fighters for the freedom and rights of the workers—has been fulfilled. But, the Ukraine's freedom has been reborn in a difficult hour. Four years of a ferocious war have weakened our Country and population, factories do not produce goods, industry has slowed down, railroads are in disarray, money continues to fall in value; there is less bread, famine looms [before us]. Mobs of robbers and thieves have multiplied throughout the countryside, especially during the times when the army has swarmed from the front, causing slaughter, disorder and ruin on our land. Due to all this, the elections to the Ukrainian Constituent Assembly could not be held on the date set by our previous Universal, and this assembly, which had been scheduled to convene today, could not meet to accept from our hands the temporary, supreme revolutionary authority in the Ukraine, institute order in our People's Republic, and form a new Government. Meanwhile, the Petrograd Government of the People's Commissars, in an attempt to bring back the Free Ukrainian Republic under its rule, has declared war against the Ukraine and is sending into our lands its armies of Red Guards and Bolsheviks, who rob the bread of our peasants, not even sparing the grain set aside for seed, and without any compensation carry it off to Russia; they kill innocent people and spread anarchy, thievery and apathy everywhere.

We, the Ukrainian Central Rada, have done everything to prevent the outbreak of this fratricidal war of two neighboring peoples, but the Petrograd Government has not chosen to meet our efforts, and continues to wage a bloody struggle with our People and [our] Republic; moreover, this same Petrograd Government of People's Commissars has begun delaying the peace and is calling for a new war, which it characterizes as holy [war]. Again, blood will flow, again the ill-fated working people shall be forced to lay down their lives.

We, the Ukrainian Central Rada, elected by the congresses of peasants, workers, and soldiers of the Ukraine, cannot agree to this at all, we will not support any wars, for the Ukrainian People want peace; and a democratic peace must come about promptly. Moreover, in order to ensure that neither the Russian nor any other government shall obstruct the Ukraine's efforts to institute this desired peace, to be able to lead our country to order, to creative work, to the strengthening of the revolution and of our freedom, we, the Ukrainian Central Rada, proclaim to all citizens of the Ukraine:

From this day forth, the Ukrainian People's Republic becomes independent, subject to no one, a Free, Sovereign State of the Ukrainian People.

We want to live in harmony and friendship with all neighboring states: Russia, Poland, Austria, Rumania, Turkey, and others, but none of these may interfere in the life of the Independent Ukrainian Republic—power in it shall belong only to the People of the Ukraine, in whose name we, the Ukrainian Central Rada, the representatives of the toiling people of peasants, workers, and soldiers and our executive arm, henceforth called "the Council of People's Ministers," shall govern until the convocation of the Ukrainian Constituent Assembly.

First of all, we direct the government of our Republic, the Council of People's Ministers, to continue on an independent basis the peace negotiations already begun with the Central Powers, to carry them through to conclusion without regard for the interference by any other part of the former Russian Empire, and to establish peace, so that our Country may begin its economic life in tranquility and harmony.

As to the so-called bolsheviks and other aggressors who destroy and ruin our Country, we direct the Government of the Ukrainian People's Republic to take up a firm and determined struggle against them, and we call upon all citizens of our Republic to defend their welfare and liberty without sparing their lives. Our Ukrainian People's State must be cleared of the violent intruders sent from Petrograd, who trample the rights of the Ukrainian Republic.

The inestimably difficult war, begun by the bourgeois government, has greatly wearied our People; it has already destroyed our Country, ruined the economy. An end must come to this now. While the army is being demobilized, we order that some [members of the armed forces] be released; after the ratification of the peace, the army is to be disbanded completely. Later, instead of a standing army, a people's militia is to be formed, so that our fighting forces may serve as defenders of the working people, and not at the pleasure of the ruling strata.

Localities destroyed by war and demobilization are to be rebuilt with the aid and through the initiative of our State Treasury. When our soldiers return home, new elections to the people's councils, district, county and city dumas will be called at a time which will be prescribed, so that our soldiers may have a voice in them: meanwhile, such local administration should be established which can be trusted and which will be based on all revolutionary-democratic strata of the people. The government should encourage the cooperation of the councils of peasants', workers' and soldiers' deputies elected from among the local population.

On the matter of land [reform], the commission elected at our last session has already worked out legislation concerning the transfer of the land without compensation to the working people, taking as its base our resolution on the abolition of property and the socialization of the land which was passed at the eighth session. In a few days the whole Central Rada will study this legislation.

The Council of People's Ministers will use all means to ensure that the transfer of land from the land committees to the working people take place without fail before the beginning of spring tilling.

Forests, waters and all mineral resources—the wealth of the Ukrainian working people—are transferred to the jurisdiction of the Ukrainian People's Republic.

The war has also taken all the manpower resources of our country. Most of the factories, enterprises and shops have been producing only that which was necessary for the war, and the nation has been left completely without goods. Now the war has ended. We direct the Council of People's Ministers to begin immediately the change over of all factories and enterprises to peace-time production of goods most needed first and foremost by the toiling masses.

This same war has proliferated hundreds of thousands of unemployed and invalids. In the Independent People's Republic of the Ukraine no working man should suffer. The government should increase the industry of the State, it should begin creative work in all areas in which the unemployed may find work and to which they may apply their strength and—[the government] should use all means to ensure [the welfare of] the maimed and of those who have suffered from the war.

During the old order, merchants and all sorts of middlemen gained huge capital from the poor oppressed classes. Henceforth, the Ukrainian People's Republic takes into its hands the most important branches of commerce, and all profit derived from them shall be used for the benefit of the people. Our State itself will supervise goods imported and exported so as to prevent the high prices [set] by speculators which are [such a] hardship to the poorest classes. To achieve this aim, we direct the Government of the Republic to prepare and present for approval legislation on this [matter], as well as on the establishment of monopolies in iron, leather, tobacco and other products and merchandise on which the greatest profit has been drawn from the working classes for the benefit of the non-toilers.

Likewise, we order the establishment of state-people's control over all banks whose credits and loans to the non-working masses aided in the exploitation of the toiling classes. Henceforth, bank loans are to be granted primarily to support the working population and the economic development of the Ukrainian People's Republic, and not for speculation and various exploitations by the banks or for profiteering.

Because of anarchy, anxiety in life, and shortage of goods, discontent is growing in a certain segment of the population. Various dark forces are using this discontent and trying to attract unenlightened people to the old system. These dark forces want to put back all free peoples under the unified tsarist yoke of Russia. The Council of People's Ministers should struggle firmly against all counter-revolutionary forces. Anyone who calls for an uprising against the independent Ukrainian Republic, for a return to the old order, must be punished for treason of the state.

All democratic freedoms proclaimed by the Third Universal are reaffirmed by the Ukrainian People's Republic, which particularly proclaims: in the Independent Ukrainian People's Republic all nations enjoy the right of national-personal autonomy, granted to them by the law of January 9.[4]

---

[4] January 9 (according to the Julian calendar) or January 22, 1918, by present-day reckoning, has gone down in history as the date of Ukraine's independence, i.e., the proclamation of the Fourth Universal. In fact, the

Whatever matters enumerated in this Universal which we, the Central Rada, will not have time to accomplish will be completed, rectified, and brought to a final order by the Ukrainian Constituent Assembly. We order all our citizens to conduct the elections most assiduously, to use all means to ensure the fastest tabulation of votes possible, in order that our Constituent Assembly—the highest ruler and administrator in our Land—may convene within a few weeks to establish freedom, harmony, and welfare by a constitution of the Independent Ukrainian People's Republic for the benefit of the whole toiling people, now and in the future.

This our Highest body will decide on the federative ties with the people's republics of the former Russian state.

Until that time we call upon all citizens of the Independent Ukrainain People's Republic to stand relentlessly on guard of the freedom and rights won by our People and to defend their fate with all their might from all enemies of the peasants'-workers' Independent Ukrainian Republic.

Kiev, 9th January, 1918.

Ukrainian Central Rada

---

third reading of the Fourth Universal was presented as a bill of the Ukrainian Central Rada, and the vote on it was taken shortly after midnight on January 12 (January 25), 1917.

It seems that the Founding Fathers of the Ukrainian People's Republic were attached to the January 9 (January 22) date because it had been the date set for the convocation of the Ukrainian Constituent Assembly. Since the Constituent Assembly failed to be elected, the Central Rada began its deliberation on the Fourth Universal on that date. Work on this legislation was held up when, on January 10 (January 23)—not January 9, as stated in the Fourth Universal—representatives of national minorities in the Rada demanded that the draft legislation on national-personal autonomy should be passed before the final vote on the Fourth Universal. The law on national-personal autonomy was passed the next day (January 11), and the second reading of the Fourth Universal followed. By then it was almost midnight, and a short recess was called. Before the third reading, Mykhailo Hrushevskyi, president of the Central Rada, made a brief introduction in which he informed the galleries that work on the Fourth Universal had begun on January 9 (January 22). This was also the date that appeared on the document when it was published.

List of Contributors

Arthur E. Adams, whose book *Bolsheviks in the Ukraine: The Second Campaign, 1918–1919* was the 1962 recipient of the Borden Award of the Hoover Institute and Library, Stanford, California, recently left Michigan State University to become Dean of the College of Humanities and Professor of History at Ohio State University, Columbus, Ohio. His latest work was co-authored with Jan S. Adams, *Men Versus Systems: Agriculture in the USSR, Poland, and Czechoslovakia* (New York: The Free Press, 1971). Professor Adams has published many articles and has written or edited numerous books in the area of Slavic studies, including *An Historical Atlas of Russia and Eastern Europe* with Ian Matley and William McCagg; *Imperial Russia After 1816; Soviet Foreign Policy: Theory and Practice;* and *The Russian Revolution and Bolshevik Victory.*

Yaroslav Bilinsky is a Professor of Political Science at the University of Delaware. Born in the Ukraine, he came to the United States in 1951, graduated with honors as a member of Phi Beta Kappa from Harvard College in 1954, and received his Ph.D. from Princeton University in 1958. In addition to many articles and book reviews, he has published *The Second Soviet Republic: The Ukraine after World War II* (New Brunswick: Rutgers University Press, 1964) and *Changes in the Central Committee, Communist Party of the Soviet Union, 1961–1966,* University of Denver Monograph Series in World Affairs, No. 4 (Denver, 1967).

Bohdan R. Bociurkiw is Professor of Political Science at Carleton University in Ottawa, Canada. A native of the Ukraine, he obtained his B.A. and M.A. degrees from the University of Manitoba and his Ph.D. in political science from the University of Chicago. From 1956 to 1969 he taught at the University of Alberta.

396

From 1969 to 1972 he served as Director of the Institute of Soviet
and East European Studies at Carleton University. He is a past
president of the Canadian Association of Slavists, former chairman
of the Inter-University Committee on Canadian Slavs, past chairman of the Inter-University Committee on Academic Exchanges
with Eastern Europe, a member of a number of Canadian and
American learned societies and fellow of the Shevchenko Scientific
Society. He has published numerous scholarly papers and articles
on church-state relations in the Ukraine, religion and atheism in
the USSR, and selected aspects of Soviet politics. He was one of
the editors of *Ukraine: A Concise Encyclopedia* (Vol. II) and edited
(with J. W. Strong) a volume on *Religion and Atheism in the USSR
and Eastern Europe* (London: Macmillan, 1974).

Martha Bohachevsky-Chomiak, Associate Professor of History at Manhattanville College, Purchase, New York, graduated
from the University of Pennsylvania in 1960. In 1968 she received
a Ph.D. from Columbia University. She was the recipient of a
Woodrow Wilson Fellowship, a Ford Fellowship, a CU President's
Fellowship, and in 1970 was awarded a Young Humanist grant from
the National Endowment for the Humanities. Among her publications are *The Spring of a Nation: Ukrainians in Eastern Galicia in
1848* (Philadelphia, 1967) and an edition of Evgenii N. Trubetskoi,
Vospominaniia (London, 1975).

Jurij Borys is Professor of Political Science at the University
of Calgary in Alberta, Canada. Born in the Ukraine, he received
a Ph.D. and a Phil.Lic. from the University of Stockholm and in
1961–62 received a Fulbright Fellowship. Among his publications
are *The Russian Communist Party and the Sovietization of Ukraine:
A Study in the Communist Doctrine of the Self-Determination of
Nations* (Stockholm, 1965) and numerous articles on Soviet political
and national problems.

George A. Brinkley, Jr., is Professor and Chairman of the
Department of Government at the University of Notre Dame. He
attended Davidson College and received an M.A. (1955), and a
Certificate of the Russian Institute and a Ph.D. (1964) from Columbia University. A member of Phi Beta Kappa, he has held several
fellowships and was the recipient of the American Historical Association's George Louis Beer Prize in 1967. Among his publications

are *The Volunteer Army and Allied Intervention in South Russia, 1917–1921* (University of Notre Dame Press, 1966), a chapter on Soviet foreign policy in W. Laqueur and L. Labedz (eds.), *The Future of Communist Society* (New York: Praeger, 1962), "The 'Withering' of the State Under Khrushchev," *Review of Politics,* XXIII, 1 (1961), "Soviet Foreign Policy and the Transition to Communism," *Survey,* No. 38 (1961), "El espiritu communista en el derecho sovietico," *Foro Internacional,* III, 2 (1962), and "The Soviet Union and the United Nations: The Changing Role of the Developing Countries," *Review of Politics,* XXXII, 1 (1970).

Oleh S. Fedyshyn is Associate Professor of Political Science at Richmond College, City University of New York. He holds a Certificate from the Russian Institute and Ph.D. from Columbia University and is the author of *Germany's Drive to the East and the Ukrainian Revolution, 1917–1918* (Newark, N.J.: Rutgers University Press, 1971) as well as a contributor to the *Slavic Review, East European Review, Social Science Quarterly,* and *The Journal of Politics.*

Taras Hunczak received his B.S. and M.A. degrees from Fordham University and Ph.D. from the University of Vienna. Since 1960 he has been teaching Russian, Ukrainian, and East European history at Rutgers University in Newark, New Jersey. His works have appeared in such journals as *Slavic Review, Jewish Social Studies, East European Quarterly, Journal of Modern History, Russian Review, Zeszyty historyczne,* and *Ukrainskyi istoryk.* He also edited *Russian Imperialism,* which was published in 1974 by Rutgers University Press. Currently he is Professor of History and serves as Director of the East European and Soviet Areas Studies Program.

Ihor Kamenetsky is a Professor of Political Science and the Chairman of the Interdisciplinary Committee on Developing Nations at Central Michigan University. Born in the Ukraine, he received his M.A. and Ph.D. from the University of Illinois. He is the recipient of the Eastern European Fund Scholarship, the W. Garner Fellowship, and the Fulbright Senior Research Award. Professor Kamenetsky has authored or edited numerous articles and books, including *Hitler's Occupation of Ukraine, 1941–1944: A Study in Totalitarian Imperialism* (Milwaukee: Marquette Uni-

versity Press, 1957), *Secret Nazi Plans for Eastern Europe: A Study of Lebensraum Policies* (New York: Bookman Associates, 1961), and "Totalitarianism and Utopia," *Chicago Review,* Spring, 1964. He is currently working on "Ukraine in German Foreign Policy Between the Two World Wars," a chapter in *Anthology on Ukrainian Nationalism,* Blochyn Boyko (ed.) (Munich, 1974).

John S. Reshetar, Jr., is Professor of Political Science at the University of Washington (Seattle). He received his B.A. from Williams College and Ph.D. from Harvard University. He is the author of *The Ukrainian Revolution, 1917–1920: A Study in Nationalism* (1952); *Problems of Analyzing and Predicting Soviet Behavior* (1955); *A Concise History of the Communist Party of the Soviet Union* (1960; revised edition, 1964), and is the co-author of several works.

Ivan L. Rudnytsky, a native of the Ukraine, lived in the United States from 1951 to 1971 and has since lived in Canada. He has studied at the University of Lviv; the University of Berlin; Charles University in Prague, where he received his Ph.D. in 1945; the Graduate Institute of International Studies in Geneva; and Columbia University. Dr. Rudnytsky has taught at several American colleges and universities and is presently Professor of Ukrainian and East European History at the University of Alberta. His publications include: *Mykhaylo Drahomanov: A Symposium and Selected Writings* (New York, 1952); "The Role of the Ukraine in Modern History," *Slavic Review,* Vol. XXII, No. 2 (1963); "The Ukrainians in Galicia under Austrian Rule," *Austrian History Yearbook,* Vol. III, Part 2 (1967); and the collection of essays on the history of Ukrainian social and political thought, *Mizh istoriieiu i politykoiu* (Munich, 1973).

Wolodymyr Stojko is Associate Professor of History and Director of Russian and East European Area Studies at Manhattan College, Bronx, New York. Born in the Ukraine, he began his higher education in Austria but completed his B.A. at the City College of New York and his M.A. and Ph.D. at New York University.

Frank Sysyn is Assistant Professor of History at Harvard University and Research Associate at the Harvard Ukrainian Research Institute. He received his B.A. from Princeton University, his M.A. from the University of London, and Ph.D. from Harvard; he was a Fulbright Scholar in 1968–69.

Constantine Warvariv is in the United States Foreign Service, presently serving as a Social Sciences Officer in the Department of State's Office of Multilateral Policy and Programs. He holds a degree in law from Heidelberg University and in political science from Columbia University.

The views expressed in this paper are those of the author and do not necessarily represent the views of the Department of State or any other agency of the United States government.

Index

HARVARD UKRAINIAN RESEARCH INSTITUTE

Monograph Series

Ievhen Sverstiuk, *Clandestine Essays,* translated with an introduction by G. S. N. Luckyj. Littleton, Colo.: Ukrainian Academic Press, 1976.

Taras Hunczak (ed.), *The Ukraine, 1917–1921: A Study in Revolution.* Cambridge, Mass.: Harvard Ukrainian Research Institute, distributed by Harvard University Press, 1977.

Paul R. Magocsi, *The Shaping of a National Identity: Developments in Subcarpathian Rus', 1848–1948.* Cambridge, Mass.: Harvard University Press, 1977.

Sources and Document Series

Proceedings of the Conference on Carpatho-Ruthenian Immigration, transcribed, edited and annotated by Richard Renoff and Stephen Reynolds. Cambridge, Mass.: Harvard Ukrainian Research Institute, 1975.

The Cossack Administration of the Hetmanate, compiled by George Gajecky. Cambridge, Mass.: Harvard Ukrainian Research Institute, 1977.

Nonconformity and Dissent in the Ukrainian SSR, 1955–1975: A Select Bibliography, compiled by George Liber and Anna Mostovych. Cambridge, Mass.: Harvard Ukrainian Research Institute, 1977.

Occasional Papers

Omeljan Pritsak, *The Origin of Rus',* Inaugural Lecture delivered at Harvard University, October 1975. Cambridge, Mass.: Harvard Ukrainian Research Institute, 1976.

HARVARD SERIES IN UKRAINIAN STUDIES

Eyewitness Chronicle (Litopys Samovydcja), Part I, edited by Orest Levyc'kyj. Munich: Fink Vlg., 1972.

George S. N. Luckyj, *Between Gogol' and Ševčenko.* Munich: Fink Vlg., 1971.

Myron Korduba, *La littérature historique soviétique ukrainienne.* Munich: Fink Vlg., 1972.

Oleksander Ohloblyn, *A History of Ukrainian Industry.* Munich: Fink Vlg., 1971.

Fedir Savčenko, *The Suppression of Ukrainian Activities in 1876* (Zaborona ukrajinstva 1876 r.). Munich: Fink Vlg., 1970.

The Galician-Volynian Chronicle, translated and annotated by George Perfecky. Munich: Fink Vlg., 1973.

Dmitrij Tschiževskij, *Skovoroda: Dichter, Denker, Mystiker.* Munich: Fink Vlg., 1974.